THE GARDEN OF EROS

The Story of the Paris Expatriates
and the Post-War Literary Scene

JOHN CALDER

ALMA BOOKS

ALMA CLASSICS
an imprint of

ALMA BOOKS LTD
Thornton House
Thornton Road
Wimbledon Village
London SW19 4NG
United Kingdom
www.almaclassics.com

First published by Calder Publications in 2013
This mass-market edition first published by Alma Books in 2014
Reprinted 2023
Copyright © John Calder, 2013

Cover pictures (left to right): Henry Miller, Patrick Bowles, George Plimpton,
Jane Lougee, Christopher Logue, Maurice Girodias, Samuel Beckett.

Printed in England by CPI Group (UK) Ltd, Croydon CR0 4YY

ISBN: 978-0-9574522-1-3

The Garden of Eros

Other Works by John Calder

Plays
Tell Me Again
The Voice
Lorca
A Happening with Robert Burns
The Twa Maisters
The Trust
After the War

Poetry
What's Wrong? What's Right?
Solo
Being – Seeing – Feeling – Healing – Meaning

Criticism
The Philosophy of Samuel Beckett
The Theology of Samuel Beckett
Four Directions of Modern Literature

Memoirs
Pursuit

Anthologies
A William Burroughs Reader
A Samuel Beckett Reader
A Henry Miller Reader
A Nouveau Roman Reader

The Garden of Eros

Introduction

This book is in part a history of the expatriates who went to Paris after the Second World War to revive the anglophone literary tradition that had ended with the German Occupation. It covers half the period and may be followed by a second volume. It is seen largely from the perspective of three publishers: Maurice Girodias, whose Olympia Press became the focus for emigrant writers from the United States, the United Kingdom and other English-speaking countries; Barney Rosset in New York, who did so much through Grove Press to introduce new authors and bridge the gap between general and academic publishing with his Evergreen "egghead" paperbacks; and their British collaborator, the author of this book. But it is also a cultural history of what resulted from the activities of a group of motivated individuals who took Paris with them as their careers led them elsewhere.

The title is borrowed from *Les Jardins d'Éros*, the second volume of Maurice Girodias's entertaining but unreliable memoirs, which have been selectively used as reference. Chronology is not strict. I have sought to bring a cast of very colourful characters to life, and to describe what they were like, what they did and how they helped to shape an age. This has meant going back and forth in time to follow individual destinies, because lives overlap with events, and to tidy up history is to distort it. Paris was a mistress or a lover to nearly everyone in this book, but the time always came to leave, perhaps to return one day; the scene had to shift – to New York or London, Tangiers or Edinburgh, San Francisco or Formentor, the expatriates always carrying Paris, the city of light, in their hearts.

My account is often very personal, adding to what is known or correcting errors in other books, mainly the biographies of writers such as Henry Miller, Samuel Beckett, Alexander Trocchi and William Burroughs. I have to thank, for their help with memories, archives and advice, many who have participated in events, including Christopher Logue, George Plimpton, Lilla Lyon, Eric Kahane, George Whitman, Richard Seaver, Victoria Moorheim, Patricia Welles, Iris Owens, Marilyn Meeske Sorel, Jerry Williams, Ann Patty (my editor – until things went wrong – and a one-time Olympia

3

employee) and Jim Haynes among many others, and the authors of the aforementioned biographies, whose names will be found in the endnotes. The character studies are my own, as are the general conclusions and descriptions of a time of excitement and pleasure we are unlikely to see repeated.

– John Calder

Chapter One

Paris after the War

1

Charles de Gaulle re-entered Paris on 25th August 1944. The symbolism of his entry and the manner of it were important: Free French Forces were only a small part of the Allied army in the Normandy invasion, but de Gaulle's intention was to give France back its pride by having a French army marching visibly down the Champs Elysées from the same Arc de Triomphe through which Hitler had driven in celebration of the country's fall four years earlier, all the way to Notre Dame cathedral. The American, British and Canadian armies, which had done most of the bloody fighting during the weeks since the landing on 6th June, although they were now also in and around Paris and shooting back at the remaining German snipers on the rooftops, had been told to play second fiddle to both the French army and the local freedom fighters, divided into two hostile groups, the Resistance and the mainly communist Maquis.

With the American army came General Leclerc's Free French Second Armoured Division and Ernest Hemingway as a war correspondent. Hemingway found his way by jeep to the Ritz Hotel and demanded his old room. He had stopped on the way from the Porte d'Orléans to see Sylvia Beach, whose bookshop was closed, but she had lived out the war on the premises. In disbelief she had rushed down the stairs of her friend Adrienne Monnier's apartment across the street when she spotted Hemingway from the window. Once at the Ritz he commandeered the bar and proceeded to order seventy-three dry martinis for his arriving friends and himself. He was the first of the pre-war "lost generation", as Gertrude Stein had once dubbed the colony of expatriate writers, journalists, painters and musicians dwelling in Paris during the Thirties, to return to the city. Many of the old crowd, not just Americans, but British, Irish and English-speaking Europeans, who had used Sylvia Beach's English-language bookshop Shakespeare & Company at 12 Rue de l'Odéon as their meeting place, had vied to be published by the many little English-language magazines, of which *transition* was perhaps the most distinguished, and had occupied the best tables of the literary cafés of Montparnasse, Alésia and the "Boul' Mich'", were now dead. Others had taken up different careers, were in the armed forces or had become part of the new arts establishments of popular culture, such as Hollywood, where refugees from pre-war Vienna and Berlin now mingled with survivors from pre-war Paris amid the glitz of a booming movie industry, from which many of them now derived a more or less precarious living.

In Paris itself the conquering Free French army soon had its new cultural commissars, led by André Malraux, who together with the heroes of the Resistance and the Maquis began to separate the sheep from the goats. Jean-Paul Sartre, Jean Cocteau and Jean Giraudoux had managed to remain creatively active during the Occupation and have their plays performed and books published – even some good quality films had been made – the Germans, many of them regular theatre-goers, not fully realizing the coded messages that lay behind the parables enclosed in works based on the classics of the past. No one suspected these writers of collaboration. Many others like Paul Éluard, Jean Paulhan and Vercors had published anti-Nazi literature underground and been lucky enough to escape the firing squads and the Gestapo torture chambers. But there were others still, who now found themselves in disgrace: Pierre Drieu la Rochelle, one of the outstanding novelists of his generation (born in 1893), who had enthusiastically attended the Nuremberg rallies before the war, had supported the German Occupation and been put in charge of one of the most prestigious literary journals by the cultural section of the German army, had already committed suicide, as had some of his fictional heroes. The poet Robert Brasillach and the most notorious collaborating journalists were shot, a fate that Ezra Pound narrowly escaped in Italy after his capture by the American army; Charles Maurras (one of T.S. Eliot's mentors) and Louis-Ferdinand Céline were sentenced to prison, but later released. Many well-known actors and entertainers who had mixed with the German officer class during the war and accepted their patronage were forbidden to perform, among them Maurice Chevalier, who managed in the immediate post-war years to find engagements in the US at a time when he was still not allowed to perform in France. Paris came back to life intellectually; ideas and conversation were more easily available than food or clothing.

The French had fled Paris in their millions in 1940 as the German army approached, and many had been bombed and strafed from the air by the Luftwaffe who would otherwise have survived by staying in their homes. The Normandy invasion, once it was clear that the

Allies would sooner or later reach Paris, persuaded many Parisians to repeat the earlier folly and flee the city that they were certain would be destroyed in a great final battle. Indeed, Hitler had given the order for Paris to be dynamited and its great buildings and monuments blown up, but the German High Command in France, led by General von Choltitz, the governor of Paris, partially persuaded, so it was said, by the officer-writer Ernst Jünger, disobeyed and surrendered. Writers who were also active communists, such as Louis Aragon, his wife Elsa Triolet and Georges Bataille, came out of hiding and tried to take control. But it was the two principal underground resistance groups, the Francs-Tireurs Partisans (FTP), who were communist-backed, and the Forces Françaises de l'Intérieur (FFI), who were not, which began to take over Paris as many German troops and the Nazi administration were hastily withdrawn.

One person who was there during the months before the Allies entered Paris and who witnessed the triumphal entry of Leclerc was Maurice Girodias, son of Jack Kahane, whose Obelisk Press had published many notable works in English before the war, most significantly the novels of Henry Miller, which were still banned in every country in the world and would remain so in English-speaking ones for nearly another two decades. Some of the best pages of *Les Jardins d'Éros*, the second volume of the Girodias autobiography, describe that period, and we are given a rather different picture of the Occupation than we find in most contemporary histories. France went on living as near to normal as possible during the war. The French with money ate good food and drank good wine. Maurice Sachs's memoir *Le Sabbat** (published in English as *Witches' Sabbath*), which appeared posthumously after the war, gives potent testament to the size, power and importance of the black market in France during the years of Occupation, and this clandestine but very visible separate economy continued for many years after the war had ended. It enabled many to live well who had the means to do so, but it also helped minorities, among them many Jews, who did not dare to take ordinary employment, to survive. And life went on normally as regards holidays and leisure activities. Girodias's sister Sylvie and her friend Claude were both sunbathing on the Côte d'Azur during the Liberation of Paris. The summer of 1944 was for many French people like any other summer, a time to go to the beaches and the mountains, to neutral Spain if they could get the visas, or even to Switzerland. Those bourgeois civilians who for one reason or another were invited to an American army mess during the Liberation – their hosts fondly imagining they were getting their first square meal in years – were shocked at American food, which they found uneatable. How could Americans put pineapple slices on the same plate with pork? How could human beings eat spam? A French dog would refuse it!

Before the reign of Napoleon III, who came to power following the revolution of 1848, Paris was a city of narrow, curving streets, tenements crammed with humanity and constant popular unrest. The French Revolution of 1789 did not just consist of ending a long-lasting tyrannical monarchy, but of constant battles between different factions, and the streets of Paris had become accustomed to regular conflict ever since, with barricades thrown up by the inhabitants of a district or *quartier* to keep out the army, the police or a rival revolutionary group. Napoleon III allowed ambitious and greedy property developers, the most notorious of whom was the Baron Haussmann, to tear down many of the old districts of Paris and push large boulevards through them, building grandiose town houses where slums had previously existed, or blocks of luxury apartments for the nouveau riche entrepreneurial class. The dispossessed went where they could: their situation was not unlike that of the victims of the Highland Clearances in Scotland, when villages were destroyed and the inhabitants forced off the land, often having no option but to emigrate in order to make way for new, profitable breeds of sheep that needed few shepherds, and to allow stags and grouse to proliferate for the sport of the wealthy. Napoleon III's brief to Haussmann was largely political: the new, wide Paris boulevards were not convenient for street-fighting. Cannon and guns could easily sweep the streets and clear away the barricades, establishing order for the government in a way that had not been possible during the popular risings of 1830 and 1848. The Paris Commune, a popular revolution that followed the fall of Napoleon III after the French defeat by the Germans in 1871, was put down without much effort by the returning French army because of the difficulties of street-fighting by poorly armed guerrillas against professionals in Haussmann's boulevards.

This created similar difficulties for the French underground in 1944, but the Germans were offering little resistance, leaving only a token force behind as the Allies drew near. The resistance groups began to emerge onto the streets, putting up large posters urging the population to rise. Other than in the working-class areas in the north and east of the city, it was largely on the Left Bank of the Seine, in the Latin Quarter, that the resistance groups began to form. Here two boulevards intersect, the Boulevard Saint-Germain and the Boulevard Saint-Michel, in the centre of the university district, which is also the area where many intellectuals and artisans live, as well as teachers and students. This crossing in the next few days became known as the "*carrefour de la mort*" (the street-crossing of death). The large boulevards were unsuitable for barricades, especially on the Right Bank where the large shopping streets and big hotels are mostly found, but this was also true to a lesser extent of the Latin Quarter; on the other hand, the small streets behind the boulevards could easily be made impassable, especially for tanks, and resistance activity was centred in them.

The Luxembourg Gardens, the only open space in the area between Saint-Germain and Montparnasse, lying just behind the Luxembourg Palace, which is currently the Senate, was the centre where the German tank division was stationed. From there, it could patrol the boulevards, but not the backstreets, but even on the boulevards the tanks were ineffective without infantry. The large buildings that were situated on these great arteries were invaded by the insurgents, not only for their strategic importance as snipers' nests, but also, according to Girodias, because they were the most likely buildings to have reserves of good food and drink: so comfortable were these requisitioned lairs that the leaders had some difficulty in getting their young activists to re-emerge into the streets to fight.

It was August and not only Girodias's sister was away on holiday. The students were away as well, mainly vacationing with their parents, who often had houses in the country, and this was also the situation with thousands of normal Parisians, including those who were hoping to avoid the imminent destruction of the city by German dynamite or artillery fire. The Resistance leaders had to man the barricades and let their members be seen in the streets to rouse the populace. Paris had a permanent population of *clochards* (tramps), and to mobilize this normally inactive segment of Parisian life the leaders had a brainwave: to take over the Halle aux Vins, the wine market, where thousands of bottles of wine were kept for auction and for sale to Parisian shops. This brought out the *clochards* in their hundreds; the one condition imposed on them was that they must look like active defenders of the streets against the nervous and mostly retreating Germans.

The taking of the Halle aux Vins, an area of poetic eminence, was a game of pleasure in every sense of the term, and the throwing up of barricades was soon doubled, both in number and fervour. At the bottom of the Rue Saint-Jacques, or of the Rue du Petit-Pont to be more precise, we succeeded in throwing up barricades of considerable proportions, effectively blocking access from the direction of the police prefecture.*

Behind these barricades the army of bibulous defenders strutted, carrying captured arms or improvised weapons, of which Molotov cocktails were the easiest to manufacture, especially given the increasing number of empty bottles that became available as they were emptied.

Dietrich von Choltitz, the General in command of what the Germans called "*Gross Paris*", had been given orders by the commanders outside Paris, Alfred Jodl and Walther Model, and by Hitler himself in Berlin, that Paris must be destroyed, the public buildings and monuments, the palaces and museums, and especially the fifty-five bridges that spanned the Seine all mined and detonated. The Gaullists had done everything possible to negotiate a truce and avoid demolition, a bloodbath and a famine, and, through the intervention of the Swedish Consul-General Raoul Nordling, von Choltitz had even been persuaded to release the senior members of de Gaulle's representatives in Paris, recently arrested, to enable them to enforce the truce and stop a general rising that would lead to an all-out battle, great destruction, and a general massacre of both the civilian population, whether combatants or not, and of German soldiers. Henri Rol-Tanguy, known as "Colonel Rol", commanding the largest organized group, the communist Maquis, had ordered all-out war from his headquarters, which lay below the Paris sewers. This, if it succeeded, would lead him to eventual victory for the FTP, the execution of the German commanders of Paris as well as their subordinates, and put him at an advantage against de Gaulle in the competition to lead France after the War had ended. The Gaullists, with amazing sangfroid and psychological manoeuvring, sent a delegation headed by Yvon Morandat and his secretary to the Hôtel Matignon, the official residence of the French President (only just abandoned by Pierre Laval, who had fled to Germany with Philippe Pétain) to take it over in the name of the Provisional Government of the French Republic. Without an objection or a single question, they were granted entry and all their orders obeyed. Other senior Gaullists arrived and, before the battle for Paris had even begun, they had appointed their own heads of ministries, given orders to the Paris police and started to negotiate to speed up the Allied entry into Paris.

General Patton, whose troops were the nearest to Paris, had no intention of entering the city. He did not want to divert any resources from fighting the German army, now preparing new lines of defence to the east, nor did he want to have to deal with the inhabitants of a starving city. Tanguy had sent out leaflets and special editions of the underground newspapers calling on the people to rise and build barricades. Behind the Allied lines a struggle was going on between de Gaulle and his principle military commander, General Leclerc, who was at the head of the only section of the French army near to Paris, and the Allied Command, to persuade Eisenhower to invade Paris before it was destroyed. De Gaulle was prepared to withdraw his troops from the Allied Command and go it alone if necessary. It was the urgent plea of Roger Gallois, sent from Paris with full information of the situation there, that swayed Eisenhower and Bradley to change their minds, overrule Patton, let the French Second Armoured Division enter the city and to support it with the Fourth US Infantry Division. Von Choltitz had held back on his orders: a loyal soldier who had obeyed Hitler's command to destroy Sebastopol in 1943, he now hesitated to do the same in Paris. The Luftwaffe Commander at Le Bourget airport had recommended bombing the north-east of the city, a militant communist district, and to flatten it in a single night: this would partly compensate for the slowness with which von Choltitz had given the order to mine the bridges and buildings at the centre, but the latter did not want to hang as a war criminal, an unsoldierly end: there could now be no doubt as to who would win the war. By authorizing Leclerc to enter Paris, Eisenhower had solved von Choltitz's dilemma. He had also unwittingly enabled de Gaulle to outmanoeuvre Tanguy.

Girodias witnessed the arriving French troops. He had joined the motley group of students, teachers and volunteers from the Latin Quarter. They built the barricades as high as they could, filling empty bottles with inflammable spirits, their necks stuffed with rags that, soaked and lit, would become lethal bombs. Various approaches to the barricades were made, one by a solitary German motorcyclist with a sidecar, who realizing he was alone, hastily turned back, another by a tank that, hit by a Molotov cocktail on the open turret, was set alight; as the crew jumped out through the flames the soldiers were killed by rifle fire from the barricades and overhead windows. For several days half-hearted sorties were made by the Germans, but their morale was low and each time they had to retreat. A hundred volunteers were asked to defend the Porte d'Orléans from incoming German tanks from the South of Paris and Girodias was one of them. They occupied a building overlooking the Place d'Alésia, and when it was sprayed by German machine-gun fire, they took refuge on the roof. There they stayed for two days, still well supplied with food and wine that had been brought from the barricaded Halle aux Vins. On the last day they saw a great crowd of both armed and unarmed civilians moving towards the Porte d'Orléans and joined them, but it was French, not German, tanks that they saw arriving. The Liberation of Paris had begun.

The tanks of Leclerc's Second Armoured Division rolled towards the Seine surrounded by cheering Parisians. Colonel Tanguy found himself frustrated, both by the successful tactics of the Gaullists and the non-resistance of the German High Command – only a few Nazi fanatics preferred to fight and die than surrender – and Maurice Girodias, who had very different battles ahead of him in his future career, threw away his FFI armband and returned to his activity as a publisher.

2

During the Thirties Sylvia Beach's Shakespeare & Company had been the principal centre for English-speaking exiles in Paris who were interested in the arts. James Joyce was the presiding genius and, in spite of frequent cavalier and ungrateful treatment from him, no trouble was too great for Miss Beach to keep him as he expected to be kept: living well, constantly flattered, protected from unfavourable criticism, with most of his problems and nuisance correspondence handled for him by others. She published *Ulysses* at her own expense, received little recompense when commercial publishers became interested, and she gave her time willingly to make Joyce and his family more comfortable and his name better known. In this she was assisted by Eugene and Maria Jolas. Maria was a Kentucky heiress whose money helped to fund Joyce, directly and indirectly, and to keep *transition* alive: this was a literary magazine that never achieved a circulation that could come remotely near covering its cost, but that published nearly all of *Finnegans Wake* in instalments as *Work in Progress* (the title was kept secret by Joyce until book publication was imminent), as well as work by Faulkner, Hemingway, Hart Crane, Gertrude Stein and the young Beckett, among very many others. Scores of French and German writers, and some from other languages, appeared regularly in *transition*, and Eugene Jolas, an enthusiastic editor, equally at home in French, German and English, through the circulation of his magazine, was making known to English readers expressionism, surrealism and the other "isms" that had Europe talking: the imagism of Ezra Pound, the Vorticism of Wyndham Lewis, the Futurism of Marinetti. By the Thirties the magazine was advocating the names of Céline, Drieu la Rochelle, Max Ernst, Franz Kafka, Man Ray, Tristan Tzara, William

Carlos Williams and others that still were little known, if at all, in American literary and art circles, and hardly more so in Britain, which was preoccupied with the Depression and the prospect of another world war. Jack Kahane was publishing Obelisk Press books, arguing with his associate, a M. Servant who printed them but disliked taking risks, and who refused to print *Tropic of Cancer* until Anaïs Nin had agreed to subsidize it herself. There were several others on the scene, Caresse and Harry Crosby's Black Sun Press and Edward Titus's Black Manikin Press notable among them.

Maurice Girodias, Jack Kahane's son, was probably the principal, certainly the most colourful personality to emerge after the war in the English-speaking literary world in Paris, although before that he had been in French publishing. As a child his father had ambitious plans for him and nearly sent him to Winchester College, but in the end decided to keep him in France. At the age of fourteen, he had been allowed to read the proofs of *Tropic of Cancer*, and his father gave him the opportunity to design the cover. As Girodias points out himself in his memoirs, Paris was full of talented artists, many of them refugees from Nazi Germany who would have done a better job for little or nothing – even Picasso would have accepted the commission – but in one day Maurice Kahane, as he then was, came up with an acceptable design that showed a giant crab of unpleasant aspect holding in its pincers a human silhouette against a large symbolic sphere. He was paid fifty francs for it by his father.

When the war broke out Maurice Kahane was twenty. His father, a patriot, wanted him to join the French army, but the young man, who had read enough about the realities of war, especially in Céline's epic novel *Journey to the End of the Night*, saw no point in imitating the hero of that book who joins the army in 1914 on an impulse and finds himself part of a uniformed rabble, led by suicidal and brutal generals and officers who were only too happy to push their men, unprepared for fighting, into battle to be massacred. Maurice refused his father's wish, and, after a massive family row, his father died of a heart attack while sitting on the lavatory. Maurice had been apprenticed to a commercial artist in 1937. He earned a little, very little, doing designs for new products, some of which were exhibited at the World Fair of that year in Paris. But apart from being in love with the girl, Laurette Filipoff, who eventually became his first wife, he wanted to be a publisher like his father.

Maurice, the eldest of four children, had opened the door to Henry Miller and his friend Alfred Perlès, who looked so like him, to Lawrence

Durrell and Anaïs Nin, who everybody knew was well known, but no one quite knew for what, to Eugene and Maria Jolas, both involved with so many writers and movements, to Georges Pelorson, friend of Beckett and devout admirer of Joyce, and to the authors who were hopeful of publication by his father. Publishing was in his blood. After the fall of France, he survived as best he could, took his mother's name, Girodias (a name typical of the Auvergne in the central mountainous region of France, and not Jewish like his father's), worked in various ways and involved himself in the black market, smuggling food to individuals and to restaurants. But mainly he kept his father's business going: he had inherited an office and employees and he kept on publishing, although no longer erotica for Anglophiles. At the invasion of Paris he was asked by anti-Nazi German friends if he would drive one of their families to Spain and thereby escape himself: being partly Jewish, although he had decided to be a Protestant during his French schooldays, they thought he would jump at the chance, but no, he had decided to stay.

While the great flight from Paris was taking place, Girodias watched from his windows the panicking crowds moving towards the southern exits of the city; those who had arrived from northern towns were spreading the feeling of terror and convincing Parisians that they too should flee. The Germans were massing north of Paris, waiting for the order to invade. Girodias spent the last day visiting familiar landmarks, including his father's offices, decided to take his mother's non-Jewish name and he bribed a barman he knew to help him get French identity cards, because his British passport – he had only been in England for a few days during his entire life, but was entitled to one as his father was British – gave Kahane as his name. The barman, about to leave Paris himself, managed to sell him several tons of canned vegetables (all of it celery hearts as it turned out) on the grounds that they would soon be worth a fortune when there was no food to buy.

Girodias, as he now was, started to publish little pamphlets recording what was happening in Paris, particularly in the theatre and the cinema, because these continued normally; his father's office, which had formerly published literary erotica, survived in a modest way. There was a boom in the cinema, mostly of old films, because the remaining Parisians desperately needed to get out of their cold apartments and escape from everyday worries into the more interesting past. Maurice, with his false identity card that could easily betray him, avoided Métro stations and checkpoints. He started to publish under one of his father's company names, Les Éditions du Chêne, in French, and planned a series of art books. At the same time he became friendly with Raymond Queneau, who had been teaching at the bilingual school founded by the Jolases at Neuilly, just north of Paris, and was persuaded by him to start a literary review. The Jolases had returned to America and the school was now run by Georges Pelorson with his Irish wife: Pelorson had been a prominent member of the Joyce circle in Paris and had spent a year in Dublin as an exchange lecturer with Samuel Beckett under an arrangement between Dublin's Trinity College and the École Normale Supérieure, the most highly regarded of the Sorbonne's rival colleges, whereby a junior lecturer from each, who was also a brilliant scholar, was exchanged every year.

During the Occupation, Maurice had one lucky escape when he was called in to Gestapo headquarters: they had somehow come across evidence of his Jewish name and part-Jewish parentage, and he was held overnight. But the next morning, his grandfather, eminent and in full naval uniform, appeared, declared himself to be a retired admiral, and gave testimony that his descendant, in spite of British connections, could in no way be Jewish, and managed thereby to convince the Gestapo to release him.

Girodias's contacts through his father remained useful, and he had made an arrangement with Hachette to have his publications distributed by them. The war years passed – years of shortage, the black market, daily danger and the boredom of living under constant restriction of movement, always suspect and liable to be raided, questioned, stopped in the street or the Métro; life had neither certainty nor freedom. The Germans demanded retribution for the war from the French and were paid with a flood of newly printed paper money and coupons; but they also took at will buildings, horses, paintings, furniture, or wines and liquors to pay the indemnities. The French were unused to shortages and the opportunities to make money with not too many risks, relatively speaking, as every human activity was now a risk, were considerable. For most of them, survival was the first priority, and increasingly the French were seducing the German invaders with their culture, their knowledge of life and pleasure, the beauty of their cities. At the same time, there were terrible reprisals against the population in revenge for the frequent activity of Maquis groups, fighting in the fields and mountains; the Gestapo and their "collabos" (French stooges who were mobilized to work for them) were constantly searching for the resistance groups who passed information to the Free French in London and to the British information services, who helped airmen shot down over France, and couriers to leave the country and cross the frontiers to Spain to get to England by fishing boat.

Life went on. Intellectuals still met and argued in cafés. Georges Bataille went to the Bibliothèque Nationale as its director; Louis Aragon, a known communist, continued to write; books were printed both underground and on official presses: there was little shortage of reading matter. Girodias ran Les Éditions du Chêne from his father's old offices in the Place Vendôme. His first book was called Le Meuble* (The Piece of Furniture). Knowing nothing of the economics of publishing, he underpriced it at nine francs and sold out in a day. But the company prospered as far as it was possible to do so in those difficult times, and he moved it to larger and plusher offices at 4 Rue de la Paix, in the fashionable street that runs from the Place de l'Opéra to the Place Vendôme; this last, built in imitation of an Italian Renaissance square, has Napoleon's statue on top of a long column in its centre. It also contains the entrance to the Ritz Hotel on one side and France's best-known jewellers opposite. Girodias kept his other premises at 16 Place Vendôme, and at the Liberation converted them into an art gallery, which was decorated by his friend Giovanni Védrès. He filled it with modern painters, among them Dubuffet, Bonnard and even Picasso.

Ten days after the Liberation, with Paris still in a fever of celebration, Girodias opened his gallery. He had engaged a white Russian, Georges, on the advice of his office manager, André Léjard (also the author of the aforementioned Le Meuble), to run it for him. No one could either remember or pronounce Georges's last name, but he quickly became known as Georges-Galerie-Vendôme, which, Girodias tells us in his book, should be pronounced with a strong Russian accent. The first exhibition was an enormous success. The whole art world came – painters, critics and the owners and directors of other galleries – to look, evaluate, talk and above all to consume the lavish champagne buffet that Girodias had somehow organized. Unfortunately no one consumed more champagne than the host himself, and he fell flat on the marble floor, passed out, and had to be taken home in a horse-drawn cab.

His great enthusiasm of the moment was for Soutine. To Girodias, he was the most Jewish of all painters, his canvasses recalling the memories of pogroms, persecution and anti-Semitic disdain, telling of his own sufferings and prophesying his eventual suicide; no one cared to have a Soutine on his wall during the Occupation, and his prices were currently at the bottom of the market. The Baron Mollet, in reality no baron at all, but a one-time drinking companion of Apollinaire, became friendly with Girodias and helped him to sniff out the Soutines from the cellars and cupboards where they had been hidden. The Galerie

Vendôme began to specialize in Soutine, buying cheaply and selling at three times the price, often within a few days: Girodias was making money. And he was also spending it and keeping up sexual liaisons with a variety of young women; the art gallery was an even stronger draw sexually than the publishing house.

For ten years, since about the age of sixteen, he had nourished a passion for Laurette, his childhood friend. Her constant refusal to become more than a friend and to allow him any physical contact inflamed his desires. She had always made it clear that she intended to be married as a virgin. In the immediate aftermath of the war, profitably engaged as a publisher and art dealer, even while taking full advantage of the prevailing sexual freedom and the number of available nubile young women, Girodias finally proposed marriage to Laurette. A two-week honeymoon was planned to follow the ceremony, which took place in the *mairie* of the sixteenth *arrondissement*; they were one of a long string of couples waiting to be married (the legal ceremony, which in France must precede any religious one, was free on Saturdays) and Girodias, distressed by mixed feelings about the forthcoming consummation of his long suppressed lust, and the price he was paying for it, wryly noted the appearance of the other waiting couples – many of the brides were heavily pregnant, and smiling happiness did not seem to be the predominant feeling – and was reminded of a Brueghel painting. In addition, he knew that he had not been Laurette's first choice – she had long maintained a chaste affection for a certain Vivian – but she had nevertheless accepted Maurice, making it clear that she wanted children early and a conventional married life. After the ceremony, they were seen off at the Gare de Lyon by friends and took the overnight *train bleu* to Nice.

Nice, however, was not what it had been before the war, a year-round holiday town for Parisians and foreigners from northern countries. The beaches were still covered with rusty barbed wire and gun emplacements; there was virtually no public transport and no fuel to make cars run, even if one could find one to hire. The town was filled with American GIs, marines and sailors, all drinking heavily and all looking for girls. MPs patrolled the streets, freely using their batons and throwing drunken bodies onto jeeps. The newly married couple ventured onto the streets warily, only to creep into the dark of the movie houses, mostly showing pre-war films, feeling more comfortable that way than in the new intimacy of their marital bed, but outside they were caught up in a river of American military uniforms; Girodias was often pulling one of his wife's arms while a GI was trying to pull the other. On one occasion, only the arrival of the MPs saved him from losing his bride to a pleasant but quite determined Texan soldier, who could not understand why this English-speaking Frenchman objected to sharing his woman.

They cut short the honeymoon and returned to Paris. It was in any case a busy time. Les Éditions du Chêne was a part of the overheated atmosphere of the Liberation: the Allied armies were still fighting German armies in the East, but Paris celebrated its freedom day and night. The bars and restaurants were full, and new nightclubs were opening up. Café life, which until recently had seen Germans occupying every other table, had returned to its pre-war buzz of gossip, political argument, flirtation, the exchange of ideas, new projects and plans for the future. In addition to the classic cafés of Saint-Germain, Montparnasse and the Champs-Élysées, there were those where the anti-Nazi underground groups had met or where black-market deals were made that had operated in semi- or total clandestinity, like the bar of Saint-Yves, well known to Girodias. And new bars were opening: one of these, La Bibliothèque, became the principal Girodias watering hole.

Although married, and rather uncertain as to how it had happened, Maurice Girodias kept up his old liaisons, one of them with a new conquest, Germaine Riedberger, whom in his book he calls Gervaise, a lively widow of wide culture, whose apartment was frequented by literary men of the left, among them Claude Roy, Jean-Francis Roland, Roger Vailland and Philippe Soupault, the last an old-time surrealist. Vailland was to become a celebrated popular writer and win the Prix Goncourt in 1957 for his novel La Loi* (The Law), while Soupault would survive all his surrealist contemporaries and live until 1990, the year of Girodias's own death. There were also Maurice Merleau-Ponty, Sartre's main rival as a literary philosopher, Robert Doisneau, the photographer, the Védrès couple, Giovanni and his wife Nicole, who together compiled a book for Les Éditions du Chêne, Images du Cinéma Français, in association with a young man, Henry Langlois, who had just opened the first cinémathèque, that gift to Parisian film buffs, showing old classics in repertory day and night. Germaine gave dinner parties to which Maurice went as if still a bachelor on his own, agreeable gatherings of writers, artists, men of letters and ideas, accompanied by their girlfriends and occasionally their wives.

To escape Laurette, Girodias spent hours in Germaine's apartment, sometimes alone, reading books. She introduced him to the work of Kafka, a new name to him, and he found close parallels to his own situation, especially in Metamorphosis. Through her, his acquaintanceship expanded; she was a hostess of genius, knowing exactly who to bring together to make an evening a success, and Maurice Girodias, as her lover and a publisher in the swing of the current excitement, received both social and commercial benefits.

Germaine was the perfect sensuous Frenchwoman, ten or twelve years older than Maurice, beautiful and elegant, who took the sex between them as something natural and uninvolving, to be enjoyed without possessiveness. Maurice, on the other hand, agonized. He was newly married! How could he be a seducer or be seduced so easily? Germaine treated his scruples with amused condescension, and when he mentioned his wife one afternoon as they lay on the bed, resting after a successful coupling, guiltily saying that such occasions could not become a habit, she turned on him with emphasis.

"I adore Laurette," she said. "I really like your wife. She has an undeniable charm, and you are very lucky to have her, my dear. Many others would like to be in your shoes." She lit a cigarette and put the *Saint Matthew Passion* on the record player, while a storm erupted outside her apartment windows. She then promised him a real passion, and as they started to make love again, he reflected on his lot, doomed guiltily to "happiness, liberty and the joy of having this crazy woman in my arms, this woman who has totally conquered me, ravaged me, possessed me, prostituted me."*

Maurice was constantly seen in the cafés and restaurants of Paris with his two women, Laurette and Germaine, a *ménage à trois* that appeared to suit all three. It was Germaine who triumphantly announced at a dinner as the winter approached that Laurette was pregnant. And the happy future mother began to prepare to make Maurice, still a child himself as he frequently protested, a paterfamilias.

3

The publishing company was prospering, especially with art books, but there were rivals on the horizon. Robert Laffont, who had been editing a poetry review in Marseille, moved to Paris and wanted to meet Girodias: was he about to take away his title of being the youngest publisher in France? Adrien Maeght started up his gallery. He had been quietly hoarding paintings during the war. Harry Abrams started publishing art books in New York. He showed Maurice the proofs of a book on van Gogh that he was about to publish. But were the colours not too bright? asked Girodias. Had the printer not made a mistake with the ink? Abrams explained that an art book would be unpublishable in America if the colours were not bright. *Life* magazine brought out an issue with articles on the French art scene under the Occupation and Les Éditions du Chêne was featured. Girodias, as a result, was interviewed by American journalists and university professors, ecstatic at being able to return to Paris, now associated in their minds with Ernest Hemingway, Henry Miller and Gertrude Stein. War correspondents with cultural interests called on him day and night. He discovered the American diet in army canteens, where he was invited, and tried not to think about it. Local prostitutes whom he met in bars complained about the sanitary expectations of American soldiers in contrast to the Germans. One of them, Suzy-Deux-Tunes, whom Girodias met with the photographer Robert Doisneau, told him that with the Germans they had to clean themselves on the bidet before sex, but with the "Ricains", they had to wash their mouths out all the time. But not everyone complained. There was no shortage of French women willing to entertain the American forces, and with money and cigarettes in short supply they did not have to pay much for their pleasures. Americans were in any case very popular, and French women felt generous. Girodias's older sister, Nicole, married an English lieutenant. Her junior, Sylvie, had proposals from both an English Quaker and a fast-talking Argentine cowboy; she chose the latter. Eric, the younger brother, who had spent the war on a farm, went to interpret for the Ninth American Air Force.

Girodias wrote to his father's most famous author, Henry Miller, who was now living in Big Sur, relieved that the war was over. He had left Paris in 1939, shortly before the outbreak of hostilities, had spent a little time with Lawrence Durrell in Crete and had then returned to the US, where, after a tour of the country with his friend Abe Rattner – a trip not at all to his liking – he had written *The Air-Conditioned Nightmare*, a damning condemnation of the US. It was of course impossible for him to earn anything from *Tropic of Cancer* and the other "obscene" novels that Obelisk Press had published in the Thirties. He did not earn very much from the non-obscene books either, such as *The Colossus of Maroussi*, which was his first American-published book. New Directions brought it out in 1941. In 1942 Miller settled himself at Big Sur where he established a small colony of artists and writers around himself, living on very little, but celebrated among those who knew his Paris reputation.

Henry Miller's attitude to the war is difficult to understand. He was a pacifist who saw no point in fighting evil. He believed in running away from it and ignoring it. The kind of evil represented by Hitler could not go away of course; it could only be fought and defeated. But Henry Miller had no understanding of that. He had an anarchist's dislike of authority and of all political systems:

Fuck your capitalistic society! Fuck your communistic society and your fascist society and your other societies! Society is made up of individuals. It is the individual who interests me – not the society.*

He had simply ignored the war and was lucky enough to be in a country where it was possible to do so.

When Girodias received a reply from Henry Miller, it was a friendly and enthusiastic one. He was pleased that Girodias had survived the war, and he liked his new name which made him think of Greece. Girodias's proposal was to bring out some of the novels in French translations, but then he also thought: why not reissue the same books in English as well? Henry Miller liked the idea. The problem lay in establishing the copyrights. Les Éditions du Chêne was really only a trading name that Girodias had taken over from his father, not registered as a company, and Obelisk Press was, of course, totally defunct. He decided to make Chêne a limited company which would then take over Obelisk and revive it, publishing books in English for sale to GIs. At the same time, he could bring out the four volumes of Frank Harris's *My Life and Loves* that he had already issued in French. Harris, an English journalist of some renown, had written a long account of his sexual conquests, which had been published by Kahane before the war. Girodias now reprinted Frank Harris in English and the two *Tropics* (*Tropic of Cancer* and *Tropic of Capricorn*), and arranged with the foreign department of Hachette to distribute them. In effect, Girodias found that he was being financed by Hachette under his contract with them, and to such an extent that he was able to reduce considerably his bank overdraft. But there were certain dangers: Henri Filipacchi was the man with whom Girodias had to deal, and this was a time when Hachette was busy buying up publishing companies that were impoverished and in difficulties, either because they had collaborated and were now under official constraints, or because they had not done so, and had no money. Girodias found that Filipacchi, representing Hachette and its financial power, and his assistant Guy Schoeller, were in effect his partners. Schoeller, a young dandy, who was later to become celebrated as the middle-aged man with whom a young girl has an affair in Françoise Sagan's best-selling novel *Bonjour Tristesse*, published in 1954, was the son of René, the man who had made Hachette a conglomerate publishing company, owning many similar ones, and with a near-monopoly of French book distribution. René Schoeller had just died. Girodias's relationship with Hachette was soon to lead him into trouble.

To encourage Henry Miller to give him all the rights to his books, Girodias calculated what Henry might make out of the deal and wrote that he could expect to receive $40,000 from the projected sales. Henry took this to mean that he was about to be paid that amount. The misunderstanding was multiplied by a drop in the value of the franc and the impossibility of anyone in France obtaining dollars to send to Miller because of the foreign exchange regulations ruling at the time. However, Girodias, by dint of buying dollars from tourists and various deals, did manage to obtain enough to enable Henry Miller to finish paying for the house he was building in Big Sur and to contemplate a first post-war trip to Paris.

Unfortunately, not everything was available. Gallimard had acquired the rights to *Black Spring* just before the start of the war and Denoël to *Tropic of Cancer*, both for translation into French. However, *Tropic of Capricorn* and *Max and the White Phagocytes*, which had been published by Jack Kahane in 1938 and 1939, were both available. The problem was to find the right French translator; Maurice now had the idea of asking Georges Pelorson to make French versions for him. Pelorson was under a cloud. A friend of Samuel Beckett since his university days, an intimate of the Jolases and of James Joyce whom he had met through them, a man with a good knowledge of English-language literature, he had put himself in danger during the war by working for the Vichy administration in the Department of Education. He was liable to be prosecuted as a traitor. He had known Miller before the war, and he was in need of money. As a collaborator in the Vichy regime on a fairly minor stratum of the bureaucracy, he was judged on a much lower level than those who had held important positions, but then he could not expect to have good lawyers to defend him, and after his arrest he had been held, not in a state prison, but by the FFI who were inclined to shoot those they had arrested, usually after a brief trial conducted more on emotional than on legal principles. When Girodias asked Raymond Queneau, a pre-war friend of Pelorson, to intervene for him, Queneau indignantly said that Pelorson deserved whatever was coming to him. He had in fact given his post, in the school that Jolas had founded, to Pelorson when he left it, and both had been adherents of James Joyce. But Queneau, like Camus and many others, was pitiless to those who had sided with and worked for the Nazis. Through a subterfuge Girodias had helped Pelorson to escape from his imprisonment, which was really a form of house arrest (he was held in a hotel with other suspected traitors), and a judge was persuaded to give him a legal release. The judge also advised him to move out of Paris and change his name, which he did – to Georges Belmont.

Pelorson was a *normalien*, a graduate of France's most prestigious university, the École Normale Supérieure, part of the Sorbonne that since Napoleon's time had trained civil servants, politicians, philosophers and intellectuals of every kind. He and Samuel Beckett had become friends under the exchange agreement. Beckett met Pelorson during his year in Paris in 1928, and the following year Pelorson went to Dublin, where Beckett introduced him to the mysteries of Dublin bohemian life and Jameson's whiskey, and they collaborated on sketches for university reviews. Helped by Girodias, Pelorson gratefully translated the two Miller novels. Girodias then rushed the translations into print, both to benefit from the publication of *Tropic of Cancer* and *Black Spring* in French translation by other publishers, and to beat the rumoured censorship which the Catholic Church was urging the new government to introduce by reviving a pre-war law against immoral and erotic literature. French publishers at the time were lobbying against the return of censorship by pointing out how much they had suffered under the German laws, and Robert Denoël, about to publish *Tropic of Cancer*, was in the forefront of the battle. Girodias spoke to him, made common cause, and was then disconcerted when Denoël was suddenly assassinated in the street at night for no apparent reason. He had apparently stopped his car, climbed out – no one knew why – and been killed. Nevertheless, the book appeared a few days later.

The publication of so many Henry Miller novels within a few days of each other attracted much attention and Miller was treated as a considerable advance on the "daring" literature that had previously come from Gide, Cocteau and even Céline. The more puritanical critics attacked *Tropic of Capricorn* more than the others and even Maurice Nadeau, while praising Miller's honesty and literary qualities, spoke of his "monstrous immorality" in his review in *Combat*. Georges Bataille, himself an erotic writer and advocate of the work of the Marquis de Sade, who had also written admiringly about Gilles de Rais as an historical personage, had considerable reservations over what he saw as a childish side to Miller's character and attitude. This was because Henry Miller, in his personality and his literary style, could hardly be further removed from the French concept of a man of letters. His honesty with himself, his willingness to expose his most secret thoughts and desires to the reading public, his rather naive pantheism, his lack of self-censorship and editorial control over what went down on the page, were shocking to the French literary establishment. Some critics, like André Ulmann and Robert Kemp, dismissed him as an incompetent and bad writer. The debate taking place in the literary pages began to sell books, and although at first Girodias found the initial sales of *Tropic of Capricorn* very disappointing, it was not long before things improved.

The reason was the return of censorship itself. It came at the right moment for Girodias, because he had by now spread himself much too thin with the art gallery, the new offices, the number of books in production and the review *Critique*, which he had launched under the editorship of Georges Bataille. It seemed impossible to avoid imminent bankruptcy. But when a prosecution was launched against him, and against Henry Miller's other publishers, under a law passed in 1939 to protect family values and young people from dangerous thoughts – a law that had never been used, because the Nazi laws passed under the Occupation were far more wide-ranging – the situation quickly changed. The prosecution was instigated by a complaint from a puritanical pressure group, the Cartel d'Action Sociale et Morale, against the publication of Henry Miller's two *Tropics*. Under the law, the publishers, the author, booksellers and even those who bought and read them, could be prosecuted and jailed if found guilty. But the case would be a long one. The publicity quickly sold Girodias's first printing of 15,000 copies, and he printed 50,000 more, while Denöel reprinted three times that number. The newspapers had a field day, asking if this was not Vichy censorship all over again and comparing the prosecution to wartime events. A public debate was organized in which Girodias, together with three literary critics, Armand Hoog (a practising Catholic), Maurice Nadeau and Pierre Fauchery, was to confront Daniel Parker, organizer of the Cartel d'Action Sociale et Morale, aided by Ulmann and Kemp. But when the latter two realized the implications of the prosecution, leading to possible imprisonment for those found guilty, they refused to appear; Girodias then had little difficulty in making his solitary opponent look ridiculous. The publicity again increased the sales to over 125,000 copies. The long Girodias war against censorship had begun.

One of his authors was the Admiral Muselier, who during the war had been head of the French Navy in London, or of what remained of it that had escaped German capture. Muselier, like many other French officers had escaped to London after the fall of France, and was senior in rank to de Gaulle, a colonel and tank commander who had promoted himself to general and contrived to outmanoeuvre and frustrate his superior officers by persuading Churchill to recognize him as head of the French armed forces. Only three such officers, including Admiral Muselier, agreed at the time to sink their pride, accept the situation and serve under de Gaulle. But according to Muselier this new, inexperienced general made tactical mistake after tactical mistake, leading to the bloody defeat at Dakar and later ones at Saint-Pierre-et-Miquelon, in Syria, the Lebanon and Indo-China. Every mistake was blamed on others, and Muselier himself was undermined by de Gaulle's secret service, arrested on trumped-up charges and dismissed. His book* was an account of de Gaulle's wartime behaviour and was intended to explode the myth of de Gaulle as a war hero and the saviour of France; it described the General's political manoeuvrings against his rivals, not only with the British, who had backed him in 1940 and afterwards, but with the State Department, which had much preferred General Giraud, his arch rival, who later wrote his own book about events, but which few read.

Muselier was no natural writer and his book was indigestibly written in a mock heroic style; he resisted every attempt to edit and rewrite, so that on publication it was, according to Girodias, naive in form but true in substance. By publishing it, Girodias was declaring war on society: it could only make him powerful enemies, and it did. At the same time, the book was hardly noticed by the public, anxious to accept any version of history that did not look too closely into its own wartime conduct and to accept the borrowed glory of its head of state.

The next political book to appear on the list of Les Éditions du Chêne was by Yves Farge, a genuine activist in the Maquis who had fought effectively during the war in the Vercors, an area where many died, including the writer Jean Prévost. It was from here that Jean Bruller, the most famous of the wartime underground writers and publishers, had taken his pen name, Vercors, under which he wrote the most successful of French clandestine novels, *La Silence de la mer* (*The Silence of the Sea*), depicting the silent, stubborn refusal of a French family to become friendly with a German officer billeted on them. His publishing company, Les Éditions de Minuit, produced twenty-five significant books under the Occupation and was later bought by Jérôme Lindon to make it the leading post-war imprint of serious French literature by new writers.

Farge captured Lyon as the Allied armies advanced from the south and when de Gaulle arrived in that town, he found that Farge had already arrested all the collaborators and put them into the local prisons. During the remainder of the war, and in the administrations that followed the surrender of Germany, Farge turned out to be an awkward administrator, incorruptible, effective and ruthless. When asked to take charge of suppressing the black market by Félix Gouin, one of the most powerful ministers in France after the Liberation, Farge agreed to do so only if the death penalty was introduced to enable him to do it effectively. His uncompromising attitude made government officials uneasy, and it was not long before he uncovered a major scandal concerning the distribution of food and especially wine – everything was in short supply and rationed – that involved many of the major figures in the administration, including the man who came second only to de Gaulle in power and importance, Félix Gouin himself. Girodias persuaded Farge to write a small book listing the facts: this appeared under the title *Le Pain de la corruption** (*The Bread of Corruption*). *Le Monde* published a major leading article that was taken up by the rest of the press, asking for a full investigation into the allegations. Gouin could not ignore this and prosecuted Farge and his publisher for defamation. The case attracted major attention, and many ministers appeared in the witness box: the obvious ways in which they covered up for each other, the bland declarations of innocence, each swearing that he had not known what the others were doing, were not convincing. After two days of hearing evidence, the judge declared that all the allegations made in Farge's book were made in good faith and on evidence enough to justify them; he acquitted both author and publisher, and furthermore ordered that Félix Gouin, who at one point in the court had hurled insults at, and nearly physically attacked, the opposing attorney, should pay all costs.

Maurice Girodias was now trying to build up his literary list. He had published some of the novels of Henry Miller and his book about Greece, *The Colossus of Maroussi*, and was looking for other American or British authors, but Gallimard had a virtual monopoly of English-language literature. His new literary director, André Maugé, saw an opportunity to reprint Russian classics that had gone out of print and of finding new Russian and East European authors, who at the time were temporarily out of fashion. *A History of Russian Literature since the Revolution* appeared on the list and new authors included Alexei Remizov, Nikos Kazantzakis (*Zorba the Greek*) and Nina Berberova. There were also anthologies of French medieval verse published, and other books of a similar nature. But Girodias had been warned by good friends in publishing that the time had come to be careful: he had too many enemies.

Henry Miller suddenly turned up without any warning in Paris. He was delighted to find that most of his old haunts from the Thirties were unchanged and that many old friends were still around. There were lunches and dinners with Girodias, son of his first publisher, who seemed to be doing well. Henry had recently become interested in the history of the Cathars, the Manichean sect that had been brutally persecuted and put down in Montségur in Provence in the thirteenth century; he had strong feelings that he was reincarnated from a Cathar and had been burnt at the stake in a previous life. The subject was one that would interest Girodias in later years. But now a large blot suddenly appeared on the horizon to spoil Henry Miller's joy at rediscovering Paris.

Girodias's lawyer, Jacques-Arnold Croquez, rang him up to warn that Henry Miller was running a considerable risk by being in Paris, giving interviews to the press and getting his name into the newspapers. His books were being prosecuted, and as the author he could be arrested. Girodias argued that Miller was a naive American, a noble savage with no comprehension of the barbarous laws that were being used to prosecute his books. But at the same time he could see that the whole matter could be turned to good advantage, that publicity would increase his sales, and that if Henry Miller could be persuaded to appear voluntarily before the court at the present time, it might all be happily cleared up. The procurator, M. Bergognon, was a civilized man; the hearing would be short, and he was fairly certain that the government was embarrassed enough about the whole matter to be happy to see it dropped.

But what should Maurice say to Henry Miller, a man who disliked all unpleasantness? Should he advise him to leave the country rapidly? Croquez warned that Miller might very well be arrested at the police control on leaving the country, and that even if he crept out quietly, the whole affair would open up new problems for Girodias. It would be better to go straight to the court and claim his rights as an artist in a country that had a long tradition of artistic tolerance. In any case, the procurator was very likely a fan of Miller. Henry was reluctantly persuaded to comply, and a separate lawyer, a Maître Villon, a man of the literary left who knew Miller's work, was engaged to represent him.

But Henry was frightened. He had always run from trouble, from wars and violence and unpleasantness. He came to court in a state of terror: the sombre atmosphere of the public building and the formal attire of the lawyers convinced him he was going to his doom. Maurice tried to keep him distracted with conversation while they waited for their turn to be heard, but Henry became more and more terrified. When asked in court to confirm his identity, all he could get out was a "Hmmm" of fright. When asked if he was the author of the works in question and if he understood that he was charged with an outrage against public morals, he turned to Maurice, asking, "What did he say?" and then, "I have a terrible need to piss. Ask if I can go." "Wait two minutes," he was told. "It won't be long."

Like a schoolboy on his first day at school, Miller sat there, wriggling and uncomfortable, while the lawyers argued their legal points and the procurator glanced at him occasionally. The glances were kindly but Miller took them as menaces. But the case was dismissed in the end and the procurator shook the hand of the terrified writer, still not sure if he had been sentenced to the guillotine or was to be released. Croquez warned Girodias to be careful in future. The Garde des Sceaux, who was responsible for launching prosecutions, was a dangerous man, and Jules Moch, the Minister of the Interior, who had given evidence against Farge in the *Pain de la corruption* case, would take any opportunity to hurt him. "Be reasonable," he said. But it was not in Girodias's nature to be reasonable.

4

French and English publishing in Paris underwent enormous changes during and after the war. The presence during the Twenties and Thirties of two intellectual bookshops on the Rue de l'Odéon, the English Shakespeare & Company of Sylvia Beach at No. 12 and the French Maison des Amis des Livres of Adrienne Monnier at No. 7 across the street, guaranteed an exchange of writing and ideas across the language barrier. Both bookshops were meeting places for writers, and their respective clienteles were to a great extent interchangeable. French writers and intellectuals would come to hear Joyce or Hemingway read at Sylvia Beach's, and some English and American literary figures, though to a lesser extent, would go to readings at Monnier's. And both bookshops sold the current literary reviews in addition to books. The English-language magazines, and in particular *transition*, translated the French literature of the day, as well as writing from other languages, and Paris was full of émigrés from Hitler's Germany, Mussolini's Italy and other countries under intolerant regimes or threatened by them.

The German Occupation of Paris was primarily dangerous for the large number of Jewish intellectuals living there, but also for communists, known leftists and anti-Nazis, and those who had enemies on the right. The intellectual leader of the French right since the Twenties had been Charles Maurras, editor of *Action Française*, which became a political movement as well as a journal. Maurras was anti-Semitic, reactionary and a monarchist, known principally to the English-speaking world for his influence on T.S. Eliot, who had published some of his essays in *The Criterion*: Eliot's political views in the Twenties were not so very different. Maurras still has his followers today, although he was greatly discredited by the war. The leaders of the left were André Malraux and Louis Aragon. Both had a communist past, but Malraux became a Gaullist and was de Gaulle's Minister of Culture from 1959 to 1969. The outbreak of war brought about an emigration from France to Britain and America. Of those who stayed behind, many died, either because of underground activities, or because they were Jewish or known leftists, and in some cases they were killed in the act of leaving. But many also survived. Aragon, Éluard, Paulhan and Jean Bruller (Vercors) produced clandestine literature and were still present after the war. Saint-Exupéry died in the Maquis, Jean Prévost in a battle at Vercors. Even Jews who had long converted to Catholicism, like the surrealist poet and writer Max Jacob, who had taken minor orders in the church, were not safe; Jacob perished in a concentration camp. Ilya Ehrenburg, who had spent much of the Thirties in Montparnasse, and was a familiar figure in La Coupole and other cafés, moved into the Soviet embassy, and returned to Russia only at the time of the pact. He had been working for a considerable time as a go-between in the Thirties, uniting anti-fascist writers in Paris with those still in favour in Stalin's USSR. Many French writers went to the south of France, some of them joining the great exodus as the Germans neared Paris. André Gide decided to stay there and sit out the Occupation. Arthur Koestler was arrested and interned, but managed eventually to get to London. Walter Benjamin was stopped at the Spanish border and killed himself. Jean-Paul Sartre and Simone de Beauvoir simply went to ground, Sartre having been released from the army immediately after the French defeat. He then resumed his university career. Samuel Beckett, who had been in Ireland when the war broke out, rushed back to France to be with his friends and joined the Resistance. When his group was uncovered by the Gestapo, he was lucky enough to be warned in time and to bicycle down to the Vaucluse with Suzanne Dechevaux-Dumesnil, whom he married nearly twenty years after the war ended. He spent the latter part of it with her in Roussillon where *Waiting for Godot* is set. Although his novel *Molloy*, written at the same time in the late Forties, would appear to be set in Ireland, its landscape is remarkably similar to that of Roussillon. Arthur Adamov, who was to come to prominence in the Fifties at the same time as Beckett, joined the flood of fleeing Parisians and eventually arrived at Marseille, where he was arrested and sent to a concentration camp because he looked Jewish; he was lucky to be later released.

In Paris at the time, the right-wing writers had the city and the literary scene to themselves: Drieu la Rochelle, an out-and-out fascist and admirer of Hitler, who had nevertheless been a friend of André Malraux, the pillar of the left and a soldier against Franco during the civil war, was made the new editor of the *Nouvelle Revue Française*, house organ of Gallimard, which collaborated during the Occupation. The previous editor, Jean Paulhan, tried to persuade Gallimard at least to change the name of the review, but was unsuccessful. Gallimard was closed for a short time but the credentials of Drieu, aided by the German officer Gerhard Heller, who had been put in charge of cultural matters in Paris, were effective in getting it reopened. The literary history of France under the Occupation is complex because many of those on the left and right had been school friends, many of them *normaliens*, and many right-wing writers protected old friends from arrest or secured their release after they had been picked up. Much the same happened after the Liberation when some intellectuals who had fought against the Germans, either in the Free French army or the underground, saved collaborators from death or imprisonment. Some other writers simply spent the war in the US or Britain.

Although many of the periodicals that nourished literary Paris continued to appear during the war, they were nearly all under new editors approved by the German authorities; Jewish contributors were banned, as well as nearly all known leftists. But although many newspapers disappeared and many publishing houses were closed, the volume of books published in France during the war actually increased. 8,680 titles appeared in 1944, about 800 more than the year before, and 3,000 more than in 1940. Many well-known anti-German writers, such as Paul Claudel, Jean Giraudoux and Jean-Paul Sartre were not only published but had their plays successfully performed on the stage. In fact, once the initial panic had subsided and many French people had returned to their homes, Paris enjoyed something of a golden age where the theatre and the cinema were concerned. Such film classics as *Les Enfants du Paradis* were made under the Occupation and many important plays had their first performances. Credit has been given to two German officers, the writer Ernst Jünger, whose wartime *Paris Diary* became a best-seller in France in the Sixties, and the aforementioned Gerhard Heller at the Ministry of Propaganda – a department of the occupying forces which consisted of specialists in French literature and culture – for this tolerance.

There were many who simply went into hiding and survived the war by not going into streets where they might be recognized, or by finding remote villages that hardly ever saw a German soldier; bad luck was more to be feared than positive German searches, which were made largely to locate hidden valuables or to find armed members of the Maquis or the Resistance. Foreign exiles and Jews were often hidden by obliging families. Raymond Duncan, brother of the dancer Isadora Duncan, spent the whole war in hiding in Paris. During the last days before the arrival of the liberating troops, he climbed over the slippery roof of his dwelling to hang the first American flag over a nearby building, nearly falling into the street while doing so.

At the Liberation, the *Nouvelle Revue Française* went back to the editorship of Jean Paulhan, and Sartre started *Les Temps Modernes*, which became its biggest rival: his co-editors were Raymond Aron and Maurice Merleau-Ponty. Aragon founded *Les Lettres Françaises*, which was, more or less, communist-backed, and *Esprit* became the Catholic literary journal. Georges Duthuit restarted *transition*, but principally in French; the only way to get paper for a new journal was to prove a connection with a pre-war one. Eugene Jolas was now an officer in the American army. His job was to interrogate Germans and to sniff out the hardline Nazis. Maria Jolas returned to her house at Colombey-Les-Deux-Eglises, which they would later sell to de Gaulle: it is now a national shrine. Soon the English-language magazines would start again.

Paris in the late Forties was filled with the American military, swarming around the popular dance halls of the Champs-Elysées, like Mimi Pinson, or the nightclubs of Pigalle. There were British and Canadian troops too, but less in evidence, and in any case they had less money. There were many restrictions, but the black market and the illegal changers of money flourished. At every street corner you could get a better rate for the franc with dollars or Swiss francs than at the banks, and bank employees were often doing the dealing, even on bank premises. There were not many British pounds to change: British currency controls were severe and were to remain so for more than a decade. Many new French films were made. Jean Vilar founded the Théâtre Nationale Populaire, giving the classics in large theatres, eventually having his own when the Palais de Chaillot was built, and he put on large summer spectacles in the open-air courtyard of the

Pope's Palace in Avignon; his principal star, alongside himself, was Gérard Philipe, the pin-up boy of France and star of many French films, such as *Le Diable au corps* and *Fanfan la Tulipe*. At the Comédie Française, Jean-Louis Barrault continued his long partnership with Madeleine Renaud, which had started in the early Thirties and was to continue into the Nineties. Jean-Paul Sartre became the literary hero of the moment. Les Deux Magots at Saint-Germain-des-Prés and La Coupole at Montparnasse were the cafés where you could see him, usually with Simone de Beauvoir and an entourage of sycophants and friends. Everyone spoke of the new existentialism, a philosophy and outlook on life that somehow became associated, because of Sartre whose lectures were widely attended, with the new nightclubs of Saint-Germain, where you could see cabaret sketches written and performed by Boris Vian, another *vedette* of the moment who also played the jazz trumpet. Vian's principal nightclub was Le Tabou on the Rue Dauphine, and among the many cellar-clubs were the Club Saint-Germain, where all-night discussions took place to the sounds of jazz and torch songs; there was also the Mephisto where political argument was the norm. Sartre would sit and drink in these places until dawn and then go to lecture at the Sorbonne. Somehow the philosophy of existentialism, a stoic view of life without God, became identified with a lifestyle that included free love and the constant search for pleasure and intellectual stimulation. After the grey years of war, Paris had become young again.

5

Maurice Girodias's long-standing affair with Germaine did not long keep its tolerant and pleasure-for-the-sake-of-pleasure tone. Laurette and Germaine became good friends, and the former almost certainly knew something of her husband's relationship with Germaine, but the beautiful and passionate mistress became more demanding. Once, when they were lost in a fog on the outskirts of a village, and had made love in the car while waiting for the fog to lift, she had afterwards pushed him naked onto the road and driven off. She came back a few minutes later, but Maurice had had a taste of her capriciousness with the unpleasant prospect of a long walk back to Paris in the nude.

On another occasion, when a whole group of them had gone off to spend Easter together in a small village, two persons each occupying a room in the two little hotels, Maurice was obliged to spend the first night sharing a room with a male friend because Laurette would not arrive until the next morning. With the greatest of difficulty, because his liaison with Germaine was not known to the others, he managed to crawl through a window when his companion was asleep (there was another couple in the next room and it was necessary to go through it to reach the door) to get to his mistress. This was very early in the morning, and on leaving Germaine, he wanted to give the impression that he had taken an early walk; at daylight he went off some distance and on his return found that Laurette had arrived and the whole group was having breakfast. He was called to the telephone: it was Germaine calling from her room, threatening suicide unless he dreamt up some pretext to escape the boring company and his just-arrived wife, and spend the rest of the weekend with her alone. Girodias told the others that a friend was threatening suicide and that he had to go to him. Germaine then drove him off. They went to the friend's empty house – he was in fact away for Easter – and they hardly ever left the bedroom.

But Germaine began to threaten suicide more and more frequently, and her capriciousness took many forms, not unlike Catherine in Henri-Pierre Roché's novel *Jules et Jim*, which became a popular film in the Sixties with Jeanne Moreau. On one occasion, when she was working with him in his office, filling in for an absent employee and annoyed that she had not received much attention from him for a few days, she asked him to come into the office next door to his. In spite of the surface coldness that she was exhibiting that day, he suddenly felt a great desire for her and made passionate love to her on the carpet. When they were finished, as he rolled over, exhausted, she told him she would have shot him had he done anything else, and proved it by producing a revolver from a drawer in her desk. She pointed it at her image in the mirror and pulled the trigger, shattering the glass. Maurice had a problem on his hands!

He also had other problems. He went away for a month's summer holiday with Laurette to Saint Tropez, then a little fishing port unknown to tourists, and in the calm of August contemplated his future. He was sinking deeper into financial trouble, was heavily in debt and had to find a way out. When he returned to Paris at the end of August, he found a vengeful Germaine waiting for him; he had by now made her a part of the publishing company, and she had considerably strengthened her position in it. Now, resenting his holiday with Laurette, she pressured him to get rid of André Léjard, his right-hand man, who had been with him loyally since the reestablishment of Les Éditions du Chêne. The Galerie Vendôme was now doing badly: there was much more competition in the art world. *Critique*, the serious literary review edited by Georges Bataille and financed by Girodias, was losing too much money; twelve issues had appeared, but it was impossible to keep financing the loss. Bataille went hunting for another publisher and found Calmann-Lévy willing to take it on. It was eventually passed on to Les Éditions de Minuit. By now the group working for Girodias at Chêne was divided into warring factions, each trying to protect his own job and undermine his rivals. Girodias became convinced that only his secretary, Genia, always loyal, always sparkling, funny and cheerful, was his true ally. She was married to a senior communist journalist, one of the editors of *Humanité*, a man who, but for Genia, would be a hardline, disagreeable party member, but because of her charm and support had maintained an air of youth and adventure. Her charm and good humour was now also Girodias's principal moral support as he tried to find a way to control his ever-growing mountain of debt, putting off until the last moment each week the decision whom to pay and with what. The habits of the Occupation, living from day to day, with little thought of tomorrow, had become too ingrained, and he had counted too long on his luck.

> At that time, the game of survival had been raised to the level of a mad gamble, to the extreme limit of defiance. I had succeeded in establishing a publishing house without a penny and amidst extreme dangers, reversing the situation as a conjuror pulls a series of unexpected objects out of his hat. Now the game was reversed. I had made a simple gamble and the virtuosity that I had gained had hidden the fact that I was throwing away my professional opportunities... instead of calmly taking stock and making rational decisions, I still relied on chance and instinct, the only law that seemed to me to be possible to follow...*

The rifts among his employees and colleagues were resulting in a paucity of new creative ideas and Les Éditions du Chêne was in the doldrums intellectually as well as financially. Germaine forced Girodias to choose between Léjard and herself; with great sadness he chose Germaine. This did not make her easier to get on with: her next target was the faithful Genia and her next victim became Laurette. Girodias stopped sleeping much of the time at Germaine's luxurious apartment and moved to a miserable little place of his own on the outer edge of Montparnasse. Germaine made a point of sleeping with all of his best male friends, and she made sure that he knew about it. He found himself engulfed in jealous rage, while the office atmosphere became ever more troubled, Germaine turning the staff against each other, while treating her ex-lover with triumphant cold disdain. And his troubles only started there.

Les Éditions du Chêne was now in the hands of a committee of creditors. They enabled Girodias to keep going, but he could sign no cheques and all his decisions had to be ratified by the financial controller in charge; his salary was the equivalent of a starting secretary's. Meetings were held in the boardroom on Louis XIII chairs, and Girodias sat uncomfortably through them. Two printers, two paper merchants, a binder and a block-maker, Monsieur Laurent, the most unbearable of the lot, all treated the office as their own, most of them fairly jovial as they drank the good wines he provided, but not Laurent, who missed no opportunity to humiliate the victim.

Girodias decided to turn his company into a limited one and try to attract new shareholders. He had lunch with Filipacchi of Hachette and exposed his plan. He was told that it would probably not work because the publishing house with all its difficulties was too small to attract investors. Filipacchi proposed instead that Girodias should have a single associate and that he would speak to Hachette about refinancing the company and taking fifty per cent of the shares. Hachette had never done such a deal before, but he was sure that he could persuade them. Girodias would run the company without interference; they trusted his literary and artistic judgement. Filipacchi knew how to flatter.

"Le Chêne isn't anything at all," he said. "What counts is you, your imagination, your subtlety, your vision, your nerve. It wasn't Léjard who created the enterprise, but you. You were right to get rid of him. It's you that counts, and now that art books are in fashion, we can invest in you and make you the first art-book publisher in the world. Not only in France, but internationally. Skira will be reduced to nothing. We have to conquer the English market, the American one and all of Europe. Only you can do it."[*]

Girodias became more than a little nervous, but he was gradually convinced. It was now June and Henri Filipacchi promised that everything could be signed and completed by early September. He also suggested that Girodias would have no need of his present offices and he would like them for a private enterprise of his own. There were celebrations that summer; Girodias reduced his staff to six people and prepared to move out of his offices and to hand them over to Filipacchi. He would move into new and larger ones in one of the many buildings that Hachette owned all over Paris. But trouble came from Laurent of the creditors' committee who claimed that nothing could be signed without their agreement, and he went personally to see Filipacchi to make his point. Girodias found a new lawyer who warned him not to make waves that might cause Hachette to think twice. The lawyer also did not like the terms of the preliminary agreement which was to lead to the final one, the date of which was approaching.

Girodias spent August outside Paris on holiday. On his return, he tried to telephone Filipacchi, now in possession of his old offices on Rue de la Paix. Filipacchi was not available, nor was Guy Schoeller, nor the other Hachette directors who had assured him that all would be signed by the middle of September. It was October before a meeting finally took place; Girodias entered Filipacchi's office where everyone involved was gathered and was greeted by stony faces and an unfriendly atmosphere. He was told that three Hachette directors were to be in charge of the new limited company that had just been formed. He was to be the manager, nothing more, and at the same low salary he had been receiving from the creditors' committee. Girodias indignantly refused the position and the salary, said that his preliminary agreement was not binding, and that in any case he had to have the creditors' agreement. Three days later he learnt that his lawyer had in fact filled in the blank forms that he had previously signed, passing over control to unnamed persons; this was the condition on which he had been allowed by his creditors to remain in business, and these forms had now been sold to Hachette. He had lost his publishing company.

During the following winter, Germaine tried on three occasions to commit suicide. Each time, Girodias went to visit her in hospital, bringing flowers, and by the third time he was receiving very odd looks from the nurses. He had received the translation in French of Henry Miller's *Sexus* and he decided to publish this under a new imprint, Les Éditions de la Terre de Feu. Knowing the risk of a police prosecution against a work that exceeded even Miller's previous novels in sexual content, he printed two versions, an expurgated one for the public and an unexpurgated one for the press, and although he announced that there were 3,000 copies of the first and only 300 of the second, the reverse was true. A right-wing popular paper, specializing in scandals, denounced the ruse, and Girodias suddenly found himself prosecuted under the law of 1881 to defend public morals. Jules Moch was still the Minister of the Interior at the time: having used the power of the state to prosecute striking miners and other sections of the workforce who created difficulties for the authoritarian regime of the day, he was now attacking publishers. Girodias was approached at this time by Jean d'Halluin, director of Les Éditions de Scorpion, who also had a novel under attack. It was called *J'irai cracher sur vos tombes** (*I Am Going to Spit on Your Graves*) by Vernon Sullivan, supposedly an American, but d'Halluin confided to Girodias that the real author was Boris Vian, who had written it in French; he had had an English translation made to deceive the police. Vian was a virtual Renaissance man during his short life: an engineer, journalist, dramatist, novelist, jazz musician, actor and music hall singer – he was a real Saint-Germain personality and celebrity, a leading member of the "Collège de 'Pataphysique" ("College of Pataphysics"), a joke institution that many took seriously. It consisted of a group of writers who were interested in words and their uses, above all in ways in which they could be twisted to give new insights into life. Other leading members were Raymond Queneau and Eugène Ionesco. If Boris Vian's best work was his novel *L'Écume des Jours* (*The Froth of Days*) and his play *Les Bâtisseurs d'empire** (*The Empire Builders*), both of which were only translated into English after his death, it was the scandal of *J'irai cracher sur vos tombes* that attracted attention to him, other than his celebrity as a performer. The story's hero was a black American revolutionary, sleeping with as many white women as possible, and killing as many white policemen as he could; it was written in a tough American slang.

D'Halluin's proposition was that they should make common cause because they were both being attacked under a statute of 1881 that had been passed originally to keep revolutionary foreign literature of a political nature out of the country. It was on the day after their meeting that Girodias was raided in his new offices by the Brigade Mondaine, the morality police. There were several dozen policemen involved in the raid, and they were led by Commissioner Fernet, the head of the Brigade. It was as if a notorious nest of assassins was being raided. The narrow street was blocked off, Baron Mollet, who happened to be in the office at the time, was put in handcuffs, and all the account books, invoices and some copies of *Sexus* were seized and examined. But fortunately the 3,000 unexpurgated copies had all been hidden away, the day before, in the premises of a library supplier on the Rue Xavier Privas; the man was interested in buying the entire edition.

Girodias was next to discover that his acquisitive library supplier was a phoney, but fortunately for him not clever enough to be a total crook. With some difficulty he eventually recovered his 3,000 copies. The raid of Girodias's office did not lead to a prosecution, but he was served with a formal notice that *Sexus* was banned and not to be sold under pain of arrest and imprisonment. This sad chapter in the career of Maurice Girodias had another unhappy ending. On

6th April 1950, Germaine finally succeeded in committing suicide. It was obvious that she did not intend to succeed, but the *pneumatique* (a form of letter-telegram sent from one Paris post office to another through a suction tube and then delivered by hand) that she sent to a friend did not arrive in time. Girodias had another meeting with Guy Schoeller at Hachette, which had effectively stolen his company, leaving him only with an edition of *Sexus*, a banned book that he could not sell. Schoeller made the meeting brief; he had a date with a girlfriend, possibly Françoise Sagan, whose *Bonjour Tristesse* would appear four years later. Nothing came of the meeting.

Girodias sat in his empty, unheated office with the telephone cut off and contemplated the future. He tried to light a fire in the grate and nearly set the building on fire, singeing the carpet.

Chapter Two

Merlin

1

In 1951, the Anglo-American literary and art scene in Paris began to revive. Many painters were coming back; Paris had always been their natural habitat, and not only was there a return of those who had frequented Montparnasse, in particular, during the Thirties, but a new generation had arrived, much of it only recently demobilized from the Allied armies and other services. Some surrealists returned, such as Max Ernst, who had been using America's desert landscapes in his work and was now an international figure; so did Dalí, on occasion with his wife Gala, the former wife of poet Paul Éluard, a hero of the underground, who had lost contact with her during the war and was now living his last years in a poverty that contrasted cruelly with the position of those who had escaped the rigours of the war and become rich. André Breton came back from New York, attacked Dalí as a fascist (Éluard defended him out of loyalty to Gala) and tried to regain his ascendancy over the French literary and artistic *tout Paris*; but the world had seen enough surrealism in everyday life, and although the movement continued and was soon strengthened by a new generation, Breton was no longer a power in the arts. The cinema flourished with a new realism, much of it imported from Italy where fashionable directors such as de Sica were the talking points. The new cultural heroes were those who had made their mark during the war, like Jean-Paul Sartre, whose three-novel sequence, *Les Chemins de la Liberté* (*The Roads to Freedom*) was a best-seller, and whose plays, alongside those of Jean Anouilh, André Roussin and Jacques Audiberti, filled many theatres.

Jean Cocteau was making films as well as writing plays and he became the centre of an artistic homosexual group that included Francis Poulenc, Henri Rabaud, Pierre Schneider and the film star Jean Marais. Picasso was still high fashion, and Sir Roland Penrose, a link between the London and Paris art scenes, crossed the channel frequently, while writing his biography of Picasso and other books on art and developing the Institute of Contemporary Arts in London as a cultural centre. Francis Bacon began to be known in Paris and other British painters like Stanley William Hayter, an English surrealist and friend of Beckett who had settled himself once again in Montparnasse, found new studios. A new generation of American composers came to Paris to study with Nadia Boulanger, the legendary martinet who had taught Virgil Thomson, Aaron Copeland, Elliott Carter and most of the established pre-war American musical figures. Her rival, Olivier Messiaen, was teaching the French, British and other young European composers, including Pierre Boulez. The GIs were slowly leaving and the expatriates landing in ever increasing numbers.

One notable new arrival was Alexander Trocchi from Glasgow. He had been a brilliant student of English and philosophy at Glasgow University, having previously done his military service in the Fleet Air Arm of the Royal Navy; he had much impressed his professors with his ability to write original essays on both major subjects, often taking a radically different point of view from that of his mentors. In English his studies had included Chaucer, Spenser, Marlowe, Shakespeare, Donne, Marvell, Milton, Keats, Pope, Johnson and others. In philosophy Trocchi had studied deductive and inductive logic, metaphysics, morality, ancient and modern philosophy and theory of knowledge. Cornerstones of his course were Plato, Aristotle, Descartes, Locke, Hume and Kant, while the modern philosopher nearest to the heart of his professor was F.H. Bradley, whose *Principles of Logic* and *Appearance and Reality* Trocchi disputed successfully enough to earn the grudging respect of the head of the department. By himself he discovered Bertrand Russell and A.J. Ayer, thereby putting himself into the school of logical positivism by self-education. Although his self-confidence and intellectual arrogance – he considered that studying for exams and revision of past work was for dullards and not for him – as well as his habit, learnt during the war when training to be a pilot, of taking Benzedrine to keep awake, lost him a first-class honours degree (because of a mistimed overdose he fell asleep during his final philosophy exam), he nevertheless obtained second-class honours and more importantly, on the recommendation of his professors, who felt that they might well have a Scottish literary genius on their hands who would bring credit to a university better known for producing engineers, scientists and architects, he was awarded the Kemsley Travelling Scholarship, worth £400. It would enable him to travel and write. Indeed he had already written many stories, some poetry and had embarked on *Young Adam*, one of the few early novels that he actually finished.

Trocchi, son of a second-generation Italian father and a Scottish mother, went to Paris in 1950, bringing with him a wife, Betty, who was a strong red-headed Scottish girl, and an infant daughter – another was on the way. Full of schemes, he intended to write a "Paris Diary" for a Scottish magazine, and make a tour of the Mediterranean, then to write a book about it to be serialized by the Kemsley Press (using his scholarship connection with them); the book, he was sure, would be a best-seller! But many things went wrong, a pattern that was often to be repeated with Trocchi: he was to have many adventures, most of them unpleasant, but his misfortunes were all created by his way of never doing things simply if a more complicated method was possible. He was clever at obtaining money, either by wheeler-dealing or borrowing, but he always spent it instantly, often on impulse on something of no real use, and he never thought of the needs of the next day.

He was now twenty-six, handsome in a saturnine way, looking rather like an Italian youth from the Renaissance world of Florentine painting, his face dominated by a prominent, beaky nose, and speaking with a strong Glasgow accent that he enunciated clearly without the rapid mumbling that makes most working-class western Scots incomprehensible to the English, and even to many fellow Scotsmen. He made friendships quickly and nearly always created a strong and positive impression on everyone he met.

After some European travel with Betty, a tour that included Italy, Greece, Turkey and Yugoslavia, he stopped back in Paris in early 1951 and began to discover the city, making friends among other expatriates. But it took him some time to become habituated and he described himself at the time as "a long-haired ill-clad creature, unshaven, an anonymous member of the army of foreign shufflers who walk Paris streets." He met painters and writers, some of whom became good friends, like Ernst Fuchs and Russell Sully, Peter Ross and Barbara Weise. He was soon short of money, had to borrow frequently, was suffering from toothache and athlete's foot, and was looking increasingly shabby as his clothes began to wear thin. Nevertheless he visited art exhibitions, went around the private galleries, dropped in on painters' studios and spent much time in cafés reading the fashionable intellectual authors of the day – Sartre and Camus, Jaspers, Heidegger, Kierkegaard – and learning French rapidly; he brought himself up to date with the current sexual obsessions and discussed literature and sexuality with strangers sitting at the next café table. Trocchi eventually found cheap lodgings for the family at Gagny, just outside Paris. He was writing and had sold a long poem to Marguerite Caetani (Princess di Bassiano), editor of

Botteghe Oscure, a highly intellectual international magazine published in Milan, which took avant-garde writing in different languages and assumed its subscribers could read them all. Trocchi had works in progress that advanced daily, and had by now filled many notebooks with ideas, projects and random jottings.

Trocchi was tall, lean and above all charming. He flaunted his erudition, loved to have an audience, could be particularly persuasive where there might be some money involved, and had the knack of showing an interest in everyone he met so that strangers were often flattered by his attention. He managed to receive a second bursary of £250 from Sir Godfrey Collins in England, a publishing magnate on whom he had made a good impression; both he and Betty began to make a little money by odd jobs, in her case by doing household work. They both worked during the summer of 1951, he as a gardener and she as a cook for an English couple, the Wilmotts, at Cap d'Ail near Monte Carlo; the duties were not onerous and it was very like a holiday, with their employers treating them socially as equals. In the early winter the Trocchis left their two infants with a couple outside Paris and returned to Britain, but they were back by the beginning of 1952 and this time Trocchi was to become the centre of a new literary venture.

2

Trocchi's own description of the Paris to which he returned on 22nd of January, a date that we can take as the beginning of the history of *Merlin*, smacks of hindsight.

> I went to France, not London, from Scotland. I found the English attitude towards existentialism – French existentialism in particular – unsympathetic after the war. They had a very patronizing attitude towards existentialism and Literature *engagé*. They thought of the term *engagé* in the old Thirties sense of "commitment", whereas *engagement* could have the sense of refusing to be identified with either capitalism or communism. You could in fact be *engagé* as an outsider.*

The Fifties were in fact a more interesting time than the much-vaunted Sixties: in the latter, the second decade of peace, a new attitude to life, previously developing in embryo, would explode into reality. With it would come the sexual revolution, full employment for young people, and a worry-free life with money easy to earn; it would also bring a youth culture largely defined and symbolized through the Beatles, the ideas of Ivan Illich, which encouraged students and even school children to take charge of their own curriculum and studies, and an anti-authoritarian view of every established institution. In the Sixties the war was forgotten and a decade of iconoclasm saw the removal of most taboos.

But the Sixties were a direct result of the Fifties and what started then. The war against Hitler had only been over a by a few years in 1951 and the cold war had immediately followed it. The Korean War was still in progress and dividing opinion, especially in France with its large communist electorate, which sometimes attracted the largest vote of any party, although never a majority. There was trouble all over the world. The big oil companies were intriguing to overthrow Mossadeq in Iran: he had recently announced his intention to nationalize the oil wells, then principally exploited by the Anglo-Iranian Oil Company (renamed British Petroleum in 1954). The first British spy scandal had erupted, with the escape of Burgess and Maclean to Russia. Stalin had ordered a purge of all liberals inside the Czech Communist Party; the Hollywood witch-hunt was in full spate in the US, and the Rosenbergs, convicted of treason, were executed in the electric chair after a trial that smelt of perjured evidence in an atmosphere of hysteria. The Truman years were about to be replaced by the Eisenhower ones.

In the US, as in communist countries, it was dangerous to discuss politics, but not in England where the Conservatives had been returned to power under Churchill, now ill and old, but still living on his wartime reputation, while the British Labour Party, torn between its different factions, still exercised considerable influence through the popular reforms it had brought in after its 1945 electoral victory, most notably in the establishment of the National Health Service, the provision of more subsidy for the arts and the BBC, and higher education to a wider spectrum of British citizens. The arrival of a new young queen in 1952 seemed to rejuvenate the country. There was much political discussion in Britain, but even more in France where the café tables hummed with argument. In Germany, facing the consequences of defeat and the guilt of Nazi war crimes, there was little public debate, but the Frankfurt Book Fair had once again made Germany something of an intellectual centre, and the literary scene had been revived by the Gruppe 47, organized by Walter Höllerer, with Günter Grass and Heinrich Böll among its members. The Marshall Plan was pouring money into the reconstruction of Germany and the country was rapidly moving towards its *Wirtschaftswunder*, or "economic miracle", under Konrad Adenauer and his brilliant economics minister, Ludwig Erhard. Italy had a socialist government with communist support. Franco still ruled with an iron hand in Spain. But in France artists had freedom and living was fairly cheap, especially for visiting expatriates from English-speaking countries. There was in general a belief in a radical future, which still had to be created by the thinkers of the day. To be "*engagé* as an outsider" in the age of Sartre and Camus was high intellectual fashion in Paris, while Britain was returning to its usual preoccupation with the class war.

The political issue that mainly interested the French was of course de Gaulle's determination to keep France's colonial empire. French troops were dealing with revolt in Indo-China and North Africa, but this interested the expatriates very little; they were more concerned with McCarthyism and the Korean War.

In 1952 there were 12,000 expatriate Americans living in Paris and about the same number of British. In addition there were the GIs for whom Paris was the favourite of all places to spend their furloughs. Soft drugs were common and the atmosphere in almost every way permissive, except that the Ministry of the Interior was still suspicious of licentiousness and subversion in literature, although less worried about languages other than French. *Lady Chatterley's Lover* was freely available in Paris bookshops in a Swedish-produced series of books by modern English and American authors, and the Miller *Tropics* were again issued in English by Les Éditions du Chêne, now owned by Hachette.

On his return Trocchi went to live in a cheap Algerian hotel in the Rue de la Huchette, frequented mainly by Arab pedlars. Shortly after arriving, he gatecrashed a *vernissage*, a party given to open an exhibition in a Saint-Germain art gallery: he met an American, Victor Miller, who told him he was about to open a new magazine called *Manuscript*. Victor Miller was staying at the Hôtel Lutetia, notorious during the war for having been the Gestapo headquarters. He and Trocchi both met a very attractive American girl at the party: she had come to spend a few months in Paris, perhaps a year: her name was Jane Lougee, and she was the daughter of a banker who owned the small Lougee Bank in Limerick, Maine. She was receiving a generous monthly allowance of $100, which went a long way in the Paris of 1951. A pretty American girl, on her own and with money, was an obvious target, and several people at the *vernissage* tried to attract her attention. Victor Miller told her that he was looking for an assistant for his magazine. Trocchi had come with the Scottish-Australian poet Alan Riddell, who also had a magazine in mind, the *Lines Review*. He tried to interest her in this as well. Trocchi suggested that they should all meet again, and a date was fixed at Miller's hotel a few days later. Trocchi had done some thinking, and he was anxious to associate himself with any literary project that might take off. At the meeting in the Hôtel Lutetia it was Trocchi who did most of the talking, mentioning his contacts with British press barons and exhibiting his erudition, and he emerged as the new editor of a magazine that was still only a vague idea and had no money to pay for anything. The discussion of seed money, as against the airing of grandiose ideas, had gone nowhere at all, and considerable hostility had developed among the men, no doubt because they were all competing for the attention of Jane Lougee, who left hand-in-hand with Trocchi.

Jane was nineteen and had already been married once to a man called Longhands, but the marriage had broken up almost immediately. She and Trocchi started instantly to have an affair. He told her that his marriage was intolerable because his wife wanted him to take a humdrum job and start to earn regular money to support his family and himself.

Jane Lougee was living in a rented studio apartment in Auteuil and Trocchi moved in with her. Betty at the time was in Newcastle-upon-Tyne where her father was dying. She received a letter there from Alex, telling her that he had fallen in love with an American girl, but that he loved her too. He was not sure what to do. Before Betty left they had boarded out the two children with a French family who spoke no English. During Betty's absence Alex never visited them because he could not bear to see them unhappy, as he told her on her return. She moved back into the sordid Algerian hotel, smelling of couscous and open drains, while Alex, visiting her from Auteuil, tried to get her to make the decision that they should separate. In desperation Betty left Paris, went blindly to Rome, but returned immediately to be with the children. She took them away from the French family, who had treated them badly, and through a friend found a small apartment on the Île Saint-Louis; then she began to earn a little money by modelling.

In the meantime Trocchi had made himself at home in Auteuil with Jane and was planning the magazine. The first thing he did was to get rid of Alan Riddell, who had intended to fill it largely with Scottish poetry, his own and that of Hugh MacDiarmid, Sydney Goodsir Smith and other members of the "Scottish Renaissance", all of whom were then largely unknown outside Edinburgh. Trocchi wrote him a cruel letter, pointing out how different their literary objectives were. Trocchi above all wanted to get away from the Scottish nationalist outlook. Alan Riddell then returned to Scotland where he lived by journalism until his death in 1972, but he did succeed in founding his own journal there, the *Lines Review*, which continued until the Sixties. He was to become one of the principal figures in "concrete poetry", a movement which flourished in the late Fifties and early Sixties but made little impression on the general public. Riddell later developed a form of poetry where his typewriter was used rather like a painter's brush, making designs on the page that gave a visual, often witty, impact to the words.

Jane's $100 a month was enough for the two of them to live comfortably and to finance the first issues of the magazine if they were careful. The name *Merlin* came from Christopher Logue, whom Trocchi met at this time. It replaced *Manuscript*, Victor Miller's title. Miller himself quickly disappeared from the scene. It transpired that he did not really have money to invest, and losing both his idea and Jane to Trocchi must have been a humiliating blow.

Christopher Logue had recently arrived from England. With fifty pounds in his pocket he reached Paris on 12th September 1951, staying for a while with a friend who had previously lodged with his mother in England to learn the language, and Christopher decided to do the opposite. He was a poet who had had a bad time in the British Army. He had been in Palestine after the war, during the period when the Zionists were trying to seize control of the country from the British, who intended to keep their Mandate, rule Jews and Arabs, and keep the peace between them. The situation was tense, and Logue, in a Scottish regiment that had been part of Montgomery's Eighth Army, fell into trouble through an illogical series of activities that he was unable to explain at the time, and years later was still unable to explain, except by reference to a certain childhood compulsion which had afflicted him until he suddenly stopped: to steal for no particular reason, except, as he put it, vainglory and boastfulness.

Logue had entered the army as a volunteer, not a national-service man (a two-year stint in the army was still compulsory in the years following the end of the war) and he had been sent to the Middle East as a private in the fourth battalion of the Black Watch in 1945. This in itself was unusual as Christopher Logue came from the south of England; the Black Watch is usually recruited north of the border. In May 1946 his battalion was stationed in a camp just south of Haifa. This was a soft posting, involving not too much work apart from routine: Logue was a Lance Corporal, was learning to drive a truck and had been put in charge of the unit library. The troops had little contact with local people and few of the soldiers understood the power struggle that was going on – the Zionists wanted to establish an independent Jewish state and get rid of the British mandate, and the Arabs tried to prevent this happening by at least keeping the status quo until an Arab protectorate could be established.

The battalion was being broken up and transferred. Paperwork and documents of all kinds were being thrown out, destroyed or sent elsewhere. Christopher Logue, who a few years later would become one of the leading poets of his generation, sequestered six pay-books and kept them. They had no value and he did not know why he did this, a gratuitous act, but having done it he boasted about it to his fellow soldiers, embroidering the act by saying that he was going to sell them to the Jews. As the Stern Gang and other Zionist activist groups were using stolen British documents to get entry to the camps and steal weapons, the theft of the pay-books by a soldier for sale might be seen as treason; a member of Logue's tent told his sergeant who told the lieutenant. The latter followed Christopher into Haifa where he was about to post the pay-books to his mother in England (again for no particular reason, except perhaps to get rid of them) and there arrested him. He was confined to camp and then charged. He pleaded guilty, a big mistake, and was sentenced to a military prison, the "glasshouse".

The battalion was disbanded and everyone who knew him and his eccentricities had left. He was in the hands of the Royal Scots, was court-martialled with no friendly witnesses present, sentenced to two years, of which he served sixteen months, and then given a "discharge for medical reasons", not as bad as a "dishonourable discharge". Many years later at the Edinburgh Festival he met his sergeant again, Steve Haggarty, who asked him why he had pleaded guilty. Everyone in the unit had known that he knew nothing of the political situation at the time and a not-guilty plea would have enabled his friends and colleagues to give favourable evidence and have him released. Logue commented to me in a private letter:

There you are. I, something of a born liar, was unwilling to lie to help myself, and harm nobody thereby. I was out for guilt. Looking for punishment. My vindictive, spiteful, almost wicked plan justified this. Have I let myself off too lightly? It is hard to keep a true balance.

When, out of the army at last and anxious to get away from the need to explain himself, he arrived in Paris, Logue was thin and cadaverous, usually dressed in a dirty duffel coat, tight trousers and – according to some who remembered him – winkle-picker shoes, which enjoyed a certain fashion in London at the time among some of the young, though now he denies the shoes. Such a costume made young men look not unlike their Renaissance equivalents, on which they were no doubt modelled. He was determined to be a poet, to live like one and find a congenial ambiance, away from the restrictive British atmosphere of the time, in the city of freedom.

After his arrival in Paris, Logue looked for odd literary jobs to earn a little money and managed to get regular employment teaching English at the Berlitz school. After a while he found two small rooms for himself at about £5 a month, which was half the train fare from London to Paris; the room had previously been occupied by an acquaintance who passed it over to Logue on leaving Paris. Christopher then settled down to enjoy the city of his choice without much thought about the future. Like so many writers and artists before him he wanted to write his poetry, survive and enjoy life, not difficult in Paris where a little money went a long way and artists lived bohemian lives, usually sharing with each other when problems intervened. This was much more difficult in London and impossible in New York where lack of money, and lack of interest in earning it with a regular job, are akin to crime and certainly could arouse no sympathy. Logue figured that if he got out of bed in the morning with £2 in his pocket he could get through the day without worry.

He first met Trocchi at the Arab hotel on the Rue de la Huchette, apparently on the staircase, although Logue could not remember what he was doing there. Their next meeting, or certainly one of the next, was in more dramatic circumstances. Christopher Logue woke up one morning with an excruciating toothache. He knew no dentist and it was in any case a Sunday morning. He dressed and left his tiny apartment, and decided to seek help from a friend who lived nearby in a *hôtel particulier* at 31 Rue de Seine. This building was owned by Raymond Duncan, brother of the dancer Isadora, the same man who had climbed over the rooftops in 1944 to erect an American flag on a nearby roof. Duncan was a genuine American eccentric who baked his own bread (in Paris of all places!), published his own books, and lived off the rent he received from having divided his house into small apartments. The friend was Philip Oxman, an American historian, who had many Paris connections. Logue had met him at an Eisenstein film in one of the many *cinémathèques* that had grown up in Paris since the war ended, and they met frequently. Logue was lucky to find Oxman in, and even luckier in that he knew a dentist personally and had his home telephone number. He rang him and the friendly dentist agreed to see the sufferer right away, and on a Sunday! They took a bus to his house where he tried to examine Christopher's mouth, but it was so sensitive that he could not bear to have it touched. The dentist pondered. "It's an abscess," he said, "a bad one. The tooth will have to come out today." The problem was that he could not get access to his surgery on a Sunday. After thinking, he put the two of them into a taxi and all three went to the north of Paris near to where the current Boulevard Périphérique separates the city from the suburbs; Christopher Logue was admitted to a building where a number of patients, most of them elderly, many only partly dressed, were wandering around the wards and corridors, flapping their arms, dribbling, hitting each other and arguing in a babble of voices and a variety of accents. "This must be bedlam," thought the unhappy Logue. It *was* in fact a lunatic asylum. The now terrified sufferer was admitted to an unprepossessing operating theatre, where he was seized by two orderlies, strapped down on a table and, overwhelmed by fear and pain, certain that his last hour had come, unable to move, felt a mask being put over his face and began to breathe the gas.

He woke some time later to find that three of his teeth had been extracted, and stumbled out to the waiting Oxman. The last thing he wanted to do on an unpleasant, cold Sunday morning was to go back to his cold and lonely lodging. Philip Oxman thought for a minute and came up with an idea. "I think I know a place where you can possibly stay more comfortably for a day or two," he said, and went to the phone. "There's a problem," he said on his return, "but let's go anyway and see what happens." They moved once again across Paris to Auteuil and Oxman ushered Christopher Logue into Jane Lougee's studio apartment. She was in bed with Trocchi, both of them suffering from hepatitis and both bright yellow in colour. "You'd better get into bed, old man," said Trocchi. Logue silently climbed in beside them and instantly fell asleep.

While he was sleeping, Jane, who was less ill than Alex, went out to buy some food. The lady who owned the studio, under the impression that she had let it to a nice respectable American girl, paid a surprise visit and let herself into the room to find two men in bed together, one of them asleep and the other electric yellow. She beat a hasty retreat. Two days later she returned, determined to find out what was going on. Jane was again out shopping and Alex Trocchi, now feeling much better, was sitting up in bed teaching Christopher Logue to play canasta, then the rage of Paris. They were both sitting cross-legged on the sheets, stark naked. Enough was enough. Jane was told to leave instantly and Christopher went back to his two tiny rooms. Alex and Jane moved to the Hôtel Verneuil. And from there they found a warehouse room, behind a shop on the Rue du Sabot, through the good offices of Richard Seaver.

Seaver was another young American in Paris, recently married to a French violinist, Jeannette Medina. He was living in a room over a shop which had a large collection of African art and artefacts, owned by a Swiss businessman, Oscar, who was more than a little mad. Seaver was managing the shop for him to earn a little money and to have free accommodation. He had until recently been in the American navy, had met Trocchi in the local cafés and knew of his plans to start a magazine. He had himself been in Paris since 1949 on a grant to study at the Sorbonne, had met many other young expatriates and had written articles for some of the little magazines, especially *Points*, was reading new books both in French and English, sometimes to review, and had been particularly impressed by the novels of Samuel Beckett that had recently been published by Jérôme Lindon of Les Éditions de Minuit, which after its wartime existence as the principal literary publisher of resistance literature, was now turning itself into an avant-garde imprint for new writing.

Seaver had been highly impressed by Trocchi, had read his novel in progress, *Young Adam*, and had shared with him his interest in Beckett. Trocchi suggested that he write about Beckett for *Merlin*. When Trocchi and Jane had to move from Auteuil, Seaver let them move into the back room of the shop and he and Jeanette moved to a room on the floor above. This building became the new office of *Merlin*, and the place of many meetings, discussions and editorial conferences. The first business address had been Jane's Auteuil apartment, then the Hôtel Verneuil, and when the magazine first appeared, it was from 8 Rue du Sabot. The street lies in the heart of Saint-Germain-des-Prés, just behind the Rue Bernard-Palissy where the offices of Les Éditions de Minuit are situated. Seaver, walking past the publishing house daily, had to notice the new novels, Beckett's prominent among them, that were exposed in the display window on the street.

Seaver's and then Trocchi's room measured ten metres by five, was unfurnished and contained a huge cupboard covered by a curtain. There was a concierge with three badly trained and smelly dogs who constantly left excrement on the stairs. The shop, managed by Seaver, was run by a girl who seemed afraid of daylight and never opened the shutters; it was hardly surprising that there were few customers, but the owner, intensely interested in African art, did not seem anxious to part with his assortment of African curiosities and adornments, tom-toms, canoe paddles, shark's-tooth necklaces, wooden sculptures, masks and the like. Here the two couples lived and discussed literature, Trocchi living largely on the food parcels that Jane's parents sent regularly from America: her allowance was largely earmarked for the magazine. Later Seaver was persuaded to go back to work for the American navy outside Paris to help finance an issue.

The *Merlin* group now included the South African poet Patrick Bowles, a good-looking, leather-clad, athletic young man of considerable literary ability, Philip Oxman, John Stephenson, a Londoner who had been trained as an accountant but was more interested in writing, Austryn Wainhouse, son of an American diplomat, and the author Henry Charles Hatcher – there were occasionally others who attended some meetings but later dropped out. They could all squeeze into Trocchi's room and Jane usually had a rich fruitcake to accompany the cheap wine that the members brought with them. Many things happened in that room, one of them reminiscent of eighteenth-century comedy. Christopher Logue was always in love and he used Trocchi as his confidant, advisor and male nurse, because Logue, in the depth of his despair, occasionally contemplated suicide. During his confessional sessions with Trocchi only Jane was allowed to be present, and this monopolizing of the leader of the group was deeply resented by the others. The latest rich fruitcake from America helped to sustain the confidences, but the others also needed Trocchi's advice, sympathy and encouragement (he loved the power that lending a willing ear gave him) and they also wanted Jane's fruitcake, which would tend to disappear during a long Trocchi-Logue dialogue. On one occasion it was agreed that the best way to find out if there was any hope for Christopher in his current obsession was for Trocchi to have a talk with the girl in question, while during their conversation, Christopher, hiding behind the cupboard curtains, would listen in. If the situation turned out to be favourable, then Logue was to spring out at the right moment with a bouquet of flowers in his hand and declare his love. But in the event, after a brief preliminary talk, Trocchi took the girl out of the room to continue the conversation elsewhere. Logue was about to emerge from hiding when the door opened again. Peering out he witnessed Henry Charles Hatcher, an occasional member of the *Merlin* group, known for his smart dressing, skill as a draughtsman and ability to make and play guitars, enter surreptitiously, produce a large knife and cut himself a big slice of the fruitcake which was lying on the table. He looked into Logue's shocked eyes and each left the room in embarrassment, the former still clutching his flowers.

The meetings were not only concerned with the editorial content of *Merlin*, although that was the ostensible reason for them. Trocchi would hold forth, as if lecturing, about his enthusiasms, especially the philosophy of A.J. Ayer, whose new work he wanted to publish in the magazine, and he was also interested in another philosopher he had recently discovered, A. Korzybski. Seaver had read *Molloy* in French, had seen Lindon to discuss translating it, and had sent a message to Beckett to express his interest. One day, while a meeting was in progress there came a knock at the door. Bowles, Logue, Seaver, Trocchi, Jane Lougee and Charles Hatcher were in deep discussion and they opened the door to see a tall, gaunt figure standing outside. He asked for Mr Seaver and Dick stepped forward. A large parcel wrapped in brown paper was thrust at him.

"Here's the manuscript," said Beckett, and turning he disappeared into the night. They opened it, found a typescript of *Watt*, which Lindon had mentioned to Seaver at the same time as he told him that Seaver's article about *Molloy* had pleased the author. *Watt* had been written by Beckett during the war while hiding in a little village in the Vaucluse. It was in English, a language Lindon could not read, and he did not know what to do with it.

They started to read *Watt* aloud, found themselves laughing, passed it from hand to hand, and agreed that they must at least serialize part of it in the magazine. Seaver then wrote to Beckett, giving the page numbers of the extracts they wanted to use, told him of the general enthusiasm and asked for permission to publish. Agreement came back very quickly. Seaver soon also discovered Beckett's *Nouvelles et Textes Pour Rien (Stories and Texts for Nothing)*, written in French, and made two attempts to translate *L'Expulsé (The Expelled)*; he finally asked Beckett for help and they worked on it together, but this was after Trocchi had made his own, not very successful attempts. 'Le Calmant' ('The Calmative') came next and created more difficulties: when Seaver and Beckett sat down together to go over Seaver's translation, they spent three hours on the first three pages. By now Trocchi and his associates had decided that the magazine should also have a book-publishing programme and that Beckett and the Marquis de Sade should be among the first volumes. The series would be called Collection Merlin. Trocchi was confident that the money would somehow be found.

The authors that had been selected for the magazine included Jean Genet, Jean-Paul Sartre, Eugène Ionesco and Pablo Neruda in translation. It would also include the English writings of the *Merlin* group themselves, as well as work by a few others, such as the American poet Robert Creeley.

The next young American to join *Merlin* was Austryn Wainhouse. He had come to Paris for a year to study and avoid the prevailing atmosphere of McCarthyism that seemed to threaten everything civilized in America. McCarthy had built a political career and achieved notoriety by persecuting everyone in the arts who had a left-wing background or known leftish sympathies. He had driven writers and directors out of Hollywood, made it impossible for many actors to find work in either films or on the stage, forced universities to dismiss professors of too liberal an inclination, made many novelists unpublishable, and created a climate in which intellectuals were afraid to talk freely or express opinions. Wainhouse persuaded himself that he was not really leaving the States, that his trip abroad would not last more than a year, and that it would help him towards his doctorate at the same time as it broadened his mind, because he had no intention of becoming an expatriate or part of a non-American culture. But the future looked uncertain on either continent and the money he had brought with him began quickly to run out, forcing him to think of ways of earning more.

Wainhouse had first been to Italy and visited the great museums, and at the Museo del Bargello in Florence had come across three extraordinary sculptures that could only be seen by special permission: they were three miniature theatres each peopled with tiny wax figures, and each representing a scene from the plague that had ravaged Italy in the sixteenth century. They were hidden from the public gaze, partly to protect them from damage and heat, and partly because the scenes were of a horror and lewdness that made them unsuitable for public exhibition. It was shortly afterwards, lying on his bed in his little *pensione* on the Arno quay, that he began reading a copy of the Marquis de Sade's *Justine, ou les malheurs de la vertu*, which he had just purchased. He read it right through, took it with him on the train north, and by the time he had arrived at the Gare de Lyon in Paris, had decided to translate it into English.

He translated both *Justine* and *La Philosophie dans le boudoir*, the latter a dialogue in which de Sade's philosophy of seduction is given an elegant shape. De Sade was in vogue after the war, and the subject of evil was one that preoccupied French intellectuals after their experience of the Nazis. The works of de Sade were published by Jean-Jacques

Pauvert, who specialized in literary erotica, but always of quality: the eighteenth-century libertine writers had exactly the right combination of historical importance and pleasant salacity to be intellectually defensible and commercially viable. The works were of course officially banned: "Tante Yvonne", as General de Gaulle's wife was popularly called, took an interest in the moral climate and encouraged the police to take action against libertine publishers, but after so many years of German censorship printers were not afraid of an occasional fine, while the climate among the intelligentsia was in favour of literary freedom, the right to know all and discover everything that had for so long been unavailable. There was a genuine interest in the relationship between evil and eroticism: Georges Bataille, Maurice Blanchot, Jean Paulhan and Pierre Klossowski were writing or had recently published books and essays on the subject. De Sade's own works were now easy to find in Pauvert's editions, not usually too obviously exposed to the public view in bookshops, but available, if asked for. Simone de Beauvoir had published an essay entitled 'Faut-il brûler Sade?'* ('Must We Burn de Sade?'). Gilbert Lely, a literary historian, was working on a multi-volume biography of the Marquis, the aristocrat who had tortured women in real life and dreamt in his writings of refined and extreme cruelty, as often as not leading to death, but who had immediately sided with the French Revolution in 1789, and as a magistrate under it had refused to send anyone brought before him to the guillotine. The link with the Nazi death camps, and with the behaviour of German soldiers in the countries they had conquered, and especially the SS and the Gestapo, was obvious. French intellectuals pondered deeply the problem of evil, brought out books on the subject, and avidly read de Sade.

Wainhouse temporarily put aside his de Sade translations to render into English instead some of the other current literature about de Sade, and he sent these to American publishers, pointing out the great French fascination that must surely apply to the US as well, but found little interest. He was told it was too soon: the market was not yet ready; he was invited to write again in a couple of years. He did not send anything to British publishers: their reputation for puritanism was too well known, and many books available in the US could still not be published there because of the censorship laws.

Conversely, many books were now appearing in Britain that could find no American publisher because Senator Joe McCarthy had frightened Madison Avenue into avoiding any left-leaning political book or novel, and their authors were turning to Britain instead. In my own capacity as a publisher I was, in the early Fifties, receiving a constant stream of manuscripts from New York, sometimes sent by American colleagues who shamefacedly explained why they had to reject them.

One day towards the end of 1952, Austryn Wainhouse received a *pneumatique* asking him to come to Le Mistral on the Rue de la Bûcherie. The bookshop still exists, but is now renamed Shakespeare & Company after the famous establishment closed since the Occupation. He went there on time and found Alexander Trocchi waiting for him. Wainhouse describes: "a great lean rascal in a raincoat, the collar pulled up, over its rim lay a long nose, claiming all the space between two little eyes, deep-set, very blue, very winning, and manifestly not to be trusted."* But they got on well: Trocchi's charm and enthusiasm, and his obvious willingness to like and make a friend of everyone he met, was irresistible to everyone. The second issue of *Merlin* had just been published. There were bundles of it on the concrete floor of the bookshop. Trocchi asked Wainhouse his opinion.

Wainhouse warily voiced approval, but thought privately that its austere and closely printed appearance in small type made it look more like a technical journal than a literary magazine. He glanced through the editorial which looked at language in terms of the logical positivism then coming into vogue, which pleaded for greater openness in literature.

Trocchi asked him: "I hear you have some texts?"

"Translations," replied Wainhouse.

"I might be interested," said Trocchi.

So began a professional relationship that was to continue for the next four years. On the same day, Wainhouse was introduced to Christopher Logue, who was later to point out to him that he had never quite grasped the true genius of Trocchi, a man who was criminal in the highest sense, without conscience or any moral sense that would allow him to hold back from a seduction or a course of action he wanted to pursue, but was capable of being a good and loyal friend, trustworthy in a crisis and an effective leader of any group. Wainhouse's first impression of Trocchi was accurate enough: they were to work together and become good friends, but Wainhouse was always alarmed by the extravagance of some of Trocchi's ideas and projects. Trocchi was often a dreamer, but it was only in his later years, when heroin addiction had totally eaten up his will power and ability to act, that his dreams became impossible to achieve and his ability to act ineffective.

One such dream – and he expected all the editorial *Merlin* group to participate in it with him – was a commercial idea that might well have succeeded. The fact is that establishments such as the one he wanted to create did exist in France during the four decades that followed the war. But the genesis of it lay in an anonymous novel published by Pauvert, entitled *Histoire d'O* (*Story of O*). In it a man takes his mistress to a quiet house near Roissy, a village near where the Charles de Gaulle airport now stands. Before stopping at the door he tells her to take off her underclothes and all her rings, to enter the door by herself and to do whatever she is told. She then goes through the rituals of becoming a sex slave, broken by the whip; she undergoes an excess of sexual use by many men and gives up all mastery over her own destiny. Henceforth she becomes the property of the male members of a secret society. The novel was being eagerly read and discussed in Paris; everyone speculated about the identity of the author, and whether it was a man or a woman: the story is told in the first person by a woman. Trocchi wanted to establish such a place, to acquire a chateau and the trimmings, good-quality whips, chains, instruments of torture and sexual aids; he claimed that he had already interested a few men into taking part, who would pay for the privilege, and had persuaded a number of women into undergoing the rituals. At the time, however, he was living in his one empty room on the Rue du Sabot and had no money to finance his idea. There are certainly people who will pay for sexual extravagance, and he could probably have found the money eventually, but the scheme never in fact materialized.

Pierre Bourgeade describes in a collection of stories* a place outside Paris where orgies took place, not far removed from those in *Histoire d'O*. Barney Rosset of Grove Press was taken there by Sylvia Bourdon, star of French porno films, who describes the orgies in which she participated in her book, *L'Amour est une fête** (*Love is a Feast*). There are many *maisons de partouze* in Paris, where orgies, usually not involving cruelty, take place. Other cities, especially in Germany and the US, have orgy centres, usually run on strictly commercial lines, but since the early Eighties these, where known to authorities, have been closed down because of the rise of the AIDS epidemic. The same has happened in New York and California. The English translation of *Histoire d'O* was in preparation at this time, soon to be published by Girodias, and it may well have been this that gave Trocchi his idea, but it is more likely that he read it in French – his French was quite good by now.

Although he had no suitable premises, Trocchi did manage to recruit a number of volunteers to whip and be whipped, mainly from people he met in cafés. In practice this developed into a series of orgies which were supposed to be classes in sexual instruction, with Trocchi as teacher, commenting while a couple made love, and hitting them with a ruler (he could not afford a whip) when they did something wrong. Most of the *Merlin* group stayed away from these sessions, and those who did participate were reluctant to talk about them in later years. Trocchi tried to recruit Austryn Wainhouse's wife, Muffie, through her husband – he thought that as the translator of de Sade's libertine novels he would give his agreement – but was dryly told that he did not think she would be interested.

It was some time after their first meeting when Trocchi first outlined his scheme to Wainhouse, and the latter estimated, on the back of a cigarette packet, that it would require between $100,000 and $150,000 to find such a house and to equip it. Having looked at Wainhouse's de Sade translations, Trocchi saw the commercial value in them and estimated that they might help to finance his scheme, but at the time they did not even have enough money to buy paper. With considerable reluctance, Trocchi dropped his project.

Book publication now preoccupied him, mainly because of Austryn Wainhouse's translation of *La Philosophie dans le boudoir*, which he realized was unsuitable for the magazine. It was then that he decided that *Merlin* should start a series of books to be called Collection Merlin. But at the time, France was going through a puritanical period: Pauvert was having his problems, as were other publishers, and fines could be severe. Even before the war, *Tropic of Cancer* and similar English publications had to be kept under the counter. A group of foreigners publishing what could be construed as pornography would immediately be expelled from France, whereas a Frenchman would only be fined, and only then if caught.

Trocchi was not worried. He saw the publication of the novels of the Marquis de Sade as a gold mine that would assure the future of *Merlin* and, in addition, line their pockets generously. He would find a way ahead, and quickly.

Within a week of this decision, Austryn Wainhouse quite independently received a typewritten letter from Maurice Girodias, asking him to meet him at Les Deux Magots. Girodias arrived second, shook hands with his left hand because the right hand was bandaged, probably from a wound inflicted by one of his more violent girlfriends. He is described by Wainhouse as dressed in a dark suit, rather restrained and "with the wooden motions of a much-depleted man",* not surprisingly for someone who hardly ever slept, kept several women more or less happy at any one time and, like Trocchi, had more schemes in his head than any normal mind can contain. Girodias spoke in his accented English, but in a low voice that Wainhouse had difficulty in hearing. He said to Wainhouse:

"Georges Bataille has spoken to me about you. I understand you have some texts of Sade."

"I have just made a translation of his preface to *Justine*."

"And of *Justine* too, I believe he said."

"And of *La Philosophie dans le boudoir*."

Girodias asked if he could see it. Wainhouse went to his nearby room and returned in a few minutes with the manuscript. Girodias read the first page, then the second, then put his glasses back into his pocket. He made an offer of 150,000 francs, then worth about £150 or $400. He said he was sorry he could not be more generous, but he had had his ennuis and was now getting back onto his feet. It was in fact half his total capital at that time. They talked, and Girodias confided his ambitious plans to bring out Henry Miller's *Nexus* and works by known authors with a strong sexual content. *The Bedroom Philosophers* (as Wainhouse's translation of *La Philosophie dans le boudoir* was called) would now be one of his immediate new titles. In fact there would be no delay at all in publication.

Wainhouse said that he would like to see more of Girodias and suggested that he might like to meet his writing friends. The offer was accepted and shortly afterwards Girodias attended a *Merlin* meeting at 8 Rue du Sabot. The meeting of Girodias and the group went well and the former shrewdly summed up the situation of *Merlin* and its editors, taking an instant liking to Trocchi, who was soon to become a boon companion and brother. Girodias questioned the others about their work and abilities. He declared that his aim was to confound puritanism, hypocrisy and censorship, and to publish in English both original works and translations. He was willing to commission novels. Although the scale on which he intended to proceed and establish himself would certainly attract the attention of the law, he in no way intended to be cowed, and was willing to take the responsibility of protecting others who were less capable than himself when it came to fighting the authorities. The Olympia Press, moreover, would not confine itself to dirty books, but produce all kinds of literature, some of it morally harmless and with no sexual content. Asking about *Merlin*, he offered to subsidize it. In fact he would pay for the next issues if all those present would bring him their new manuscripts. In a little over an hour, during which he never touched the glass of Nescafé that they offered him on arrival, *Merlin* was in effect taken over by Maurice Girodias and his new Olympia Press.

A few days later, Austryn Wainhouse had arranged to read his translation of *La Philosophie dans le boudoir* to a group of about ten friends. They gathered together in Trocchi's room and the reading began. At a particularly salacious moment, there was a loud knocking on the door and the group took fright. Had the police heard of this private event? The US State Department was believed to have spies in Paris, keeping watch on expatriates and those running away from McCarthyism. But it was Girodias, who was arriving late for the reading. He listened for a while and then once again began to outline his plans for Olympia. Within three months he had received ten books from the *Merlin* group.

Maurice Girodias was a spendthrift with money when he had it. He was soon achieving good sales from the first Olympia titles in the tourist resorts of France, but his books also managed to get to other European cities, and they sold particularly well in those seaports where American sailors could buy them on shore leave. The many GIs in Paris were a rich source of revenue and the Traveller's Companion series of Olympia Press paperbacks, with their plain but distinctive green covers, were a familiar sight except in English-speaking countries, where thousands were smuggled in but never seen in bookshops: they were seized by customs or the police if discovered. The *Merlin* writers would frequently visit Girodias, first in his office on the Rue Jacob, a fashionable street that ran parallel to the Boulevard Saint-Germain, then in larger premises on the nearby Rue de Nesles. He would pay by the page for translations and give a lump sum for original manuscripts, but often, if he had the money on him in cash, he would pay out something on account for work in progress.

Trocchi became a constant companion to Girodias, advising him on manuscripts, imparting to him much of his recent educational knowledge and his literary taste; they shared copious lunches, always well washed down with good wines, and it was Girodias who paid for them. They both liked eating, and eating well. Christopher Logue would often see them emerging from a restaurant around the Boul' Mich' at four o'clock, not walking too steadily.

Under the pen name of Frances Lengel, Trocchi became one of the most prolific of Olympia's authors. He was now a guru, not just to his own circle, but to other expatriate groups, including those who followed *Merlin* by publishing the *Paris Review*, in particular the editors George Plimpton and Peter Matthiessen, and to some French intellectuals like Jean-Paul Sartre whom Trocchi had gone out of his way to meet, and who had been favourably impressed by him. Trocchi even managed to get an agreement from Sartre that he could use material from his currently fashionable review *Les Temps Modernes* without asking prior permission and without payment. And through Girodias he met more French people in the media, including some of those whom Girodias had come to know through Germaine Riedberger, prominent members of "*Le tout Paris*", the smart set.

Trocchi and Girodias had an amazing amount in common: this has become more obvious since the death of the latter in 1990, and the contradictory aspects of the two men can now be seen in perspective. They are both variously described by those who knew them well either as basically highly moral, albeit not in any conventional sense, or conversely as dangerous lunatics, caring for nothing but their own obsessions. Both had charm and good looks, Trocchi in a rougher mould than Girodias; they liked meeting people and were amusing and good company. Each had a strong streak of paranoia; neither ever thought about what today's actions might lead to when tomorrow came, and each was prodigal with money when the means were at hand. When Maurice Girodias had money rolling in from the American rights of *Lolita* and *The Naked Lunch*, he treated the money as absolutely his own, to be spent on whatever current folly interested him, without a thought for the author who was entitled to half of it or more, nor did he worry about the bills that he knew were coming in next month when the cash flow might stop. Trocchi borrowed copiously and in various ways procured money from the rich and credulous to put into *Merlin* and his other enterprises, and as often as not paid the donor in sex. Although there is no real hard evidence, it seems extremely likely that he was bisexual, not by nature, but because he had no emotional prejudice against sexuality of any kind, and he was always curious. He had a wife with him when he first went to Paris, where he quickly acquired a mistress, but he slept with every new sexual opportunity that caught his fancy, abandoning wife and offspring to the goodwill of anyone who might be able to help them. When he had run through the bursary from Kemsley and he needed money in a hurry, he went to the Isle of Man, not to see his wife whom he had temporarily sent there, but to borrow money from his brother who was lodging his family.

Both Trocchi and Girodias were renowned lovers, ladies' men of the first water, libertine in their literary tastes as well as their physical appetites. Each had a brother of compensating sanity, who were fortunately not prigs who preached. Each counted on his brother to help in an emergency and for frequent small loans. Each had a taste for luxury which certainly did not develop from their family backgrounds, and considered himself a natural aristocrat who deserved the best from life. They shared a messianic dream, an obsession with projects or causes that were pursued relentlessly. And finally both Trocchi and Girodias had power complexes that made them need to be the centre of their particular group of sycophants, sometimes inspiring fierce loyalty from their followers, who would be rewarded with kindness, affection and the feeling of being part of a very special circle.

The character of Don Juan, as created by de Molina, Molière and da Ponte, can be seen as a role model for them both. It must be remembered that da Ponte's hero, created for Mozart's opera, was closely modelled on his friend Casanova, who was a political radical as well as a seducer. Don Giovanni's final outburst when his nemesis finally catches up with him, "*Vivan le femmine! Viva il buon vino! Sostegno e gloria d'umanità*" ("Long live women! Long live good wine! Support and glory of mankind!") could hardly have been more appropriate for these two *bons vivants*. Girodias was impassioned about censorship, about breaking down taboos, making the world randier, and about fighting the hypocrisy of the *bien-pensant* bourgeois world. Later he was a radical anarchist, and the same can be said of Trocchi. A libertine personal life and political radicalism often go together, and with it a cavalier attitude towards women, who exist for personal pleasure and use; such men are usually much loved by women who often remain loyal and forgiving, willing to work for their men as well as love them, and accepting a marginal role in the man's preoccupations. Both Girodias and Trocchi took full advantage of their attractiveness to women, and exploited them. And both of them, by the time they met, had had considerable experience as seducers and lovers.

3

Girodias's account of his first meeting with Wainhouse differs considerably from the latter's.* In the cafés of Saint-Germain, Girodias had started to notice a group of young men who met and talked at the cheaper cafés, the Old Navy and the Monaco on the Boulevard and the Café Tournon near the Senate. One day he was sitting before an empty coffee cup when he was approached by Wainhouse, speaking excellent French; not only did the young American know his name, but his past history as well, and even that of his father. He had been watching him for some time and had asked questions.

"My wife and I were married at university when students," Wainhouse told Girodias, "and as soon as we graduated we left for Europe. We wanted to get away from the States and to find a more stimulating climate. Above all I wanted to be a writer." He related how he had travelled all over Europe on a scooter with his wife hanging on to his back. He knew French literature well and especially the eighteenth-century writers. And he had translated the Marquis de Sade's *La Philosophie dans le boudoir* as *The Bedroom Philosophers*. Girodias was impressed by his knowledge, style and humour. But the coincidence was that Girodias had already thought of having this early de Sade work translated, and he had talked to a young art critic whom he had met in Paris, David Sylvester, about it. But Sylvester was lazy and had not even started to do the translation. The first issue of *Merlin* had recently appeared, but not too many copies had been sold. In fact there were only two points of distribution, Le Mistral and Gaït Frogé's English Bookshop. Although Trocchi wanted to publish *The Bedroom Philosophers*, partly in *Merlin*, but also as a book on its own, his group were nervous, afraid that they might well be expelled from France. There are discrepancies between Girodias's and Wainhouse's descriptions of the course of events, although Wainhouse's is probably more accurate, because Girodias, in his own book, confuses places, dates and meetings very frequently.

Girodias then met the whole group. Austryn Wainhouse was the most political of them, decrying McCarthyism in the US and French colonial policy in Algeria. His father was a diplomat and more than a little nervous of the effect that his outspoken and radical son might have on his own career. Christopher Logue contributed poetry and did some editing for *Merlin*; although he spent some time with Trocchi, he was more often on his own, often going over to the Right Bank, perhaps the only member of the group who did so on a fairly frequent basis, visiting the glossier nightclubs and jazz clubs that attracted tourists rather than the young people of Saint-Germain. Logue at the time was principally concerned with a series of girlfriends, all of whom caused him problems of one sort or another, and he wanted to enjoy to the full the fabulous city of Paris, while writing his poems and reading others for *Merlin*.

From this point there is general agreement about the merging of *Merlin* with Olympia Press. *Merlin* remained under the editorship of Trocchi and his closest associates, subsidized, but only partly, by Girodias, and then on a haphazard basis. Girodias's accounts were never properly kept and he dealt much of the time in cash of which he kept little record. Individual writers were often able to take advantage of

Girodias's vagueness and get paid twice, and some money destined for *Merlin* may have gone elsewhere, most probably into Trocchi's pocket. Beckett was published. Both *Molloy* and *Watt* came out in editions that were designated as Collection Merlin, but also as Olympia Press. They were very different in appearance from the green Traveller's Companion paperbacks. Seaver was the main contact with Beckett, but Trocchi was also an enthusiast, and he and Beckett got on well after they met. Although Beckett always retained a considerable respect for Trocchi's abilities and liked his ebullient personality, he eventually became tired of Alex's continual demands on his time and attention, and retired more and more into his privacy. *Watt* appeared first in a hardcover edition and *Molloy* first in hardcover and then in paperback in an unusual format with an abstract cover. During the negotiations, Seaver heard that the Office de Radiodiffusion Télévision Française (ORTF), the French national radio, was to broadcast a portion of a play by Beckett, *En attendant Godot*. He met Roger Blin who was directing it and asked if he could come to the studio. Through the influence of Jeanette, his wife, he was given permission, but was disappointed that Beckett never turned up in person. This was, of course, before the Beckett appearance at the Rue du Sabot. It was to be nearly another year before *Godot* opened on stage.

Merlin had another problem at the time of its negotiations with Girodias. Not only did the editors have no money, but the legal status of the magazine was in doubt. No company had been set up, but it was nevertheless trading, on however minor a scale; the law required foreign enterprises to have a French *gérant*, a managing partner in effect, although such a person did not necessarily have to be active: Girodias was willing to be the *gérant*. He would also find money.

The first important collaboration was over *Watt*. Once Seaver had decided that the novel was unsuitable for serialization it was agreed that Olympia could publish it, but Girodias apparently (although not in his own account of events) had a number of reservations. Having read it, he knew that this was not a dirty book for tourists, although it did have a fairly salacious incident in the opening chapter. Beckett had known Jack Kahane before the war and had been commissioned by him to translate *Les 120 Journées de Sodome* (*The 120 Days of Sodom*), de Sade's last book and his masterpiece, into English. He had started the translation of what, by any standard, is a long book in the late Thirties, and had finished approximately half of it when war broke out, but the manuscript was lost during the Occupation. Beckett attended a meeting with *Merlin* and Girodias, where it was agreed to proceed with a printing of 2,000 copies of *Watt*, which was quite a small edition, under the dual Collection Merlin-Olympia Press imprint. According to Deirdre Bair, Beckett hoped that the publication of a modest edition in this way might help him find a British or American publisher.* He had problems with Girodias who was requesting cuts, largely on the advice of Trocchi, especially of the musical sections. There were also a number of eccentricities and oddities, such as the phrases, poems and paragraphs written for later inclusion in the main text, but simply put as addenda at the end of the book: Beckett's tongue-in-cheek comment on these extracts, or rather frustrated intracts, was: "The following precious and illuminating material should be carefully studied. Only fatigue and disgust prevented its incorporation."

Although by this time Beckett had largely taken the brilliant, enthusiastic Lothario under his wing – Beckett always had a penchant for talented rogues – *Watt* undoubtedly created tension between them. Trocchi, however, recognizing that he now had a major talent involved with *Merlin*, always gave way in the end. It was later said that Girodias had fought many of the oddities in the text and had published it under the impression that he was bringing out another "db" (dirty book) for GI consumption, but he always denied this and claimed that he considered *Watt* to be Beckett's major novel and that he had recognized its brilliance from the beginning. It is certainly the funniest of the post-war works, and its humour and occasional erotic incident is broader than in the *Molloy* trilogy, which he wrote subsequently, the appearance of which, in French, had first attracted Seaver's attention.

The first issue of *Merlin* appeared on 15th May 1952. The printing was 1,000 copies and cost 250 francs, which was 3/6d. or 60 cents. Sales were slow and, as had been customary among English-language and other foreign publications produced in Paris since the Twenties, many copies were sold hand to hand in cafés by those willing to earn a few francs in this way. Both English-language bookshops on the Left Bank, Le Mistral and the English Bookshop, displayed the publication in their windows and sold it regularly. Material came in from everywhere. Trocchi had made a point of getting to know French writers and magazine editors, and his agreement with Sartre gave him access to well-known names and rich literary material. Prestigious French names guaranteed that the magazine would be noticed by the literary press in both Britain and the US. This in turn would lead to French novels, translated by Trocchi and his colleagues, appearing under the Collection Merlin imprint, although it was often Girodias who was both the source and the real publisher; his close relationship with Pauvert gave him out-of-copyright authors for translation: Pauvert was bringing out handsomely produced editions of de Sade, Restif de la Bretonne and other earlier libertine writers, mainly of the eighteenth century. But there were many other controversial authors that interested Girodias, such as Jean Genet, published by Gallimard and highly praised by Sartre, who saw in his writings a practical demonstration of his theory that one is what one is seen to be, or otherwise becomes it, even if one did not originally match the image that the world sees. Genet was perceived as a criminal by society, therefore he became one. And he was not apologetic about his criminality in his novels. Girodias started to publish Genet in English: *The Thief's Journal* gradually became a cult book among those literati in the US and the UK who kept up with the new French literature, especially when English translations were available. Bernard Frechtman did the translation, not a very good one, but it remained the only English translation until after Frechtman's death in the Eighties. The most famous banned eighteenth-century English novel was John Cleland's *Fanny Hill*, a natural for Olympia, and it needed no translator. James Broughton's *Almanac for Amorists* was in the same collection, as was Christopher Logue's first book of poetry, very different from an Olympia Press db, *Wand and Quadrant*. Girodias was keeping his promise to publish "pure" as well as erotic literature.

Everybody in the *Merlin* group was now writing novels for Girodias, and without question Trocchi was the best of them. He used his memories, many of them relying on hearsay and what had been reported in the press, of the Glasgow gangs and their razor kings, who lived and operated mainly in the Gorbals, a slum district of tenements very different from Hillhead, the fairly genteel area near the university where he had grown up and attended school. He gave a colourful and mostly negative picture of his native city, the Gorbals with their fierce neighbourhood loyalty, standing together against authority and the police from whom these inner-city-dwellers expected little sympathy – residents were tolerant about the criminals in their midst, especially when their own families were involved. Sex and violence was part of the Gorbals life, steeped in a sordid pub culture of hard drinking, and Trocchi described the Glasgow gangs with colour and style. The razor kings dominated the pubs on weekend nights, choosing the women they wanted and marking their thighs with their razors as a sign of possession. The fights were largely between the young, rising thugs and the experienced older men who knew every trick of combat and how to kill or maim. The masochism among these women, who became attached to local figures of power and prestige, was sometimes strong.

Trocchi brought all this out in those novels that were based partly in Glasgow, such as *Helen and Desire*, which appeared under his pen name, Frances Lengel. The law of the jungle, of the sharpest tooth and strongest claw, was one he knew well, and he turned it into literature. *Helen* was followed by *The Carnal Days of Helen Seferis*, *Young Adam* (in a version that Trocchi "dirtied up" for this first published edition), *School for Wives*, *Thongs*, and *White Thighs*. In addition, he wrote the pseudonymous fifth volume of Frank Harris's *My Life and Loves*, a brilliant literary fraud in which he perfectly captured the style of the libertine English journalist, whose earlier volumes of disclosures about his sexual life had been published before the war by Jack Kahane. In 1953 Trocchi, together with Dick Seaver, also translated Apollinaire's *Les onze mille Verges* (*Eleven Thousand Penises*) under the title *The Debauched Hospodar*, using the pen name Oscar Mole. There were other translations that he started but never finished, like *Les Exploits d'un jeune Don Juan*, which was completed by Seaver. From all these novels and translations only *Young Adam* was regularly republished and made available during the next decades. It has had different American and British editions and has been pirated in the US on more than one occasion. During this time Trocchi was carrying on a host of other activities: editing and writing articles for *Merlin*, getting his name into other periodicals, contacting people who could be useful to him and living a full social and sexual life.

Christopher Logue wrote *Lust* under the name Count Palmiro Vicarion, and later *Count Palmiro's Book of Bawdy Ballads* and *Book of Limericks*. John Stephenson, the young accountant who had become the business manager of *Merlin*, wrote fictional erotic biographies of the Borgias, Spartacus and Ramses II, as Marcus van Heller. One of the best of the Olympia authors was Iris Owens who took the pen name Harriet Daimler and wrote *Innocence*, *The Organization* and *Darling*. Later she was to become celebrated for *The Woman Thing*, which achieved commercial publication in New York after its appearance on the Olympia list. Bill Bryant, who some years later was to marry Jane Lougee, wrote *Until She Screams*, and Mason Hoffenberg, who later would write, jointly with Terry Southern, the best-seller *Candy*, produced *Sin for Breakfast* under the pseudonym Faustino Perez. The American painter Norman Rubington, who had lived in Paris since leaving the army where he had worked during the war in American intelligence and as a war artist, was recruited by Olympia and wrote some excellent dbs as Akbar del Piombo. These included *Cosimo's Wife*, *Skirts*, *Who Pushed Paula?* and *L'Anticame*, and he also put together collage novels in the style of Max Ernst's *Une Semaine de Bonté*: *The Boiler Maker*, *The Fetish Crowd* and above all *Fuzz against Junk*, a satirical semi-comic-strip satire on the drug scene and the New York police. John Glassco, a Canadian poet of some reputation, wrote *The English Governess* under the name Miles Underwood. There was a young English teacher, a good-looking young Englishman, whose real name has never been revealed, teaching in a school for young girls of good family, who wrote some of the best sado-masochistic titles under feminine names, Ruth Less, Greta X and Angela Pearson. Pierre Loüys had his name anglicized to Peter Lewys for a translation of *Les Trois filles de leur mère*, to which significantly more erotic detail was added. Other French classics suffered an even more erotic transformation as they were freely adapted into English pornography.

Girodias himself was often choosing the titles, all of which shouted their lewdness as brazenly as possible: *The Chariot of Flesh*, *The Enormous Bed*, *Roman Orgy*, *Cruel Lips*, *Until She Screams*, *The Pleasure Thieves*, *Wisdom of the Lash*, *A Gallery of Nudes*, *Inch by Inch*, *Busy Bodies*, *Tender Was My Flesh*, *There's a Whip in My Valise*, and so on. Girodias compared himself, nurturing his titles, to a gardener lovingly growing the most beautiful flowers.

A line would gather outside Girodias's door every morning, waiting for the publisher, who was usually short of sleep because of the lady with whom he had spent a passionate night and more than a little hungover, to arrive. Money was handed over in driblets, sometimes on production of a manuscript. Girodias gave out between ten and thirty thousand francs at a time: he was theoretically paying about 300,000 francs or £300 or $800 a manuscript, although some authors ended up with as much as £750 or $2,000. He was normally printing about 5,000 copies of each edition and it would take him six to nine months to sell them. He did not bother about royalties, but paid a new lump sum when he reprinted; it is probable that the authors earned more this way than if sales had been properly accounted and regular royalties paid, but of course they didn't see it that way, and with time many of them became convinced that they were being cheated as they had no way of knowing exactly how many copies were being sold and how well Girodias was doing out of it. His flamboyant lifestyle contributed to their grievance. It had never occurred to Girodias in those days that with changing times some of the books he published in the Olympia Press Traveller's Companion series might have a later commercial life in Britain and the US. He was to become a little more careful later on, but his natural lack of interest in routine and organization would always leave him open to losing the fruits of his discoveries and commissions.

Writing pornography kept most of the *Merlin* group alive, but others did it for fun. George Plimpton, then editor of the *Paris Review*, started a novel for Girodias based on Robert Louis Stevenson's *The Suicide Club* but in which sex replaced death to unite the club members. He made some progress with it, but, realizing that writing fiction was not his greatest talent, and perhaps under some pressure from the other well-brought-up, ambitious young Americans who surrounded him, he abandoned it. The quality of the manuscripts accepted was uneven, and the worst of them – those with no redeeming merit other than the pornographic content – were published under Girodias's secondary imprint, Ophelia Press, in pink covers that soon became recognized by devotees as less difficult and more titillating; they were soon selling better. The group of literary expatriates was large and growing and *Merlin* was not its only centre: the *Paris Review*, subject of the next chapter, was only established a little while after *Merlin*, and there was also *Points*, a friendly rival that looked for new young writers, but on a less highbrow level, and it was not politically *engagé* like Trocchi's magazine. There was also the *Paris Magazine*, put out by George Whitman, owner of Le Mistral, for which Trocchi both contributed and did editorial work. Many other little periodicals were started but none of them lasted for more than a few issues, many only for one.

Points, edited by Sinbad Vail, the son of Peggy Guggenheim and Laurence Vail, who was apparently given his first name on the grounds that it would dissuade him from becoming a writer (no writer with such a name could be taken seriously!), did have some significance, and Trocchi tried hard to form a link to get some of the Guggenheim money. He managed to meet Peggy, and spent a weekend with her in Mégève, but although the rich heiress was always willing to accept a new, potent lover, she was by now hardened to demands for money to support their careers, and Trocchi does not appear to have obtained anything other than a taste of luxury for a few days. Trocchi tried hard to get some money, either as investment or loan from Sinbad, but the rival editor treated all of the *Merlin* group with caution, especially Alex, and in particular he kept his girlfriend from contact with the notorious seducer so that, as he put it to Terry Southern, he could not "suck the cervix clean out of her!"

But social life within the *Merlin* group was active and fun. Everyone took advantage of the splendours of Paris, the exhibitions and *vernissages*, the parties, the hours spent in cafés discussing politics, literature, their own work and the magazine. Girlfriends were exchanged regularly and everyone was falling in or out of love. Christopher Logue's affairs were especially messy and Trocchi was always his advisor, mentor and father figure. On one occasion Logue had fallen in love with a rich sixteen-year-old Brazilian girl called Vera Pedrosa, whose family could hardly have viewed him as a desirable boyfriend, and took her rapidly out of the country when they suspected a love affair was developing. In despair, the young poet decided, unknowingly aided and abetted by a South African painter, Louis de Wet, to commit suicide, and decided to do it poetically by taking a boat out to sea and sinking it. He took a train to Canet Plage in the Pyrenées, found he did not have enough money to hire a boat, let alone buy one, and bought a tin of mixed sleeping pills instead. Trocchi, having learnt of his plan and his whereabouts, followed him to Canet Plage and found him on the beach, disconsolately trying to open the tin by smashing it on a rock. He looked up and said, "Alex, I can't open this." A minute later, realizing the oddity of the situation, he added in surprise, "Alex, what are you doing here?"

"I'm here to embarrass you," said Trocchi, confiscating the tin. "Come on, Christopher, enough of this. Let's go into town and talk... d'accord, old man?" They went to a café and that night took the sleeper back to Paris, first-class – Logue never discovered where Trocchi had found the money – had an excellent dinner in the dining car with two bottles of wine and much brandy, and arrived back in Paris in the morning, the cause of the trip largely forgotten. Trocchi then managed to lodge Logue with his friends the Hellers, who lived on the Rue Vaneau for a few days. It was probable that he obtained funding for the mercy trip, on the grounds that he was saving a life.

The second issue of *Merlin* was published on 15th September. In it Trocchi declared his intention to make it iconoclastic, initiating new forms and new ideas. *Ulysses* had broken the mould of the novel and changed literature: it must be followed by new innovation. New moulds must not be allowed to form and harden. They must be broken over and over: "All categories are utilitarian; when they cease to be recognized as such, they become obnoxious," said his editorial. *Merlin* attracted contributors from everywhere and published Jean Genet, Paul Éluard, the exiled Turkish poet Nâzım Hikmet, William Sansom, Eugène Ionesco, Tristram Hull, Italo Svevo, Arthur Adamov, Robert Creeley, Patrick Brangwyn, Daniel Mauroc, Vasco Pratolini, Pablo Neruda (later to win the Nobel Prize and become Chilean ambassador to Paris, until he was dismissed after the fall of Allende's socialist government in a CIA-backed coup), W.S. Graham, and, of course, Henry Miller and

Samuel Beckett. Austryn Wainhouse's translations of the Marquis de Sade were now making money for both Girodias and *Merlin*: one issue was entirely paid for by *The Bedroom Philosophers*. Copies of the magazine were being sold in London, Amsterdam and other European cities with English-speaking populations. There was a certain exchange of contributors with the *Paris Review* and with *Points*. In London, *Horizon*, the most prestigious literary magazine of the Forties, had closed, and *Encounter* had started in its place, edited by Irving Kristol, who was soon known to be a CIA agent and who received his backing from the Congress for Cultural Freedom, which was also CIA-backed. The *Paris Review* was also believed to have CIA connections and Peter Matthiessen, one of the early editors, was later to admit his temporary involvement. Little magazines like *Mandrake*, edited by Arthur Boyars, an undergraduate student at Oxford, which admittedly imitated *Merlin*, appeared like mushrooms, many of them largely devoted to poetry, such as *Poetry Manchester*, edited by Howard Sergeant, *The Glass*, which was typeset and printed by hand by Anthony Borrow, and John Sankey's *The Window*. Sankey was a printer who began to specialize in little magazines, produced some poetry in pamphlet form and he subsidized his publishing by a variety of jobbing printing. Villiers Press was both a publisher and a printer.

The only serious musical figure involved with the *Merlin* group was Alexander ("Sandy") Goehr, son of the famous conductor Walter Goehr, who had moved to England from Germany because of the Nazis in the early Thirties. Sandy Goehr had studied at the Royal Manchester College of Music and was later to become celebrated as a leading member of the "Manchester School" that began to dominate English music after the Britten generation. He moved to Paris in 1954 and found a room near the Odéon where Christopher Logue and Trocchi helped him, with much effort, to lift a hired piano up the stairs and into it. The Café Tournon and the Old Navy were Goehr's normal hangouts until he began to spend more time near the Conservatoire, where he joined Olivier Messiaen's musical composition class. There was a war at the time between the two great musical teachers in Paris, Messiaen and Nadia Boulanger. The latter taught primarily young American composers, while most Europeans and some British went to Messiaen. The quarrel involved both musical style and politics. Although Messiaen himself was a devout Catholic, most of his pupils were on the ideological left, some of them communists, much involved with writers like Sartre, Éluard and Aragon, and those German composers who now had East Berlin as their headquarters, such as Paul Dessau and Hans Eisler, who also worked with Brecht on occasion. The Boulanger group were either little interested in politics or tended to the conformist right, not surprising as a musical career in America at the time was impossible for anyone of known left-wing views. René Leibowitz was also teaching the same group at the Conservatoire as Messiaen, but Leibowitz was a Schönbergian as well as a communist supporter, and musically apart from both Messiaen and Boulanger. Some believed he was also a Comintern spy. Pierre Boulez had studied with both these French composers, and had also become at this time Jean-Louis Barrault's musical director. His own later music was to owe much to Messiaen, although Schönberg and Webern were his main enthusiasms at that time. Trocchi was aware of the musical politics of Paris but they were tangential to *Merlin*.

Many US universities had literary magazines coming from their publishing presses or were helping those edited by well-known members of the staff. And writers were travelling, meeting each other, calling on magazine editors. Tangiers, Majorca, Amsterdam and the Greek islands each had their colony of writers and artists, and Paris was a very central point that most of them wanted to visit, coming from as far away as San Francisco, Durban and Sydney. From the first issue *Merlin* managed to create an excitement that had nothing to do with its modest sales; the people who mattered were reading it, and Trocchi, with his energy, ego and faith in his good luck and powers of persuasion, was profoundly confident. He persuaded many rich people who were willing to be associated with the arts and literature to make donations, while Jane Lougee, who spent three years with him, still had her allowance. She became the "Publisher" of the magazine, a code word for backer. Sometimes, with her Siamese cat Fuki sitting on her shoulder, she would stand around the places that Americans visited, in particular the American Express on the Rue Scribe, catching the eye of American tourists and trying to persuade whoever stopped there to buy a copy. The American Embassy was cooperative for a while in selling copies, but after one issue carried a Trocchi review of a book by Sartre, who was considered a "commie" in those McCarthyite days, *Merlin* was knocked off the list of approved publications. Peter Matthiessen, who was in London during the early days of *Merlin*, had written asking if he could distribute it there, but was turned down. He might well have joined it had he had any encouragement, instead of starting the *Paris Review*. But some people helped both publications. Plimpton gave money to Trocchi, both in those early days, and later after *Merlin* folded. John Marquand Jr, son of the famous author and a budding writer himself, was another soft touch, and there were quite a few others who helped all the little reviews in Paris.

The city was full of anglophones, and many were studying in French or involved in the cultural scene. P.J. Kavanagh has written in *The Perfect Stranger** about those Paris days, and his enrolment in a drama school behind the Hôtel des Invalides run by René Simon, a retired Comédie Française actor who had the ability to draw any emotion he wanted from his students by tactics that often bordered on the sadistic, pulling their hair or twisting their faces to make them overcome their diffidence, and putting on pyrotechnical displays of Corneille and Racine that succeeded in convincing his student audience of the greatness of the French classical theatre. Those were the unforgettable days of the Comédie Française when Madeleine Renaud, Marie Bell, Pierre Fresnay and Jean-Louis Barrault were nightly astonishing audiences with dazzling, often Artaud-influenced performances at the Salle Richelieu and later the Théâtre de Marigny of a wide repertory of modern and classical plays. The Théâtre National Populaire was performing with Jean Vilar and Gérard Philipe at the Palais de Chaillot. The political plays of Sartre and Camus, the bittersweet comedies and tragedies of Jean Anouilh, and the puzzling new plays of the absurd theatre – although it was not called that yet – with their subliminal appeal to the subconscious, were drawing American and British audiences as well as French. Richard Wright, whose *Native Son** had been a wartime best-seller, was only one of many black Americans who found the essentially non-racist atmosphere of Paris more comfortable than that of many American cities. Many of them learnt fluent French and became more a part of the French scene than the expatriate one. Wright wrote about Paris in his novels and one of his characters, Fishbelly, was based on Ishmael (Cobra Kelly), a con man from Alabama who had used a series of elaborate ploys to defraud American tourists. Many such shady characters were known to the *Merlin* editors. Kosta Alexopoulos was a Greek sculptor whom Trocchi met, who seemed to have a finger in many dubious dealings, but was nevertheless a source of some revenue to both Trocchi and *Merlin*. Both found money where they could and Trocchi's facility at picking up women and introducing them to others undoubtedly helped the finances. His charm and disingenuousness covered a total lack of conventional morality.

Trocchi certainly exploited others to the extent of their willingness to be exploited. Dick Seaver was persuaded to take a job at an American army base to help produce revenue. It was a job he hated. Trocchi made a trip to Spain both to meet authors and to negotiate cheaper printing than he could find in France. He borrowed a motorcycle from Shinkichi Tajiri, a Dutch-American sculptor, and ran it down to Majorca. He had hoped to meet Robert Graves there, but Graves was away. Betty and her children were on the island at the time, part of the reason for the trip, which he had to explain to Jane on his return. Jane at this point was expecting him to get a divorce and marry her. He did see Robert Creeley, and the visit is described in Creeley's novel *The Island*: "He was tall, taller, had a crooked face with a strong nose, it was that one was first aware of, the beak-like strength of that nose, then the eyes, blue, sharp in no simple sense, set into that projecting forehead..."* He returned with a few Creeley poems and a new printing arrangement that saved the magazine some money. But much of that saving he put into his own pocket. The others were aware of this, but shrugged their shoulders: Trocchi would always be Trocchi!

His meeting with Betty was indecisive. He slept with her again and she later became pregnant; it was not long since she had her last abortion, and now she would need another. Nor did the renewal of sexual contact help him to get from Betty what he wanted – a decision made by *herself* to divorce him. Trocchi could never bring himself to take blame or to say outright that he no longer loved Betty, who he had pursued relentlessly some years earlier, overcoming her initial reluctance and her parents' strong opposition.

3,000 copies of *Merlin* were printed in Spain, but most of them were lost: a thousand sent to England sank with the boat and another thousand sent to the US never arrived; it is likely that they never left Spain, either because Trocchi had forgotten to pay for transport or because he had not filled in the documents properly. Less than a thousand actually arrived in Paris. The issue was a disaster. Trocchi not only had to mollify the other members of the *Merlin* group, who had made every sacrifice that Trocchi demanded of them for the magazine, but he also had to make his peace with Jane. He promised that he would get a divorce and marry her, and they talked of adopting his two daughters if Betty would allow this.

Trocchi then thought it politic to take Jane away for a holiday in the south of France, and they stayed with his Paris friends Clement and Matilda Heller who had a house near the coast, but as the Hellers made it clear that they were welcome for a few days but not for the summer, they went on to Spain, hitchhiking. Jane was the bait for truck drivers to stop and she was furious at Alex's complaisance when she was molested by them. He saw no reason why they should have to walk because Jane was reluctant to allow a little amorous molestation.

They went to bullfights in Barcelona, sat in the cafés on nearby beaches and sent postcards to Paris. But by now Jane was becoming rapidly disillusioned and Trocchi was balancing in his mind the advantages of Jane's allowance against the growing staleness of the relationship.

Back in Paris at the end of the summer Trocchi returned to work on another issue of *Merlin*. They had by now, in addition to magazine contributors, a large number of manuscripts that had been offered for book publication, and the appearance of *Watt* and the Wainhouse translations brought in more. The Hellers agreed to have a party for the magazine and in early December 1953 they organized a reception in their apartment. Among those who came were the photographer Georges Brassaï, who had chronicled the low-life of Montmartre and Montparnasse, several painters including Max Ernst, Stanley William Hayter and Alberto Giacometti, and a diversity of writers including Sidney Chaplin, Richard Wright and other Americans mainly associated with the *Paris Review*. Among the French were Eugène Ionesco, Arthur Adamov, Raymond Queneau and Jean Paulhan. The mix of intellectuals from different disciplines, and the mixture of English and French with a smattering of other languages, was reminiscent of Shakespeare & Company in the Thirties. It was also a clear sign that *Merlin* had arrived, in the sense that it was now recognized by the more avant-garde French literary establishment as part of the Paris art scene.

4

By 1954 Paris had become its old self. There were restrictions resulting from wartime shortages, but they bothered very few people. The country was alive, once again a tourist paradise, and exporting wines, perfumes and luxury goods. Paris haute couture once again dominated the world of fashion and new developments were taking place in the arts. American action painting was modish and found its Parisian echo in tachism: painters threw paint haphazardly onto canvas, then drove bicycles over it, rolled in it, or did whatever would produce easy, interesting, aleatory patterns. André Masson became high fashion.

Masson was one of the three painters that Samuel Beckett, now re-established in Paris, had selected for a series of dialogues, which were reconstructions of his discussions about painting with the art critic Georges Duthuit while they played chess in cafés, amusingly and penetratingly bringing out their disparate points of view in a stylized fashion. These dialogues appeared in Duthuit's *transition*: he had revived the pre-war Jolas review, principally to get the entitlement to a paper ration. The dialogues, which are most revealing about Beckett's mindset and aesthetics, go deeply into the nature of artistic creativity. Besides Masson, the other painters discussed are Pierre Tal-Coat and Beckett's friend, the Dutch painter Bram van Velde, not well known at the time; all were abstract painters.*

The ideological arguments of the days were wide-ranging, painting being prominent as always in Paris, but they included politics, the cold war, the freedom movements against neo-colonialism, McCarthyism, the atom bomb, and the conflict of paternalistic authority with the demand for total freedom, including, naturally, artistic freedom. Commitment was much discussed: should the artist use his art as a form of propaganda and put it at the service of a cause, as was demanded by the authoritarian right and the Communist Party, or was the artist's real commitment only to his art itself? Sartre wavered between the two positions, while Camus was for commitment. The literature of the new Germany was grounded in neo-expressionism: the immediate past made it impossible for the artist to ignore politics. In Italy the arguments were similar to those in France, the different ideologies all trying to recruit the intellectuals of the day to their colours. But the public was increasingly attracted to abstraction in all the arts: it saw the new theatre of Beckett and Ionesco as an equivalent to action painting, to tachism, and the abstract expressionism of Jackson Pollock and Willem de Kooning. The *nouveau roman* was in existence in the early Fifties, but not called that yet: the literary papers spoke of "a-literature" (from "atonal" in music) and "anti-literature", featuring antiheroes. But signals were confused: Beckett was considered in Poland to be the most political of committed authors, his work seen as a protest against the conformism of state art and a repressive communist society, while in France he was attacked for not taking a recognizable political stance in his writing. Marguerite Duras, having been a communist, had increasingly found it impossible to write as the party wanted her to do, and she left the party; one of her boyfriends, Dionys Mascolo, wrote an immense book called *Le Communisme*, the argument of which can be stated as follows: every writer of sensitivity would like to be a communist, but as a writer he finds it impossible to submit to the discipline the party demands; this is a problem and a pity!

Michel Butor, Alain Robbe-Grillet, Nathalie Sarraute and Claude Simon, the four leading members of "a-literature", while claiming they had nothing much in common, found that what they did have was a mutual dislike of committed literature and of novels which told a chronological story, served a cause, pointed to a moral or were simply adapted to the comfort of readers who wanted entertaining reading that might also teach some new ideas. To them, and the other *nouveaux romanciers* writing at about the same time or following their example, what mattered was to describe the world though the only vehicle capable of making sense of it, the human mind. The human mind therefore became the new hero (or antihero as the press put it). As each mind is different and no one can ever be quite sure of the sanity of even his own mind, everything observed in the world and described by the novel becomes subjective and open to interpretation. The only commitment possible for the writer, said Robbe-Grillet, is to his own writing.

Merlin followed all this and Trocchi, as the principal leader-writer for the magazine, came down on the side of commitment. His editorials became more and more portentous. In his later days, Trocchi was to talk much about the *coup du monde*, a world revolution to be brought about by a massive international change of heart. The kernel of the idea first appears in his writings in *Merlin*. At the time he was above all in favour of art questioning itself, and using its influence to create change, the old argument of the expressionists, who felt that if you do not like the world about you, you change it, if necessary by revolution. Dick Seaver became more important in making decisions for *Merlin* as Trocchi was increasingly occupied with his other writing, and his affairs and outside activities, which by the end of 1954 included experiments with drugs. Hashish was of course very common in Paris and easily obtainable from Arab pedlars, especially around the Rue de la Huchette where Trocchi had lived for a while with his family. But hard drugs were not difficult to obtain and there were several opium smokers. Sadeq Hedayat, a friend and disciple of Sartre's, who is now recognized as the most important Persian poet since Omar Khayyám, was a confirmed smoker and had died of it in Paris in 1951. But such examples did not deter artists and writers looking for new experience, and certainly not Trocchi.

It has been suggested that it was the circle of Jean Cocteau, which Trocchi came to know, that persuaded him to try hard drugs, and that Cocteau was therefore at the root of his addition, but there is no hard evidence for this. In any case it didn't matter. Trocchi was persuaded that the world had much to offer and that everything must be tried. He believed he was so strong in his natural health and will power that he was above addiction: nothing could harm him. As he came less to the office, Seaver took over; he was increasingly in disagreement with Trocchi's theories of total libertarianism and commitment to commitment.

Seaver tried to tone down Trocchi's growing extremism and he took a large part in deciding what went into the magazine. Several Trocchi short stories appeared there under different names: one of them was James Pidler, and there may be others that will never be recognized as his because he did not necessarily let his colleague know all his pen names. He always had the ability to use different styles and to imitate other writers, and this has created difficulties in identifying his work.

The group kept together, but it became smaller in time as the more marginal writer-editors left Paris, concentrated on their own writing or simply made money by writing pornography for Girodias. The evenings of discussion and readings became a thing of the past. Trocchi had been an excellent improvisational cook: over the solitary gas ring in his room on the Rue du Sabot he had turned out complete meals for the *Merlin* group, often finishing with Jane Lougee's fruit cake; on one occasion he even cooked African lobsters. Pea soup was his speciality and among those who attested to its excellence was Brendan Behan, who ended many of his drunken nights in Paris sleeping across three chairs in the same room as Alex and Jane. But after Jane's departure Trocchi moved to ever-smaller lodgings, frequently writing to her and asking her to return. He obtained a divorce from Betty through a French lawyer in a Mexican court, promising Jane at the time that they would then get married by proxy, also in Mexico, but without having to go there. (He later obtained a second divorce in Mexico.) But Jane had by now had enough of Alex's antics and, although she undoubtedly still loved him, she felt that the time had come to make a total break. But shortly before she left Paris for good, there was a last act of extravagance.

The Bal des Quat'z' Arts had long been a celebrated and notorious festival of sex, organized by the students of the École des Beaux-Arts. Brassaï the photographer took famous photographs of this event, in which the students paraded naked – or nearly – through the streets, disguised in masks and covered in dye, drinking heavily, banqueting in university halls and ending up in the Salle Wagram, where the doors were locked at ten p.m. and only opened again at dawn. Straw was scattered around the walls for couples to copulate. The whole event was a gigantic orgy where everyone, in theory at least, was available to everyone else. The students provided their own police, a "*cadre noir*" armed with wooden clubs to separate any coupling where one participant was unwilling and to spare her from rape. A military band played throughout the night from a balcony and a wandering spotlight picked out scenes from the boxes around the theatre. Art students organized still-life *tableaux* for the moment when the spotlight came around to their box and a prize was awarded to the best. A group from *Merlin* and the *Paris Review* decided to participate in the Quat'z' Arts ball of 1954, which took place in early July to celebrate the end of the university year. The group included Trocchi and Jane Lougee, George Plimpton, Christopher Logue and some others. They dressed, according to the theme of the year, in Grecian dress – scanty togas and blue dye – Jane wearing only bikini bottoms. The scene was a wild one, with totally abandoned dancing to the military band, much drinking and the throwing away into the shadows of any clothes that had not previously been torn off, as the atmosphere became warmer and couples and groups tangled together on the bundles of straw around the walls. The more faint-hearted, or those already exhausted by lovemaking, watched the scene from the balcony and the boxes. Although the majority were students, the event was open to all who could pay the entry price and there was no shortage of single and willing young women, many of whom had travelled up to Paris from the provinces for the occasion. Trocchi was excited and entranced by the whole event. When the moment came for "*Le spectacle*", the moment when the spotlight travels around the boxes and balconies, illuminating for a few seconds the prepared *tableaux*, Trocchi suddenly decided that he too wanted to participate. One group of art students had created the beautiful *trompe-l'oeil* effect of a naked woman suspended in space, painted a cerulean blue from head to foot, the whites of her eyes clearly visible in the light. The crowd called for the spotlight to return to her, shouting out "*La bleue, la bleue*!" Trocchi excitedly told his friends that they would put on their own spectacle: Jane was to lie naked on the edge of their box, on her side, and he would face her and make love while the others, also naked, fanned them with palm fronds. Jane was sent upstairs to the box to get into position and Trocchi, after telling the others to pick up a few bunches of straw to look like palms, and to follow him up the box, started to follow Jane up the stairs. But Trocchi was tall and in his haste he knocked himself out on the low ceiling to the stairs. George Plimpton managed to get into the box on time, but he was the only one fanning Jane when the spotlight settled on them. The crowd was puzzled by the symbolism of a naked girl being fanned by a naked man. When Trocchi regained consciousness he was very angry. "Why didn't one of you take my place?" he said. "We might have won the prize."

When Jane went back to America on 10th August, her allowance went with her and Trocchi moved back to the Hôtel Verneuil and then to a small room in the Rue Campagne-Première near the Montparnasse cemetery, where Kosta Alexopoulos, his shady Greek friend with whom he shared many traits, including an appetite for women, helped him to construct a large bed that nearly filled the whole room: this was intended to be the scene of future orgies. Trocchi was working prolifically at this time; many of his stories were written in this room, as well as editorials and books for Girodias. He also corresponded frequently with Jane and Betty.

The latter, before leaving for New Zealand, had returned briefly from Spain to Paris, claiming alimony and money for the children, but this was impossible for Trocchi. Previously he had been able to divert some of Jane's money to pay the children's school fees, but Betty had been obliged for some time to make do with the little money she earned from looking after an American colonel's children in addition to her own. From August to December, Trocchi wrote thirty-three love letters to Jane, but, even while asking her to come back, he was boasting in these letters about his many female conquests; he was hardly going the right way to persuade her. During this time he seduced Alexopoulos's Chinese girlfriend out of pure bravado, had a fling with another Jane who worked for UNESCO, and wrote to New York that he had tried heroin and found it wonderful. His addiction had begun. Betty succumbed to him once again in Paris after Jane's departure, again became pregnant, and had to return to Spain for yet another abortion. Trocchi told a friend at the time that she was having "a dirty weekend" with a boyfriend.

Only seven issues of *Merlin* appeared altogether. It was Trocchi's organizational drive that got it going in the first place, and there was a creative and exciting period when everyone in the group was convinced that they were making literary history, and believed in Trocchi as their leader. Seaver announced in those early days that Trocchi would be the new Hemingway. Not only did *Merlin* hold readings in private, but often its members read out-loud to crowds in cafés, with Trocchi standing on a table and declaiming the bawdiest passages he could find from his own work or that of others. It could hardly have pleased the waiters or the proprietors of the cafés.

Jane did return for a week in January 1955 and although she consented to sleep with Trocchi she made it clear that she was not returning to him. Nor did she have any money for *Merlin*. After her departure Trocchi suddenly discovered that he had picked up gonorrhoea and wrote that he hoped he had not given it to her.

Austryn Wainhouse and Richard Seaver became the working editors of the later issues, with Trocchi writing for *Merlin* and raising money, much of which he kept for his own needs. There was a conspiracy among his associates to gloss over his peccadilloes, once they began to realize what they really were. He was not easy to pin down, lied convincingly, and when he knew that truth would out had a way of exerting his charm in such a winning way that he had to be forgiven. They respected his energy, knowledge and talent even when it began to be sapped by sex and drugs and when he was becoming increasingly unreliable and unrealistic. His lack of any scruple when it came to sex, giving the women he seduced (quite apart from Betty and Jane) every expectation of a settled relationship, from which he walked away when it suited him, or when some new opportunity came his way, troubled them. Less worrying was his taste for orgies, which was widespread enough at the time in Paris – the orgy idea appealed to and excited even those who did not participate – and he was not the only one who indulged in sexual exchanges involving the women of the others in the group. After all, that was what they were all writing about for Olympia, and their sexual experiments were quickly transformed into erotic literature. Trocchi claimed that jealousy was not in his nature and he constantly stated that love was stronger than sex; everyone could enjoy another experimentally without injuring his marriage or permanent relationship with a lover. He persuaded Baird Bryant's wife, Denny, to spend the night with him and Bryant, who worshipped Trocchi at the time, acquiesced. To test Trocchi, the group arranged for Jane to spend the night in a hotel room with Sinbad Vail with a bottle of wine. Nothing happened, nor was intended to, but Trocchi then bedded several other women in a move that could only have been intended to anger Jane, and it did. Trocchi also behaved very boorishly at parties when some new face attracted him, especially if the woman was with a husband or boyfriend: he strutted around, boasting of his intentions and making obscene gestures. Paris had gone a little too much to his head!

Recriminations did no good. His disingenuousness, and way of circumventing any awkward situation in which he found himself, usually made his accusers back down, unconvinced perhaps, but aware that they would never get anywhere with him. Although his dishonesty, his philandering and his deviousness can only make him appear unsavoury in retrospect, the fact remains that those who knew him in his Paris days continue to remember him with respect and affection, and they draw a veil over his misdemeanours. Even the only Trocchi biography, subtitled *The Making of the Monster*, by Andrew Murray Scott, has difficulty in assessing his extremely complex character. Seaver talks of his kindness and has referred to him as "a very moral man". If the facts, looked at many years later, do not seem to bear that out, it must be because the man's actions and his manifest intentions were at odds with each other and that he himself never quite discovered who the "cosmonaut of inner space", as he was later to describe himself, really was.

Trocchi's novels do tell us a little about him, in particular *Cain's Book*,* written as a result of his later American experiences. The decline came with the heroin addiction, but this did not surface obviously until 1956. The end of the magazine was less dramatic: it simply petered out when Trocchi left Paris and his colleagues found new occupations. There was a hiatus from 1954 to 1955 (numbers five to six). On 10th June 1955, Trocchi wrote a letter to the *Times Literary Supplement* in reply to a news item that had appeared there about the *Paris Review* in which it was mentioned that, "*Merlin*, unpublished for almost a year, is about to begin again, under the editorship of Alex Trocchi, Austryn Wainhouse and Christopher Logue."* Trocchi's letter denied that the magazine had ever ceased publishing, insisted that its future was secure and would continue under the first two named editors with the addition of Richard Seaver ("Mr Logue was never officially connected with *Merlin*").

Merlin was only to continue for another year and Collection Merlin would cease at the same time, although Girodias was to continue publishing many of its titles. *Merlin* had been praised, among others, by Sartre, Camus, Stephen Spender, Bertrand Russell and Sir Herbert Read. Read had written: "in its pages one can find the best experimental work in the arts that is being done on both sides of the Atlantic."* From it sprang many writers who have stood the test of time and its influence on literary history, although less well-known, is not necessarily less than that of *transition* in the Thirties.

Chapter Three

The Paris Review

The *Paris Review* was a largely American phenomenon as compared to *Merlin*. It never set out to change the world, to define what literature should be about, or to preach. The group that founded and edited it was largely interchangeable with the *Merlin* group as people: they all knew each other and frequented the same cafés, had good times together and lived similar lives, but the *Paris Review* group were not really bohemians: they had been to good American universities, sometimes followed by good British ones; they were typical Ivy-League young Americans with a desire to make a name for themselves in literature and to have a good time as well. *Merlin* aimed at high seriousness; the *Paris Review* simply wanted to exist for the benefit of its editors and contributors, and it never had a manifesto.

Peter Matthiessen was a young man who after Harvard went to Cambridge in England, where at one point he suggested to *Merlin* that he might represent the magazine in London. He arrived in Paris in the spring of 1951 with his beautiful new wife Patsy, looking for a literary opening. He met another American, Harold L. Humes, in Le Dôme, the Montparnasse café and restaurant that had been a literary haunt for generations. Humes was to distinguish himself over the years as an unusual and genuine eccentric. He had just started a magazine called the *Paris News Post*, which was designed to look as much as possible like the *New Yorker*. Matthiessen told him that he was working on a novel, which eventually emerged as *Race Rock*, and that he wanted to start a purely literary magazine. Humes became enthusiastic and, talking excitedly, they decided to start such a publication together and call it *Manuscript*. Matthiessen described Humes at the time as an elegant, flamboyant young man, wearing a cape and carrying a silver-headed cane, who laughed a lot.

> ...a lot of style to him; he was appealing, aggressive, warm-hearted, curious, yet with convictions on every subject... all of which made him impossible.*

Humes was always referred to as "Doc", both then and later in his career, although no one quite knew why. He asked Matthiessen to become fiction editor of the *Paris News Post* and in a short time Matthiessen came up with a short story by a young American writer called Terry Southern. This was so much better than anything else in Doc's second-rate magazine that they agreed to start all over again with a new periodical and this became the *Paris Review*. They then began to gather an editorial group together, it being understood that Humes would look after the publishing and production side as well as being managing editor. That was exactly what he did not do: he suddenly began spending his time in Montparnasse cafés with a glass of beer in front of him, reading American classics. His job was done instead by John Train, a Harvard graduate who had been editor of *The Harvard Lampoon* and had a master's degree in comparative literature. Train was also an eccentric and fond of practical jokes. Then George Plimpton, another young American who had known Matthiessen at Harvard, joined the group and eventually became both the organizer and the editor.

Among the recruits were William Styron, Jane Fonda, Frances Fitzgerald and others who were destined to make successful careers. They would meet in Matthiessen's apartment in a backstreet in Montparnasse and discuss editorial content and fund-raising. Plimpton gave the magazine its name, and it was decided to play down critical writing and theory and to concentrate on creative work. French magazines were all heavy on theory, political and literary. *Engagement* was the fashionable word in France, everyone had to be "committed", but the group that gathered around Matthiessen and Plimpton were all bright young men from good families and universities, remote from the Depression, the Thirties and the war that had turned a generation of intellectuals to the left (giving Joseph McCarthy and the Un-American Activities Committee its chance to get publicity and power by attacking such easy targets). These young Americans were by instinct loyal to the class they came from, even if not positively right-wing. Most of them were barely aware of politics. Peter Matthiessen was later to admit that he had himself once worked for the CIA, but he has never said what this involved; several of the editors and contributors – and there were many of both over the years to come – may well have worked for the CIA, which was anxious to recruit agents from the world of culture as well as politics and business. But this is a large issue that I will look at more closely later in this chapter.

The editors themselves were not consciously political as far as their editorial functions were concerned: the established situation, a moneyed status quo, was normal to them and there is no evidence of political intent in the *Paris Review*, then or later. Certainly William Styron, who was a little older than the others and a published novelist, and who had much to say in the early policy-making discussions, declared his lack of interest in anything that might be described as "Zeitgeist". Peter Matthiessen was well heeled enough to be able to supply apparently endless quantities of whisky and other drinks during the editorial sessions, but money to live was never much of a problem for the *Paris Review* group as compared to the editors of *Merlin*. From Matthiessen's apartment they would move on to a café and, other than *Le Dôme*, the *Chaplain* became a favoured spot, a bar with a piano that was played almost continuously by music students, who thereby gained the experience of playing in public and practising on an instrument that was usually in tune. There was no applause, but the performances were usually listened to attentively. Here, in the thick smoke, with a background of piano music, the first issues were planned and the manuscript submissions discussed.

Through a friend at Les Éditions de la Table Ronde, one of the more popular imprints at the rather staid publishing house of Librairie Plon, a small office was obtained without rent in Plon's big building at 8 Rue Garancière. The motivation for giving the space seems to have been the hope by one of the Table Ronde editors that out of the material sent to and published in the new magazine there might be literary work of interest for translation into French. After all, major literary works had emerged from the pre-war little literary reviews.

The Plon structure was a large square building, dating from well before the French Revolution, with a courtyard that could only be entered from a central gate, and only very senior directors were allowed to drive their cars into this space. It was later to become the offices of a big publishing group that took over Plon, Les Presses de la Cité, which in addition bought the fashionable post-war publishing house of René Julliard. When Julliard fell victim to cancer and had to retire, Christian Bourgois, a younger brother of another well-known publisher of reference books, was engaged to manage his company, and used the opportunity to start his own imprint, Christian Bourgois, which largely replaced it. Bourgois soon became one of the most fashionable of literary French publishers, much of its material being translations from English. Bourgois also masterminded the paperback series 10/18, so named for the physical dimensions of the books in centimetres.

The problem was that the *Paris Review* editors, and others who worked in the small room they were assigned, were not entrusted with a key, and the concierge locked up as soon as the employees of Plon had left. The *Paris Review* group kept irregular hours, often working late: they had to arrive when the doors were still open, and they developed a system of leaving, when they were locked in, by lowering themselves out of the window and onto the street, dropping the last few feet, a risky procedure for the girls and the shorter men. George Plimpton remembered many amusing incidents from those days. Sometimes they would be leaving the building just as the Garde Républicaine, mounted ceremonial soldiers rather like the British Life Guards, were returning to their quarters on the other side of the Rue Garancière. The editors must have looked rather like cat burglars leaving the scene of the crime, but they never received more than a glance, nor were the police ever called.

Because of its proximity to Plon, a café in a parallel street became the meeting place for the *Paris Review*. This was the Café Tournon at the very beginning of the Rue de Tournon, a smart street with several small comfortable hotels, some discrete larger houses and, on the Rue de Seine extension nearer the boulevard, a number of fashionable boutiques. The café was open until about two in the morning and provided chess sets to those who asked for them. During the day a number of literary types could be seen reading, writing and correcting proofs. Café Tournon was considerably cheaper than the larger cafés of Saint-Germain and Montparnasse and was situated conveniently between them. Here the Plimpton crowd began to meet, during the day, after office hours and on weekends; some of the *Merlin* editors also came to use the café because of the prices and the proximity of their English-speaking rivals. Trocchi, Seaver, Logue, Wainhouse and Jane Lougee exchanged gossip with Matthiessen, Plimpton, Styron and the others. The café became a draw for others with manuscripts to publish.

One of Plon's authors was General de Gaulle himself. On one occasion when the General came to visit his publishers, the entire staff was drawn up in the entry hall to receive him, rather like troops being reviewed. The *Paris Review* group were asked to be part of this assembly, thereby demonstrating what a large and varied number of people made up the staff. He shook many hands and made a small speech.

Much of literary Paris lies around the Saint-Sulpice area. The church dominates a large square and is one of the finest examples of Romanesque church architecture in Paris. The Rue Garancière runs from the church to the Rue de Vaugirard; two streets away, on the other side of the

Rue de Tournon, is the Rue de Condé which joins Vaugirard, but also has a small street named after Crébillon, the eighteenth-century libertine writer, that links it to the Place de l'Odéon, dominated by the Théâtre de l'Odéon. The Place is impressive and elegant, built in a uniform half-moon crescent which contains a famous restaurant, La Meditérranée, small boutiques, publishers and, between the theatre and the Rue de Condé, the Hôtel Michelet Odéon, named after the great French historian, novelist and prose stylist Jules Michelet. Henry James frequently stayed here, and it is where Jean Genet hid for two years while writing his later plays and Maurice Girodias was to live for a while after he returned to Paris from America in the early Eighties. Sylvia Beach's old bookshop had been parallel to the Rue de Tournon on the Rue de l'Odéon, which faces the theatre. It is a street with many specialized bookshops, antique shops and small publishers situated between the hotels and large double carriage doors that lead to interior courtyards and often luxurious apartments. It was a highly desirable area to be in, and in the Fifties it was still cheap, because those with money, even successful intellectuals, wanted to live in the fashionable *seizième* near the Bois de Boulogne, or the *huitième* with its luxurious shopping streets, or on the big boulevards constructed by Haussmann between the Louvre and Montmartre.

On the Rue de Tournon were many hotels. Eugene Walter, one of the contributors to the *Paris Review*, lived at the Hôtel Helvetia, just across the street from the Café Tournon itself. A southerner from Mobile, Alabama, he was well versed in literature, but also knew much about the art of cooking, ballet, opera, costume and set design and other such things. He eventually became an advisory editor. A colourful eccentric, he was popular with the whole group and left some useful reminiscences of those times:

The day I arrived in Paris, I had moved into the Hôtel Helvetia across the street from the café. The hotel, an eighteenth-century townhouse, was immaculately clean, and I liked the marmalade cat who came up with M. Jordan, the proprietor, when he brought breakfast. The Café de Tournon was close; coffee there was good. I liked their Irish setter, Arnauld, a real silly dog who, with one enthusiastic lashing of the tail, could send whole trayfuls of drinks crashing off the little round tables outside on the sidewalk. Seeing people correcting proofs, and reading over their drinks, I realized I had found the appropriate climate.*

His nickname was "Tum-te-Tum", because these were the first words the editors had heard him say when, summoned to meet them in the boardroom of La Table Ronde, borrowed for this as for many other occasions, he was told that his submission had been accepted for publication. This was a story entitled 'Troubador'. As an editor he turned out to be as eccentric as so many of the others, signing his letters "Professor James B. Willoughby", often prefixed with the greeting "*mille fleurs*". He managed to introduce such a number of articles and illustrations into the magazine on his hobby-horses, of which cookery was a principal one, that Archibald MacLeish, who had taught many of the editors at Harvard and was keeping a fatherly eye on the issues they sent him, began to wonder if it was not getting a bit too fey.

Eugene Walter was a monkey-lover, keeping a stuffed one in his room that travelled with him, and "Monkey" was a favourite word of endearment, sometimes bestowed on the girls who adorned the staff of the *Paris Review*. There were many of these, nearly all unusually pretty: the magazine was a magnet for well-heeled young women with time on their hands, anxious to be where things were happening, and willing to work for little or nothing. They were given the general name of "*Apotheker*" (German for pharmacist) in the early days, a name invented by John Train – nobody later remembered why! Among them were the previously mentioned Frances Fitzgerald, later to write *Fire in the Lake*, Jane Fonda, daughter of Henry, who would later become a star herself, and Gail Jones, the daughter of Lena Horne. The male volunteers were called "Musinkys" for a while, after the first of them, but the nickname did not last. Their principal function, other than the duller editorial drudgery, was selling the magazine around the cafés and any place where Americans might be found. The young English writer, Colin Wilson, then working on *The Outsider*, the kind of book that every undergraduate dreams of writing but no other ever did, was one of the volunteers. Another, Peter Moscoso-Gongora, already considered himself to be a genius, and he numbered his stories instead of titling them. Like nearly all the young men he only wanted to be a successful writer, but he had to put in time selling the review as well. One of the best of the street-sellers was an Italian philosophy student, Vittorio Abrami, who had to be relieved of the cash he had collected at the end of his rounds or it would be rapidly spent, after which he would go into hiding from shame. His career as a *camelot* (street-seller) ended when he shaved off his hair to win the love of a pretty French student – hardly a recommended procedure in those pre-punk days – and found himself unappealing to both the girl and potential customers.

Christopher Logue, poetry editor of *Merlin*, offered work to the *Paris Review* and was accepted; he also became the principal link between the two groups and frequently appeared at the Café Tournon, the most favoured watering hole. Among the young hopefuls who frequented the place were writers like Richard Wright, already a celebrity, Max Steele, William Gardner Smith, Mary Lee Settle, Sissel Lange-Nielsen, Jean Garrigue, whose novel *The Animal Hotel* used the Helvetia across the street as its model, Renata Vitzthum von Eckstadt, the Finnish art historian and Gurney Campbell, the playwright, as well as such senior figures as Igor Stravinsky, Clara Malraux and Jean Duvignaud, pillars of the establishment. Beckett would stop by occasionally for a beer, a coffee or a game of chess. Some of the old pre-war crowd were seen there: Alice B. Toklas, Natalie Barney, Raymond Duncan, and the Hellers, who later hosted the big *Merlin* party. Matilda Heller was later to become the Duchess of Argyll and acquire a bijou apartment in one of the grand courtyard houses of Rue de Tournon, a little further up the street from the café.

Patti Hill, a beautiful ex-model from New York, had work accepted and began to live in the quarter. She was encouraged by Plimpton to write about cats, her particular passion, and the *Paris Review* printed everything she wrote. She had plenty of talent, but so did many others, and her astonishing good looks certainly contributed to the editors' willingness to see her as often as possible and print her material. She was at the time more than a little disturbed by her lack of success with major New York publishing companies, although she did eventually get two novels accepted. She should not be confused with another Patty Hill, also very beautiful, who wrote a little for Olympia Press and was a sister of Marilyn Meeske, another Girodias author.

Natalie Barney was one of the most celebrated American ladies in Paris. She had moved there from Ohio at the turn of the century, and she held a weekly salon to which, little by little, the editors of the *Paris Review* gained admittance. Most who attended were of the older generation who remembered Sarah Bernhardt, had seen Mary Garden's Mélisande, and had known Proust. They would recount their annoyance at having been portrayed by him in his novel, or else at not having been. The large room had a round table covered with food and there were divans in each corner, each containing a celebrity or famous beauty who would hold court from there while the genial hostess wandered about from group to group, dropping into this conversation and out of that one. The editors met Colette there, and others of her ilk, with awe, wondering if one day they too would be as well known.

That, after all was why they were in Paris, city of opportunity and literary beginnings!

Little by little the *Review* became more established. George Plimpton happened to be in the Ritz Hotel at a wedding reception one day when he saw Hemingway stop at a kiosk there to buy a copy, the only time that he had ever seen anyone actually doing so. He approached Hemingway and asked him if he would give an interview. Hemingway invited him for a drink at the bar and eventually agreed. But he did not like Plimpton's idea that the interview should be conducted during a walk around Paris that would take in all the old literary haunts, especially those associated with himself. He would give an interview if he had to, but he was not going to tramp around Paris to do it: this interview eventually appeared in No. 18.

The first of the *Paris Review* interviews – no feature in the magazine has contributed more to its reputation than its interviews – was with E.M. Forster. This was a direct result of George Plimpton's time studying at King's College, Cambridge, where Forster was the presiding great man, living in rooms overlooking the great lawn of the college and taking an active part in its activities. Plimpton was much impressed by the intellectual atmosphere of Cambridge, where literary curiosity and knowledge was shared by all the academic community, and Forster was part of that tradition, kind to undergraduates who were treated as equals. He took an interest in the new magazine and agreed to the interview, which was conducted by P.N. Furbank and F.J.H. Haskell. It established the formula for future interviews: questions about the craft of writing, the author's difficulties with his texts, his future intentions, his feelings about his own success in doing what he had set out to do and so on. It was to prove a successful formula. The interviews have usually had a second life, appearing in book form in anthologies edited by George Plimpton.

The two most remarkable things about the *Paris Review* have been its longevity and the great number of people who have been associated with it. It has always offered prestige in place of salary, which means that its editors have needed other means of support. To be named on the masthead (the title page) as an editorial member of the staff has been offered as an honour that could lead to a literary career and certainly look well on a CV. But this creates great difficulties in any assessment of the individuals who are responsible for the magazine's continuing success. The big names are obvious, but many people have figured as editors of the whole or the part. *Paris Review* No. 79, celebrating thirty-five years of publication in 1981, featured sixty-eight

names as editors, advisors, consultants and so on, not counting the
"Squaw Valley Community of Writers". Some of these names are there
for historical reasons – past services – others in return for help of one
kind or another, but many current names listed on the issue were still
doing the hard work at the time this was written.

Although there was general agreement from the beginning about the
tone of the magazine, William Styron put the policy in a public letter
to the editor, which was intended for publication. He referred to the
writers of his own age as the "Waiting Generation":

> ...people who feel and write and observe, and wait and wait and wait.
> And go on writing. I think the *Paris Review* should welcome these
> people into its pages – the good writers and good poets, the non-
> drumbeaters and non-axe-grinders. So long as they're good... I still
> maintain that the times get precisely the literature that they deserve,
> and that if the writing of this period is gloomy the gloom is not so
> much inherent in the literature as in the times. The writer's duty is to
> keep on writing... he *must* go on writing, reflecting disorder, defeat,
> despair, should that be all he sees at the moment, but ever searching
> for the elusive love, joy and hope – qualities which, as in the act of
> life itself, are best when they have to be struggled for... If he does
> not think one way or another, that he can create literature worthy of
> himself and of his place, at this particular moment in history, in his
> society, then he'd better pawn his Underwood, or become a critic.*

Writers of fiction who appeared in the early issues included Samuel
Beckett (an extract from *Molloy*), Italo Calvino, Evan S. Connell, Philip
Roth and Terry Southern, while the numerous poets included Robert
Bly, Thomas Gunn, Geoffrey Hill, Richard Howard, Ted Hughes,
Philip Larkin, W.S. Merwin, Christopher Middleton, Louis Simpson,
George Steiner, Charles Tomlinson and James Wright. There was also
much non-fiction, and of course the famous interviews. Donald Hall
was the first poetry editor. Two of his oversights were Frank O'Hara
and Allen Ginsberg; the latter wrote to complain to Plimpton that
Hall would not recognize a poem if it buggered him in broad daylight.
Plimpton did not always like Hall's choices, and he suggested to him
that too many poems published were either about animals ("I am not
opposed to animals, only to a magazine that smells like a zoo") or were
lamenting the loss of Christian faith. Donald Hall listed his problems
as poetry editor as follows: "lost manuscripts, threats of murder, lost
issues, overstock, fecklessness breeding like smallpox in the Paris office."

Hall was in the same class as Plimpton at Harvard in 1950, which was the first year of Archibald MacLeish's English course, soon to be legendary. He then went to Christ Church, Oxford, where he won the Newdigate Prize for poetry. Plimpton then persuaded him to join the magazine in Paris, where the first issue carried the prize poem, suitably entitled 'Exile'. He stayed with the *Paris Review* until 1959 and went on to a distinguished career in poetry and literature.

William Pène du Bois, the son of a well-known Paris painter of the "Ashcan" school, and who was to become well known himself as an illustrator of children's books, was an early member of the team and the first art editor. He designed the cover logo of the *Review*, usually called "the bird". It shows an American eagle carrying a pen, but also wearing the French *bonnet rouge*, which represented liberty during the Revolution, and which had been borrowed from Greek times: it was the Phrygian cap given to the slave when he had earned his freedom. It appeared on the first twenty-six issues. In addition to providing the logo, Pène du Bois gave the *Paris Review* its basic appearance and designed the first four issues. Afterwards, realizing that he would be doing this in perpetuity for nothing, he became more of a contributor and art editor than magazine designer. One of his successful ideas was to go around Paris restaurants examining their *livres d'or* (visitors' books) and then to reproduce twenty-odd pages of the sketches and notes left in them by celebrities: one such page featured a Toulouse-Lautrec line-drawing that was subsequently picked up by *Life* magazine.

George Plimpton shared a house for a few months with Pène du Bois. It had been loaned to him rent-free because the rest was paid by a state department employee who had been transferred to another country. Because of official American thinking at the time, the refrigerator was full of hot dogs and baked beans: the man was hedging his bets against a communist takeover of the country which would result in no food being available. William Styron would come around periodically with fresh eggs and there were many meals there of hot dogs, beans and omelette.

John Marquand Jr, son of the well-known novelist, was an early advisory editor, using the pen name John Phillips to differentiate himself from his father. He interviewed Lillian Hellman for the magazine, published some of his own fiction in it, discovered a neglected novella by Malcolm Lowry, *Lunar Caustic*, which created considerable interest, and generally gave good literary advice to the *Review* and personal advice to the other editors. Inspired by the American critic John Aldridge, whose book *After the Lost Generation* was the first to examine the new breed of post-war expatriate writers (which he found much inferior to their pre-war precursors), Marquand made a trip to Paris with Tom Guinzberg, later to become senior editor of Viking Press. They had intended to have a look at the Paris scene and then go on to Africa in search of other literary adventures, inspired probably by Hemingway's African stories, but they did not get further than Paris. Part of the intention of the trip was to investigate Aldridge's claim that the post-war American writers had no moral values: the *Paris Review*, being the obvious centre for American writers in Paris, was to be the start of the enquiry.

Marquand and Guinzberg were met at Orly on a cold, dank morning in November 1952 by George Plimpton and Peter Matthiessen. George Plimpton was tall and gangling, not unlike Jimmy Stewart, the film actor, in appearance and manner. They were driving a beat-up old car that had belonged to "Doc" Humes, left behind when the latter departed for the States earlier in the year, and its appearance was enough to arouse suspicion. Stopped by the police on the way into Paris, Plimpton, talking French, did a passable imitation of Stewart's boyish innocence, pretending to know nothing of policemen, of being stopped, of the need to have a passport or identity papers on him, and especially car papers. Under questioning he claimed that he was a student of *beaux arts* (the fine arts), which impressed the cops enough to let him go. It transpired that Humes had left them no car papers anyway, or that they were false.

Paris was of course still in the full grip of the post-war fever of freedom and search for pleasure. Abundant available sex was a large part of that search, easy to find in Paris, and young Americans – both those who had come there as GIs and as the products of American universities, where puritanical principles were still the norm and getting a girl into bed without marrying her first, or promising to do so, was very difficult – took full advantage. Marquand had this to say:

Through the long winter I was repeatedly impressed by the sangfroid and savoir-faire with which the founders of this journal withstood the lack of moral values. They knew their way around town better than I and that bothered me; I was jealous. I had been in France long before them – while a soldier, if you please, during the Second World War. It was hard to make my point without sounding vainglorious, and yet I wanted them to know that I, too, had been in Paris. I had roamed the Place Pigalle when we soldier chauvinists called it Pig Alley and GIs in filthy fatigues and muddy boots were hauled in from the front and dumped loose on a forty-eight hour pass... In that sea of cocksmen, the angels of Pig Alley could afford to be choosy. I was keen in my recollections but the jaded sophisticates of the *Paris Review* found them mostly boring.*

He was shown Paris by night as it had then become: brothels of every denomination, where orgies and pornographic exhibitions were commonplace and no one worried much about venereal disease. Professional whores knew how to protect themselves and their clients, and exciting the imagination was in any case more important than just sexual release. Plimpton took Marquand to the Hôtel Bar Americain in Pigalle, a brothel with a bar where one could first inspect the girls. Marquand, in a fit of enthusiasm and trying hard to get the girls to reveal themselves in all their naked charms before striking a financial bargain with them, ordered champagne for the house. When at last they went upstairs with two girls, Marquand, about to embark on a promising session of pleasure, was interrupted as the door burst open; it was Plimpton's girl screaming that her client had no money on him. The two were thrown ignominiously out, broke and unsatisfied.

The *Paris Review* crowd were cultured in their speech, talking in the languages and accents of Harvard and Yale. Occasionally, a different kind of American came into their orbit. One such was Terry Southern, who had made as his headquarters the Old Navy, a café that was considerably downmarket, but not far down the boulevard from the smarter cafés of the literary establishment, the Café de Flore and Les Deux Magots. His language was that of the new "beats", but not called that yet: the demotic speech that we know largely from the novels of William Burroughs, where "man" is the standard form of address in every sentence: "Say, man", "Hey, man", "No, man". Southern was not gregarious, but he had his own circle, some members of which had done the drug scene in North Africa as well as in America. One friend of his, who had had his ear lobe bitten off in Rabat by his girlfriend, would pour liquid opium over his couscous in Arab restaurants around the Boul' Mich' and expound as he got higher from the drug: "You have to burn out. Burn out, baby. Go beyond art." Marquand felt it was his duty as advisor to commission work from the Old Navy crowd; much that was written for him was lost or mislaid, because his colleagues were less enthusiastic, and this included a poem of sorts from Al Avakian, the lobeless poet. But Terry Southern was published frequently in the *Review* and was soon to start writing for New York publishers and Maurice Girodias.

John Train was with the *Paris Review* from its early days until 1954. He did much of the hard work of publishing and getting the magazine out, and developed a certain professionalism, learnt by trial and error. He was a rapid talker and wit, presentably dressed, and it was, according to Pène du Bois, his aura of confidence that persuaded the others to make him managing editor after Humes went back to the States. He was one of the most indefatigable workers when it came to reading the manuscripts that poured in faster and faster. Subscribing to the non-ideological tone of the magazine, he decided that he wanted to publish only prime matter, except for the odd "newsy piece on what was brewing up on the European literary and artistic scene". He mentions a walk with Bernard Berenson, then perhaps the most prestigious and distinguished art critic in Europe, at least where the Renaissance is concerned, although his reputation has become somewhat tarnished since his death. Berenson told him, after Train had declared his intention to work for a doctorate in comparative literature, that "comp lit is as dead as cold mutton", his point being that one should look at art itself, not words about art. Train never did take a doctorate, but he achieved a master's degree – in comparative literature! Well known for not receiving fools gladly, he had the most caustic personality of any of the editors, and the printed cards that he gave to the unwary when they asked for his address referred callers to a vacant lot, invisible behind a sheet-iron gate to which he had glued one of his cards with the additional words: "PLEASE KNOCK LOUDLY".

The early days of the *Review* were fun, not very professional, and full of incident. But play was gradually hardening into serious work. The fun consisted of seeing every interesting side of Paris, getting to know people, especially what remained of the pre-war crowd of expatriates. There were play-readings and other literary activities, and even dancing in the streets. Edith Schor taught them the words and the tune of the old French revolutionary song, 'La Carmagnole', which has a catchy melody, and they would form a circle on an empty street, sometimes outside Café Tournon, singing and dancing a song that did not exactly please the French bourgeoisie:

Ah, we'll see it yet,
We'll see it yet:
We'll hang the high-born from the lamp-posts!
Dance, dance the *Carmagnole*!

Max Steele was on the fringe of the group, an established short-story writer who hated French people, refused to learn any French, and lost no opportunity to abuse and denigrate them. He was on the rebound from an unhappy love affair in the States and had put himself into the hands of a woman psychiatrist who he hoped would cure him of his lovelorn melancholy. He liked to trick the French, ordering such a non-existent (but possible) drink as hot coca cola, in the hope that the French would imitate him. He made a play for Patti Hill and after a long and boozy lunch they decided to go back to her place and make passionate love. But something went wrong: a stop on the way to pick up some papers and problems arising out of them killed off the appointed time, so that the tryst was put off to another day that never came.

Sinbad Vail was well known to the *Paris Review*, and some authors were published in his magazine *Points* who also appeared in the *Review*. He was of course much closer in background and class to the Plimpton crowd than the *Merlin* one. His father, one of Peggy Guggenheim's husbands, had once had an association with *transition* and had signed Eugene Jolas's 'Revolution of the Word Manifesto', which appeared in that magazine in June 1929. Some of the more provocative lines from the manifesto are as follows:

The Revolution in the English language is an accomplished fact.

The imagination in search of a fabulous world is autonomous and unconfined.

Narrative is not mere anecdote, but the projection of a metamorphosis of reality.

We are not concerned with the propagation of sociological ideas, except to emancipate the creative elements from the present ideology.

Time is a tyranny to be abolished.

The writer expresses. He does not communicate.

The plain reader be damned.*

Vail was serious about his magazine, but he did not form a group around himself. He did all the work personally, was unconcerned with meeting deadlines, and of course could always pay the printer out of his more than adequate income. He met the other young literati socially, took part in their various activities, but professionally preferred to remain a lone wolf, looking for new young talent and publishing it. His influence on the literary scene was small, but not insignificant. Trocchi made every effort to get him into the *Merlin* group and probably borrowed money from him fairly frequently, as he did from Plimpton and others, but Sinbad Vail had Trocchi well sized up and he was cautious. The difference between his own situation and that of Vail, Plimpton and his *Paris Review* associates infuriated Trocchi. All he could try to do was to make the rich young Americans feel guilty at their better fortune; it was of course their parents who had the money. But although Trocchi was tolerated, and his special abilities to a great extent appreciated, and he was admitted to social get-togethers organized by his rivals, everyone was interested primarily in his own work and career; in any case the aims and attitudes of the others were very different. Trocchi could only try to control his envy and accept that his obvious brilliance had to be frustrated. But there is little doubt, given his profligate nature, that even had he found a generous backer it would have made little difference. And it should not be thought that Plimpton and his friends, *jeunesse dorée* as they may have appeared to others, were simply subsidizing the magazine out of their pockets. There were endless schemes for raising money and many of them succeeded; like Trocchi they were always looking for backers, but they were also more likely to find them, because their social contacts were better. The final straw for Trocchi came when the *Paris Review* managed to capture Prince Sadruddin Aga Khan, second son of the Aga Khan, and brother of the Ali Khan, to both finance and become publisher of the *Review*.

After two years the *Paris Review* had become known, not only in Europe but increasingly in the US as well. "Doc" Humes kept a connection with it and, furious that his name had been left off the masthead of the first edition to reach the States, intercepted the shipment and stamped his name on as many of the title pages as he could. Thereafter he managed to have his books published and was able to exhibit his eccentricities in many ways. Two novels, *The Underground City* (1957) and *Men Die* (1959) were published by Random House, but the author wanted to be involved in every stage of publication and would go to the printing plant to watch the presses printing the copies. He once parked his large motorcycle in Bennett Cerf's anteroom at the publisher's Madison Avenue offices, and frequently spent nights there sleeping on the couch.

Not too much is known about the backing of the *Paris Review*. It has always been accused of receiving funds from the CIA and certainly some of the group may have been involved with the Agency, but Plimpton insists that he was not, and that he received no money from it. And what use could these young men have been to Washington? Some have asserted that they were paid to keep an eye on other Americans in Paris – there were many of them, mainly from Hollywood, but there were also writers, journalists, musicians and academics who had been "named" by someone as communist sympathizers. They could have spied on their more political compatriots, but it is doubtful that any information that came their way was of much use except to add to files probably already full. It is more likely that those who agreed to work for the Agency did so more out of a sense of adventure than for any other reason, and that any money that came to the *Review* was a token to keep close to it for some possible future advantage.

Although many people were named as editors over the years, the constant factor from the time of his arrival in Paris was George Plimpton. Others concerned themselves with the details of publication or with certain editorial functions but Plimpton was the de facto editor from 1952 onwards and his name over the years became synonymous with the magazine. Matthiessen, although he kept a connection, went on to write his own books and, with the exception of Styron, has been the most successful writer to emerge from it.

2

Until Prince Sadruddin Aga Khan came on the scene in 1954, the finances, of which little detail has been given in Plimpton's various summaries of the *Paris Review* history, appear to have been a mixture of hopeful schemes and odd amounts put in from time to time, sometimes as donations, sometimes as loans by well-wishers and the editors. Plimpton had the idea of providing literary material to the Paris edition of the *New York Herald Tribune* – in effect, making up a literary page for them – and getting regularly paid for it. This did not develop into anything positive. By now part of the editorial work was being done in New York in any case, as the editors moved back and forth. But Sadri, as he came to be called, started his association by funding a fiction prize to be given in the name of the Aga Khan, his father: the first prize was $300 and the second $200: the contest immediately began to bring in a higher quality of submission. Plimpton succeeded in persuading Hiram Haydn, Brendan Gill and Saul Bellow to be the three judges and their established names were a help: every prize of an artistic nature basically has only the prestige of the people who give it. Issue No. 12, which appeared in the spring of 1956, carried the winning entries. The first prize went to Gina Berriault and was shared with John Langdon; the second was won by Owen Dodson. George Plimpton felt that the three winners were all good stories, but that the judges had overlooked some that were as good or better, but he made sure that most of these appeared later. The same issue was notable for carrying Jean Stein's interview with William Faulkner.

Robert Silvers was associated with the magazine by then. George Plimpton had returned to New York and was editing the magazine from there, but there was still a Paris editor; in fact the direction of the magazine was split between the two cities. The *Paris Review* was still printed in Europe, but most of the editors were in New York. Bob Silvers first went to Paris with a note from George Plimpton. He had been accepted as an undergraduate at the University of Chicago at the age of thirteen, and at seventeen he was the youngest ever student at Yale Law School. But he dropped law to become a reporter and was accepted as press secretary to Connecticut Governor Chester Bowles at the age of twenty-one. Silvers was to follow Bowles to India when he was appointed US Ambassador to that country, but instead was drafted into the US army and sent to France, where he spent his leaves sitting around the literary cafés of Saint-Germain, hoping to catch an occasional glimpse of Jean-Paul Sartre, Simone de Beauvoir and other writers he admired. He became the Paris editor in 1956.

He was described in those days as a chronic insomniac, always tired, often falling asleep in front of people and eating a great deal to keep up his energy. The first important step that he took as editor was to improve the quality of printing and the appearance of the cover. He went to a Dutch printer in Nijmegen and ordered heavier and whiter paper. The improvements were obvious in No. 12. Blair Fuller, later to become editor himself, accompanied Silvers to Holland, where there were long meetings and some dinners with Mr van Zee, the printer – Silvers allegedly fell asleep at one such meal. This was the first of many such trips, during which a taste for Dutch Geneva gin was developed and Dutch contributors brought into the *Paris Review*. On the first trip Silvers met Gerard Kornelis van het Reve, who had already corresponded with the *Review* in a jocular fashion; he showed the two Americans some of the juicier sides of Amsterdam: the student cafés, the red-light district, where the girls read magazines and did their knitting in big picture-windows while waiting to be hired by passers-by, and the wide variety of bars, each attracting a different kind of client. It was Silvers who changed the editorial content of the magazine by actively looking for European writers to be translated; until then the *Paris Review* had published almost entirely American writers with a smattering of others from Britain and the Commonwealth.

Silvers moved the offices to a loft rented from Éditions Stock in the Rue Casimir-Delavigne, another little street of small hotels near the Odéon theatre. This was still only about three minutes walk from Café Tournon, no longer the principal meeting place since Train, Hall and Plimpton had all returned to America. Other cafés were used by Silvers, some on the other side of the Boulevard Saint-Germain, a busy, crowded criss-cross of streets just south of the Seine where a large number of people live and work and one of the most colourful parts of Paris. The Rue Saint-Louis and the Rue de Buci had less leisurely cafés, and they reflected the accelerated pace of Silvers's editorship. He met painters like Pierre Tal-Coat, Jean-Paul Riopelle, the expressionist French-Canadian artist, and James Lord. He tried to meet the elusive Maurice Blanchot who was recommended by Patrick Bowles. Christopher Logue sparked off his interest in the sprung rhythms of Gerard Manley Hopkins, the nineteenth-century Catholic poet.

Silvers was invited by Natalie Barney to her salons. He went the rounds of French publishing houses, met editors and their writers. There were still many Americans in Paris. Richard Wright was now frequently back there, having researched the book he was writing on Ghana, the recently founded African republic, which he titled *Black Power*, a phrase to be much used in the next few years. Excited by the Bandung Conference, a meeting of newly independent Asian and African states that took place in Indonesia in 1955, he was announcing the birth of a "third world", but could hardly have guessed the grim connotation the term would acquire by the end of the century. Alfred Chester made himself noticed as a shrieking gay on the Left Bank – Silvers published a collection of his stories under the title *Head of a Sad Angel* – and Irwin Shaw was living across the river in an American colony of successful writers and film celebrities. Many artists had their work examined in the *Review,* including Eugène Berman, Pavel Tchelitchew, André Masson, Ottaviano Zev, Jean Jones, Anita de Caro and Oskar Kokoschka, whose large retrospective exhibition visited most European capitals and revived interest in the German and Austrian expressionists at around this time. Genet was seen around Saint-Germain, often drinking in Le Village, one of the more expensive bars with an atmosphere more American than French. Genet appeared in the *Review*, as did Kenneth Tynan, frequently visiting Paris from London, and the writer-painter Henri Michaux.

Other bars, on the Right Bank, attracted American journalists like Art Buchwald, who came to write for the Paris edition of the *New York Herald Tribune*. His light, humorous articles were soon syndicated in other American papers. A mixture of political commentary and social observation, they coloured the way Americans saw France and appeared later in several book collections. Harry's Bar on the Rue Daunou, near the opera, once a favourite haunt of Hemingway, was where you could find the more bohemian Right-Bankers, while the established senior correspondents of major English-language papers favoured the bar of the Hôtel de Crillon on the Place de la Concorde. This latter was the place for political gossip and rumour; it was only a short distance from the Hôtel Matignon, where the head of state resided, as well as the major ministries.

In late 1956 Silvers managed to rent a Thames River barge that was moored by the Pont d'Alma, the bridge that leads to the Avenue Georges V on the Right Bank. He went to live there and to edit the magazine from this floating office, sharing the living accommodation with a jazz musician, Peter Duchin. There was no telephone, and contributors coming with their manuscripts frequently found themselves in the middle of a jam session. George Plimpton arrived from New York and stayed on the barge, but he was not comfortable as his legs were too long for the bunks. Plimpton, who liked to keep up appearances, would walk up the street to the Hôtel Plaza Athénée, one of the smartest Right Bank hotels, and use the notepaper to write home, assuring everyone he was very comfortable there.

The river flooded the following spring, and the barge had to be anchored in mid-stream. Silvers was effectively isolated: he could not get ashore and no one could visit him. But he managed to arrange to get food winched over to him in baskets, as well as the mail and manuscripts. The editors accomplished more than usual, while watching the flotsam flowing rapidly by; it included a dead cow.

Blair Fuller worked with Silvers and succeeded him in 1960. He had worked for several years in West Africa, where he had started a novel, *A Far Place*, which he finished in Paris while working on the *Review*. He too set out to meet as many people as possible. He encountered Stella Adler, teacher of actors and directors, and her husband Harold Clurman, founder of the Group Theater in New York. Stella was very concerned that her past beauty (although she was still beautiful) should not be forgotten, and brought it up frequently in conversation. Fuller became marginally involved with Right-Bank Americans, while Silvers moved ever more in French circles, getting to know actors and dancers as well as writers and publishers. He also went to political cafés like the Café de Maine where he met journalists outside literature, becoming friends with Nathalie de Bosquet, Colette and Jacques

Duhamel, Jean Daniel and François Bondy, editor of the *Tribune de Genève*, an influential right-wing newspaper. He met Sartre at the bar of the Hôtel Montalembert, a hotel near Gallimard's offices, and Henri Michaux, who showed him a series of drawings he had made under the influence of mescaline, which resulted in a portfolio in the *Review*. He came to know homosexual Paris through Natalie Barney, who had dancers, artists and movie-makers in her salon, and through Cocteau who also held salons.

Silvers travelled more than any other editor to find material for the *Paris Review*. He interviewed John Lehman and Stephen Spender. He brought Gaby van Sweelen from Holland, a country he visited frequently from the time he began printing there, and she was a competent assistant who kept him informed about her own country. Many French friends like Pierre Schneider, a successful novelist, kept him in touch with new French writing. His effect was to give the magazine a more professional and international appearance and more influence than it had had before. It was the beginning of a distinguished editorial career. Silvers's connections with the CIA are a matter of hearsay and speculation. Certainly he knew many agents, and some of his European contacts were certainly CIA cultural operatives. It would have been surprising if he had not been contacted during his army days, given his educational background and time spent with Supreme Headquarters Allied Powers Europe (SHAPE), the central command of NATO military forces, before he went back to the States, after the army. But it was literary ambition that drove him, whatever other use might have been made of his talents and knowledge. He returned to the US to work at *Harper's* in 1958. When the *New York Times* was unavailable because of a strike in 1963, he started the *New York Review of Books*, and has been its editor ever since.

3

It was at the end of Bob Silvers's editorship that the *Paris Review* moved to the Right Bank, to an office on the Rue Vernet, near the Place de l'Étoile, which is now called the Place Charles de Gaulle. This is a small street at the edge of the *huitième*. Blair Fuller became the next editor, and when he returned to the States he was succeeded by Nelson W. Aldrich, Jr. At this point Joan Dillon, daughter of C. Douglas Dillon, who was to become Secretary of the Treasury in the Kennedy Administration, was working for the magazine; she was later to acquire the title of Princess of Luxembourg, and later still, Duchesse de Mouchy; as one might imagine from her subsequent career, she was a lady of determination as well as charm, accustomed to order, and she was the first to keep the files in a tidy system; previously they had been chaotic and the cause of much grief to authors whose manuscripts were lost, mislaid or sent to some reader and forgotten.

One day at about five in the afternoon, two "horrors", as she put it, pushed their way into the Rue Vernet office, speaking an incomprehensible (to her) American "Beat" language. She could barely understand the words, and the obscenities she didn't want to. They were Allen Ginsberg and Peter Orlovsky, doped to the hilt, she didn't know on what, and they wanted to look at the magazine's correspondence with Ezra Pound, which they were convinced was in the files. Joan Dillon resisted them, and they threatened to become violent and to force her to let them look at the filing cabinets. Eventually they tried another ploy to make her leave the room: they undressed and began to make love on the floor. Several people dropped in to ask Joan out for a drink, but fled hastily. Then Nelson Aldrich rang and was appalled to hear that there were hippie visitors present, and misbehaving. He was wearing a tuxedo to go to a smart dinner, and felt it would be wrong to be seen in it at the office under such circumstances. So he told her to cope as best she could, and to call the police if necessary. She was saved by a well-dressed English friend who came in, also to invite her out for a drink; he took in the situation, untangled the lovers, and with his best English patrician accent put them out in the corridor. Joan Dillon was to meet Ginsberg and Orlovsky again some years later, when they had become successful literary figures in suits and ties: they laughed off the incident.

From 1956 the work of the *Paris Review* was increasingly done from New York. Plimpton's apartment on East 74th Street, overlooking the East River, was office, meeting place and party centre. Parties have always played a large part in the fun atmosphere of the *Review*, which has become eminent as much for its longevity as for its contents; the literary public has a short memory and dead reviews and magazines are quickly forgotten by all except literary historians and past editors. As Paris became more expensive and the art scene switched to London and New York in the Sixties, the city ceased to be the main centre of activity, but a succession of editors kept the Paris office going. Most of the best anecdotes are nevertheless about the first five years of the *Paris Review*'s history. It was a social centre and a place to meet new boyfriends and girlfriends as well as an office. Terry Southern recalls coming into it one afternoon and seeing two members of the staff, both wearing trench coats, busily copulating on one of the desks. Certainly sex was one of the attractions of working there: the *Paris Review*, after all, had a succession of good-looking and reasonably well-heeled young men and many attractive young girls, some of them spectacularly so. One must assume that there was much sexual activity going on and that promiscuity was the norm, but on a different and less sordid level than the bohemian sex described by Henry Miller in his novels of the Thirties. And Paris was cheap, the dollar fetching large numbers of francs in 1952.

It would not be unfair to call the original group who founded the *Review* dilettantes, who used it to justify being in Paris – city of pleasure and sexual freedom. It gave them a focus to their young lives, a justification for their education, a boost to their literary ambition and the satisfaction of seeing something concrete – a printed magazine – after all the effort. The same could be said of the Camerata, the group of cultured and musical Florentine noblemen who, trying to recreate the Greek theatre as they imagined it might have been, more or less accidentally invented opera at the end of the sixteenth century. One has to judge by the result. Both Art Buchwald, living in Paris for much of this time and writing for the *Herald Tribune*, and Gay Talese, who documented Paris life and the *Review*'s activities in an article in *Esquire*, saw them as dilettantes. But if one looks at the word in the original Italian or in eighteenth-century English sense, describing persons of wide culture who take delight in the fine arts and wish to further them, we come closer to the truth. The fact is that most of the young men in question went on to have successful literary careers of their own, and would have done so without the *Paris Review*. It brought them together as a community, created a cross-fertilization of ideas and the mutual encouragement which has always been characteristic of Paris artistic life, but which is rare elsewhere. If they also enjoyed the experience, that too is more apposite to Paris than elsewhere. It is true that the *Merlin* group were more serious-minded as well as poorer: but Trocchi ended pitiably, a self-deluding drug addict, Seaver became an editor and then a publisher, whose career after leaving Grove Press had little to do with literature and more with earning a big salary, and Wainhouse faded from the literary scene; only Christopher Logue, as much connected with the *Paris Review* as with *Merlin*, can be said to have had a continuing career as poet, writer for the theatre and producer of fiction. In a later chapter I will trace what happened to some of the *Merlin* editors.

The *Merlin* group, together with some contributors to the *Paris Review,* like Terry Southern and Chester Himes, made some money by writing books for Girodias. But it was mainly Trocchi, Logue, Wainhouse and those associated with no particular literary group, like Norman Rubington, a painter with a literary facility, who did this, most of them earning about £375 or $1,000 a book. Only Plimpton, who was perhaps the *Paris Review* editor least suitable to a creative literary career in those early years – he only later emerged as a writer outside his connection with the magazine, unlike Matthiessen – tried to write an Olympia db, and that was for fun, not money. And he abandoned the project half way. Perhaps it would have embarrassed his father, a successful stockbroker in New York, or perhaps there were better ways of spending his time. He did not really need the money. But he did develop a reputation as a successful writer on baseball in later years.

Irwin Shaw, who was a personality in literary Europe in the Fifties, and a generous host to young literati, contrasted the bohemian young writers he had known in Greenwich Village – sitting around drinking coffee, trying to write the great American novel, doing any kind of literary hack-work to earn a few dollars, despised by their parents for refusing to take good respectable jobs, going to Coney Island with "drab, but insanely virginal girls who condemned them to nights of desperate celibacy or desolate marriages" – with the "literary hopefuls of the Paris contingent":

…the latter spoke in the casual tones of the good schools and could be found, surrounded by flocks of pretty and nobly acquiescent girls, in chic places like Lipp's or on the roads to Deauville or Biarritz for month-long holidays. They were mild-mannered, beautifully polite, recoiled from the appearance of seeming ambitious and were ready at all times to drop whatever they were almost secretly composing to play tennis (usually very well), drive down to Spain for a bullfight, fly to Rome for a wedding or sit around most of the night drinking… One guessed that there were wealthy and benevolent parents on the other side of the Atlantic.

There is little doubt that the magazine could have continued quite comfortably even without injections from "Daddy" or those who came later willing to be "publisher", which in newspaper or magazine terms means the backer or angel. But when Prince Sadri was helping, the $500 that an issue cost was far less important than the prestige of his name and the implication that limitless funds were there if needed. He also used his palatial home in the Bois de Boulogne for parties, and most notably for a giving a prize to Philip Roth, who had won a Paris Review award for a short story.

As an English-language magazine published in Paris, it was inevitable that there would be some difficulties sooner or later with US Customs, always on the lookout for obscenity and regularly stopping parcels from Olympia Press and other known producers of erotica in English, as well as searching returning Americans carrying such forbidden items in their pockets or luggage. The *Paris Review* could hardly have been further in intention or reality from a publisher of pornography, but a suspicious mind will find obscenities anywhere. In Britain, Beckett's *Waiting for Godot* was heavily censored, some of the most innocent lines, like one referring to flies (insects) which the censor thought might apply to trousers, having to be excised. US Customs were subject to the same delusions. Plimpton, knowing this, was always careful, and he used his own censorship powers on copy, something which sometimes aroused the ire of authors. In the very first issue, in a story by Terry Southern, he changed the line "Don't get your shit hot" (used in a perfectly realistic context by a state trooper to an irate motorist), substituting "crap" for "shit", and then omitting that too. Southern was furious and wrote a long letter of protest in which the word "crap" (the letter was printed in the next issue) could again not be used. Art Buchwald wanted to make a story out of the incident in the *Herald Tribune*, but the paper would also not print the word "crap".

When Plimpton returned to New York in 1956 he found himself frequently having to visit Mr Demcy, the customs officer in charge of literature, at Varick Street, south of Greenwich Village on the West Side. He was mainly concerned with the depiction of pubic hair, which had to be airbrushed from any depiction of nudity. Mr Demcy read every arriving issue, mindful of young readers who might be susceptible. Usually Plimpton was able to get each issue through with not too much argument: it was obvious that the magazine was not for collectors of pornography. He had trouble with No. 21, however, which arrived on the eve of a longshoremen's strike. He assured Mr Demcy that there was nothing salacious in the issue, but forgot about an extract from Trocchi's *Cain's Book*. Demcy, a thorough reader, found the line: "Give me that spike quick or I'll split your fucking throat!" Outraged, he demanded that all copies be rendered to him from the warehouse where they had arrived. US Marshalls would bond the issue the next morning and probably burn it in the city dump. Plimpton, normally very law-abiding, refused to tell him where the books were on the docks, and the next morning led a group of *Paris Review* people to the warehouse from where they smuggled the edition out and hid it in various cellars in the Village.

Washington eventually reviewed the issue after the Customs had made a formal complaint, and cleared it. The US Mails were at the time more liberal than Customs as a result of a number of court cases, especially that of Roth versus the US in 1957 (no relation to Philip). US subscribers received their copies of No. 21. When Demcy retired in 1965, he wrote a book, *How to Cope with US Customs*, and sent Plimpton a complimentary copy.

American subscribers became accustomed to receiving their copies late and only a few complained, one of them a Cleveland businessman whose complaint was sent to the Better Business Bureau. Delays had many causes, some to do with tardy publication, the vagaries of shipping or the speed with which American distributors sent out copies after receiving them. On one occasion a boat carrying an edition was sinking in New York harbour while the editors daily scanned the newspapers for the latest news, but with a month's delay the issue finally went out.

The *Paris Review*, like the Roman Empire in the fourth century, divided itself into an eastern wing (in Paris) and a western one (in New York). The weight of the name countered the much heavier weight of the American workload. But Paris was still the centre for translated material and for contributions from Britain, some of these rather resented by American writers who felt that it should be entirely, and not just predominantly, an American magazine. Editors came and went, but did not really leave: there was nearly always a continuing interest and a sense of gratitude on the part of past editors and staff, who were now established as writers; that was, after all, why they became editors on the magazine in the first place, with very few exceptions: to start their careers as writers. Plimpton records that William Styron, coming through Paris in the early Seventies, dropped into the office on Rue Vernet to ask how the magazine was doing and how many European subscribers there were. He was disappointed that there were only two hundred and thirteen. Such unexpected visits were frequent in Paris; in New York it was more a matter of dropping into a party or taking part in the fund-raising "Revels".

It is perhaps to William Styron that the principal credit must go for making the *Paris Review*, at its onset, purely a vehicle for creative work and not for theory or critical comment. It started without any manifesto, other than to publish the best available writing, and it has stuck to that formula. If it received funding from time to time from the CIA as has often been claimed – after all the CIA scatters its money widely, without always being sure what it can expect in return – then there is no evidence of this in the work published. Unlike *Blast*, *transition*, *The Exile*, *The Criterion*, *Horizon*, *Partisan Review* and hundreds of other literary magazines, down to its early contemporary *Merlin*, short-lived but remembered, it had no cause to push. Styron's 'Letter to an Editor', defining the "Waiting Generation", has remained its non-manifesto to the present day.

Chapter Four

The Paris English Bookshops

Sylvia Beach's Shakespeare & Company was the most famous pre-war English bookshop in Paris. It was well situated on the Left Bank, home of the intellectual and bohemian, near the Sorbonne. There were other bookshops, then as later, which sold English-language books, but they were mainly conventional establishments with little atmosphere, catering to tourists rather than residents, and run on purely commercial lines. Those who worked in them did not know the customers personally and usually knew little about the books they had on the shelves.

Two bookshops came after the war to replace Shakespeare & Company, and the best of them, although not the longest-lasting, or even the best-known, was the English Bookshop at 42 Rue de Seine, started in 1951 by Gaït Frogé, an enthusiastic Frenchwoman with a penchant for writers and artists. The other was founded by an American, George Whitman, as Le Mistral, but he later changed its name to Shakespeare & Company. Both post-war bookshops have been second homes for writers, their proprietors taking a keen interest in their work and promoting their reputations.

The difference between the two bookshops lay in the personalities of their proprietors, and in their different motivations. Whitman was a groupie by nature, wanting to pick up some of the reflected glory of the new generation of post-war writers, but his stock has always mostly consisted of a random selection of second-hand books with a smattering of new ones. His shop has an antiquarian look, not unsuitable for its excellent situation overlooking Notre Dame on the Île de la Cité, an oval-shaped island that divides the Seine, and only a few doors away from La Bûcherie where Girodias was to stay for some time; La Bûcherie plays some part in this book. The English Bookshop, by contrast, was a typical small literary bookshop, carrying a wide range of titles in current demand, but also the products of small presses and avant-garde literature, books that one was unlikely to find at WH Smith, Brentano's or Galignani on the Right Bank. It rapidly became a centre for the Anglo-American colony of writers and artists; it was in fact more than a bookshop, having an art gallery in the basement. There was not always a current exhibition, and the basement was otherwise used for storage and sometimes for meetings, but many American and British painters showed their work there and occasionally sold a painting. It was a small shop and the shelves were never very full because Gaït was not able to pay her bills very fast, and as a result it was often on the "stop list" of publishers, who would not supply her orders until she had paid for the last shipment, which often took months. But it was still a discriminating stock of good literature that she carried, with a preference for authors she knew and those who lived in Paris. There were always writers hanging about the bookshop, often borrowing books they could not afford to buy, sometimes borrowing money from Gaït as well. Kind-hearted and generous, probably too much so, genuinely interested in good writing, but in a less elitist fashion than Sylvia Beach, who had had the advantage of the help and French literary contacts of Adrienne Monnier, she was always short of cash; money that should have gone to pay publishers was often subsidizing writers and painters, and some of them were her lovers.

The *Merlin* editors were among the group that used the bookshop in which to spend time – you did not have to use money to buy a coffee or a beer as in a café – and you could sit and read; above all the bookshop was warm in winter, when cheap rooms were usually not. There were chairs and there was company. The *Paris Review* crowd, being better-heeled, would come in to see how the magazine was selling and to buy books, but spent little time there. Maurice Girodias counted on the English Bookshop to sell his publications, but his big sales were on the Rue de Rivoli and the Avenue de l'Opéra on the Right Bank where there were more tourists and fewer discriminating readers of erotica. But all his offices – he moved fairly frequently in the Fifties – were nearby; he would drop in frequently and became a friend of Gaït Frogé's.

It was in fact Girodias's authors who used the bookshop most, other than the Left Bank anglophones who bought their reading material there. William Burroughs, once he had settled in Paris, would drop in from the Rue Gît-le-Coeur and from the little hotel there that became known as the "Beat Hotel": it is described by his friend and collaborator Brion Gysin in his book *The Process*.* Gaït Frogé organized the odd reading in the bookshop: one such evening had Burroughs, Gysin and Sinclair Beiles, a South African poet, reading extracts from their works in progress. These she afterwards published under the title *Minutes to Go*, a little pamphlet that is now a collector's item. One of the most frequent denizens of the English Bookshop was Norman Rubington, an American artist who had lived some years in Paris. He had been in

American military intelligence as a war artist and he had a special gift at the time for analysing aerial photographs and reinterpreting them for bomber pilots. He had won the Prix de Rome as a painter and spent the obligatory year in that city. During the Fifties he was known as a ladies' man, frequently changing his address, and with sexual liaisons in many different parts of Paris. Much of Rubington's painting was erotic, although he also produced much religious art. Some of it was later to hang in American cathedrals in San Francisco and Boston.

Gaït Frogé had many lovers, perfectly normal in the climate of that time on the Left Bank, but there is no doubt that Norman Rubington was the serious one. He was a big man, enthusiastic, full of charm, a seducer who would pick up girls – American, French, Swiss, Italian – and who frequented the cafés, but he had stable sexual relationships as well. He was a New Yorker with equally large capacities for work and sex, a sense of humour that overflowed in all directions and an excellent conversationalist in a variety of languages, which he had picked up without difficulty. He had no compunction about being largely supported by the many women who adored him, and he made little effort to sell his paintings or to earn much money. He saw society as being overly concerned with filthy lucre and success and wished to have no part in it. He was receiving money from the American government under the GI Bill of Rights, found ways of getting additional subsidies from the US, and although he was married at the time to a pharmacist and had a comfortable apartment in the eleventh *arrondissement*, he preferred to spend most of his time in the sixth. He used the apartments of different women as it suited him, treating many of them as studios in which to paint. He knew that his talent enabled him to do whatever he wanted and he ignored success. The books he wrote and put together for Girodias were written as much for fun as for profit.

He told Girodias that his name, as with so many Americans whose ancestors had immigrated into the US from Europe at the end of the nineteenth century, was a deliberate accident. His grandfather had come from Łód in Poland, and had given his name on arrival at Ellis Island to the immigration officer as Rubenstein, but as this official had already admitted several other Rubensteins that day, he changed it to Rubington and let him in under that name. Girodias often commented that most of his New York authors were from Jewish immigrant backgrounds – Iris Owens, Marilyn Meeske, Mason Hoffenberg, Norman Rubington – and that they were among the more imaginative and productive producers of high level erotica. He noted the contrast with George Plimpton and his colleagues with their privileged moneyed backgrounds and Ivy League voices, manners and preoccupations. But were they really so different? They were all looking for the same things: a good time in Paris, enough money to live reasonably well, a career in the arts, and as much sex as possible; and some of them also found love. For most of the writers around Girodias, Henry Miller was the model, although they were also aware of Joyce. For the *Paris Review* crowd it was Hemingway.

Rubington – the "Rube" to his American circle – was one of the most colourful characters in the quarter, adored by the bistro waitresses, who all knew him, and whose charms he did not overlook, and the principal habitué of Gaït Frogé's bookshop as well as her bed, which she shared with her Afghan dog. Norman's paintings were the most frequent ones to be seen in the basement gallery and his presence helped to sell one occasionally. As an Olympia author, he was the most reliable, always on time with copy, and, with Trocchi, the most prolific. The flights of imagination and descriptive extravagance in the novels that were written under the pen name Akbar del Piombo plumbed the carnal depths of humorous pornography: he could be as cruel as the Marquis de Sade in describing the sexual infliction of pain, but his fiction delighted in the orgy. He was the perfect masturbatory author, but always had a sense of fun. Rubington was unfortunately the inadvertent cause of the closure of the bookshop. When he decided that the time had come for him to return to America, he said his adieus, kissed many a teary eye, and departed, promising to be back at some future date. Gaït Frogé, on an impulse, decided to follow him. She hastily put her bookshop up for sale and left for the US, but on arrival found that Norman was anything but free – he had other family ties in New York – and, disillusioned, she returned to Paris. There she tried to recover her bookshop, but it was too late: she had signed the transfer of her lease to an antiquarian furniture dealer and he refused to sell it back. Accepting the situation she returned to New York. There she met a Texas businessman, unfortunately not a rich one, and went to live in the Lone Star State. But the marriage did not last long, and she returned once again to New York where she found employment as a freelance editor.

Gaït came from Brittany. Although no beauty, her charm, gaiety, bright eyes and self-confidence gave her a typical Gallic appeal, and her forthrightness and warmth made her attractive sexually to heterosexuals and a good, even motherly, friend to homosexuals; both frequented the bookshop and spent much time there. She had a wide knowledge of both English-language literature (she knew her customers well enough to suggest books for their tastes), and for French, stocking many translations. In fact, French writers dropped in on her to see if she had their books in English. Arthur Adamov, the more political of the "absurdist" French playwrights, lived much of the time at the Hôtel de Seine, fifty yards away, but as he was usually drunk, always dirty and unshaven, smelling from both his breath and feet – he apparently owned no socks as his large feet were always encased in old sandals – he was not the most welcome of visitors. His large, prominent eyes were likely to frighten the more timid, especially young American women, and he would quickly empty the shop. Although he probably received the odd handout from the soft-hearted Gaït – Adamov made it a principle of his life never to do any work other than writing and to borrow from anyone who could be persuaded to lend, that is to say *give*, to him – he was the only person in the quarter to speak disparagingly of her. "That woman has a *sale gueule*," he would say, which, repeated to Gaït, drew the response that he was not so pretty himself.

The other significant bookshop, and the one that has survived until the present, was Le Mistral, which was started by George Whitman in 1951. Whitman was born in East Orange, New Jersey, and moved as a child to Salem, Mass. He served in the merchant navy and was based in New Orleans for a while: he remembers seeing the streetcar line called "Desire". He started his first second-hand bookshop in Taunton, Mass., but it was always his intention to go to Paris, which had an almost mystical attraction for him. When the opportunity presented itself in 1946, he sold his bookshop and moved to France, spending some years living on what he had saved from the Taunton sale and discovering the city of light. His first Paris bookshop was called the Franco-American Bookstore on the Rue de Courcelles. He learnt about Paris from there, but he wanted a more picturesque address to correspond to his romantic view of the city. In an interview many years later, he said: "Perhaps the ideal situation in life is that of a seventeen-year-old girl in Paris in the springtime, ready for her first love." The sentiment also applies to the young men ready to offer that love, although it is not always of a totally romantic nature. One of Henry Miller's most quoted adages was: "Women came to Paris looking for love, but would settle for sex."

George Whitman was eventually lucky. He found an old grocery shop that was about to go bankrupt. It was a crumbling building, but it was on the Rue de la Bûcherie on the Paris quays in the *cinquième* with an unrestricted view of Notre Dame. In front of him, lining the river, were the small bookstalls, locked up in their boxes at night, that are a browser's Garden of Eden, selling both new and antiquarian books, mostly in French. A more ideal situation would be hard to imagine. He acquired the grocery shop and opened it as "Le Mistral", after the name of the Chilean poet Gabriela Mistral, whom he much admired; it is also the sharp northerly wind which periodically interrupts the normally mild climate of the Côte d'Azur during the winter months. In 1964, after the death of Sylvia Beach, Whitman changed the name to Shakespeare & Company. Sylvia had visited Whitman on previous occasions and once gifted him a brass plaque reading "Shakespeare & Company – Writers' Guest House", giving him permission to use the name for his shop. Although the locations of the old and the new Shakespeare bookshops are about a mile apart, George Whitman never did anything to reduce the impression visitors got that the two bookshops were one and the same. If directly challenged, he would admit the truth. Nevertheless, first editions of Joyce that have come into his hands are displayed in glass bookcases, and as much Joyceana as possible is shown on the front tables. On Bloomsday he used to offer a free but not very appetizing punch to those in the shop. Whitman also liked to give the impression, although more in his early days than later, that he was descended from Walt Whitman, the poet. The unlikeliness of this became more evident when Walt Whitman's sexual proclivities became better known in the Sixties. Here too there is no connection with reality. But his father was called Walter. There was much mythomania in George Whitman, but with time he has become enough of a myth himself, and a famous Parisian character, to be able to dispense with any supposed connections with the pre-war literary scene; he played a large enough part in the post-war one.

The shop still has much atmosphere and is filled with books. The tattiness comes mainly from the age of the building and the large number of volumes in various conditions of decay on the shelves, of which an increasing number consists of new books, although for the most part these are popular paperback fiction. The antiquarian stock is not cheap: it was acquired by Whitman partly from Parisian people with books to sell, broken-up libraries in auctions and acquisitions from second-hand stores in the States and London. Many people wanting a few francs or euros would come in with a handful of books to sell. He paid little for them and marked them up as high as possible. Whitman edited and published some literary magazines, including the *Paris Magazine*, for which Trocchi did some work, and issued anthologies from time to time.

Le Mistral was one of the sales points for the *Paris Review* and *Merlin*, which had its editorial base there for its first four issues. Whitman always stocked books that were published in Paris, but never in more than token quantities. It was mainly a second-hand shop, always with interesting things to be found, but there was much junk too. It was never a prime sales point for Girodias, because he wanted to sell large quantities and be paid quickly: fast payment was never a Whitman habit. Although money was not the primary object of George Whitman, he knew the value of out-of-print books for which there was a demand. In his way he was a good businessman.

The bookshop has always been a meeting place for Paris anglophones, literary visitors and writers. For over fifty years, Whitman encouraged young poets and hopeful fiction writers to stay in his guest room upstairs, where there was a library and where you could spend the day reading or talking. This was never the home from home of Gaït Frogé's very different, albeit far less ideally situated, establishment: her stock consisted almost entirely of new books, and she knew exactly what she had on the shelves, whereas Whitman would take anything offered to him cheaply enough. After the English Bookshop closed, Whitman was able to pick up much extra business; he also increased his activities with readings by authors, talks and literary meetings.

In a sense Le Mistral-Shakespeare & Company continued Whitman's previous activity from his very early days in Paris. On arrival, staying in the Hôtel de Suez, he began to collect books for himself, and he would often find after returning – one did not necessarily lock one's hotel room in those days – that other residents of the hotel were using his room as a library. When he owned Le Mistral he was able to keep those books that he did not want to sell – his own collection – on the upper floors, where there were also a number of sofas; these became a library where those he knew or trusted could sit and read. He liked to have American and British writers and poets staying there, and many took advantage of his hospitality. Among those was Lawrence Ferlinghetti, whose City Lights bookshop (once described by Ferlinghetti as "Shakespeare & Company's 'brother bookstore'") has long been the most famous literary establishment on the West Coast. The two shops are however very different. Ferlinghetti is also a publisher and a well-known poet, as well as being perhaps the central figure, because of his bookshop, in the Beat movement, which came into existence at about the same time as the literary exiles in Paris were organizing themselves.

The American writers who frequented Le Mistral included James Jones, Langston Hughes, Anaïs Nin, Richard Wright, James Baldwin and many others either living in Paris or visiting it. There was always a large Irish contingent, among them Brian Coffey, Brendan Behan, Aidan Higgins, Séamus Ó Néill and many who never became as well known. Such international names as Julio Cortázar and Octavio Paz were frequent visitors, the former calling it "the most humane bookshop in the world". In the Sixties, among those who were most often seen there were Allen Ginsberg, Peter Orlovsky, Gregory Corso, Alan Sillitoe, J.P. Donleavy and William Burroughs; the last divided much of his non-working time between the two English bookshops, paying several visits a week to each. One of the most frequent visitors until his death was Lawrence Durrell, who did many readings there, and Whitman gave parties for him. *The Alexandria Quartet* had the kind of universal success that made him one of the writers whom readers most wanted to meet, and he did not mind being used as a draw by booksellers: he was a frequenter of many, and could also often be seen in Bernard Stone's very similar Turret Bookshop in London.

Whitman kept up his relationships with other booksellers, exchanging stock, looking out for special editions and carrying out searches for customers on occasion. In the Fifties he kept in touch with Peter Russell, who from London edited a rather elitist magazine of the intellectual right, largely devoted to the resuscitation of the work of Ezra Pound, called *Nine*. Russell eventually opened a second-hand bookshop in a small town in Kent and then moved to Florence, where a fire in 1991 destroyed most of his large and rare collection of literary first editions. Whitman himself had a fire in 1990 that burned many of his own rare literary volumes, although it did not harm the shop itself.

George Whitman allowed his bookstore to become the publishing address as well as sales point for several little magazines, the *Paris Magazine* (which he owned and financed), *Two Cities* (a bilingual magazine), *Points*, *New Story* and others that did not survive beyond one or two issues. Whitman had a particular admiration for the *Merlin* crowd, and Patrick Bowles in particular. He thought him the literary figure most like Hemingway, combining literary talent with a penchant for adventure, an athlete who was also an intellectual. This was only partly proved true by Bowles's later career; he spent some time in London doing various forms of literary work before moving back to Paris to work for French radio, and then went to the Congo, where his activities included working for the World Health Organization. Like so many of his colleagues, Bowles was a ladies' man, making many conquests without having to try very hard: he saw sleeping with women, of all types and ages, as a kind of public service. Good-looking in a dark, saturnine way, lean and adventurous-looking, he often resembled the prototypal German SS officer, normally being dressed in black leather with riding boots. He had a sense of mystery about him that women found attractive: the London artist Marion Wilson would frequently refer to him as "my fascist boyfriend", because of the macho leather, not his politics. Some also found him alarming as if some deep violence lay under the calm exterior, like Lady Caroline Lamb's description of Byron: "Mad, bad, and dangerous to know".

Of the *Paris Review* crowd – not many of them spent time in bookshops – Peter Matthiessen was the principal frequenter of Le Mistral, and he still returned there on visits to Paris years later. Whitman considered him the most talented member of the group, and he was certainly the most successful writer.

British politicians have often made Shakespeare & Company a favourite place to call. Whitman used to point out that they tended to be on the left, with Dennis Healey and Michael Foot, the more literary of Labour Party politicians, being among the most frequent. During the McCarthyite Fifties, Whitman had many American film writers and directors, as well as novelists, among his customers, exiles who could find no work in America after being "named". He said that he could detect FBI informers among them when they came asking questions. One of them was McCarthy's aide, Roy Cohn.

At certain points in this book the author has to introduce himself into the narrative and speak in the first person. I have been myself a frequenter of the two bookshops, and of others founded later that will feature in later chapters. I was more at home with Gaït Frogé than with George Whitman, principally because of a common interest in certain authors with whom I had either a friendly or a professional relationship, but also because she was a valuable customer, stocking the books I published – those written in English by Samuel Beckett, William Burroughs, Henry Miller, Aidan Higgins, Alan Burns and Ann Quin, writers in vogue in the late Fifties and early Sixties, as well as translations from French and German, mainly of Alain Robbe-Grillet and his colleagues in the *nouveau roman*. Gaït was an adventurous bookseller who also read and could persuade visitors to buy authors of whom they had not yet heard. Such booksellers were rare, even in Britain, where I was based. She also became a good friend, and I lost both a client and a confidante when she abruptly sold the shop and made her ill-fated move to America. Whitman did not buy new books, and I only visited him as a browser. Gaït could tell me what was happening in literary Paris: she knew what people were writing and was creatively interested in their work, whereas Whitman was more involved in writers as personalities, established ones because they were already successful, and beginners because they might be one day. He wanted to be part of the success of others and thereby was self-serving in a way that Gaït was not. His claims, which he later dropped, to be descended from Walt Whitman the poet, and that his shop was the same as Sylvia Beach's, did him harm in the long run, because he lost credence thereby. He nevertheless gave his life to books and bookselling and, after a little carping, is due much credit for it. But he never was the kind of bookseller that leads taste by stocking new books and new talent as did his contemporary Frogé and those other English bookshops that were to come later.

Chapter Five

The Rise of Olympia

1

At this point I must return to the earlier career of Maurice Girodias. He was at a low ebb after the suicide of Germaine and the loss of Les Éditions du Chêne. He had no money, and his morale had sunk to its lowest level. He was dispirited, lacked energy and saw no prospect of escaping the failure that had befallen him at the age of thirty-two. He was living apart from his wife and two children, whom he had in effect abandoned. He had lost the fruits of ten years' work. He asked himself why, if his spirit could survive his body after death, he should have to wait any longer to separate the two. He was sharing a room with his brother now, the cheapest they could find. He had hurt his right hand and the wound would not heal, while the bandage was never really clean. For a time they stayed in the apartment of a friend of Eric's on the Rue de l'Université on condition that they fed the Siamese cat. The cat had a strong smell and regularly pissed on the piano, and the ceilings were low so that they banged their heads if they stood up too hastily. Eric, less accustomed to the luxury that Maurice had known in recent years, supported the situation best. When they had to move, it was Eric who found a small room in a cheap hotel on the Rue Jacob. While they were waiting in the lobby for the room to be ready for them, they saw two municipal employees, who should have arrived the previous day, carrying a coffin down the stairs: a Yugoslav painter had committed suicide in the room they were about to occupy. The manager was embarrassed that they had arrived at that particular moment and reduced the rent for the room.

Maurice had always believed in his luck. There was an uncle, the elder brother of his father, who had been evicted from the family home in Manchester for stealing the diamond cufflinks of Maurice's grandfather; he had gone to South Africa to fight in the Boer War. Perhaps, thought Girodias, he had made a fortune there that would now come to his brother's children! That Christmas Maurice and Eric shared a sausage, a piece of bread and their future plans. Where to move next? They thought of Rolande Canado, an old girlfriend of Maurice's, whose husband was away. When approached, she agreed to take them into her apartment for a while. Maurice began to think about publishing again. The new owners of Les Éditions du Chêne had turned down the first volumes of Henry Miller's *Rosy Crucifixion*, entitled *Sexus* and *Plexus*. If he could pay a printer he would be able to publish and sell them easily, with only a certain risk from the morality police, which was worth taking. He ran into Jean-Jacques Pauvert, who was publishing the major novels of the Marquis de Sade in a semi-clandestine way. Pauvert offered him the use of his office.

Girodias went to a doctor who told him that he was physically run-down and exhausted. He knew of a treatment that a Swiss doctor had developed, based on injections of monkey glands, which had been developed to slow down senility. There were certain risks – possible blindness was one – but he did not think they were too great for someone of Maurice's age. The treatment was not yet legal in France, but the doctor wanted to experiment and would give Maurice financial credit if he tried it. He did and felt his energy returning.

His brother Eric left for England after a few months, and Rolande told him he could not stay any longer; he eventually found other rooms. With his sexual energy returning, he met a beautiful Canadian girl from Toronto, Shirley, and shared her apartment for a while, and then found other beds in which to sleep. He moved into Pauvert's office and met two printers who were willing to give him credit. By now he had encountered the *Merlin* editors and had accepted Austryn Wainhouse's *The Bedroom Philosophers*, his translation of de Sade's *La Philosophie dans le boudoir*. Impressed that Girodias had previously published *Critique*, the journal edited by Georges Bataille, Trocchi suggested translating some of Bataille's short erotic novels, which had appeared under his pen name, Pierre Angélique. Bataille was interested, but only if the translations were well done. Austryn Wainhouse then undertook them and also agreed to start on a complete translation of de Sade's masterpiece, *Les 120 Journées de Sodome*; it would be worth the years of his life that it would take to complete. Olympia Press was now in business and soon it would begin to flower.

Girodias had kept the list of some four hundred buyers of erotica from his father's Obelisk Press. He also knew the principal booksellers of Paris, Amsterdam, Nice, Geneva, Milan and other cities where there was a market for books in English, especially those considered pornographic. He sent leaflets announcing works by de Sade, Genet (*The Thief's Journal*), Bataille, Beckett and Henry Miller. In a short time he received a flood of letters and orders, cheques and telegrams. His old confidence began to return.

With his new team of writers and translators, and with increased credit from printers, now more confident of being paid, Girodias increased his production. The non-literary pornography came out under the imprint of Ophelia Press – crude novels of sexual narrative description, catering to the tastes of both hetero- and homosexuals, voyeurs, masochists and sadists, with every possible perversion included – but these lacked the imagination and the style of the authors of the Olympia list which sold in more places than the pink Ophelia titles; booksellers were more willing to have them on view because the names of Apollinaire, Genet and de Sade had a certain cachet to them, and Beckett, after the success of *Waiting for Godot*, had become a cult figure, increasingly interesting to academics. Within a short time he was to become the most written-about author of the twentieth century and the one most studied at universities.

It was Philip Oxman, with his interest in psychoanalysis, who had persuaded Girodias to go to the doctor. Oxman had in the meantime himself become an Olympia writer. Girodias went every week to visit the doctor in his office on the Butte Montmartre at the top of the city, and continued taking his monkey-gland injections. Not only had his old energy come back, but he was "suffering", if that is the right word, from satyriasis: he could not have too much sex and no one woman could satisfy him. He worked hard in the office all day and made love most of the night. It was the beginning of his almost sleepless existence, which was to continue up to the late Sixties. He still enjoyed good food and wine, indeed more than ever, now that he could afford such things again. There were frequent lunches with Trocchi, whose brains he picked on many subjects, and who, together with Pauvert, became his principal literary advisor. Authors came to see him from the US and from Britain, with manuscripts that they could not publish in their native countries because of what the editors in the big publishing companies saw as obscene content; often this was very minor and absolutely necessary for the validity of the novel in question. But in those days Hollywood films had a code whereby no couple could be alone in a bedroom unless the woman had at least one foot on the floor, and women produced babies without any apparent sexual intercourse; it was little wonder that many young girls thought they could get pregnant from a kiss. "Fuck" or "cunt" in a novel would lead to automatic prosecution. Clients of all kinds came directly to the Olympia office to buy Girodias's books, some of them eminent literary figures like Cyril Connolly, whose pre-war novel *The Rock Pool* his father had published, and Desmond MacCarthy and Sir Herbert Read, both pillars of the English intellectual establishment.

Girodias always liked money, but was careless with it. It has already been said that when it flowed in he spent generously and without a thought for the morrow, a characteristic he shared with Trocchi. The tap once turned on would surely never turn itself off! He was a crusader always sure of his crusade, although it changed from time to time, as his enthusiasms did. As an enemy of all censorship he followed in his father's footsteps, and saw himself as the scourge of hypocrites. His ideas on religion were vague and fluid. He had once decided to go to a Protestant school, a compromise as his background was half Jewish and half Catholic; his parents had raised no objection. He became interested in religious history insofar as it concerned heretics and others who had been persecuted and suffered at the hands of authority. His publications of de Sade, Bataille, Miller, Apollinaire and Beckett, all of them authors who had defied authority and conventional morality, he saw as a declaration of "total war against ordinary morality and against the old religions of the West". He pictured himself at the head of a group of writers who between them would play a large role in bringing down the old attitudes and the hierarchy that supported them, and that would finally bring society out of the Middle Ages.

> It was not religion as such that I was attacking, but the political God of the Christians, the Jews and the other monotheists, the followers of a jealous God who commanded wars. The God of St Dominic, of Simon de Montfort, of the Borgias and Henry VIII, the bloody ogre... the God of the conquistadores and the slave merchants... In the name of which the spirit of hate and vengeance is established on the earth – because it is that God which gave birth to Hitler and to Stalin.*

Sexuality was one of the means by which that savage monotheistic God could be attacked. What he liked about Jean Genet, who was being translated for him by Bernard Frechtman, was his defence of his own sexuality, homosexual love, often rough and brutal, but unashamed in its open and joyous animality. Authority did not want society to know about its own sexual potential. It wanted a military discipline, a military aesthetic, one that promoted virginity and innocence, praising honour and patriotism as the supreme virtues. There was officially no promiscuity or homosexuality in the armed forces, or in the prison system. Genet had exposed the hypocrisy of official thinking, and he had done so without all the camouflage practised by Proust and Gide in order to make their homosexuality acceptable to the literary establishment.

Girodias saw his readers as the solitary men – mostly American but also British and from the Commonwealth – who were shut up in military camps in Germany and elsewhere in Europe, and constituted the armies of occupation after the war. He saw them also as tourists from puritanical countries, where love scenes in films excluded sex, and novels could not describe it realistically. His readers found reality in the books he published as well as imagination-freeing fantasy, and thereby also found enjoyable release through masturbation, still frowned on, seldom admitted and stigmatized as "self-abuse". During the war, Dr Eustace Chesser, a Harley Street doctor and author of many books on sexuality, had been prosecuted at the Old Bailey in London for a very mild book of sexual instruction for married couples. He had defended himself without lawyers, and, looking at the jury, had challenged it directly: "Let any man among you who has never masturbated now stand up!" No one did. A fortune was to be made by satisfying the need for erotic fiction. Had Girodias simply done this he would have become and remained a rich man, assuming that he stretched the limits of acceptability gradually, and avoided the most emotionally charged taboos. But such restraint was not in his nature.

Girodias made the publishing of erotica into a crusade, took pride in producing his books on good paper and in choosing good authors and translators. Certainly many of his clients looking for masturbatory material must have been disappointed by Beckett's *Watt* and *Molloy*, philosophical novels that broke new ground in fiction, but in which the sexual content is both sparse and not intended to excite. And some other Olympia authors wrote well above the understanding of the average GI. But soon the Traveller's Companion titles were being bought, increasingly, by readers of modern literature, more interested in the new ideas and styles that were emerging from Beckett, Genet and Bataille than in the sexual content, sophisticates whose own sex lives were active and free from inhibition and guilt. Publishers in Britain and the US began to eye the Olympia list with interest, waiting for the moment when their own moral taboos would begin to crumble.

Girodias remembered that, although the four volumes of Frank Harris's *My Life and Loves* now belonged to Hachette, owners of Les Éditions du Chêne, his father had had a contract for a fifth volume that had never been delivered. He went in search of it, and even took a train to Nice to try to trace Harris's widow, Nellie, but it was several weeks before he finally received a letter from the nonagenarian lady in question, asking him to get in touch with a Paris lawyer, Maître Adolphe. He was eventually received by this gentleman, who started off by saying that he felt obliged to offer the manuscript to Hachette, who now owned the benefit of the old contract and the titles in print. Girodias proposed a ten per cent royalty.

"That's all very well," replied Adolphe, "but what interests my client is the size of the advance that you would pay on signature of the contract. Something solid, young man, something solid."

"Well, yes," murmured Girodias, "at least 400,000 francs. I can't really say much until I've seen the manuscript."

"Young man, that's not very serious," said the lawyer. "Your father made a fortune from the first four volumes of Frank Harris, which tells you enough about the value of the fifth. Come on now, how much?"

"And the manuscript, do you have it?"

"Of course I have it. It's here in the drawer."

In the ensuing discussion, Maurice Girodias was not to see the manuscript, if it was indeed in the drawer, but he raised his offer to a million francs. Maître Adolphe said that he would take note of the offer and come back to him, making him confirm it in writing on the spot. He would contact him in due course.

Girodias knew perfectly well that his offer, especially now that it had been put in writing, would simply be used to obtain a higher, or at least the same, from Hachette or another publisher. But at least he had put the price up!

Temporarily putting Frank Harris out of his mind, he went off with Shirley, the Canadian girl who was one of his four mistresses at the time, to Alsace where the *vendanges* had begun. It was a beautiful time of the year in the picturesque little villages of the Alsatian wine country, and between wine-tasting and the beautiful white body of Shirley, Frank Harris was soon forgotten.

Three weeks later Adolphe telephoned him, said there was good news, and asked him to come again. He was friendlier this time. Yes, he would accept a million on signature of a contract.

"And the manuscript, can I see it? The manuscript was in your drawer."

"I told you. Give me a certified cheque for a million francs and I will give you a contract signed by my client. After that, I will give you the manuscript. A million, that's all. The sum you proposed yourself."

"But things aren't done that way. It's against all normal practice." And so it was. But Maurice Girodias gave in. It was not easy to find such a large sum; it took him several days. Then he telephoned the lawyer.

"Fine, fine," said his torturer. "Don't forget to bring my fees."

"Your fees?" moaned Girodias. "But you're not my lawyer."

"Now look here, young man," said Adolphe, "I'm an old man, and I don't much like the manners of the young today. I have acted as a go-between in all this and in your interest. In spite of your bad character and your reluctance to complete the matter, I have persuaded Madame Harris to accept your offer. *Instead of Hachette*. Think of it! It seems to me that 50,000 francs is a very reasonable fee."

He went back the next day, apprehensively, with a further cheque. What did this manuscript consist of and what was it really worth? After verifying the cheques and obtaining Girodias's signature on the contract, Adolphe produced a small packet wrapped in green paper. Taking it away and resisting the impulse to throw it in the nearest dustbin, he eventually opened it back at home. There were a few notes and articles on yellowed paper, padded with some blank white pages! What had he really expected, after all, but to be cheated? But, on thinking about it, Girodias had an idea. He had the widow's signature, a proof that a fifth volume existed. There were about fifty pages of a manuscript of a sort. He spoke to Trocchi, who agreed, for another 50,000 francs, to reconstitute a fifth volume, using the few pages in existence and doing a fictitious imitation of Harris's style. He would have to sell over 10,000 copies to break even on his investment, but it would be a literary event. And it would certainly annoy Hachette.

2

Sharing an office with Jean-Jacques Pauvert gave Maurice Girodias the advantage of having a congenial colleague in whom he could confide, and a partner in the occasional joint book – one would publish the French original and the other the English translation. They shared the Marquis de Sade, Georges Bataille and some others, including the anonymous *Histoire d'O*, writing with obscene content but high literary quality. Pauvert was a genial, literate, convivial man, respected in the profession in a way that Girodias never was. He produced books of art as well as literature, and was one of the publishers most interested in surrealism, which, after its initial vogue in the Twenties and Thirties, was now recognized for its historical importance in the development of art and literature, and was continuing through the work of a new creative generation. Surrealist art books now enjoyed the same success that had been characteristic of French impressionism in the Forties.

Pauvert's editions were beautifully produced, and even the literary titles had carefully selected illustrations to accompany the obscene material where it existed. The good taste, sophistication and high production standards of Pauvert's books were such that no one had to hide them or feel they did not belong on their bookshelves. When he exhibited them at the Frankfurt Book Fair, so many were stolen that he eventually had to put chains on them. When he put on show volumes that were only dummies of pasted-up proofs, he could use his figures of theft to decide how many to print.

Laid-back, unexcitable, a man of the world, fond of sunshine holidays and skiing in the winter, Pauvert was far more in the image of the big establishment publishers like Gallimard or Grasset than the emotional, accident-prone, easily deceived Girodias. He would never have been taken in by Adolphe. He was a useful collaborator for Girodias, both in his professionalism and his persona. He had production managers, accountants, sales managers and office personnel who did their jobs in a normal fashion, unlike the chaos that always surrounded Girodias.

The offices at 8 Rue de Nesle, in the heart of the teeming backstreets of the *cinquième*, which contain hundreds of art galleries, boutiques, jewellery shops, bookshops, little theatres, brothels, bars, big and small hotels, clubs, cinemas and hundreds of restaurants, were in an old building, and for the *quartier* they were fairly large and comfortable. Underneath them was a famous art dealer, Maeght.

Things were beginning to go well for both publishers, and Girodias also found a place nearby to live. This came about by chance: he began to believe that his new-found creative and sexual energy, following his course of injections of monkey-gland serum, had also brought him back his old luck. He met Genia Courtade, his previous secretary who had been so faithful and supportive in earlier days when others were robbing him or leading him in the wrong direction, and she introduced him to another lady from the same Russian colony in Paris. This was Elizabeth Maupoil, who had bought an old crumbling building on the Paris quayside facing Notre Dame. It was situated on the corner of the Rue Saint-Jacques near the church of Saint-Julien-le-Pauvre, an area that Girodias knew well from his perambulations over the years. Le Mistral was two doors away. In spite of her French name, the residue of a marriage to a colonial administrator who was killed in the war, Elizabeth was very Russian, outgoing, emotional, generous and attractive. She also had an explosive temper. She could be as stingy as the worst financial manager on a tight budget when in a bad mood, and extravagantly generous to those she liked. She also had a mania for chess. She had just opened a restaurant, La Bûcherie, a place of charm that was more like the lounge of a skiing hotel than a Left Bank restaurant. An open fire blazed in the middle where customers could sit in comfortable armchairs with a drink; you could have a light snack or a full meal in a totally relaxed atmosphere. Genia brought Maurice there, introduced him to Elizabeth, and they drank a bottle of vodka together. They all got on famously and Maurice lost two games of chess. He was encouraged to relate his personal problems, and in the end was offered a small but comfortable room at the top of the building, better than anything he had slept in for a considerable time, for a tiny rent, although it included an unspoken obligation to keep Elizabeth sexually happy on occasion. But Elizabeth liked other women, was not possessive or jealous, and she became one of his four current sleeping partners. His memoirs are sometimes vague on names, but at the time they included Shirley, and a beautiful and sensual Italian lady.

Girodias's collaboration with Pauvert might have included the acquisition of a novel by a young student of nineteen who was about to enter the École Normale Supérieure. He had previously written an essay on Henry Miller, which Girodias remembered, and now he suggested an idea for an erotic book on Defoe's *Robinson Crusoe*. It was commissioned, written in two months in French, and Girodias expected Pauvert to publish the original while he had it translated. But Pauvert eventually turned it down, on the grounds that he had enough on his plate without publishing modern novels with which he had little sympathy in any case, and it eventually appeared only in English as *The Sexual Life of Robinson Crusoe*.

On one occasion they had a visit from a group of plain-clothes policemen of the Sûreté, charged with discovering and seizing pornography. Pauvert and Girodias were natural targets. The offices were inspected, proofs and blocks looked at: one was the frogs' song from *Watt*, a rhythmic representation of the sound that frogs make in chorus. They could make neither head nor tail of it – some English code, no doubt fetishist. Girodias had for some time now been attracting the attention of British Customs and the Home Office, and the Obscenity Squad was putting pressure on the French to curtail his activities. But Pauvert with his urbane charm usually managed to get rid of the police with little incident, arguing always that all literature had an erotic element, that it was part of life, and that in any case his books were so well produced and expensive that they were luxury objects that could only be bought by the rich and those no longer young.

One day Pauvert entered the office with a manuscript that had been given to him by Jean Paulhan which intrigued him greatly. Much in the spirit of de Sade, it was a modern story of sexual bondage and slavery. The title was *Le Bonheur dans l'esclavage* (*Happiness in Slavery*), which Pauvert decided was too provocative and he changed it to *Histoire d'O*.

"Listen," said Pauvert. "I want you to do me a favour and give me your advice. Can you read it by tomorrow? Paulhan has written an introduction. It's de Sade the other way round. The cruelty and masochism is written from a woman's point of view and it's very well done. Good writing, very cold, which suits the story very well."

Girodias asked why he wanted another opinion of a book he already liked.

"It's like this," said Pauvert. "It seems to me to be the first of a new kind of literature, flying in the face of public morality, as the police call it, without being just a pornographic novel. But it's also a contemporary novel, and I've sworn to keep away from them, unlike you…"

"I don't understand you," Girodias said to him. "Isn't a work of de Sade's a novel? Here you have something of the same quality that you like, and with a preface by Jean Paulhan, a big name. You have an automatic success on your hands. What's your problem? Either you want to publish it or you don't."

"Listen," insisted Pauvert, "you always oversimplify things. You specialize in this kind of dirty book. I need your practical advice. I don't want to be dragged into interminable legal prosecutions which will affect my other publications. I specialize in republishing books that are out of copyright, with guaranteed sales and no royalties to pay. As you're now interested, read it for me tonight. I'm having lunch with Paulhan tomorrow and I've promised him an answer."

Returning to La Bûcherie with the manuscript burning his fingers, Girodias took his telephone off the hook and sat down with a glass of Burgundy on the table next to him. He left the Paulhan preface for last, read the text with excitement, noted down a few criticisms, regretted the alternative endings, but was sure he had a masterpiece of its category in his hands. The next day he went to see Pauvert and told him that he *had* to publish it; after all, he was protected by Paulhan, the grey eminence of Gallimard and one of the most respected critics in France. Also, he added, he wanted to bring out an English translation at the same time.

Girodias then asked who the author was. Pauvert wriggled, said that although he knew, he had promised not to tell. It was better, in any case, for Girodias not to know. Maurice could get nothing out of him. In fact, the identity of the author of *Histoire d'O* was one of the best kept literary secrets of the twentieth century until the end of it: the question was asked countless times of everyone who had any involvement with the novel and always the person interrogated tended to put on a knowing look and say that he or she had promised not to tell. I repeated the same question to Girodias many years later at the end of his life, having done so many times over the intervening years, and he still gave the same stock reply which he had received from Pauvert. My own conviction was that no one, except the author, knew for certain the real name of "Pauline Réage". Paulhan was often suspected of being the author, although this was most unlikely. It is now believed to have been Anne Desclos, an editor with Gallimard who was Paulhan's mistress at the time, and who also wrote under the pen name Dominique Aury.

Girodias then looked for a translator. Wainhouse was occupied with de Sade, Bowles with Beckett (he was translating *Molloy*), Trocchi with his own pornographic novels. He settled on a young American couple who had submitted work to him that was reasonably well written, Baird Bryant and his wife Denny; he told them he needed it quickly. The translation when it came in was not very good, but Pauvert was about to publish in French and Girodias could not wait, so he published it anyway.

There was a little Basque restaurant near the Rue de Nesle where Girodias and Pauvert frequently went for lunch, sometimes meeting the other two Paris publishers who specialized in literary and artistic eroticism, Claude Tchou, a Chinese Frenchman, and Eric Losfeld. The restaurant was not frequented by other, more conventional publishers, to whom these four constituted a certain danger by making literature controversial and therefore less likely to attract state support. Girodias was there alone one day when Pauvert burst in, a legal summons in his hands. It had been served on him by Inspector Laffont of the Brigade Mondaine. He had to appear at the police station the next day to answer questions, and he had been warned that the interrogation would go on all day. Another summons was waiting for Girodias when he returned from lunch. What Inspector Laffont particularly wanted to know was the real name of Pauline Réage. Pauvert had protested that he must keep professional confidences, but he knew he had a tough ordeal ahead of him. The day after that the police wanted to see Girodias and their questioning would not be confined to the one book.

The following evening Girodias, Pauvert's wife Christine, and a few friends were all waiting on the terrace of a café to hear the news. Pauvert arrived in a state of concentrated fury from which they divined that he had been harshly treated, but had defended himself well.

"It's incredible," he declared. "They've got it into their heads that Lucie Faure wrote the book. I don't know where they got that stupid idea, but it must have come from someone high up. They put me through the wringer all day, threatened me with prison, beating-up... as usual they made themselves look as stupid as they really are. I stuck to my guns. 'I know who wrote *Histoire d'O* and I'm not going to tell you. This interrogation is illegal. You're wasting my time and I want to go.'"

The next day was Maurice's turn. He had to present himself at the Ministry of Justice on the Seine, near Notre Dame. To get to the Brigade Mondaine offices in the building he had to pass cells full of prostitutes, drug dealers, pickpockets and petty criminals – the catch of the night. They were all the responsibility of the Brigade Mondaine. He ran the gauntlet of their taunts and insults. Laffont knew he had something a little different in front of him, an English-language pornographer. He took Girodias to another room where he found himself in front of the commissioner who was the head of the Brigade.

"Sit down," he said. "So, you are the famous Girodias?"

"Yes," replied his victim, humbly.

"So," grunted the commissioner, "are you pleased to find yourself here?"

"Moderately so, Monsieur le Commissaire."

"Well, I hope you will enjoy our hospitality. These gentlemen are going to look after you."

Surrounded by half a dozen police officers like a dangerous criminal, he was led to another office, where he found himself facing a senior inspector while surrounded by the others. They all asked him questions while Laffont periodically delivered little kicks against the legs of the chair that Girodias was sitting on. They told him that they already knew from Pauvert who the author of the book was, but they wanted his confirmation. "Who is it?"

Girodias could not stop himself laughing. It was like a scene from the worst film he had ever seen.

"How can I answer when I don't know? But if you'd like to tell me who Pauvert said it was, I might then know."

"He didn't tell us who it was, but he said he knew."

"Ah, that's another story. Well, what can I say?"

"Who wrote *Histoire d'O*?"

129

"It's a good question," Girodias said. "I hear it all the time. I can't go out to dinner without being asked by everyone there, 'Who wrote *Histoire d'O*?' I'd like to know myself. But I don't."

"Well then, tell us who you think Pauvert knows to have written it?"

"How can I know anything? Pauvert thinks he knows who wrote it, but can he be sure? He has no reason to think that whatever he thinks he knows is true. It might all be an illusion."

"Well then, if you think he's wrong and that it's not the person who he thinks wrote it, tell us who you think he thinks *didn't* write it."

"That would really be a large number of people. It would be millions of people, without even going as far as China. It could be anyone capable of writing. It could be Pauvert himself. He owns a pen."

"So," said the inspector, "you think it's Pauvert himself. The publisher is also the author… and why not? All this is to throw dust in our eyes. Now it becomes clear. When Pauvert told us he knows the author he was telling the truth. Of course he does, since it's himself. You've told us now yourself."

"But no," protested Girodias in alarm, "I only said he owns a pen. It's a metaphorical way of saying that it could be anyone you suspect."

"Metaphorical? So you're telling us more lies!" he went on grimly. "You're going to answer us. We're not here to waste our time."

The interrogation went on for three hours. The name Lucie Faure was brought up. The questions were repeated. How could he, having a contract to publish the book in English, not know the name of the author? Finally they released him and he went to join his friends, drinking their apéritifs at a restaurant across the river.

"Well, Maurice, did you finally find out who wrote *Histoire d'O*?"

3

In spite of occasional annoyances and set-backs, by the end of the decade Olympia Press was well established. Books were seized from time to time by the police, but they were all in English, which practically no French policeman could read. The raids were usually on small bookshops, and only a few books were seized, which was mainly to give some satisfaction to the British Home Office. US Customs only worried about books that actually arrived in the States. And censorship was gradually being whittled away there, as more cases were won by publishers; the American situation was fluid as every city had a different attitude and moral code.

In 1959, a new Act was passed in the UK because of an obscenity case involving *The Philanderer*,* a novel by Stanley Kauffmann published by Secker & Warburg in 1954, which was lucky to find itself in front of a civilized and liberal judge. Not only was Fred Warburg, the publisher of the book, treated with courtesy and not made to stand in the dock, but the spectator benches of the court were filled with well-known literary and public personalities, whose presence gave implicit support to the publisher. In those days expert witnesses for the defence were not allowed to appear. In his final summing up to the jury, the judge, before finding the defendant not guilty, went on to say that literary standards could not be based simply on what was suitable for a fourteen-year-old girl to read. A great public debate followed the case and much of it took place in Parliament. Liberal reforms were in the air and the Conservative government did not have too much time before the return of Labour to power which would bring with it a rapid series of new laws and the abolition of old ones, to limit the persecution of minorities and extending civil rights. But the first such reform was passed under the Conservatives by Roy Jenkins, a Labour MP, as a private member's bill: this was the Obscene Publications Act 1959, which for the first time allowed expert witnesses to be introduced by the defence in a prosecution. It also brought a new concept into the law, that the obscenity of a book (its tendency to corrupt and deprave) had to be balanced against its literary merit. Books could henceforth be vigorously defended by publishers who had the financial means to do so, and with a good chance of winning.

In the meantime, the pace of change was accelerating in the US. McCarthy was dead and McCarthyism discredited. Authors who had been under a cloud were published again, and the new ones included the beats, who were producing a radical literature that reflected a lifestyle that was anti-authoritarian and counter to the values of conventional society. The Civil Rights movement had started, and Martin Luther King had, from 1956, established himself at the head of the battle for desegregation. A new generation was looking for a civilized ethos, and it was much larger than its predecessors because the population of the US was then growing by more than three million a year. In his influential essay 'The New Mood in Politics', Arthur Schlesinger Jr. said:

> If something does not pay its way in the marketplace, it is felt to be hardly worth doing at all. Is our land really dedicated to the notion that only things that pay their way deserve to survive? If so, we are doomed, because very little of genuine importance – from education

to defence – pays its own way in the market… Our trouble is not that our capabilities are inadequate. It is that our priorities – which means our *values* – are wrong.*

Young people were in revolt, but it took different forms. The beats were basically apolitical: they were not radicals or left-wing reformers but a subsection of a new young generation that wanted to opt out totally from society. They never really defined what was wrong, as many new gurus were soon to do. They simply wanted to create their own, different world; art played a large part in this, an art that was free, immediate and disposable. They wanted heightened awareness and found it in drugs as well as in art. They were abetted by some established writers like Norman Mailer who encouraged them to be militant as well as dismissive. Free sexuality was a tenet of that militancy.

As the Fifties drew to a close, there were an increasing number of court judgements favouring the release of books on sexual subjects. The culmination was Grove Press's publication of *Lady Chatterley's Lover* in 1959, which received even greater publicity than the court decision in favour of *Ulysses* before the war. It was followed two years later by the American publication of *Tropic of Cancer*, also by Grove Press. By now Barney Rosset had become the white knight of both the new radicalism and the Beat movement, and his magazine, the *Evergreen Review*, reflected an approach to life and the arts that owed much to Saint-Germain-des-Prés, as well as to the jazz and poetry clubs of San Francisco that he frequented. But he also supported the Civil Rights movement and desegregation. Students began to make demands for more than just an education aimed at fitting them into jobs. The intellectual cowardice of their parents and elders sickened them. Eric Goldman, who later became an advisor to Lyndon Johnson during his presidency, wrote an article in *Harper's Magazine* in 1960 in which, deploring the complacency, stupor and anti-intellectualism of the time, he said: "We live in a heavy, humourless, sanctimonious, stultifying atmosphere singularly lacking in the self-mockery that is self-criticism. Probably the climate of the late Fifties was the dullest and dreariest in our history."*

Minorities were no longer stirring: they were ready for revolt. Black Americans stopped being "coloured" and insisted they were black; they began to overcome the fear and Uncle-Tomism under which they had lived for so many centuries and to demand a share of the wealth and opportunity of the richest country on earth. Homosexuals came out of the closet to demand recognition and the right to live their lives openly without guilt. The Beat movement gave them an umbrella and they became an important part of it. The exiles who had left the US for London, Paris, Tangiers and elsewhere had become known and respected; some of them, like Paul Bowles, had written best-sellers, and had thereby influenced the new nonconformism, and some were returning to America to continue their careers in a climate that was becoming more congenial, because a recognizable alternative to the status quo was emerging. It would soon be the dawn of the Kennedy era, bringing with it an intellectual revival of high culture and a rejuvenation of popular culture: a new liberalism was growing.

Although these events would in time affect the profitability of Olympia, Girodias was still flourishing. He had long had a taste for fine Burgundy, and now that he could once again afford it, he was certainly drinking too much, but without his ability to work and to function sexually being affected. In the early days of his association with the *Merlin* group, he had been invited one evening to have dinner with the Wainhouses in their tiny apartment and had been impressed with the gourmet dinner that Muffie Wainhouse had served up, all cooked on a small spirit stove and accompanied by an excellent Chambolle-Musigny. The Wainhouse marriage was breaking up, and soon after that evening Muffie moved into her own apartment, but kept the address secret. She then started an affair with Girodias, visiting him in his room over La Bûcherie. He was never able to understand how it had all started, but he woke up one morning with a slight Burgundy headache and there was Muffie in bed beside him. They became not only lovers but good friends, and for a while he considered monogamy. Muffie, far from jealous, did not ask for this, but she was concerned about his drinking.

Manuscripts arrived from the four corners of the earth. He had stabilized his printings at 5,000 copies and sold each edition fairly rapidly, many copies directly for cash: cheques, postal orders and bank-notes arrived daily at his offices. He had for some time put many of his titles under the imprint of Atlantic Library and these were often his financial best-sellers. He was starting to sign contracts for some titles with publishers in the UK and the US, some of them with myself. His principal sales were made in the summer with the arrival of hordes of tourists, his smallest in the winter, but they never stopped. In preparation for the spring season he would put out a catalogue of authors and titles, many of them at the time fictitious: he and his colleagues would dream up subjects for books, give them titles and then look for a writer to produce them in a hurry for a lump sum. If the book was reprinted the author was given an additional payment, but Girodias had no head for figures, hated routine and bookkeeping and seldom gave normal royalties to his authors. In this way he cheated himself more than his writers, because many of them, by being a nuisance and calling frequently at his office, earned more than their sales justified, while some of the more timid may not have done as well as they should. In later years he was accused of systematically cheating them, but there is no justification for this: he simply never knew what he owed and usually gave the author the benefit of the doubt.

In September 1954 Girodias received a letter from a Mr J.P. Donleavy, an American living in London. It said that he had a manuscript of about 125,000 words, which had been refused by a New York publisher because he considered it obscene. The letter went on: "The obscenity is very much a part of this novel and its removal would detract from it." Donleavy's letter looked interesting and Girodias wrote back asking to see the manuscript. When it arrived he liked it, but felt that it was too disorganized and wordy. Muffie confirmed his opinion and he wrote back that he would accept it if the author would incorporate his editorial suggestions. Much correspondence followed, and in several letters Donleavy asked him for a contract.

Maurice Girodias at the time had little experience of contracts. In his case they usually consisted of a few words scribbled in longhand on a piece of paper, buying or commissioning a new work for a sum of money with no mention of royalties. Most of the time he was dealing with young writers interested in immediate money: they would take an advance and bring back the work to get some more. Adolphe, who cheated him over the non-existent Frank Harris manuscript, was an exception, and it is likely that the publisher never even read the legal document for which he had paid out a million francs and 50,000 more in legal fees. Girodias claimed in his autobiography that a contract was an invitation to break it, and that he was better off with a handshake, a sentiment which it is unlikely he ever seriously believed. He was certainly to regret his carelessness about contracts in later years. But a contract was eventually given to Donleavy. The author wanted £250 sent to him in London but this was difficult for Maurice with existing exchange controls. He arranged for the money to be delivered by a Soho bookseller called Cliff Scheiner, a man who made frequent trips to Paris to buy Olympia books and then smuggled them into England. Donleavy worked at revising his novel along the lines suggested, largely by Muffie, who took charge of the project. Eventually *The Ginger Man* in its revised form arrived. Muffie's past experience of living with a writer, knowing his working habits and how to cajole him, had paid off for Girodias.

Donleavy eventually came to Paris. By now Girodias had become very enthusiastic about the novel and felt that he might have a money-maker on his hands. He would publish it first in hardcover, an honour he had given to only a very few books of a literary rather than erotic nature, such as *Watt* and Paul Ableman's *I Hear Voices*. He organized a big dinner for Donleavy, sent Muffie to the Gare du Nord to meet him and take him to his nearby hotel, and then to his studio over La Bûcherie. He had invited a few friends who spoke English and had read the book in manuscript or in proof. This was the period when Girodias was selecting and drinking the great wines of Burgundy, and he sat waiting for his guests while sipping from a newly opened bottle of Morey Saint-Denis. Donleavy arrived. He was dressed in heavy tweeds and looked ill at ease. Throughout the evening he was surly, suspicious and had little to say. Girodias put him between his brother Eric and Michael Gall (who had written *The Sexual Life of Robinson Crusoe* under the pen name Humphrey Richardson), but neither was able to get more than a monosyllable out of him. Great wines were opened and Muffie turned out a superb dinner, but the author drank slowly, looking ahead of him as if sleep-walking. The conversation turned gradually towards subjects other than *The Ginger Man*, Donleavy getting drunker but saying nothing, while the man on either side of him tried vainly to get him into conversation. The evening passed and it was well after midnight when it became obvious that the author could not stand up. They were at the top of the building and it was quite a problem for Maurice and Gall, holding up Donleavy with his arms over their shoulders, to manoeuvre him down the stairs and into the street. Eventually Maurice, who had himself imbibed heavily, managed on his own to get Donleavy back to his hotel.

At this point Donleavy sobered up enough to look him in the eyes and say with a drunken smile: "I've seen you before. Are you Girodias's brother?" He had confused Maurice and Eric!

The next day Girodias had many problems to deal with and he sent Muffie to see Donleavy and take him to lunch. She reported later in the afternoon that the author had eaten nothing but *biscottes* (rusks), drunk mineral water, looked at her glassily, and said nothing. Girodias's dinner and idea of drowning everyone in good Gevrey-Chambertin had served no useful purpose. In fact, it had been a disastrous mistake. In any case, said Muffie, it was time he controlled his own drinking which was affecting his judgement, his health and his pocket.

A letter came from London a few days later. Donleavy complained about what the wines had done to his system – his way, Girodias concluded, of saying thank you. Girodias had pointed out to Muffie that in *The Ginger Man* all the characters drank all the time, but she reminded him that not all fiction was based on real people and real events. Girodias sent off a few copies of some of his more prestigious fiction titles to show Donleavy the company he was in.

The Ginger Man appeared in print and did more or less as well as his other Olympia titles, although this novel about a young American, Dangerfield, getting himself into and out of scrapes in Ireland, usually in a state of alcoholic abandonment, in spite of Donleavy's statement that it had been refused in New York for its obscene content, had practically nothing erotic in it. Then Girodias received a visit from Paul Dinnage on behalf of Neville Armstrong, a London publisher. He was interested in British rights for *The Ginger Man.*

Paul Dinnage, in his role as ambassador, told Girodias that Armstrong intended to publish *The Ginger Man* in Britain, that he (Girodias) did not have a proper contract, and that the exchange of letters that Girodias up to then had considered to be contract enough was only for a single printing. The contract did not apply to Britain and in any case – this emerged in the subsequent correspondence – Donleavy claimed that on his visit to Paris Girodias had authorized him to make his own British arrangements for publication and for his own exclusive benefit. The correspondence was to include references to letters that Girodias had never received and he was sure had never been sent.

How was Armstrong going to manage to publish a book that might have difficulties with the British obscenity laws? Very simple! Donleavy intended to remove one short chapter, in which Dangerfield, on a train, had forgotten to close his fly; the reaction of the other passengers, from embarrassed young women to elderly gentlemen, was the stuff of high comedy: but its removal would inevitably impoverish the book. Other dubious passages could also be removed. Although Donleavy, in his first letter to Girodias, had pointed out that the obscenity was essential to the book, he had now agreed to expurgation.

One of the first persons to be shown the book by Girodias was myself, and shortly after French publication I had signed a contract with him, and acquired British rights. At this point I already had other contracts with Olympia, most notably for *Watt* and the English translation of *Molloy*. I knew Beckett well at this point, had contracts for his other novels written in French with Les Éditions de Minuit, and with Beckett directly for his own translation of these (he revised the *Molloy* translation after Patrick Bowles had finished with it, but thereafter did his own without help). But Girodias was dealing with a different kind of author when it came to *The Ginger Man*. He had to defend his copyright without a proper contract, and had already given a sub-contract to me for Britain and negotiated another with Grove Press for the US. He went to Michael Rubinstein, head of Rubinstein, Nash & Co., the doyen of British publishing solicitors, who agreed to represent him for a sizeable advance payment on his fees.

A letter arrived from Armstrong telling Girodias he had no rights over the novel, that he had never made a valid contract and had no recourse to law. Girodias now suspected that Donleavy and Armstrong had been in league all the time, and that in all probability Armstrong had already contracted *The Ginger Man* before Donleavy had approached him. He had wanted to receive an extra advance and have an edition of the complete, unexpurgated novel in existence. His character Dangerfield was well named: poor Girodias had walked into a field of danger indeed! He took the plane to London, found the Dickensian firm of Rubinstein, Nash & Co. more interested in tea arriving at the proper time and in the proper form than in anything else. They assured him that they would negotiate and that he would hear from them in due course.

Correspondence ensued between Rubinstein and Armstrong's solicitors. At one point there was an indication that Armstrong, whose own reputation was not of the best, might concede some acknowledgement of Girodias's claim to copyright and pay royalties to Olympia instead of directly to the author. But expenses were mounting and a court case would be financially disastrous for everyone. The lawyers were of course interested in keeping the dispute going, but out of court, because in litigation one of them would lose, not money, but some prestige if their client lost. No agreement was made. In the meantime, I too had threatening letters promising to sue me if I published his book under my Olympia contract. I had no intention of expurgating it – I had already taken risks with other books that had frightened other publishers, the novels of Beckett among them – but I decided on this occasion to withdraw. Although I felt that I was legally entitled to publish, I had no intention of going against the author if I could not persuade him to accept me, and it soon became evident that Donleavy was not someone whom publishers – a breed he obviously disliked – could persuade.

4

Denise Clarouin was a literary agent who had been representing mainly British authors in France since the Thirties. Maurice Girodias met her occasionally, knew she had been friendly with his father, about whom she always spoke glowingly, but she never brought him any of the writers she represented. One day she telephoned him to say that an associate of hers wished to see him in connection with an interesting Russian author. Doussia Ergaz came to his offices and told him that she represented a Russian whose forebears she had known since childhood. He came from an aristocratic St Petersburg family, had been educated at Cambridge, and had then gone on to the US, where he was teaching Russian literature at Cornell University. He was a poet, critic and novelist who, in the years since leaving Russia, had tried to write in the languages of the various countries where he had lived: German, French and English. Some of his past work had been published in Russian in the West and was known to educated emigrés. But now he had decided to write only in English. He had just finished a rather "specialized" novel. It had been shown to four New York publishers who knew his past work and respected him highly. But they had been shocked by it. She was certain that Girodias, a publisher known for his taste as well as his courage, would be enchanted by the novel, even seduced by the heroine, whose name was Lolita.

That night Girodias dreamt of young girls and had to wake Muffie to relieve his sexual excitement. The following morning Doussia Ergaz brought him a thick manuscript. The author's brief personal details on the first page did not increase his enthusiasm. Vladimir Nabokov had been born in 1899 in St Petersburg, where his father was then a Minister of State, an elected Liberal member of the Duma; his grandfather had been Minister of Justice under Alexander II. He had been educated internationally, had not returned to Russia after the Revolution and had been an American citizen since 1945. He had carried out advanced research in zoology, was a professor of Russian literature, had been awarded a Guggenheim Fellowship twice for his own writing and had been elected a member of the American Academy of Arts and Letters. Here was the whitest of White Russians! Girodias reflected on the dual nature of so many Russians he knew: Elizabeth, his landlady, whose surface respectability hid a passionate nature and a voyeuristic capacity for sexual intrigue, was only one that came to mind. It was also evident that Doussia Ergaz must have had a flaming affair with

Nabokov in her teens. When he started to look through the manuscript he was startled by its satanic, elegiac quality, its extravagance, its obsessiveness. He took a day and a night to read it. Muffie read it with him and confirmed his reactions.

"There's not even a word that needs changing," she commented. "There's not the slightest fault in grammar or any misprint. When I think of all the work I had to do on the horrible Donleavy!"

"It proves the superiority of the old school over the moderns, what do you expect?"

"I've never heard of this Nabokov. All this passion for entomology!... And butterflies and little girls!"

"And Quilty?"

"Ah, Quilty!"

"And the motels?"

"And what do you know about motels? You've never even set foot in America."

"That's the whole point. This book lets you feel what they're like. This travelling from motel to motel has given me a profound insight into deepest America. I understand it all now... Only a Russian could do that. But I don't like the ending. It's a cinema ending."

"You're not going to ask him to change the ending, I hope?"

"Of course not. But there are other things. He uses too many French words, and of another age, St Petersburg French perhaps."

"That's true. But you're not going to upset him with that. He'll tell you to go to hell."

Girodias telephoned Doussia and expressed his enthusiasm. This was a mistake since she now asked him for an advance of two million francs; he was thinking of offering a quarter of that. But then he thought that it was a long book and he could publish it in two volumes in his Traveller's Companion series. Then he could cover the advance with half the printing. He would like to make a few changes however. He would send suggestions to the author, who would surely understand that they were for his own benefit.

"We'll see," said Doussia. "If I were you I wouldn't complicate matters. He has asked questions about you and he's a little nervous. You've published Miller, Beckett and de Sade; that worries him. He doesn't want to lose his university post."

Girodias protested that it was Nabokov who had approached him through her good offices, not the other way round. He was not very happy when he was then told that Nabokov wanted the book to appear under a pseudonym. He had chosen Sirine as a pen name. But then, she pointed out to Maurice, it could make little difference: his name was not well known to general readers. If he wanted the book he should make no difficulties.

Girodias invited Doussia Ergaz for a drink in Harry's Bar, still the meeting place of American journalists and one of Hemingway's old haunts. He agreed, against all his earlier principles, on a properly drawn-up contract on American lines. Donleavy had taught him a lesson, and in more than one respect, and because of the large advance she was demanding, he also asked for a third of any royalties if the book was ever sub-contracted to another publisher in English. The risks were high, and in French publishing, half of subsidiary rights was in any case the norm. She agreed and wrote to the author.

Nabokov replied directly to Girodias, insisting that he never mention the name of his university, Cornell, although he could say in his publicity that the author taught literature at a big university. Nabokov, in further correspondence, promised to read the proofs himself and even to make some changes that Girodias had asked for. From the ensuing exchange of letters Girodias began to build a picture of his new author in his mind. Nabokov was icily polite in his missives. It became obvious that this covered up his contempt for this pornographic publisher, his only hope of getting his book into print. He was an old-style aristocrat, unhappily teaching American students, his major novels ignored by the literary establishments, his plight as an exile causing him considerable humility, his pride constantly jolted by the crudity of the Americans he daily encountered and by the necessity of accepting the unclean money of this unsavoury Girodias. He must be in a constant state of inner rage.

The letters that arrived had been typed out by his wife Vera, who served as his secretary and probably also as his chess partner. Was this feminine hand not also pushing him to destroy himself? Girodias detected that Vera was an anti-nymphette, the opposite of a Lolita and his terrible dragon. She undoubtedly played a subtle role in toning down the letters, to ensure that the appearance of his book would not be prejudiced by his inner feelings about his new publisher. For Girodias, *Lolita* was to play a determining role in his future. It would bring him wealth, but also sow the seeds of his destruction.

5

One of Girodias's authors was Mason Hoffenberg, an American in Paris, married to a vivacious French girl called Couquite, with whom he had three children. Outwardly a large-eyed, blond, naive American boy, he had intricate ways of torturing his wife and upsetting people. People would laugh when they looked at him without knowing why. He had a suggestive look about him, a deadpan expression suggestive of secret knowledge. He was the author of *Until She Screams*, *Sin for Breakfast* and other commissioned Olympia titles. Now he suggested a new idea to Girodias: a collaboration between himself and Terry Southern, who was being successfully published in New York and already had a reputation as a writer of quality. They had known each other since schooldays and were great friends, and Hoffenberg was convinced that together they could write a commercial novel for Olympia. Their idea was to create a modern version of Voltaire's *Candide*. Girodias agreed with the plan, gave them a contract and an advance, and they started to write *Candy*. Mason Hoffenberg had described it as an ultra-modern satire, in which a Midwestern little adventuress would move to Greenwich Village in New York, and there undertake every possible perversion and opportunity for amorous adventure. Girodias knew them both; he waited expectantly for the result.

The only problem was that Terry Southern was then living in Geneva which made the collaboration difficult. Southern corresponded with Girodias from the end of 1956, pointing out that *Candy* was to be a morality tale in which the heroine gets "raped by Negroes, robbed by Jews, knocked up by Puerto Ricans, etc., finally taking up religion (where she seduces the priest) and turns to Buddhism, dying with the Buddha's stone nose up her vagina when the temple is blown up during the war."* It was obvious that Southern was the dominant partner in the Southern-Hoffenberg co-authorship. And Southern, with other novels being offered by his New York agent, felt that a pen name was needed for *Candy*. He chose Maxwell Kenton and invented a life for him as a principled nuclear scientist who had left his profession for reasons of conscience.

The contract provided for payments in instalments as chapters arrived in the Olympia office. But the two writers had to correspond and send what they were writing back and forth. As they did they became obsessed with their heroine, and sexually excited by the devouring sexuality of their own creation. Only occasionally did Southern come to Paris; his wife had a job in Geneva. But the book progressed because they both needed money, and a wad of manuscript arrived periodically, always accompanied by an urgent demand for cash.

Candy was published with Maxwell Kenton as author and some copies were immediately seized by the police. Girodias changed the title of the second printing to *Lollipop* and republished it as such. Although his correspondence with Southern and Hoffenberg was mainly amicable – the latter was particularly keen to co-author another Maxwell Kenton novel – they both, especially Hoffenberg, became anxious later when royalty statements and money failed to arrive. When the second edition was printed in 1963, Terry Southern tried through a New York attorney to withdraw rights. In the ensuing correspondence, Girodias claimed that, as he had originally commissioned the book for an outright payment, he owned it absolutely. He had subsequently agreed to sign a contract, principally because he recognized that *Candy* was not just a db, but a work of literature, and to enable the authors to enjoy a share of foreign and subsidiary rights, as well as continuing royalties. He had in fact given a great concession for nothing, and the authors now wanted to penalize him for his generosity! Girodias offered to reduce his share of the still-unsold American rights to twenty-five per cent, which proportion could be retained by the authors until they were up to date with royalties. He was at that time in deep financial difficulties. He also commented to his American lawyer, Leon Friedman: "I know that Terry Southern is furious at what he judges to be a total lack of concern on my part for other peoples' difficulties and problems. If I were that kind of person, I would certainly be rich and safe from trouble."*

Girodias also received the manuscript of *Quiet Days in Clichy* from Henry Miller. It had been turned down by New Directions, which had by now published most of his non-obscene books. New Directions had also successfully brought out a *Henry Miller Reader*, which used some material from the banned works, and was edited by his great friend Lawrence Durrell. But *Quiet Days* contained enough explicitly erotic material to frighten James Laughlin, a good publisher but the inheritor of a Calvinist conscience, who had no desire to be prosecuted. It was a small book and Girodias had the idea of padding it out with illustrations of the little suburban town of Clichy, just north of Paris, where Henry Miller had spent some time in the late Thirties. He approached Georges Brassaï, photographer of Paris low life, who was perfectly attuned to catching the atmosphere of period Paris with its underlying feeling of sensuality. Brassaï agreed and took photographs for the book, finding in his files others that were perfectly suited to the locale and style of the novel. And so another Henry Miller came out with Olympia Press.

By the end of the Fifties Girodias had re-established himself as a publisher, and developed an international reputation as the leading producer of erotica in English, but he had also attracted the attention of those critics who were interested in new writing that took a different direction from normal fiction. He also had his enemies in the Home Office in London and in US Customs. The latter were not liable to pay much attention to the Civil Rights interpretations of the freedom of the press under the Constitution, where the Supreme Court was frequently coming out with liberal judgements in favour of books that had been seized by the police. "Banned in Boston" was often the phrase that made the book sell everywhere else. The Sixties, with their iconoclastic breaking down of social and cultural barriers, were not far off. Olympia had much-admired authors on its list and Girodias's office was constantly visited by literary notables, including critics curious about his next publications.

For some time he had been living a practically – nothing was ever absolute with Maurice Girodias – monogamous existence. Muffie was his very capable secretary, his principal editor and his mistress; real friendship was part of their intimacy, the kind of friendship that Girodias had rarely known. He was of course married, but did not live with his wife, who seemed largely unconcerned by this, nor did he often see his two children. He was as happy as he was ever to be.

Then things changed. For three days Muffie did not come to see him, nor did she appear in the office. He was not too concerned, but it was unusual. One Friday morning he walked into the office and Muffie was there. She told him, very calmly, that she was leaving – the job, the office and him. She needed to be alone. She gave no reason. She had advertised for a secretary for him in the Paris *Herald Tribune*, had interviewed several possible women, had selected the most suitable, someone very beautiful, very capable and very well informed about literature. She was waiting in the next room. Muffie brought her in. Her name was Miriam Worms. She was Jewish, from Danzig, and most of her family had been killed in the war. She had been educated at Oxford and the Sorbonne. She introduced them and left. He was not to see her again.

He had a new personal assistant who would be only that. She was ravishing-looking, but married. The reason she had to work was to help her husband, a young sociologist, to finish his studies.

Chapter Six

The Trials of Girodias

1

After three years of sharing an office, both Girodias and Pauvert found that they needed more space. Their staff had grown. Pauvert told Girodias that he had seen an old building at 7 Rue Saint-Séverin, almost next to the church of the same name, and the building was empty. He had made enquiries and it could be rented. Why didn't Girodias move there? Girodias asked why it had to be him to move. They tossed a coin and Girodias lost, doubly so if one looks at the long-term consequences.

Girodias knew the street well, just around the corner from La Bûcherie, which he had recently left after a falling-out with Elizabeth. It was also not far from the Rue de Nesle. He found it to be an old, crumbling building with an enormous amount of space on five floors, going back to the fourteenth century, some of it to the twelfth. It had big rooms, a big cellar, but no modern amenities whatsoever; it was also very damp and much of the timbering was rotten.

Girodias's reason for leaving La Bûcherie was a new relationship in his life. After the departure of Muffie, he had taken to sitting alone by the stone fireplace that was the special feature of La Bûcherie. It had a comfortable armchair on each side where lovers often spent time over a drink, looking into each other's eyes. In cold weather a large log fire blazed all day and was kept going until the restaurant closed in the early hours of the morning. He was sitting alone one day, gloomily looking into the flames, when he saw a hand offering him a large balloon glass. It contained Armagnac and the hand belonged to the hostess or manageress, a tall, charming, very attractive lady he had vaguely noticed from time to time.

"I thought this might cheer you up," she said with a friendly smile. "You look so sad. My name is Michelle by the way. May I join you?"

She had recently been put in charge of the restaurant by Elizabeth, who was away for a few weeks. During the conversation she mentioned that she had a commission to carry out. Maurice was considerably behind

144

in his rent. Girodias had in the previous few minutes already fallen under her charm, had just invited her out to have dinner with him, an invitation which was politely refused, but they had been getting on well together. And here suddenly, was business: she was doing Elizabeth's dirty work under the guise of a flirtation. He felt a real enmity towards his landlady for humiliating him in this way.

That evening he dined alone at La Bûcherie and on impulse scribbled on a corner of his newspaper: "What about that dinner, Michelle?" He tore the message off and gave it to her the next time she passed his table. She glanced at it, then at him, and he felt that an electric current had passed between them. The dinner, a day or so later, had been anticipated by them both with excitement. A good bottle of Burgundy, the soft conversation and the rising sense of occasion affected him strangely. Back in his car, with Michelle beside him, not knowing where to go next, he began driving out of Paris, and he did not stop until he reached the sea in Normandy. A new love affair had begun.

Michelle was breaking up a marriage, and had a small daughter, who was then staying with her grandmother. It was not possible under the circumstances for Maurice to stay in his room over the restaurant, nor for Michelle, also beholden to Elizabeth, who had taken her under her wing, to stay at the restaurant. They decided to flee together and live together. Early one morning they each left their separate lodgings and moved to a hotel, the Lutétia, because Maurice had always liked its romantic Gothic architecture. They met for lunch at La Brasserie Lorraine on the Right Bank and then moved to the hotel. Feeling like teenage young lovers, they had actually eloped! Elizabeth was sent flowers and a present. But she did not forgive them.

Michelle had for some time been interested in opening her own restaurant, and it occurred to Maurice that she was unlikely to find a cheaper rent in the Saint-Michel district than the building he had just inspected at the instigation of Pauvert. In the middle of the fifth *arrondissement*, it was an area jammed with small hotels, jazz clubs and boutiques, largely an Arab quarter, with the narrow streets packed with tourists. He knew it better than any other part of Paris.

Michelle Forgeois saw the commercial possibilities of the building with its big spaces, and she became the driving force of its conversion. She soon felt a compulsion to fill it completely. All Maurice needed for his publishing activities was one floor or part of one floor and this left at least four that could have other uses not counting the cellar. An architect was needed and Michelle thought of one who answered Maurice's description: he had to be young, original, in need of work and with a touch of genius in his character. It would not be easy to modernize such a dilapidated building and turn it into a restaurant. Girodias, his enthusiasm now rising, began to see the ownership of a restaurant as an excellent idea: it would provide steady cash flow and give another string to his bow; he began to picture himself as a successful restaurateur. Such people are treated like royalty in France, and it would give him the kind of respectability he had never enjoyed. And then Michelle had all the right qualifications to run it. She had flair, was a good organizer, enjoyed parties, had good taste and knew what Parisians wanted.

Michelle's architect was called Jean-Pierre: he was suitably brilliant and incredibly eccentric. He went everywhere with a crow perched on his shoulder, and carried a piece of putrefying meat around with him to feed it. He never washed and looked as ill as his crow, whose feathers were constantly dropping off. He spent much time wandering around the building, looking at it, and began sleeping in a corner, but he never came up with any concrete ideas. They realized they had to start looking for a new architect, but Girodias at this moment had many other matters on his mind, and he left the problem of finding one to Michelle. He had at least installed his office on the first floor and could get on with his work.

Shortly after moving in, he received a visit from Inspector Laffont, the same Brigade Mondaine policeman who had interrogated him about the *Story of O*. Laffont had heard about *Lolita*, which had just been published in two volumes. He wanted a copy.

"Do you want to buy it?" asked the publisher.

"You're joking," said the policeman. "And I advise you to take another tone. You're in deep trouble. It's very clever to publish pornography in English, but don't think you'll get away with it because of the language. I want a copy of every book you have in stock."

Eventually he left with twenty-five different volumes. Fortunately many others were out of stock at the time. The atmosphere between the two men was electric.

An hour later Girodias lunched with a printer, M. Lefevre, who had produced books for both Pauvert and Olympia Press. Lefevre already knew all about Laffont's visit; he had just talked to him. He explained that as a printer he had to be on good terms with the police. He didn't want any trouble. Maurice's defiant attitude was not very wise, he said. But he had some advice to give him.

"He's a very dangerous man, Laffont," he said. "He can be very nasty and you'd do well to humour him. Now, I have a suggestion. He's just had an accident with his car and he has some heavy damages to pay. He hasn't told me about all this for nothing. You could help him out and he'll help you. He knows that *Lolita* is a serious novel, not just a bit of pornography. He can ignore it, or he can take action against it. It's up to you."

"If I start paying Laffont, I'll have the whole Brigade Mondaine to deal with. They'll all want a pay-off and I can't afford it."

"You'd better think about it seriously. He's given you a chance."

Girodias did think about it, but decided to do nothing. Time passed. Then, on 20th December, the *Journal Officiel* was published. It contained the announcement that twenty-five books published by Olympia Press were officially banned under Article 14 of the Law of 1881 against subversive literature. They were not to be distributed or sold anywhere in France. Laffont had gone to the top, and had managed to get every title he had removed from the Olympia office put on the list, including novels by Beckett, Genet and Queneau.

The Queneau novel was one of the best-sellers of the day in French: *Zazie dans le métro*. Girodias had bought the English-language rights and asked his brother Eric Kahane to translate it. It was also being filmed by Louis Malle. Raymond Queneau was one of the most revered literary figures of the moment, the nearest France had produced to a James Joyce, whom Queneau had known in the Thirties. Queneau was a man with an ability to use the French language as a philosophical tool, a source of humour, and a semantic game. His novels, written on many levels, could also delight on many levels. *Zazie dans le métro*, a story about a little girl from the provinces in Paris for the first time and staying with unconventional relatives while her mother spends the weekend with her lover, had its erotic moments, but was certainly not pornographic. Queneau was also a mathematician, philosopher, poet and the editor of the very prestigious *Encyclopédie de la Pléiade*, and he had his own offices at Gallimard, where he acted as advisory editor on different projects. Now his current best-seller could not be sold in English.

Gallimard became very nervous, because they had bought the French rights to *Lolita* and Eric Kahane had also translated that for them, this time from English into French. The attention that Girodias was getting could easily rub off onto other publishers, and affect the translations of Henry Miller and other authors if the 1881 law and the later one of 1949, passed by Jules Moch, were both enforced. Girodias had no choice: he had to go to court to defend his books, and his lawyers did not offer him too much hope of success.

It was *Lolita* on which everything turned. This story of a fourteen-year-old nymphette who seduces her guardian after her parents are killed and then travels all over the US with him so that he can cover up their relationship, does not lack humour or literary quality; the situation of this parody of American motel life is more provocative than the actual text. But no one ever knows how judges will react to literature which tends to outflank legal definitions. The lawyers that Girodias consulted all used the same metaphor: he was Don Quixote charging windmills. It was Maître Jean Lemanissier who finally took up the case and appeared for Olympia Press in the Cour de Cassation, the High Court, to which only the top rank of legal counsel is accredited to plead. Girodias had not done well in the courts previously, and in the expectation of losing he decided to at least make it a scandal of importance. With the Dreyfus Case in mind, he started to prepare a pamphlet to be called 'L'Affaire Lolita'. Lemanissier also wrote to the Minister pointing out that the whole case against Girodias was unjust and would make the government look ridiculous in the eyes of all civilized people. Nabokov was asked for a statement to appear in the pamphlet. He wrote: "My defence of the book on the moral level is the book itself. I feel in no way obliged to say anything further... and on the aesthetic level I am totally indifferent to the opinion of judges, either French or English, or to other tribunals, or in general to all the mentally retarded who want to bring their judgements against my work."

Girodias did not consider the author's statement very helpful, but he went ahead with his pamphlet. 5,000 copies were sent out – to the press, well-known authors, politicians, judges and other members of the legal profession. The book had been read by Graham Greene, who praised it. This led to an attack on him in London by John Gordon of the *Daily Express*, a professional philistine if ever there was one, who had of course not read the book, but never missed an opportunity to attack anything intellectual in a way that could titillate the lowbrow readers of his newspaper. British Customs, surprisingly, cleared the book, Girodias's first important victory in that respect.

Over a drink at the Café de Flore, Raymond Queneau, the first French voice to praise *Lolita*, agreed to help with the campaign in France. It was he who had accepted the book for Gallimard and he would stick to his guns, and speak personally to Gaston Gallimard, the aged founder of the company. Although now retired, he still had a patriarch's influence over his son Claude, a rather timid businessman, who had taken over the company after the death of his elder brother Michel, who was killed in a road accident together with their most celebrated author, Albert Camus. Claude was no crusader and he had a great deal to lose if he attracted the unfavourable attention of the Minister of the Interior and the police. Queneau also had much influence in the serious newspapers.

Girodias went to see Georges Bataille as well, another *éminence grise* of the French literary establishment, an author who had written fiction of extreme erotic perversity, some of which had been translated by the *Merlin* group for Olympia after having been first published by Pauvert. Queneau and Bataille were both respected members of the literary establishment with an underlying interest in cerebral and erotic sexuality, and both had written pornographic works under pen names, Sally Mara (Queneau) and Pierre Angélique (Bataille). Many other French intellectuals promised support and the correspondence columns of the press discussed *Lolita*, which became, although no one could now obtain it, a cause célèbre.

Not only in France! It was discussed in the American and British press as well. Girodias now had several propositions for foreign rights. In America there were several interested publishers; McDowell, Obolensky was the first to make a serious offer. Ivan Obolensky, one of the two partners in this new publishing firm, the son of one of the best-known White Russian figures in New York, who led the Czarist movement there, came to Paris, and Girodias went to meet him in the Hotel Lotti. Obolensky said that he wanted to build an avant-garde list and *Lolita* would fit very well. He had little money and proposed that instead of giving an advance and normal royalties, they would pay twenty per cent, instead of the normal ten per cent: no up-front money, but a fortune in royalties if the book sold well, which he was sure it would. Barney Rosset of Grove Press was also interested, but Girodias did not trust Barney and was sure that he would not come up with any sizeable sum of money (in that he was wrong – Barney had money and could afford it). Money *now*, in a lump sum, was Girodias's principal priority.

At this time Maurice also had other problems. Several new imprints had started up in Paris, publishing commissioned pornography in imitation of Olympia. Although none of them approached the quality of Girodias's authors, either those with established literary names or those writing under pseudonyms, they were making a considerable dent in his market, both in Europe and outside. After all, few of the readers and collectors of pornography were interested in literary quality: they wanted to be sexually aroused. But none of his competitors were making much money: they did not know how to distribute their books, they had trouble in finding authors, and practically none of them knew enough English to have much idea of what they were publishing; the competitors were mainly little gangsters in any case. Usually, after a while, they offered their stock and imprints to Girodias.

Maurice had also lost money on books seized by British Customs. He had a prime customer called Cliff Scheiner, who operated in Soho, selling through little backstreet pornography shops, the same man who had obliged him by giving money to Donleavy. Cliff had a friend who imported Olympia books to London in a truck, hidden underneath fruits, vegetables and other goods, hundreds of copies at a time. But the friend, Tony, was caught and sent to jail for six months. The books were confiscated and Cliff naturally did not want to pay for what he had not received.

But his biggest problem was of course the Cour de Cassation. Usually a few months after a new title was published, it would appear on the official list of books that could not be sold, distributed or offered for sale in a bookshop. Sales had to be secret and the books had to be kept under the counter, which considerably reduced the numbers bought, or else bought directly from his offices. Time after time he was brought before the Tribunal correctionnel, a magistrate's court. The charge was "*outrage aux bonnes moeurs par la voie du livre*" (outrage against good morals by means of books), "OBM" for short. He was not charged with the offence of publishing several books at once; that would have shortened the pleasure of the operation. Each book was a separate trial, and each time he was condemned to three months' imprisonment and forbidden to practise the profession of publisher for three years. His lawyers always succeeded in getting the sentence suspended, at least for the time being, and having developed the habit of leaving the court in temporary freedom, Girodias basked in a false security. Most of the time his lawyer was Maître Emile-Jean Bomsel, who obtained an amnesty from imprisonment until the next presidential election, when the censorship laws might be relaxed – they might also be hardened.

On one occasion he was charged with a book called *Lust in Samarkand*, published with no imprint on it by one of his rivals. Laffont had done him the honour of assuming it was his book. He was formally accused in the court.

"*Monsieur, le président*," said Maurice to the judge, "I've never seen this book in my life before. I would never publish a book with such an idiotic title."

"It is judged that you have published a pornographic novel in English called *Lust in Samarkand*," went on the judge, ignoring him, "and you are hereby condemned to three months' imprisonment, and for three years you are forbidden to exercise the profession of a publisher."

"But this is pure Kafka."

"How dare you. A serious insult to the judge. That will be nine months' imprisonment."

Girodias was certain that the judge had never heard of Kafka or of his masterpiece, *The Trial*. And even if he had, he had probably thought it a scatological book.

"Clerk of the Court, note it down. Nine months for insulting the bench. Next case…"

Lolita was another matter, because he was appealing against the sentence, citing the fact that the book was in print with Gallimard, and had been praised by Queneau and others. Three days before the judgement, on 14th February 1958, a telegram came from New York, telling him that Nabokov had agreed to give the American contract to Putnam, a well-known New York imprint. But it was now too late to introduce new evidence. Girodias sat in the court while the judgement was read. He had noticed that French lawyers all seemed to have the ability to sleep on their feet in the courtroom while the case was being tried, and Maître Lemanissier was no exception. He rocked gently while the judgement was being read. Girodias was not sure if he was listening or not. But the words electrified the defendant.

"We've won, did you hear?" he said to his counsel.

"So we have," exploded Lemanissier, suddenly awake. "Well, well… Mind you, I was always sure we would win. Are you happy now?"

"Well, of course… But are you sure? Did you really hear it? I haven't made a mistake, have I?"

It was a historic day for Maurice Girodias and he celebrated it properly. A telegram was sent to Nabokov: "YOU WON L'AFFAIRE LOLITA, CONGRATULATIONS. GIRODIAS."

2

In Britain I had already offered Girodias a contract for *Lolita*, and after a minimum of negotiations he signed it. But problems immediately arrived. Nabokov wanted to know who his publisher was going to be. He had approved Gallimard, but my name was not acceptable. A few enquiries had turned up the information that during the early Fifties

I had published many American authors who, because of their left-wing activities or previous books, had been unable to continue being published in the US: Alvah Bessie, Albert Maltz, Martha Dodd, John Wexley, Corliss Lamont, and especially Alger Hiss, whose book on his own trial had gained me the reputation in some circles of being soft on communism: anything that was not of the unthinking doctrinaire right was so described in those days. Vladimir Nabokov, like nearly all émigrés from Russia and Eastern Europe, was very right-wing and opposed to liberalism of any kind. He made it clear to Girodias that he did not want me to be his British publisher; various approaches through third parties failed to soften him in any way. Barney Rosset of Grove Press was asked to help and tried to do so, having failed to obtain the book himself, and being at the time a friend and collaborator of mine on many other books; but when he realized that the objection was political, he desisted.

The American publisher was to be Walter Minton, a brash young man who had taken over Putnam on the death of his father. The way he became interested in *Lolita* will be related in the next few pages. My first meeting with him was unexpected and unpleasant. I returned to my office from a lunch date one day to find a strange man sitting at my desk, his feet up on it, busily reading my private correspondence.

"What the devil are you doing?" I exploded.

"Are you Calder?" he asked, in no way discomfited and keeping his feet where they were.

"Yes. You're sitting at my desk and reading my private letters."

"Yes, very interesting too. I'm Walter Minton. I've come to tell you that you're not going to publish *Lolita*."

"I have a contract for it."

"Yes, with Girodias. But Nabokov's not going to let you. And you know why? Because you're a commie. He's checked you out. And he'll sue if you publish."

My first meeting with the charming Walter Minton!

3

Nabokov's attitude was a major disappointment to me. The book carried certain dangers with it, but it was obviously a milestone in current fiction and likely to be a best-seller. Publishing at the time much worthy but not very commercial literature, by authors whose fame lay largely in the future, I had great need of such a book. But I could not very well go against the total opposition of the author. The answer must lie in a collaboration with another publisher.

I approached George Weidenfeld of Weidenfeld & Nicolson. George was himself an émigré who had come to Britain from Vienna before the war. I suggested to him that I would share the benefit of my contract with him if his name was acceptable to Nabokov, and, failing Nabokov's agreement, help him, through Girodias, to become the nominal publisher, while I remained co-publisher, sharing the risks and benefits as a secret partner. It would prevent legal conflict and, most importantly, get rid of any competition from other publishers. Many of my British rivals were now interested, most notably André Deutsch, who had already been in touch with Minton in New York. There also remained the very real risk of a prosecution for obscenity, even though the book in the Olympia two-volume edition had succeeded in getting through British customs.

I had at this point known Maurice Girodias for some years. I had contracted *Molloy* from him and the next two Beckett novels written in French, *Malone Dies* and *The Unnamable*, from Les Éditions de Minuit and was preparing to bring them out in a single volume as a trilogy, which was the author's wish. *Watt* was also contracted and waiting to appear, but to keep down my capital commitment I was importing the American edition from Grove Press. However, although Girodias and I were much in contact in the late Fifties, in his own memoirs he gives the impression that we first met at the time of *Lolita* and recalls that meeting as follows:

At the end of the afternoon I was alone with Michelle in my office when the door opened and a little compact gentleman came in, looking like a traveller in a hurry. His short moustaches, in the RAF style, looked unreal.

"Excuse me for bothering you, the door was open, and I'm looking for Maurice Girodias... Sorry to disturb you..."

"It doesn't matter, the harm's done. You've found him. I'm Maurice Girodias."

"My name is John Calder," he said in correct French. "I'm a London publisher..."

Michelle left the room with an amused smile, and the publisher's eyes followed her out with the speculative look of a man who likes women. Something in his favour! His little red moustache intrigued me: why was he walking around with a false moustache? I asked him to sit down and he told me about his London publishing house, his hope of finding new and interesting writers, his admiration for Olympia... the kind of speech I had learnt to distrust, because I had heard it too often before.*

Girodias then relates that I invited him to have lunch with Barney Rosset the next day at Quasimodo, a restaurant on the Île Saint-Louis. Although I have no recollection of that occasion, it was certainly a favourite watering hole of mine at the time, and such a lunch probably happened, but not after a first meeting. I had in any case shaved off my moustache by the beginning of 1958. If *Lolita* was the topic of lunch, it happened in 1958, otherwise much later. But it may well have been the beginning of what Girodias describes: a three-sided alliance of publishers who saw their activities as a form of intellectual adventure, each discovering new talent and sharing it with the others. The image that each of us was developing in the eyes of the book trade, and the journalistic publisher-watchers of the day, was one of non-commercial quality publishing, the promotion of literary lists that were iconoclastic, bucking current literary trends fostered by the establishment that did most of the reviewing, and politically anti-authoritarian and libertarian. "Idealism" was in the air, appealing to a new generation, not then the dirty word – synonymous with uncommercial crankiness – that it was to become twenty years later. All three of us had already had problems with censorship, and the future was to increase and deepen that experience. A bond was formed that in spite of later quarrels, recriminations and even lawsuits, was never broken. It is also fair to say that all three of us were, in different ways, eccentric, stubborn and motivated by our own literary convictions, which were far from identical, but most of the time coincided near enough.

It was at the Frankfurt Book Fair that I struck a deal with George Weidenfeld, and introduced him to Girodias, who then put George's name to Nabokov as an alternative to mine. Nabokov agreed. I signed a contract with Weidenfeld whereby I was to be a secret, but equal, partner. We began to prepare for British publication, but several problems intervened almost immediately.

Weidenfeld decided that legal advice was necessary (I did not) and brought in the firm of London solicitors that had the greatest experience of libel law, although it had never been much concerned with obscene libel. The Obscene Publications Act 1959 had not yet been passed and the watershed of the *Lady Chatterley* trial was still some time in the future. But there was a general feeling among educated people that the law was an ass where obscenity was concerned; the authorities were in any case more bothered about the appearance of four-letter words in print than anything else, obscenity being ill-defined as "a tendency to corrupt and deprave". There was much discussion in the press about obscenity and Parliament was already debating the new bill that would eventually become an Act, which, as discussed previously, incorporated a recognition of literary merit as a justification for what some people might see as obscenity. The problem with *Lolita* was that a fourteen-year-old girl was the heroine, that she was sexually active, and Peter Carter-Ruck, the solicitor, warned that a prosecution was likely: he advised that publication not be rushed. To me it seemed that the climate was exactly right: we knew of well-known writers like Graham Greene who would defend the book, and it was available in other countries. Weidenfeld, however, had a second problem: his partner, Nigel Nicolson, was a Tory MP in Bournemouth, an ultra-conservative constituency full of *Daily Express* readers. Nicolson had already invoked the wrath of his constituents by rebelling against Anthony Eden at the time of the Suez Canal Crisis and had resigned as a junior minister. To be involved with a controversial book might well end his political career. In fact, in the end, it did!

The expenses incurred by employing Carter-Ruck, and Weidenfeld's practice of making his own decisions without consulting me, were such that I realized that the role of sleeping partner was an unenviable one. Weidenfeld was indecisive and nervous about proceeding to publish. Expenses were going up, I was asked to contribute to them with no immediate prospect of any return, and because of the need for secrecy where my role was concerned, I was at a constant disadvantage. In the end I agreed to give Weidenfeld the entire benefit of the contract and to receive ten per cent of the profits. Not only did Weidenfeld have a best-seller when he did finally bring it out, but he subsequently published all the other novels of Nabokov and had another world-class author in his catalogue.

Gallimard also published the book in France where it did well, and Rowohlt made it a best-seller in Germany, and in many other countries, as it became translated worldwide, it did equally well. It made a fortune for Girodias, especially from the American sales. It was in many ways the most important event of his professional life.

4

While the Paris trial of *Lolita* was still in the future, and before Laffont's visit to Girodias in his new office on the Rue Saint-Séverin, Walter Minton, the young New York publisher, who had recently inherited G.P.

Putnam from his father, went to a cocktail party, where he met and was intrigued by a tall, well-shaped showgirl called Rosemary Ridgewell. She was the star of a nude review at the Latin Quarter, a New York nightclub. This magnificent creature caught the eye of most of the men present, and Minton remembered that he had seen her dancing nude in her show. He started a conversation.

"What's a girl like you doing here?" he asked her.

"A girl like me probably knows more about contemporary literature than an ignorant publisher like you, joy boy," was the response. "If you'd listen to me, I could make you a fortune."

"Yes? How's that?"

"If I tell you what to publish and you make a million, how much will you give me?"

"Well, that depends," he hedged.

"I mean big money, real millions. I know of a book that's dynamite."

"You'd get the usual scouting fee, two per cent… if it really sells."

Walter Minton was not a reader. He had inherited a publishing company, but he had little idea of how to run it. But he did want to make money. Rosemary told him about *Lolita*, which she had bought and read on a recent visit to Paris. As a result Girodias received a letter a week or so later asking for American rights. At this point Nabokov had made it clear that he did not want either McDowell, Obolensky or Grove Press as his American publisher. He wanted an established company with a literary reputation, but none of the obvious ones were interested. He had however heard of Putnam and agreed that they were suitable. Girodias finally offered a contract to Minton: the advance of $6,000 was not big, but he negotiated a royalty of 17.5 per cent, having produced Obolensky's letter offering twenty per cent. This, compared to normal royalties, which start at ten per cent and rise to a maximum of fifteen per cent, was exceptionally good, providing of course that the book sold well. To Nabokov $6,000 sounded good. He was always worried about money and Girodias, observing this, later recalled the events in his memoirs, and used his negotiations with Nabokov to air his credo:

For the analytical intelligence and imagination of a man like Vladimir Nabokov to be pushed into a corner by the arrival of financial considerations onto the scene seemed to me to be depressing and sad: money, the lack of it, the worry about penury, are as much the leitmotifs of an artist's life as of a tramp's, of the little employee as of the rich, and by definition of all the world's without exception, whether one has money or not, a great deal or a little, often or never.

Because money is in reality only a feeble myth, something never quite attainable that has the passing allure of reality because we constantly forget that it has no concrete existence but is only a convention that is fluid and deceiving. The laws of credit, the hazards of the stock exchange make it clear enough: it is enough to see how we live, and why we live, to be able to say that the fiction of money has substituted itself for all authentic values of life, love and beauty, the spirit, pleasure. Money is an anorexic malady which we allow to conquer us, an abandonment of the will to live, like other illnesses, which end by falling in love, with their own sickness. Alas, three times alas!

If I utter a few vain sighs on the subject of money, it is because this fetid presence has never ceased to pursue me from one end of my existence to another, and that the act of rejecting it, despising it, trying to exclude it from my life, has only aggravated my dependence on it: I am therefore the victim of my own insight.*

This may sound a little unconvincing coming from a man who was always looking for money, certainly enjoyed it when it came his way and spent much of his career veering from poverty to riches and back again. But his very refusal to allow money or the lack of it to affect in any significant way his lifestyle or outlook (and he was certainly never miserly at any time, nor was he concerned about the future in money terms by trying to protect it when he had it, or economize when he didn't), says much for him. He was no hypocrite and always generous when he could be.

5

Lolita came out in New York. Girodias suddenly received a telegram from Walter Minton, announcing that he and Rosemary were coming to Paris to celebrate. It was no surprise: only a short time earlier he had received a cable to tell him that *Lolita* was number one on the *New York Times* best-seller list. Maurice was passing a few days in the south of France at Biot with Michelle when the news arrived. It made him the happiest man in the world at that moment: what better than to be in love, to be away from all problems and to receive news like this!

Lolita had sold more than 200,000 copies in hardcover in the US and the publisher Fawcett wanted to do the paperback, offering an advance that represented a sale of more than two million copies. It remained on the best-seller list and, although it was dethroned eventually by *Dr Zhivago*, it remained solidly in second place. Girodias began to build hopes of selling other books to Minton, especially Iris Owens's *The Woman Thing*, a novel in which the New York spirit is transposed to Paris; Girodias saw great possibilities in this novel which he described as being sulphurous, perverse and carnal, and capable of seducing the Sphinx of Giza.

The first Girodias-Minton meeting took place at L'Hôtel d'Orsay, a surprising place for a rich young American to stay. It was an old hotel on the Left Bank, much gone to seed, usually putting up travellers arriving at the station underneath it. It was later to become Jean-Louis Barrault's theatre, and even later a state museum. Girodias arrived in time for the appointment at noon, announced himself, and waited in the hall until down the stairs came a young businessman wearing glasses, and beside him the most perfect pair of legs that Girodias had ever seen. As he looked upwards towards the great nineteenth-century curving stairway he saw that the rest of the body perfectly suited the legs: it was Rosemary, the cabaret dancer, who had recommended the novel to Minton.

"Hi, Maurice," said Minton. "At last we meet… let me introduce you to Rosemary Ridgewell." He had left his wife behind with the excuse that he had to pay a short, urgent visit to Paris on business, and Rosemary had insisted on taking her place. She wanted to meet Maurice Girodias. Her presence explained the choice of hotel; he was unlikely to meet other Americans there.

Girodias asked where they would like to lunch and Rosemary immediately answered that she had heard the best place was La Tour d'Argent. This, the most expensive restaurant in Paris, was not on Maurice Girodias's current budget, but he acquiesced with the best grace he could muster. Rosemary was something else!

At lunch, in the elegance of the restaurant overlooking Notre Dame, a view Girodias knew well from another angle, that of La Bûcherie, she behaved exactly as a vamp from an old Hollywood film would have done, putting her pearl-grey spectacles into a drinking glass, bringing a golden swizzle-stick on a chain out from between her magnificent breasts and signalling with it at the sommelier to indicate that she wanted champagne. A magnum of *Dom Perignon* was soon produced. Girodias chewed his lips at the thought of what this was going to cost him at Tour d'Argent prices. Throughout the meal she was giving Minton little kicks under the table. She did most of the talking.

"What I must tell you," she said, "is that without me, Walter would never have heard about this book."

And without me, thought Girodias, neither would she! She told him that she had been offered a two per cent commission, but Walter was trying to get out of it as he was paying a 17.5 per cent royalty to Girodias. No doubt she would eventually get the promise in writing as a proof of his feelings for her after she had completed her seduction. But she was giving him a difficult time at table, concentrating on Maurice, now totally under her spell. Claude Terrail, owner of the restaurant, alerted by his staff that some unusual Americans were there for the first time, came over to their table, employed all his Gallic charm, and kissed Rosemary's hand. A bottle of vintage Gevrey-Chambertin followed the magnum of Dom Perignon; Maurice mentally totted up what his *addition* was coming to. Rosemary and Walter quaffed the wines like seltzer without tasting them. Walter was finally forced to admit, his mood getting blacker, that he had never read the book. He was talked about by Rosemary as if not present, while Maurice was given the full force of her presence, her eyes and jutting breasts hypnotizing him. Walter, picking at the *canard pressé*, said he wanted to go back to the hotel, but she ignored him and ordered *crêpes suzette* for everyone. After coffee and Armagnac, they were given a tour of the wine cellar by Terrail, while Girodias tried furtively to count the money he had on him. Would he have enough left for a tip?

But back at the table when the bill arrived Rosemary took it, handed it to Minton, smiled at Maurice, and said that Walter would of course pay for lunch. The much-relieved Girodias then suggested that they could see each other again in the evening and he might bring a friend.

He took them back to their hotel, arranged to meet them for a late dinner, got through the afternoon in his office with the help of Alka Seltzer and eventually went to the Café de Flore, where he had suggested they gather. With him was Iris Owens. His purpose in bringing her was to interest Walter Minton in her writing, but she was at that time a fairly constant companion, a good friend, albeit one whom he preferred not to sleep with given his other sexual commitments. Iris was not particularly pleased by this reserve on his part, but she accepted it for the time being. And she certainly wanted to have an American publisher. Girodias told her about the lunch, pointing out that American publishers in general were usually about as unexciting and ignorant as Walter.

"You should go there yourself, Maurice," she told him. "You would do very well in the States."

"I think I belong in Paris," he answered. "They don't drink good Burgundy in America."

"But now, after *Lolita*, you'd never look back. And think of all your condemnations to prison! They'll get you eventually. Especially with de Gaulle in power. You need an escape route."

A taxi drew up and a gorgeous leg appeared as the door opened. "That's her," said Maurice excitedly to Iris. "Rosemary and her legs! I wonder if they've been fucking this afternoon."

"I don't think so," said Iris. "He looks too grumpy. So that's Walter! What a pity."

There were introductions. Rosemary brushed her lips against Maurice's cheek, while squeezing her thigh against his. The two women sized each other up. Iris was wearing a shiny black raincoat which showed off her glistening dark skin, high-heeled black deer-skin shoes and, to all appearances, nothing else. Walter looked her up and down questioningly... He wanted to know if... There was considerable tension in the air. Rosemary took her champagne swizzle-stick from between her breasts, but Walter with a gesture made her put it back. Girodias quickly ordered a glass of champagne for Rosemary.

"Ah, thank you, darling," cooed Rosemary, pinching his leg. Neither of them had any intention of having dinner, and Maurice assumed that they wanted to see Paris by night. If they wanted him to take them to the Lido or the Folies Bergère, they had better think again.

"I know an amusing place," he said. "It's a lesbian club, a little depraved, but at least there are no tourists."

Rosemary showed enthusiasm, but Walter only scowled. Probably he had wanted to go to the Folies Bergère. A little while later they had a table at the Montagne Sainte-Geneviève where wild dancing was going on to a paso doble, and the atmosphere was frantic. Walter remarked sourly that no doubt Rosemary felt at home there as she earned her living by— But his words were cut short by a resounding slap to his face, which was followed by an uppercut back from Walter, after which she seized the whisky bottle on the table and cracked him over the skull with it. Iris and Maurice tried to separate them as a transvestite waiter came up with the bill and an order to leave. Girodias stuffed some banknotes into the waiter's hand and they left hastily. Walter Minton pushed Rosemary into a taxi, and, without a word and a desultory wave of the hand, they drove off.

Girodias slept badly, waking frequently after a series of nightmares, but he had fallen at last into a deep sleep when the telephone rang. It was Rosemary on the line. He was still in his room at La Bûcherie at this time, in a big bed that had been designed by Elizabeth before she had offered him the room. It had little shards of mirror, angled in different directions and in different colours, which had always inspired the laughter and the erotic interest of the series of ladies who had been there with him.

"Hello, darling," she said in a clear and seductive voice. "Are you awake? Would you like some croissants for breakfast? Make some coffee, I'll be right over."

He shook himself, remembering the night before. Rosemary, croissants, coffee! Where were the aspirin? Was he still dreaming?

The doorbell rang and she walked in, a little bag of croissants in her hand. She threw her arms around his neck, sipped the coffee he had just made, threw her beret in a corner and started to take off her clothes. At the same time she was inspecting the room, and laughing with each new discovery.

"Now look, Rosemary!"

"How dark it is in here."

She laughed delightedly at discovering the large satin bed, the little mirrors set into it at different angles, and the other erotic eccentricities that had been designed by Elizabeth. Girodias, still in a daze, put Mozart's *Prague Symphony* onto his record player. Rosemary took him by the arm and pulled him towards the bed.

After two passionate hours Girodias began to sip his cold coffee and suddenly asked: "But what about Walter? What happened?"

"Oh, Walter! He left early this morning. Just got up and packed and walked out... back to New York. At least the hotel's paid and I have my ticket to get back."

"He didn't even leave you some flowers?"

"Nothing. Not a cent. Not a word. He's a bad boy. I hate him, he's so stupid."

Girodias contemplated the situation. He was just as badly off, worse, than Walter Minton. In financial terms he had probably just lost his best American contact. Minton would turn Nabokov, already suspicious and disdainful, against him totally.

Rosemary liked the bed and didn't want to leave it, but a man had to give his body a chance to recover, after all! He eventually managed to get her outside to see a little of Paris – the Eiffel Tower (she insisted on going to the top), the *Tchamps Elayzis*, the Bois de Boulogne – and then on to a candlelit dinner, followed by a silent return to the room and the mirrored bed.

It was a long night of lovemaking. They both knew that Rosemary had to leave the next day. Exhausted, Girodias tried to keep awake by caressing her, but sleep overtook him. He woke to hear glass breaking in the bathroom. Rosemary was pulling all the drawers out of a little cabinet and breaking all the bottles of toiletries in them, throwing everything into the rubbish receptacle. Most of them had obviously been left there by other ladies. Seeing him, she threw a pot of ointment at him.

"But Rosemary…" He followed her into the bathroom and they looked at each other panting, then seized each other and started to make love again.

Their final embrace was at the check-in desk at Orly.

"My little Velvet-nose," he breathed in her ear, his nickname for her since the night before.

"Darling, I'll be back, I swear," were her last words before tearfully going through the immigration barrier with her passport. Girodias returned to his problems.

6

Lolita was to solve many of those problems and bring new ones. The first large cheque to arrive for American royalties amounted to $300,000 and it was soon followed by more. Girodias could go ahead with his restaurant. He started to spend money on decoration and continued publishing from his first-floor offices, which he later moved to the second. Terry Southern and Mason Hoffenberg finally finished their collaborative novel *Candy*, and Girodias published it. It was more than an erotic book: it satirized New York smart society with its pretensions and snobbery. He also published an unusual novel that was very far from the commissioned pornography of Trocchi, Rubington and Iris Owens. It was Paul Ableman's *I Hear Voices*. This was a serious social novel by a good writer who happened to come to see him because he was in Paris and had not found a British publisher. But because of the lack of sexual content the sales were poor. Girodias was learning that the Olympia imprint did not automatically guarantee success and that the more up-market he went as a publisher the lower his Paris sales would be. But his real income in future would not come from his own sales, but from his contracts to other publishers.

Girodias sometimes cast a wistful eye on the old Obelisk Press titles that Hachette were selling well, Henry Miller's two *Tropics* and Frank Harris's *My Life and Loves* in particular. His old employee Léjard was now working for Hachette. Maurice did manage to persuade Miller's agent in Paris, Dr Michel Hoffman, to sell him other Miller works; no one at Les Éditions du Chêne ever thought of doing more than continuing to exploit what they already had. Girodias signed contracts with Hoffman for *Black Spring* (a collection of short pieces that had originally been written between the *Tropics*), *Max and the White Phagocytes*, *Sexus* and *Plexus* (the first volumes of Miller's trilogy, *The Rosy Crucifixion*), and also for *The World of Sex* and *Quiet Days in Clichy*. The third part of the *Rosy Crucifixion* trilogy would not be finished for several years: Miller was already working on *Nexus* but he had developed a superstition that it would be his last book and that, once completed, he would die.

Barney Rosset was now coming regularly to Paris and he wanted to publish Henry Miller in the US. He had read Miller's best-known novel, *Tropic of Cancer,* when a student at Skidmore and hoped to acquire and publish it. He proposed an advance of $50,000, but Miller was now reluctant to get involved in legal hassles in the US, and after years of living on very little, large sums of money meant little to him. In fact, he was frightened of any amount that represented more than a month's expenditure. There were meetings in Paris. Miller was getting on well with Girodias and he had brought his current wife, Eve, with him, for whom Maurice quickly developed an attraction. There was a reunion between Henry and his old friend Alfred Perlès; they had shared many pre-war experiences together, including many women. One of the nightclubs where they met on occasion was very near La Coupole, Elle et Lui, which had a big lesbian clientele: Girodias, dropping in one night, saw Eve dancing in a frenzy with another woman. Later that evening she confided in him that her relationship with Henry was not an easy one. The artists' colony in Big Sur where they lived was dominated by men who put their art first, and money and women a long way behind. Henry did not really believe in the large advance that Barney Rosset, a rich young man, had offered for *Tropic of Cancer*, but she advised Maurice that the best way to get Henry to agree to any proposition was to go through his Big Sur friend, Emil White, a painter: Henry trusted him to keep away nuisance visitors and fans, and to vet financial offers. Eve pointed out that Henry Miller was a puritan at bottom, who disliked the idea that people were only interested in his books because of their sexual content. He also distrusted Rosset, a new arrival on the publishing scene in New York. He would feel more comfortable with an offer from one of the big established publishing houses. Girodias pointed out that Random House and Alfred Knopf were not proposing big advances or showing much inclination to take the risk of publishing a book that might involve them in prosecution, and that James Laughlin of New Directions, who had brought out all of Miller's non-obscene books, was even less interested in notoriety and defending his publications in the courts.

Lawrence Durrell was also in Paris to see Miller, and Girodias tried to persuade him to add to his own pressure and Rosset's, to get Miller's agreement to American publication. At the same time Girodias was trying to overcome Durrell's own reluctance to see his most Millerish novel, *The Black Book*, come out in print. Durrell was now the celebrated author of the successful *Alexandria Quartet*, four novels drawn from his experiences as a diplomat at the time of the early Arab-Jewish conflict, and he was not happy at seeing the products of his bohemian youth, previously published by Jack Kahane, return on the Olympia list. He hedged and kept putting Girodias off, but when promised a large advance he agreed to think about it, but without enthusiasm. He was now established as a poet, novelist and playwright; the appearance of bohemian early work might attract critical censure. There was also British censorship to be considered and the possibility of legal action. But he agreed in the end: Durrell was always a pleasant and accommodating man.

Girodias's motives for involving himself in the negotiations between Rosset and Henry Miller were twofold. First he wanted, if only symbolically, to be involved once more with the books that had established his father's name, and secondly he had plans to distribute the American edition himself in Europe. He also hoped for some remuneration for his good offices in the form of a commission from Grove Press. When Miller finally did agree – his agent Dr Hoffman, who had much to gain himself from the appearance of an American edition, was probably the decisive factor – Girodias still had to strike a deal with Hachette. However Guy Schoeller liked the suggestion that Grove should publish in English, pay all costs and legal expenses, whatever they should be, and give him forty per cent of the royalties.

All this took two years, from 1959 to 1961. In the meantime a German edition had appeared with Rowohlt in Hamburg; Heinrich-Maria Ledig-Rowohlt had gone out of his way to be friendly with Miller, who in the Sixties fell in love with his secretary, Renata Gerhardt. After a brief affair with her, Miller backed her financially out of his

German royalties to start her own literary publishing company in Berlin. Many other countries were also interested now, because the censorship barriers were falling internationally after a number of daring books had met little obstruction. Grove Press still had another problem: the copyright law in 1961 did not protect American authors whose books had been printed abroad if more than 1,500 copies had been imported. Hundreds of copies of *Tropic of Cancer* had been seized by American customs officials over the years and it was safe to assume that many thousands of other copies had slipped through. When Rosset published his edition he not only had to deal with many local prosecutions in towns that had active puritanical pressure groups, but he also had to cope with pirate editions that took advantage of the anomaly in American copyright law whereby American authors lost their copyright if published abroad. The US Post Office, after some hesitation, decided not to impede the book's sale, but *Tropic of Cancer* was banned in Massachusetts, Texas and some other states. Barney Rosset had to spend more than $250,000 in legal fees and fines. Then came the news that a pirate edition had appeared in Chicago. After much legal correspondence Rosset agreed to buy the whole edition in exchange for a recognition of copyright, but this also forced him to bring out a mass-market paperback much earlier than he had intended. As a result there were more prosecutions. 100,000 copies had been sold in hardback and probably many times that number would have been sold in the following year at $7.50, too high a price for most juveniles; but the appearance of a 95-cent paperback made it much more accessible to all, not only in bookshops but at newspaper kiosks and wherever popular books were sold. Two million copies were sold in the year amid much outcry. Grove Press received a great deal of publicity, but had to suffer an overall loss, the extent of which has never been admitted. But it put Grove Press and its owner Barney Rosset on the map. Now he was one of the best-known figures in American publishing and would remain so for the next quarter of a century.

7

The rise of Barney Rosset plays an important part in the post-war New York publishing scene, and in many ways it had its effect on Paris. Kurt Wolff, the great German expressionist publisher and discoverer of Kafka, who because of Hitler had moved to New York in the late Thirties, used to say that all a real publisher needed was enthusiasm and taste. He forgot to mention money. Barney inherited lots of it. His father left him a considerable fortune on his death in 1952.

Rosset was born in 1922, the son of a Chicago banker who had come close to bankruptcy during the Depression but made a remarkable recovery during his last years. His father was a Jew who had converted to Catholicism, the religion of his Irish-American wife, which was one of the many similarities in background between Rosset and Girodias. The young Rosset was brought up in the windy city in an affluent neighbourhood where his half-Jewish ancestry was not acceptable to many of the families on the street, and he was excluded from the homes of some of his schoolmates, including that of the future Nancy Reagan, whose parents adhered to extreme right-wing causes. He had great difficulty in seeing Joan Mitchell, the girl he had known in school from infanthood as they grew up, because her parents did not want her to know him or be friendly with him. It was only after Joan was sent to Europe to study as an adult, and he had joined her there, that he was able to continue his courtship, and they were eventually married in France. Joan was to become one of the best-known American painters of her generation. Before that Rosset had attended a number of good schools, had been to Swarthmore, UCLA and the University of Chicago, where he joined the army. He was commissioned in 1943, becoming a war photographer. Rosset became the first American to enter Shanghai, by accidentally wandering into an area believed still to be occupied by the Japanese, although it was in fact evacuated; he took many interesting pictures before the other troops arrived. Barney was to remain a warrior all his life, but his battlefields would change.

After leaving the army Rosset returned to the University of Chicago, where one of his professors was Wallace Fowlie, from whom he learnt something of modern literature. When still at the university he met Robert Phelps and John Balcomb in New York, young men who had started a small publishing house that they named Grove Press, after the street in the West Village where their office was. They had only published three books and had run out of money. Rosset paid them $3,000 for the firm and decided to keep it going. After finishing at the university, and after the death of his father, he moved to New York. He was now wealthy with a large income, but most of the capital would only come to him in tranches over the years up to his mid-thirties.

A natural barfly and frequenter of jazz clubs and bohemian hangouts, Barney occasionally visited those cities, other than Chicago and New York, that had an artistic subculture, and in particular went to San Francisco hoping to see his idol Henry Miller. While there he came across the Beat poets, some of whom he had noticed as individuals in New York. But in San Francisco they had become a group, with the City Lights bookshop as their pivotal centre, and they now thought of themselves as a school. The bookshop, which Lawrence Ferlinghetti had started in 1946 with help from the GI Bill of Rights, also published a magazine of the same name. This was edited by Peter Martin, son of an Italian anarchist, Carlo Martin, who had been assassinated in New York in 1943. *City Lights* published Ginsberg, Kerouac and Neal Cassady, but the review also had regular contributions from such other rising writers as Pauline Kael, Robert Duncan and Jack Spicer in its pages. Lawrence Ferlinghetti was himself a poet and he started a series of cheap poetry editions, very different from the expensive and luxurious volumes that came from other small literary presses in the Bay Area, both for his own work and that of the writers and poets who frequented his bookstore at 261 Columbus Avenue, between North Beach's Little Italy and Chinatown, a raunchy, commercial part of San Francisco with many cheap restaurants and bars, nightclubs and strip shows, cheap motels and brothels. It attracted both tourists and itinerant poets. Barney Rosset quickly became at home there and in bars like Tosca, across the street from City Lights, he met many of the best literary figures, mostly still unpublished, and became interested in their work. He also met Donald Allen, whom he engaged to go to New York and join him as an editor. He then commissioned Allen to put together a large collection of poetry that would include all the new emerging schools, and especially the beats. This resulted in a large anthology, *The New American Poetry*, published in 1960. It featured many new names unknown to literary editors, but it was widely reviewed and, being a well-produced large-format trade paperback, still a novelty in those days, it sold well and soon became legendary. It helped to establish the reputations of Ginsberg and Kerouac.

The San Francisco connection was to become important to Grove, although the mercurial Rosset never developed the connection as well as he might have; other publishers took advantage of his distraction and his insufficient appreciation of City Lights. Ferlinghetti was in touch with Paris through his friend George Whitman at Le Mistral, with whom he corresponded frequently, and City Lights stocked *Merlin* and the *Paris Review* among many other little magazines. It became the west coast centre for alternative literature. Ferlinghetti's Pocket Poet Series took some time to get into eastern bookshops after 1955, when the series first came out, but Ginsberg was back in New York shortly after that, and he became a tireless campaigner for the work of his friends and himself, pushing those publications that were available to booksellers, and trying to meet as many editors and reviewers as possible to put over the Beat school and get more books published. Donald Allen realized more than Barney Rosset that something new was developing in America and he persuaded Rosset to devote a whole issue of his new *Evergreen Review* to the San Francisco scene in 1957. Had Barney been less interested in his private occupations and nocturnal activities he could easily have cornered the market in Beat writing as he eventually did with the new avant-garde French writers.

Barney's other significant editor was to be Richard Seaver. Both Trocchi and Seaver moved to New York in 1956, but quite independently of each other. Trocchi arrived after a trip to the Middle East and a brief period of hesitation in London. George Plimpton, who had frequently helped him financially, was back in New York, and Trocchi counted on him and his contacts to help him to get started there; he also had a contract with a New York literary agent for his future work. Seaver had met Barney in Paris some years earlier and had been offered a job at Grove Press, one that he had thought about seriously. But Barney had no reputation then, and he was vague about his publishing plans; the offer was turned down. It was only after his return to New York, and subsequently working for two years for George Braziller at the Book Find Club and Seven Arts Book Club that Seaver, in 1959, finally moved to Grove Press, and became involved with the acquisition of new French literature and the publication in the US of Samuel Beckett, thereby renewing his old contact.

Barney Rosset probably first heard about Beckett from Sylvia Beach, whom he met at a party in New York. He published *Waiting for Godot*, which was first staged in America in Florida in January 1956 as a farcical comedy; it obviously had a puzzling effect on the audiences to which American managements misrepresented it, a play that is above all philosophical and poetic, two words which were never used in its publicity. It was only after it had been redirected for New York in an off-Broadway theatre with more suitable advertising, that it began to acquire its reputation among intellectuals. Alan Schneider had directed the first production in Miami, where the audience had expected easy, light humour, and because of the fiasco, he was subsequently sacked, but he soon after became the only American director ultimately to win Beckett's confidence. Barney was by then more interested in the novel *Murphy*, first published unsuccessfully in England in 1938: he read it and talked about it all over New York. Although much of the theme of *Murphy*, a fictional representation of the body-mind conflict that has interested philosophers for centuries, may have escaped Barney, he found an echo in many of its episodes of his own erotic obsessions. Murphy, the hero, is in love with a prostitute, Celia, who supports him financially. The masochistic overtones of much of the novel obviously appealed to Rosset, an avid reader of erotica since his schooldays, whose nights were largely spent in search of similar adventures.

Wallace Fowlie relates that Rosset, then a student, came to him one day and said: "Please, sir. I've just bought the Grove Press. What should I publish?" If so, he was the first of the many advisors who recommended titles and authors to Rosset. A kitchen cabinet developed over the next few years that included Donald Allen, Herbert de Graf, Fred Jordan and Dick Seaver. Barney's volatile personality – the Jekyll and Hyde on which Girodias would later comment – was largely a result of his lifestyle: he took wake-up drugs to boost his energy in the mornings after nights of debauchery, which ended with sleeping pills to overcome the uppers that had kept him awake, and got through the day with the help of a variety of stimulants, always accompanied by much alcoholic consumption. Barney needed constant excitement and had moods of great euphoria and energy; but in a flash he would become a different person, suspicious, negative, incapable of listening, and blaming others for the consequences of his own previous impulses. He would remember only what he wanted to remember, deny previous promises or verbal instructions and turn viciously on anyone who happened to be at hand when he was irritable. Not surprisingly his kitchen cabinet changed frequently: the longest survivors were Seaver and Jordan.

But in the Fifties Barney Rosset created much excitement in the publishing world and became newsworthy for his willingness to fight censorship battles, publish unconventional and controversial books, and not worry about the consequences. In his theatre collection he published most of the new playwrights from France, who became known as "absurdist" after Martin Esslin's book *The Theatre of the Absurd* gave them this generic label. Beckett, Ionesco, Arrabal and Pinget were all published in America by Grove and subsequently or simultaneously performed in the theatres of Greenwich Village, or further uptown near the Hudson River, west of Broadway. Their English-language equivalents, Pinter, Arden, Stoppard, Albee and Jack Gelber, also came out with Grove. Barney started the *Evergreen Review* as a house journal that became the voice of the "underground", as the new culture began to call itself, taking a European wartime term to reflect the hostility of the dominant middle-class commercial establishment against the attitudes it represented. Advertisements in the press for the

Evergreen Review invited readers to "Join the underground". Grove was perfectly placed to become the avant-garde publisher of the day and to be the most representative voice of the Sixties. Barney Rosset published *Lady Chatterley's Lover* in 1958, taking advantage of the same anomaly in the copyright law that made a book public property if more than 1,500 copies had been imported, legally or not, into the US; it would later be used against him when he published *Tropic of Cancer*. He placated the D.H. Lawrence estate by paying royalties voluntarily, but it never forgave him for proceeding without a proper contract. Quixotic, unpredictable, volatile, excitable, newsworthy, infuriatingly two-minded, and rich enough to do whatever he wanted during those crucial years from the early Fifties until the late Seventies, he was without question the most interesting American publisher outside the Madison Avenue establishment, especially during the Sixties, his heyday, when youth culture exploded.

At the time of his elopement with Joan Mitchell in 1958, Barney Rosset had wanted to be a writer. He met Joan in Paris, where they were married, and they went on honeymoon to the south of France, renting a villa at Saint-Tropez. Rosset had brought with him a large, handsomely bound volume of blank white pages, into which he intended to write his first novel. Every morning Joan set up her easel in the garden and started to paint; by sunset there were always one or two finished canvases. But the white pages remained white. After scratching his head for half an hour, Barney would give up and look for a tennis partner, and then go swimming. By the end of the honeymoon he knew he would never be a writer.

Joan was ultimately to settle in Paris after their separation and divorce. She later lived with the French-Canadian artist Jean-Paul Riopelle, and after he left her she moved to Verteuil outside Paris, where she established her studio. By the late Sixties she was one of the best-known American artists of the de Kooning school. Barney Rosset has had many women in his life, and at the time of writing this book had four wives and as many divorces behind him. His more successful and often longer-lasting relationships have on the whole been non-marital. For a time he branched out of publishing into films: having successfully distributed a Swedish sex film, *I Am Curious (Yellow)*, in the US, he started a small cinema near his office in Greenwich Village and distributed other films, but his venture was ultimately a loss. He also decided to go into film production, and to this end commissioned scenarios from three of his most prestigious authors living in France: Beckett, Ionesco and Marguerite Duras, but only the Beckett was ever produced by Rosset. It was entitled *Film* and Beckett asked for Buster Keaton, by then long retired, to play his protagonist. Barney then obtained the services of Boris Kaufman, the cameraman who had made Jean Vigo's *Zéro de Conduite* in the Thirties, a particular Rosset favourite, and he engaged Alan Schneider as director.

Beckett was persuaded to come from Paris for the filming. It was his only visit to the US. Much of that visit was spent at Barney Rosset's house in East Hampton where there were many conferences sitting around the swimming pool. Barney installed a microphone under the poolside coffee table to record the conversations and planning sessions for posterity. They hunted for a location to film around the older parts of New York and found a section of crumbling wall in lower Manhattan near the East River, as well as a sufficiently dilapidated building to use for the interior: here *Film*, a short of about twenty minutes, was made. There was no dialogue in it, only a single sound, a "Shss" – Beckett was really putting his producers to the test – but this necessitated a complete soundtrack for what is really a silent film. Schneider had never directed a film before and the result, in terms of finished quality, must be left to the individual opinions of the Beckett buffs who see it (it is usually only shown at special Beckett festivals and conferences). The Ionesco, *How to Boil an Egg*, although published, was never made, and Marguerite Duras eventually used her scenario to make her own film.

Except for the time spent on location in lower Manhattan, when Beckett was staying with Barney Rosset and Christine, his third wife, at their fortress-like house on Houston Street, which had no exterior windows, the author saw little of New York. It was the hot July of 1964 and it took three weeks to film the scenario with a puzzled Buster Keaton, who saw no point in a script where he was allowed no comic routine and none of his suggestions were accepted – he did it purely for the money. Keaton resisted Schneider and Beckett at every point.

Beckett walked around Greenwich Village in the evenings and accompanied Barney to his favourite bars, but otherwise showed no interest in seeing New York. The film finished, he returned to Paris. On the last morning, when he was booked on the morning plane from Idlewild (later JFK), he sat patiently, packed and ready to go, on a chair in Barney Rosset's hall at East Hampton while his host overslept, until, waking suddenly, Barney had to drive frantically to the airport, only just making the flight for Beckett at the last moment.

When *Film* was cut and edited, a copy was sent to Paris, and for a week Beckett arranged to show it in a small cutting room projection cinema. I was invited to see it and was told by Beckett that the professionals, potential distributors and exhibitors, were coming early in the week, and old friends towards the end. I flew from London on the Saturday. After the showing, the thirty or so invitees went to Le Falstaff, a Montparnasse bar and restaurant much frequented by Beckett, which was always open until the early hours of the morning. There we discovered that a lavish champagne spread had been ordered for all by Beckett, and no one was allowed to contribute to the cost of it. It was a long night in which the author relaxed with old friends and drank rather too much, the actor Patrick Magee had to be pulled away from a fight with a stranger at the bar by Beckett, and I missed my plane to London by several hours, dossing down on a bench at Orly airport at five in the morning. Beckett had organized at Le Falstaff a similar post-showing supper every night of the week at his own expense, thereby spending much more than he could ever have earned from Barney Rosset's little film venture.

Beckett was one author who cemented the link between Barney Rosset and myself, and he was often caught in the crossfire when we quarrelled.* By the late Fifties, Grove had taken on a number of writers from my British company. I sold Rosset another Irish author, Aidan Higgins, who had first come to me with a recommendation from Beckett, and Barney subsequently published his early short stories, *Felo de Se* and his prize-winning novel, *Langrishe, Go Down*: both depicted decaying Irish families that had lost their money, and the decline of individuals through self-destruction, either by alcoholic addiction or the ineptness of those who had never been trained to work at dealing with the world. Higgins was himself a good example of the class he described and after four brilliant works of fiction based on detailed observation and a very Irish preoccupation with language, he declined into one of his own characters, but re-emerged in later life. Rosset was to receive many begging letters from Higgins, and he occasionally sent him drinking money, but he was little interested in his work, and showed no desire to keep him when another American publisher offered a substantial advance for his third novel, *Balcony of Europe*, which was runner-up for the second Booker Prize. Grove also took on Eugène Ionesco, Fernando Arrabal, Alain Robbe-Grillet, Robert Pinget and Marguerite Duras, all of whom I had acquired for Britain; I was anxious to have an American contribution towards the cost of translation. But Donald Allen, who preferred to make his own translations of Ionesco, sometimes frustrated me in this, and he held up many decisions until Barney was convinced, for or against cooperation. Things became somewhat easier when Seaver moved to Grove, but Rosset would still make lightning changes of mind on an impulse. Robbe-Grillet's *The Voyeur* was the first of his novels to appear in English because Barney Rosset, himself a voyeur, liked the title, although it was not the first to be contracted and translated. I had to wait a year before he would cooperate on *Jealousy*, which in the event sold much better. From Grove, who had bought world rights to Beckett's *Murphy*, I acquired the British rights, and I later contracted Trocchi's *Cain's Book* because of its success with Grove. It was the first of the titles to appear in America as a "Paperback Original", with possibly a simultaneous hardcover edition; it was a time when the student market for offbeat literature was expanding rapidly, and students would not pay for hardcover editions. It became something of a best-seller for Rosset. *Cain's Book* was followed by Kerouac's *Dr Sax* in the same large paperback format once usually identified with hardcovers.

I had first met Barney at a small office he occupied on Fifth Avenue, at a time when he had only acquired a handful of titles to publish but was already supremely self-confident. Realizing that I was like-minded in many ways, he telephoned me at my hotel shortly after our first meeting and invited me to dinner at an expensive French restaurant, where I also met his current girlfriend, Link, an artist. He was at the time estranged from his German second wife, Loli, who had also been his California sales representative, a lady I never met. Link looked like a blonde New York cover-girl, well-groomed, soft-spoken, full of charm, and intelligent as well. I liked her very much, and she complemented Barney's restless, excitable personality. I learnt more about Barney at table that night, because he talked incessantly, ordered an expensive wine that was not very good, one that tourists in the south of France tend to go for because of its pretty pink colour and elegantly shaped bottle, and he obviously was not very interested in the food he was eating. But he had enthusiasm: it gushed from him. He spoke jerkily and used his hands a great deal. He had retained his army brush-cut; in those days he went to have it cut twice or three times a week, and as a mannerism liked to run his hand over it. A long relationship began that night.

Within a short time Barney and I were doing deals. It started with exchanges of information, leading to each taking some book titles from the other, then to our most important one, when I agreed to import his paperback series, Evergreen Books, into the UK and sell them there. I could not sell the entire list – some titles had their own British publishers – but it became the first "Egghead Paperback" group of titles to appear in Britain and, given the nature of the books, it was immensely successful. Evergreens were not cheap by British paperback standards, but they had a strikingly different look to them, with cover designs by Roy Kuhlman that looked like modern art, and they were in a format associated with hardcovers, which suited books of an often highly intellectual or specialized nature. In the climate of the time they were quickly accepted by the more adventurous British booksellers and the more literate members of the reading public. Almost immediately, I began to imitate them with my own paperback reissues of my hardcover books: I called the series Calderbooks and sold them in tandem with the imports. At the same time I imported a series that complemented them, books on theatre under the imprint Dramabooks, which were published by Hill & Wang in New York. My own economic resources were slender and I was very stretched at the time, having also acquired many new books for my own list, but as many of these were also accepted by Grove through my recommendation, and appearing as Evergreen editions, it often seemed wise to import the American edition until I could afford to produce my own. Then Barney and I started a joint series of new, smaller paperbacks, based on one published in France by Les Éditions du Seuil. They were heavily illustrated, semi-academic titles on history, art history, music and the like. We eventually bought English-language rights to all the Seuil series, commissioned new titles in English, and called them Profile Books.

Within a short time of that first dinner, I had seen much evidence of Barney's eccentricities, and the high cost of them. He spent $15,000 on a whole-page advertisement in the *New York Times* book review section, which carried two words: "EVERGREEN BOOKS", or, if my memory fails me, it might have been "GROVE PRESS", in large letters on the centre of an otherwise blank page. I asked him what the point was, advertising an imprint and not a single title or author, without even an address. "You never know," was his reply, and he could not be persuaded that it was money down the drain. About this time he added an Englishman to his team. John Pizey had been sent to the US by Sir Allen Lane, head of Penguin Books in London, to see if there was a market for those Penguin titles that had no American copyright. His exploratory tour was successful enough for him to be sent back to the States as the unique Penguin salesman. Barney heard about him and persuaded him to become his sales manager. I met Pizey in Chicago one day, staying at the Palmer House Hotel and spending money on his expenses in a way that would never have been countenanced by another publisher. "I know what Barney likes," he confided to me over brandy that night after dinner. "He likes to spend money." This was true. Barney seemed to have no sense of budgets, or of profit and loss, as something to worry about. He had the money and he spent it. But only on his interests, as Pizey was later to discover.

By the early Sixties the transatlantic connection was in operation, a triangle between Girodias in Paris, initiating many titles that were co-produced, Rosset in New York cooperating when it suited him, often backing out of deals that had been agreed by the other two, and myself in London.

In my early days I had published mainly European classics in translation, then moved on to American fiction and non-fiction that had come to my notice through friends and those New York publishers who had the courage to defy Senator McCarthy, like Angus Cameron, previously a senior editor with Little, Brown in Boston, who had founded Cameron and Kahn and the Liberty Book Club, and Leo Huberman and Paul Sweezy, who edited and published the periodical *Monthly Review*. I also acquired titles from some of the larger publishers. At the same time I was bringing out books on serious music, reflecting one of my major interests, one I did not share with Rosset and Girodias. An *Opera Annual*, appearing every year, was joined by an *International Theatre Annual*, edited by Harold Hobson, the theatre critic of the *Sunday Times*, who was a particular enthusiast for the current French theatre, which helped to keep me up to date with new plays appearing in Paris and elsewhere. As a result I was able to build a stable of good theatrical authors, meeting them on their home ground, going to many first nights, and gaining privileged insight into their present and future work. Other annuals appeared, covering world literature, film, concert music and art, and they attracted more authors to the list.

By the late Fifties I was publishing too much, owed too much to printers and authors, and was finding myself in similar difficulties to Girodias a decade earlier. I advertised for a partner with capital, and Marion Lobbenberg, a bored housewife looking for an occupation, answered the advertisement. After negotiations that took years rather than months (as a result of the attempts made by Roy Jones, her lover as well as accountant and financial advisor, to dissuade her), she bought half the company, which is to say that she received half the shares for nothing in return for an injection of £10,000; the reason it was for nothing was that her accountant made it a condition that I too had to find the same amount and put it into the company, which needed £20,000. Marion Lobbenberg, who was later to become Marion Boyars, was lucky in her timing: our best and most affluent period was about to begin.

8

Some of Girodias's difficulties had arisen out of political books that had exposed corruption or questioned the orthodoxy of the day. He was not quite finished with attacks on the political establishment, even though his principal activity had switched to confronting censorship with books that outraged conventional morality. It was an Irish scandal that he tackled next.

Girodias had read much modern history out of general interest, and during his first summer on the Rue Saint-Séverin he was reading *The Accusing Ghost, or Justice for Casement*, an account of the Casement trial by Alfred Noyes. Girodias became very excited by this famous trial and decided to find out more about it.

Sir Roger Casement was an Irish patriot who had been hanged by the British following the failed 1916 Easter Rising in Dublin. His career before the First World War as a civil servant had been distinguished. He had been posted to a number of countries oppressed by colonial regimes, and had in particular observed conditions in the Belgian Congo and the remoter areas of South America. Casement had brought the continuing presence of slavery in Africa and Amazonia to public attention in Europe, and because of the outcry the governments concerned had been obliged to initiate reforms. He was a popular hero to liberals and had been knighted for his services to humanity. But on returning to his native Ulster (he came from Anglo-Protestant stock), he realized that the attitude of the Protestant Ascendancy, the minority that ruled Ireland and owned most of it, was very similar to the situations he had encountered when investigating slavery. That minority was currently opposing, and in 1906 was willing to take up arms against, the popular desire for Home Rule, which the British government, with the Liberal Party in power, was willing, after centuries of conflict, to concede. Only the beginning of the First World War in 1914 prevented it. Casement switched his allegiance to Sinn Fein, the militant movement for Irish national independence, and went to Germany to try to persuade the German High Command to send an army to back a popular rising in Ireland. But he only succeeded in being sent back in a German submarine with a cargo of outdated arms for the rebels. The British had been warned and were waiting for him; he was arrested and tried. Normally a man of his public popularity, and with his background as a reformer, would have had the death sentence for High Treason commuted by the king, but to prevent this the British Home Office took an unusual step. They claimed that they had discovered Casement's secret diaries at the time of his arrest, and that these contained hundreds of references to his practices as an active and obsessive homosexual; his encounters with other men were described in detail in these diaries, and with full descriptions of the genitals of his partners and conquests. Copies were made of these diaries and circulated in confidence to the most influential of the journalists covering the court case; the purpose was to evoke horror and disgust, and to prevent the newspapers from reporting the trial and the comportment of Casement in any light favourable to the defendant. The prosecutor was F.E. Smith (later Lord Birkenhead), who had just become Attorney General in succession to the notorious Sir Edward Carson, leader of the loyalist Ulster Unionist Party; Smith was a leading barrister and Queen's Counsel. Carson and his party were the greatest enemies of the Catholic peasant class and of all nationalist aspirations. Casement was convicted and hanged. After the trial all copies of the diaries were supposed to be returned to the Home Office, but it was believed that some journalists had kept them, declaring them lost.

Reading Noyes's book led Maurice Girodias to make his own investigation, and he decided to obtain a copy of the diaries if it were possible. He was particularly interested in the legal act under which Casement had been sentenced to death: this was an Act of 1351, passed in the reign of Edward III, and worded in Norman French, a language with which not many modern judges were very conversant. It was of course open to interpretation. Reading more widely, Girodias found that many writers, including T.E. Lawrence, had considered writing a book on the Casement trial. The Home Office had never admitted the existence of the "Black Diaries", nor their own behaviour in circulating them. When southern Ireland achieved its independence in 1922, the new Irish government was not interested in having one of its national heroes revealed as a practising homosexual of a particularly virulent type, and it too was silent. Lawrence had called for an independent investigation into the case. Why should it not be by me, thought Girodias?

After many telephone calls he was lucky enough to trace and speak on the telephone to Peter Singleton-Gates, an elderly, retired journalist, who told him that he did indeed have a copy of the Black Diaries, which in 1916 had been hidden away: the Home Office had been told that the copy was lost and they did not dare pursue the matter. There was another publisher interested at the time, Anthony Blond, but Blond's lawyers had told him that the risk of prosecution was too great, and he had decided not to proceed. Singleton-Gates immediately realized that Olympia's interest was another matter altogether. Girodias was outside the jurisdiction of the British courts, and the French government was hardly likely to take much interest in an old dispute concerning Irish independence.

The following day Girodias flew to London and met Singleton-Gates and Blond in a pub in South Kensington. After a while Blond wished them good luck with the proposed book and left. The journalist had three perfectly legible and complete volumes of the Diaries, which had been mimeographed by the Home Office. Much of the writing was in a personal code which it was not difficult to decipher, referring to the length of penises, an obsession of Casement's, the duration of couplings, and the like. An Olympia edition would need an adequate introduction, a biography of Casement, and the complete text of the diaries, with the telegraphese style and code words extended into normal language. Girodias realized that he himself would have to do the essential editorial reconstruction of the volume and, given Singleton-Gates's reluctance to involve himself further in the project, he would also have to write the introduction and the biography. This would require much time and research. But he would do it.

He spent many months on the project, and it was during this same period that Michelle was transforming the large building on the Rue Saint-Séverin into a restaurant at considerable expense. There was no architect now: they simply told the builder what they wanted done, and, little by little, room after room was restored, then decorated. Olympia Press was continuing to publish books in spite of Laffont, and money was coming in from other countries for books sub-licensed to foreign publishers, but mainly from *Lolita*. Girodias was living in unaccustomed monogamy with Michelle. One evening he gave an excited shout and told her to open a bottle of champagne. The Act of Edward III – which invoked the death penalty for a series of crimes that included coining false money, raping the queen or the eldest son of the king (and so on) – ended with references to treason committed against the king *par ailleurs*, a phrase which had been taken to refer to treason committed "outside the country", in this case in Germany. But Girodias realized that the old use of the term – and he checked this with an appropriate authority – meant "by other means". Casement was therefore executed under a faulty interpretation of the law. Girodias's discovery was perhaps not as important as it seemed to him at the time. The leaders of the 1916 rising were shot under quite different Acts of Parliament, and it was in the middle of a war in which thousands sometimes died in a single day. But the use of the Black Diaries to suppress sympathy and prevent a reprieve was a savage act of ministerial malice that recalled the Oscar Wilde trial, still fresh in the public memory at the time.

Girodias proceeded to publish his book on the trial, which included the Black Diaries *in toto* and looked for publishers in other countries. Barney Rosset, remembering his Irish ancestry, agreed to take the book for the US, and I said that I would take the risk of doing it in Britain. But then Girodias, often unreasonable in negotiation, was true to form and insisted that, although he would give me publishing rights to bring out the book in whatever form I wanted, he reserved the right to send his own edition into Britain and the Commonwealth at any time; it would take me at least six months to bring out my own publication, while his own would be immediately available to whatever libraries and bookshops were willing to take the risk of stocking it. The contract was not very tempting. I told Maurice, not for the first or the last time, that I would rather be his friend than do bad business that would lead to recrimination, bad will and even legal action. The deal I was offered left me with the full responsibility for defending a prosecution, while my sales would be much diminished by the prior sales of another edition.

In the end, Girodias, his own edition selling very badly in France, where there was little interest, made a contract with James Knapp-Fisher, the canny head of Sidgwick & Jackson, who bought 1,500 bound copies from him under their own imprint. All these disappeared on the day of publication. Strangely, not a single copy seems to have been seen in a single bookshop. Not a single review appeared, and newspapers, later asked if they had received a review copy, could not remember seeing one. There are only a few copies to this day in British public libraries; the prestigious London Library, owned by its subscribers, has a copy, but it is not available for perusal. Sidgwick told Girodias that they had sold out on publication and had decided not to reprint. There is only one possible explanation: that the entire edition was bought by a single purchaser, who no doubt paid a sufficient compensatory sum to persuade the publisher to abandon the book. The obvious suspect must be the British Home Office, but it is not impossible that the Irish government was also involved.

Chapter Seven

Tangiers, the Other Paris

Everyone who was around in the Sixties has his or her own memories of a decade that was lived under the continuing shadow of nuclear war, but was, nonetheless, for those who inhabited the more fortunate countries of the western world, unrivalled as a time of opportunity, freedom, iconoclasm and pleasure. But the freedom of the Sixties in the UK, the US and other anglophone countries had already been present in Paris (for students and bohemians) and Tangiers, which is why expatriates went there. When they returned to their own countries, they brought that freedom back with them and contributed more than a little to the liberalization of their home countries. The expatriate diaspora became reversed in the Sixties.

One community that has not yet been mentioned was the anglophone group that had made Morocco its base. The country was ideal for artists, and Tangiers, with its status as an "open" international city, was a natural draw for eccentrics, artists, sexual minorities who were not tolerated in their own countries, deviates of every kind and criminals wanted elsewhere by the police. The indigenous population tolerated them and lived its own life; the police were not interested in the foreign population as long as criminality and outré sex practices did not affect them or become too blatant. The administration was a French colonial one, and it was only when growing native nationalism, and the intolerance that always accompanies it, began to touch the lives of the foreign residents, that this little paradise became less attractive. But Tangiers was largely interchangeable with Paris as far as artists were concerned: less bohemian, but with more freedoms.

Paul Bowles, the central figure among the expatriates in Tangiers, had moved there in 1947. He was already a successful American composer who, once he had settled himself in North Africa, turned to writing and eventually nearly eclipsed his wife, Jane Bowles, an established and critically admired playwright and prose writer. Married since 1938, they were a strange couple, devoted to each other, but in each case with proclivities towards their own sex. The Tangiers group became known principally as a homosexual enclave where pederasty, in particular, did not incur legal risks. Among the Americans who were attracted there were Tennessee Williams, Truman Capote, Brion Gysin (really an Americanized European), William Burroughs, Jack Kerouac, Peter Orlovsky, Allen Ginsberg and Alfred Chester, and, among the rich set, pre-eminently Barbara Hutton, the Woolworth heiress. The British included the fashion photographer Cecil Beaton, a succession of dissolute or lecherous aristocrats and some writers and artists, among them Francis Bacon and his entourage. There were film stars, actors, celebrities and, after the more reserved early years of the anglophone colony, an influx of hippies. This gathering together of a community of English-speaking exiles took place in the middle of an international city where the laws applied mainly to the indigenous population, and international crime operations involving drugs, gunrunning, money-laundering, gambling and prostitution could flourish unchecked.

Morocco had been since 1912 a protectorate of France and Spain. Entry was refused to no one, but in practice one had to have a means of support, which for a foreigner could be difficult to find in Tangiers. Everything could be bought and sold there, and fortunes were made and lost on the stock exchange or the money market, or in the various rackets that used Morocco as a base of operations but traded mainly outside. It was also a centre of piracy, but safe enough for the city's residents. For those who had money arriving regularly from outside and kept to their own circles, it was a virtual paradise: every known sexual taste could be practised without attracting attention and every desired sex object was on tap, the social scene was varied and interesting, creativity and privacy were respected, and no one was judgemental. The only barrier was a class one; until the arrival of the hippies, virtually everyone had a higher educational background or came from the more affluent classes. But there were class hierarchies even then.

Paul Bowles, although primarily a composer in 1947, had many other talents: he was both a poet and a linguist with many translations to his credit, including an English version of Sartre's *Huis Clos*, which he translated as *No Exit*. He had written operas and scores for plays. He was also a recognized and perceptive music critic, with his own column in the *New York Herald Tribune*. He was thirty-seven and at the height of his powers when he arrived in Tangiers. His wife, Jane, was also a public success, author of many successful short stories and some short novels, and had been praised by Tennessee Williams as "the most important writer of prose fiction in modern American letters". Paul too, before moving to North Africa, had written short stories that had attracted attention, and he had a contract from Doubleday for a novel that was not even formed in his mind.

Paul and Jane had had enough of New York with its superficiality, its way of drowning celebrities in unwanted attention and of making each success a hurdle for the future. Paul Bowles needed privacy, difficult to find when you are famous, and he was looking for an exoticism far from the glitter of Broadway. The move, and the choice of Morocco, was the result of a very vivid dream he had experienced in May 1947, in which he recognized a medina and the Tangiers he had seen on an extended visit before the war. By the summer he was there.

Paul Bowles's background was already an exceptionally interesting one. A pre-war pupil and travelling companion of Aaron Copeland, he had toured Europe with him and been more than marginally involved in the literary circle of Gertrude Stein in Paris, through whom he had come to know Gide, Cocteau, some of the Joyce circle, and Ezra Pound. He had visited Tangiers in 1931 with Copeland, who could not bear the place and went on alone to Berlin, leaving Paul behind to travel around the country and see something of its splendours. His adventures at that time had left an abiding memory, and when he woke from his dream he knew that it was to Tangiers he had to move.

He was not the first American to establish himself there. Barbara Hutton had bought a palace the year before, outbidding General Franco to get it, and she imported many friends to keep her amused and fill up her parties. But Bowles did not mix with other Americans. He worked steadily on his first novel, which became *The Sheltering Sky*, and acquired a long-term Arab boyfriend, Ahmed Yacoubi, while Jane fell heavily for a Berber grain-seller, Cherifa, who was to remain her lover and companion for many years, and was believed by many to be a witch.

The Bowles led their own lives, but became marginally involved in the expatriate scene: given their celebrity it was difficult for them to remain entirely aloof. One of the main hang-outs was Dean's Bar on a small street near the Minzah, one of the main avenues; the proprietor, rumoured to be the model for Rick in the film *Casablanca*, was also believed to be involved in the raffish side of Tangiers life; he was a middle-man involved in many deals who could use his barman's post to his own advantage. But his bar was also frequented by international celebrities, especially from the film world: Ava Gardner, Errol Flynn, Ian Fleming and Francis Bacon were all clients when in town. Dean was a great raconteur and told many stories, some of them true, and amused his listeners with gossipy details about the foreign residents and their visitors; the stories were probably invented by others, but hilarious at the time of telling. Jane was more involved in Tangiers café life than her husband, who went on frequent trips to research other parts of the country, and he stayed mostly in seclusion when in town; she would meet other artistic and social residents in the local meeting places to gossip, and in general she made herself socially available. The Bowles' good friend, Tennessee Williams, came to Tangiers several times, first of all in 1948, when he was accompanied by a new grand passion, Frank Merlo, an ex-sailor, who created a rift between them because Williams suspected that he was also seeing Bowles. Cecil Beaton, who had photographed royalty, the theatre, opera and ballet scene and the London celebrities of the day, began to frequent the town. Other friends of the Bowles' included the torch singer Libby Holman, Édouard Roditi and Truman Capote, all frequent visitors. But there was a host of noticeable eccentrics of every kind in their milieu, ranging from Russian nobility to animal collectors who neglected their pets so scandalously that they became the talking point of the international, and especially Anglo-American, community. Many amusing anecdotes are related in Michelle Green's vivid *The Dream at the End of the World*.*

One prominent new resident, who arrived some time after the Bowles couple, was David Herbert, second son of the Earl of Pembroke, who, like most second sons of the British titled aristocracy, was given the best possible education and then a modest allowance to live on, which would often cease with the death of his father. Cultured, witty, intelligent, a good conversationalist, he became a central figure in the Tangiers social scene. He was homosexual and artistic, and a close friend of Cecil Beaton's. Raised in a stately home, he knew a great deal about style, talked about it, practised it, and was connected with the most fashionable public figures, especially in the theatre, counting among his acquaintances Alfred Lunt and Lynn Fontaine, Elinor Glyn, Mrs Patrick Campbell, Tallulah Bankhead, Cyril Connolly, Noël Coward, Nancy Mitford and much European royalty. He also knew the Sitwells, Greta Garbo, Harold Nicolson and most of the rich international crowd who frequented Monte Carlo and Cannes, Biarritz, Madrid and Bermuda, and the more glamorous cities of Europe, as well as New York and Hollywood.

David Herbert and Barbara Hutton became the social leaders of Tangiers. Hutton's palace, Sidi Hosni, was the scene of extravagant parties, where the ambitious social climbers of the city sought invitations, and when they failed to receive them, tried to crash. No expense was too much for the Hutton fortune: she seemed to feel that she was

Cleopatra, and during her grand balls she would sit on a large jewel-encrusted throne, wearing the emerald and diamond tiara that had once belonged to Catherine the Great. She liked, according to Paul Bowles, "everything around her to show an element of the unreal in it, and she took great pains to transform reality into a continuous fantasy which seemed to her sufficiently *féerique* to be taken seriously."*

Drugs were common and cheap, especially kif (a mixture of cannabis and tobacco), hashish and *majoun*, and most of the artistic colony used them regularly. Every kind of sex was on offer: there were brothels for homosexuals, where boys would perform any service demanded, prostitutes and gigolos were easily available. These conveniences, and the exotic nature of a city where the international and the native communities existed side by side without friction, made Tangiers a natural draw for artists and playboys of all kinds, especially those with unconventional tastes. Some found the atmosphere too heavy and did not stay long, like Tennessee Williams, who was more inclined to see menace than charm in Morocco; he came principally to visit Paul Bowles, who had written the music for his play *Summer and Smoke*. Truman Capote alternated between Paris and North Africa with his lover Jack Dunphy, his main dissatisfaction being that whereas he was a celebrity in Paris he was unknown in Tangiers. As the author of *Other Voices, Other Rooms*, with its delicate handling of homosexual erotic attraction, he was one of the most discussed new novelists of the day in New York and in Europe. He became a close friend of Jane Bowles, and had parties given for him by Cecil Beaton and other members of the artistic community.

Brion Gysin arrived in 1950 and soon became a central figure in Tangiers. An early member of the surrealist group in Paris, he had been expelled by André Breton. Born in Britain, he had lived in Canada and the US, had worked at a variety of more or less exotic jobs, some of them blue-collar, but his stories about his past were so wild and colourful that no one really believed them. His paintings had been exhibited alongside those of Picasso, Dalí and Max Ernst. Gysin had been part of the famous 1935 surrealist exhibition in Paris, but Breton had removed his paintings at the last moment; Gysin had simply shown them on the street outside. A man with an easy charisma, Brion Gysin quickly became a centre of interest. A good talker, he had a wide knowledge of the world and opinions on everything, was casually promiscuous, seemed to have read everything, and could hold forth for hours on subjects ranging from remote mythologies to the modern arts.

Paul Bowles had met Gysin in Paris before the war, and a second chance meeting there led to Gysin's move to Tangiers, where for a while he shared Bowles's house. Like his host, Gysin made several trips to the remoter parts of the country, studying the folklore and taking part in the religious and secular festivals of the Berbers. After two years in Tangiers he made a long retreat into the Sahara where, fascinated by the light, he painted the desert and filled many sketchbooks. He had long been interested in the history of slavery, a subject on which he had written a book which had earned him a Fulbright scholarship, and he was also interested in black culture: much of the time he preferred black lovers. The Sahara fascinated him and he returned to it frequently. It was there that he met Felicity Mason, a beautiful British-born woman who travelled widely, mainly in search of sexual adventures. They became like brother and sister, each looking for men and delighting in each other's company. In Tangiers they became inseparable, which at first surprised his friends as his misogyny was notorious: he considered women to be either harpies or amazons and said so frequently. When William Burroughs later wrote that women were "a biological mistake" he was really quoting Brion Gysin. Gysin got on less well with Jane Bowles, who considered him a manipulator and something of a phoney, although she liked homosexual men in general and was herself a practising lesbian.

In 1954 Brion Gysin created a restaurant together with his Arab boyfriend, Hamri, an excellent cook. It was bankrolled by wealthy admirers and he called it The 1,001 Nights. It was furnished in Moroccan style, located in a wing of the Menebhi Palace in the Marshan, and on the walls hung his paintings of the desert. In the main room a troupe of musicians played traditional Moroccan music, and there were acrobats and fire-eaters to entertain the guests. The restaurant was an instant success and Gysin's natural talent as a host came into its own. He began to make money.

William Burroughs arrived in Tangiers at the beginning of 1954, having spent some time in Rome with Alan Anson, whom he had met in New York through Allen Ginsberg. Anson wanted to get into the literary life and did so by attaching himself to literary figures in the homosexual world, whom he went out of his way to meet. He was a classical scholar, but it did him little good. He had worked for W.H. Auden as his secretary, but rather than assisting Auden with his work, he was only allowed to do routine tasks, such as paying bills, fielding telephone calls and keeping Auden's personal accounts. Burroughs took to him, suggested they travel together in Europe, and first rendezvous in Rome. He took a cheap passage on a Greek liner, which was dirty and had inedible food, and arrived in an unhappy state in a cold Rome which, since he did not share Anson's interest in visiting churches and the monuments of the ancient civilization, he simply wanted to escape. As a Latin scholar Anson spoke some Italian, and he managed to make successful pick-ups, while Burroughs remained lonely and miserable in an unheated hotel room. They soon parted, Anson for Venice, where he would stay for some years, while Burroughs, inspired as much by Bowles's *Sheltering Sky* as anything else, went on to Tangiers.

He was there on 5th February for his fortieth birthday, a watershed date for both sexes. It is an age when men should, by tradition, be well advanced in their careers, knowing what the rest of their active lives will be like, while for women of a conventional mould it is a date for settling down with what they have or else of losing hope for improvement. Burroughs had accomplished nothing of note. His friends Ginsberg and Kerouac, companions of the drug scene, and of the years of bohemian road travel from one hippy meeting place to another, believed in his talent as a writer, but only *Junky* had been published, and that by a paperback company with no hardback to precede it. He was still living on a family allowance. He believed to some extent in his own magical powers, that he could put a curse on an enemy through telepathy, but his largely unfocused occultism was undoubtedly connected with his dream life and hallucinations under drugs.

Burroughs's sombre appearance and habit of walking straight ahead without looking to the right or left earned him the nickname in Tangiers of *"El hombre invisible"* from the Arab street boys. He wanted to meet Paul Bowles, whose novel had much influenced him, and he called on him, using his recently published *Junky* as an excuse: he said that he wanted Bowles's advice on his contract, which was pronounced unsatisfactory from the author's point of view. Bowles vaguely remembered having seen Burroughs occasionally on the street; he found him disquieting at first, but then, on further acquaintance, began to think him more interesting. Burroughs at this point was very much into his heroin addiction, but this did not put him in any danger of arrest in Tangiers.

Bowles, according to his own account, introduced Burroughs to Brion Gysin but Gysin seemed to remember that they first met at an exhibition of his paintings in the gallery of the Rembrandt Hotel. Burroughs had very much the appearance of a junky then and Gysin, although he used all the locally available soft drugs himself, had a horror of narcotic addicts. "Hamri and I decided, rather smugly, that we could not afford to know him," he is quoted as saying at the time. But it was not long before they became inseparable friends and collaborators.

Burroughs at forty had been through many adventures. He came from a conventional home in St Louis, where his father had made money by inventing an adding machine; Burroughs would later use this as the title of his collected essays. As a young man he had married Joan Vollmer, an experienced and adventurous young lady of exceptional good looks who had been previously married. She was intelligent, interested in the occult, older civilizations and a variety of cultural subjects. Burroughs learnt much from her, and some of his later preoccupations had their origin in her interests at the time he met her.

During the course of a drunken game in Mexico in 1951, where Burroughs and his wife, both revolver freaks, had shot glasses off each other's heads, which they called their "William Tell act", he had put a bullet through her forehead. The Mexican authorities, after a brief investigation, termed this a "*crime d'imprudence*" and released him as there was no proof that it was anything other than an accident. Since then William Burroughs had travelled in search of the forbidden and the perverse, the main subjects of his writing, convinced that occult evil forces influence our behaviour, and that beings from other planets are constantly trying to exercise control over our minds.

Burroughs had by now experimented with a wide variety of drugs, was writing in a desultory, disorganized way out of his drug experience, his work being not unlike that produced by the early surrealists through automatic writing, which is to say that the fingers that wrote or typed were not always governed by the thinking, planning brain. From the mix of his preoccupations, dreams, observation, memory and creative drive, texts were emerging. These were fragmented episodes or "routines", only occasionally linked, and, being more interested in writing than in organizing his texts, Burroughs left them that way. He had been for a considerable time in love with Allen Ginsberg, who was very willing to be his friend and correspondent, but not his lover. Their first brief sexual encounter, some years earlier, had not been satisfactory for Ginsberg, and he did not want to repeat the experience. They wrote to each other frequently and Burroughs's descriptions of the delights of Tangiers did eventually succeed in luring Ginsberg to North Africa. Burroughs had been very much alone during his early months there, and he had a great need for conversation and contact with other writers and artists. He missed the long nights talking in bars until dawn with a group of friends, or listening to jazz in a drug-induced daze in good company. Writing in his disjointed, fragmented way, he was unsure of his own talent, but obsessed with his special vision of the world. The film of *The Naked Lunch*, made by David Cronenberg and released in early 1992, is perhaps at its best in the way it catches Burroughs's frame of mind in those early Tangiers years. Burroughs now wanted to kick his heroin addiction, but money was still being sent to him by his family, and he constantly put off the necessity of taking a cure.

In a letter to Jack Kerouac and Allen Ginsberg, Burroughs complained that he had been coldly received by Paul Bowles, and he described Gysin, with whom he was not yet friendly, as having "a paranoid conceit"; he complained of his "glacial geniality", but this quality, he realized, was just right for a successful restaurateur. He predicted that Gysin "will get rich by acting like he is rich already".* He was already referring to Tangiers as "Interzone", the fictional city where so much of *The Naked Lunch* is set. Increasingly Burroughs began to realize that he had no ability to write in a popular or commercial vein. Continuity not only did not come easily to him, but he seemed to be incapable of organizing his own work into any kind of a sequence. He was developing a dislike for the Arabs, whom he called a "gabby, gossipy, simple-minded, lazy crew of citizens", and he also resented the affluent Mountain set, who lived with their pretensions on the higher levels of the town. He complained in his letters that he was not made welcome in the more fashionable bars like Dean's, but it was in fact his unprepossessing appearance, the shabbiness of his shiny clothes, his look of a "gaunt undertaker", as Paul Bowles once described him, that was responsible for this. He was receiving $200 a month from his parents, which just enabled him to eat quite well in good French restaurants, pay for his drugs, sleep with street boys, as well as afford a few other luxuries. Most drugs could be bought over the counter at a pharmacy, while heroin and morphine of good quality were readily available in the street. *Majoun* in particular he found to be a good stimulant to his writing, inspiring wild flights of fancy.

Gradually Brion Gysin began to realize that there was more to Burroughs than he had at first thought, and that behind the haunted look there lay a debauched kind of creativity. The Bowleses now began to receive him and to take an interest in his work. He met Francis Bacon, a frequent visitor staying with Paul, who liked to paint in the town and was teaching Bowles's Arab protegé, Ahmed Yacoubi, to use oil paint. Burroughs, in letters to his friends in the States, described Ahmed as fanatically jealous and a practitioner of black magic.

Early in 1956 Burroughs realized that his $200 a month was devalued by rising prices and his increasing heroin addiction. He was writing very little, was "junk sick" most of the time, and in considerable danger of having his allowance cut off. He was told of a Dr John Dent in London, who had successfully cured other addicts. He appealed to his parents for $500 to enable him to go to London to take a cure, and, when he received the money, left as quickly as he could obtain an exit visa. Dr Dent accepted him and Burroughs then underwent the apomorphine treatment that had originally been developed for alcoholics, but that Dent had discovered was equally effective in the treatment of heroin and morphine cases. It was a two-week course, with Burroughs hospitalized in Dent's small clinic in West Kensington, but it was successful. Burroughs was enabled to comprehend the chemical nature of the cure, which interested him very much, and although he was to use drugs again, more moderately, in future years, he was always able to avoid disabling addiction. He returned to Tangiers and continued with what was to become *The Naked Lunch*.

Paul Bowles paid a visit to Burroughs's lodgings one day and found that he was using it as a shooting gallery: the walls were heavily pitted with bullet holes while the growing pile of manuscript lay in fragments on his desk. He had a little cooking stove on which he made hashish candy. Burroughs would read from his manuscript at random to visitors, which usually made them laugh, after which he would normally embark on a harangue about some world event that was preoccupying him at the time. Once he was off hard drugs his lifestyle changed for the better; he made a more favourable impression on people he knew only slightly, and began to make new friends, even building a small circle of fans. He began to see the good side of Jane Bowles, whom he had previously considered to be an intellectual snob, only interested in knowing successful people. He even got on with Jane's girlfriend Cherifa, who thought that Burroughs was some kind of mystic.

Jack Kerouac finally responded to Burroughs's constant invitations and came to Tangiers in February 1957, sailing from New York on a Yugoslav freighter. Kerouac, the most prolific of the Beat writers at that time, had long been a supporter of Burroughs, and he was just beginning to be successful himself. *On the Road* had been published by Viking Press, and Grove had accepted *The Subterraneans*. Burroughs found him a hotel room and introduced him to the many shady pleasures of the city, of which Kerouac, who drank and whored hard, took full advantage. Kerouac read the various routines of Burroughs's manuscript and found the right title for it, *The Naked Lunch*, although Burroughs was later to define the title differently: a "lunch" in homosexual slang is a penis. During the visit Kerouac over-indulged in soft drugs and speed and heard much about Bill's continuing love and passion for Ginsberg. He knew that Ginsberg was now living with Peter Orlovsky, and he begged Kerouac for a description of his rival. He was assured that Allen was still his devoted friend and disciple, but also that he had no intention of sleeping with him again: their brief sexual encounter of many years earlier was remembered without pleasure. Burroughs pleaded with Jack to persuade Ginsberg to come to Tangiers, even with Orlovsky in tow, and promised not to be jealous. The end of Kerouac's visit saw Burroughs becoming increasingly maudlin; he realized that Jack was homesick and anxious to leave this colourful city, the pleasures of which were beginning to pall.

Allen Ginsberg and Peter Orlovsky did finally arrive on 21st March. They were now an established couple and Ginsberg – who had for a time tried to become heterosexual and acquire an image of middle-class respectability – had finally made up his mind that he would remain a bohemian poet and follow his own lifestyle. He was beginning to be successful, particularly with his public readings, while *Howl and Other Poems* was selling well in the alternative bookstores. Ginsberg had become the leader of the "Beat poets", who were now being called that, and of what the establishment sometimes referred to as "the new barbarians".

Burroughs found this new visit difficult. His feelings for Ginsberg were as strong as ever, and he could not control his jealousy and dislike for Orlovsky, who at twenty-three was eight years younger than Ginsberg and nearly half the age of Burroughs. Paul Bowles did not take to Orlovsky either: the latter's butterfly mind seemed incapable of following a line of thought or a conversation and he was not stimulating company. Burroughs turned surly and sarcastic, refused to take part in the many excursions that Ginsberg planned for them, and stuck to his work routine, writing until four in the afternoon, then entertaining his friends with brandy and kif. Kerouac, anxious to leave, did his best to keep the peace between them.

Tangiers had by this time changed quite considerably since Bowles and Barbara Hutton had first established themselves there. The French were gradually giving up their authority after much political agitation against them, and the new nationalists were not friendly towards the international community. The party was nearing its end. Paul Bowles moved from the native centre of the town to a less picturesque, but safer, area where the terrorists were not likely to be active. But the atmosphere was changing, and with a native administration the era of tolerance was over. Not only were there crackdowns on known criminals and racketeers, but there was a moral purge as well. Ahmed Yacoubi, Paul Bowles's painter-protegé and now former lover, was arrested for seducing a German boy, and everyone who had slept with a local Arab of either sex began to fear possible arrest. The prostitutes and the street boys disappeared from sight and there were new laws and regulations to be observed. The city still had a charter guaranteeing its economic independence, but the financial institutions began to leave, and there were fewer good French restaurants and places catering to European tastes. New import duties were introduced and the cost of living nearly doubled.

During his stay in Tangiers Ginsberg spent some time putting Burroughs's manuscript in order, trying to find some sequence to the episodes of the novel. Two hundred pages were now finished. But the hostility between Burroughs and Orlovsky continued, and after a particularly pointed taunt from the former, Peter took out a hunting knife and ripped up the front of Burroughs's shirt. Ginsberg realized that the time had come to leave, and he went to Spain with Orlovsky, taking a draft of the novel with him. Things were not going well with the Bowleses either: Jane had a severe stroke that slowed down all her movements and made it very difficult for her to write; it also impaired her eyesight. Paul Bowles was called in for questioning several times in connection with the Yacoubi affair. The new Algerian police chief was not willing to turn a blind eye to sexual deviants and Bowles realized that his Moroccan days were numbered. He made plans to return to the US where his books were now selling well. Brion Gysin also had his troubles. After a fight with Hamri, who had dominated the kitchen and the staff, Gysin bought him out, but Hamri started a second restaurant and took much of the business away. Brion had been studying Moroccan magic and had kept notes and made sketches of local magical practices, which his workers discovered. Furious that their secrets had been discovered by an infidel, they twice tried to poison him, and then used their own witchcraft; one day he found an amulet in the ventilator, of a kind used to cast an evil spell; inside it was a cabalistic grid with a message, calling for him to leave and never return. Shortly thereafter, Mary Cooke, one of his principal backers, told him he was fired. She too had been persuaded by his enemies. In January 1958 he moved to London where he sold some of his paintings and then went on to Paris.

Parts of *The Naked Lunch* appeared in the magazine *Big Table* in Chicago. Ginsberg had offered extracts to the editors of the *Chicago Review*, which was subsidized by the University of Chicago, but the authorities would not allow the issue to appear. As a result the editors resigned and started *Big Table*, although the first issue was immediately impounded by the Chicago post office. The editors ensured that the ensuing censorship debate received maximum publicity, and this finally decided Maurice Girodias to publish the text. He had turned it down, provisionally, two years earlier in 1957, as too chaotic to be a db. Burroughs at this time was having his own difficulties with the Moroccan police. A drug smuggler had been caught with half a kilo of opium. On his person at the time was a letter from Burroughs to a friend, proposing a plan to export kif in camel saddles, a plan that should not be taken as much more than a joke. The arrested man, a Captain Stevens, in order to divert attention from himself, claimed that Burroughs was a central figure in the drug trade. Burroughs was given warning of imminent arrest (the police did not realize that he was still in Morocco), and he moved quickly to Paris where he ran into Gysin in the street; the latter brought him to the Beat Hotel at 9 Rue Gît-le-Coeur. But the Moroccan police persisted and traced him, and the author was eventually brought to court in Paris, where Girodias engaged Maître Bomsel to defend him. Well accustomed to defending literary figures by now, Bomsel read extracts from the author's work (the more poetic passages, not the strongest) into his plea that Burroughs was a man of letters who had been mistaken for another. He was released.

Burroughs returned for a short time to Tangiers, as did many of the other expatriates, but they all knew the party was over. Burroughs wrote to Ginsberg: "Tanger [sic] is finished. The Arab dogs are upon us. Many a queen had been dragged shrieking from *The Parade*, *The Socco Chico*, and lodged in the local box where sixty sons of Sodom now languish… The boys, many beaten to a pulp, have spelt a list of hundreds…"* He moved back to Paris and took up long-term residence at the Beat Hotel, where Ginsberg, Orlovsky, Gysin and Gregory Corso were also living. Brion Gysin's novel *The Process* gives a fictional description of the life of the hotel, perhaps not unlike Henry Miller's Villa Seurat in the Thirties. Burroughs accommodated himself to a small hotel room, which most of his bedrooms for the next thirty years would resemble: it contained a small wooden table with his typewriter on it, stacks of typescript on the floor alongside books, magazines and other reading matter, with one or two upright chairs and a small wardrobe. Here he finished off *The Naked Lunch*, Ginsberg once again helping to put the text into some kind of a sequence. Eventually it was all delivered to Girodias. Burroughs was now leading a normal life, free of heroin, although he still occasionally had to use apomorphine and methadone to regulate his body. He liked drinking, but other than the odd glass of wine if he went out to lunch, he followed Gysin's rule to touch no alcohol until sundown.

On the day after Burroughs's return from Tangiers, Ginsberg announced to Girodias over the telephone: "The man's in town." He arranged to bring him over and introduce him to Maurice the following day. It was a walk of about two hundred yards from Rue Gît-le-Coeur, across the Place Saint-Michel and the boulevard of the same name, to Girodias's office, which now had the restaurant underneath it. Within five minutes Girodias felt that he had a new friend, while the American publicity generated by the post office case and the anti-censorship stance generated by the editors of *Big Table* were reason enough to publish. His hesitations gone, he had begun to appreciate the black humour of Burroughs, and he realized that he was about to tap a new market, that of homosexual eroticism, and one that would also appeal to adventurous heterosexual readers, as Genet had. The Casement book had not done that: it had in the event been an all-round loss; his own edition had sold badly, Rosset had sold very few copies in the States, and the American press had shown as little interest as the French newspapers in the "*Affaire Casement*". Girodias had been paid for the 1,500 copies sold to Sidgwick & Jackson, which was hardly a recompense for the research and editorial effort it had taken him to put the book together. But *The Naked Lunch* was a different situation altogether. He realized that Burroughs was a total opposite to the unfriendly Donleavy: he was grateful to be published, to have someone interested and enthusiastic about his work and to be interested in him as a person. "Simple, well-meaning and full of wisdom" was Girodias's judgement. Maurice began to compare *The Naked Lunch* to *La Chanson de Roland*, the anonymous twelfth-century heroic poem in which the hero prepares himself for an ecstatic death.

In rapid succession Girodias published *The Naked Lunch* and its two sequels, *The Soft Machine* and *The Ticket that Exploded*. The latter two increasingly showed Gysin's influence. Having talked to Burroughs about the way he created collages in his paintings to produce accidental results, and having in his writings and manifestos advocated "freeing the word" to invent a new literature, he excited Burroughs intellectually, who began to experiment and look for ways of producing similar aleatory results in his prose. Burroughs pondered, then sat down with scissors, paste and a variety of texts, whatever was close to hand, and by experiment began to develop his fold-in and cut-up method. This consisted of taking two separate texts, which could be as different as a page of a newspaper and a novel by Proust or Kafka: the two pages were then lined up and Burroughs would read across the two pages, copying out half of what he saw on the left and half of what was present on the right, then editing the new lines so created. This would yield a new text that would then be lined up with a quite different one. The result, after an indefinite number of linings up, was then edited to make some sense of the sentences run together, adding or subtracting words. Alternately a page would be folded or cut vertically in half and lined up with another folded or cut page to produce a similar result. In this way the *New York Times* or *New York Herald Tribune* was mixed with Beckett, Genet, Hemingway or Burroughs's own previous work. Strange stories began to emerge from cut-ups and fold-ins. Gradually Burroughs began to believe that he was creating magic. On one occasion he came up with a story about a plane crash in South America. The next day he read in the newspapers about a real plane crash that had happened about the time that he was producing his unfinished, edited text. The name of the Captain of the aircraft was very similar, and so was the place of the crash. Burroughs believed that he had made it happen: literature could really produce magic! He became increasingly convinced that he had the power by "freeing the word" to discover a whole new world of arcane and mystical experience, reinforcing his natural interest in the occult, which had been stimulated by Joan, his dead wife.

Maurice Girodias

Liberation of Paris, 1944

Reception for Merlin, Paris 1953. Back row, left to right: George Plimpton,
Corneille, Richard Seaver, Mary Smith, Patrick Bowles, Gaït Frogé,
Jane Lougee. Front row, left to right: Christopher Logue,
Austryn Wainhouse, Christopher Middleton

Alexander Trocchi

Lyn Hicks

Alexander Trocchi and
Jane Lougee

Eugène Ionesco and
Alexander Trocchi

John Calder with Maurice Girodias (top left), with Barney Rosset (bottom left)
and with Jérôme Lindon (right)

Some of Olympia Press's iconic editions

Chapter Eight

La Grande Séverine

1

At great expense and after many setbacks Girodias opened his restaurant. His contractors had illegally tunnelled under the graveyard of the church to extend his cellar, removing the earth and the remains of old coffins and their contents at night. There had been floods when the nearby river rose, and rain came in from the defective roof overhead. The other residents of the street, mainly Arab traders and the owners of small, cheap boutiques and restaurants, were not friendly, and the priest was also hostile, suspecting that a brothel was opening next door. When La Grande Séverine finally opened, it was as a de luxe establishment at street level with a big spacious basement under it containing more tables, where the decor consisted of old polished stones from the middle ages. There was a bar in the American style at the entrance. People began to come out of curiosity, and soon Rolls-Royces, Déesses and Mercedes began to block the narrow street, park on the concrete, and make the windows of the small traders invisible to passers-by.

For some time Michelle had begun to realize that the money being poured into rehabilitating the building from a medieval slum into a fashionable restaurant, and the considerable overhead that Girodias had incurred by employing waiters, chefs, barmen and cleaners, was unlikely ever to come back. She was tired from the work and needed a holiday. In short, she was disenchanted, disillusioned and sick of the whole crazy project. Maurice had promised to take her to Greece, but it was obviously impossible for him to be away for long, and reluctantly she agreed to settle for a short holiday on the Côte d'Azur. They left for Nice on 26th August by the night train. They were awakened early on their first morning by a telephone call from Sylvie, Maurice's sister. There had been a fire at the restaurant the previous night. They returned instantly to Paris and surveyed the ruin. It had obviously been sabotage, but there was no proof; the firemen were unconvinced, and could not identify the source or the cause of the fire. The offices were also mostly destroyed, although Girodias's own room was spared, as well as the adjoining office of Miriam Worms. The building was still smoking when they arrived and Girodias realized that the conflagration might easily have spread and burnt down the whole quarter.

The parrots that Miriam kept in the main office were roasted in their cage, manuscripts and proofs were turned to ashes, expensive kitchen and restaurant equipment totally destroyed. A crowd had gathered in the street and the overheard comments of Girodias's neighbours were not friendly. Girodias had under-insured the building and the insurance agent, who had come to inspect the damage, told him that any insurance paid would be purely symbolic. The employees of the restaurant began to turn up, one by one, to contemplate the scene of their lost jobs. Marcos, the contractor who had built and decorated the restaurant, surveyed his wasted work. Girodias made a decision.

"How long would it take," he asked Marcos, "if you worked flat out, to rebuild the kitchen, the cellar and the bar?"

Marcos was an enthusiast. He contemplated the smoking scene. "Perhaps three weeks to do only that, and to camouflage the rest."

"Do it then," said Girodias. "We'll have a grand opening in three weeks. All this will give us publicity."

"Count me out," said Michelle. "If you're so stupid as to start this folly all over again, do it on your own. I'm exhausted. And I'm leaving."

"But Michelle—"

"Goodbye then." And she was gone.

Marcos tapped him on the back. "We'll start tomorrow," he said. "I'll have it ready in three weeks. And she'll be back for the opening, I guarantee it, I know women."

But he was wrong.

2

Girodias had made another decision, one hardly sensible for a man also rebuilding a restaurant in Paris: to start another publishing house in the US. His dealings with publishers like Walter Minton, and others whose working methods consisted of doing only that which would make the most money while avoiding all risk and any kind of publication that was different from current popular taste or that offered a sense of adventure, had convinced him that with his special flair he could put them all to shame. The very size of the American market beckoned him. His books would sell millions there. But this project had to wait.

Although he was to see Michelle two or three times more, it was purely for brief physical reunions. Michelle had come to realize, during the short life of the restaurant, the full scale of Girodias's folly. From the beginning there had been theft by the staff. The cellar emptied itself of the fine wines it contained in a way that had little to do with what the customers drank, and half the food disappeared by the kitchen door. A business that operated on liquid cash had to be properly monitored, and Girodias was incapable of doing that. The fire could have been a godsend, but for his stubbornness. It was Sylvie, his sister, back from the Argentine, who now took charge. The cellar could take a hundred diners, and it was full most of the time. People came out of curiosity to see the building – there were rumours that Girodias was involved in the criminal world and that rivals had burnt him out; many came just to have a drink in the bar and to look around. He rebuilt his offices on the third floor and made a large salon one floor below where the old ones had been, in the style of Louis XVI. The "Winter Garden" on the street floor was gradually rebuilt.

Both on the street level and the cellar underneath, there had originally been a wall with nothing apparently behind it. As no architect had been involved with the building since the disappearance of Jean-Pierre, and Girodias had never applied for any licence to do what he wanted in the way of construction, there had been no inspection of the building or the work done on it. Marcos was always ready for anything, and to enlarge the premises they had delved behind the interior walls, both before the first opening and after the fire, only to find bones buried in the earth. Skulls, backbones and ribcages were pulled out by pickaxes and shovels. This was consecrated ground, where most of the time the poor had been buried without coffins, many no doubt victims of the plague. The excavation had to be carried out in secret, and the human and other debris taken out late at night. Girodias occasionally had a twinge of conscience. He was a grave-robber.

Mason Hoffenberg now became a nuisance. He could not understand why Girodias had not succeeded in selling *Candy* to an American publisher to repeat the success of *Lolita*. It had been offered several times but had been turned down, even by Barney Rosset. Girodias vaguely thought of publishing it himself in the US. It would inaugurate his career as an American publisher. But he was not yet ready. Hoffenberg was often seen standing outside the restaurant, looking disapprovingly at the customers turning up in their big cars, and going in to an expensive dinner. One night he came into the bar and sat down next to Girodias, who offered him a drink. Hoffenberg asked if he could borrow his pen.

Girodias had to leave the bar for a minute, and when he returned the author was gone and so was the pen. Maurice had valued it: it was the pen with which he signed contracts, and he was just about to leave for the Frankfurt Book Fair. Was this voodoo? He was to understand the symbolism of the pen a little later.

In Frankfurt that year he was given a big dinner outside the town by all the European publishers of *Lolita*. They had all done well out of Nabokov. At the end of the evening Ledig-Rowohlt made a toast and a little speech. He ended by saying: "We're between friends now. Tell us, what is the title of your next best-seller?"

Girodias stood up, thanked his hosts, and calmly announced. "Its name is *Candy*."

On his way back to Frankfurt in his rented Mercedes, Girodias, a little drunk and euphoric at the prospect of more fat advances from his hosts, who were all willing to buy *Candy* for their respective publishing houses without even seeing it, drove into a ditch. As a result he did not bother to go to the Fair the following day, and failed to keep his appointment with Walter Minton, who had not been present at the dinner, and was returning to New York. It was a serious oversight on Girodias's part. Back in Paris he learnt that Hoffenberg had just signed a contract with Minton, who had stopped over on the way back to the States. He had used Maurice's pen to sign it.

Girodias's own contract with the two authors of *Candy* included American rights, but Minton could now claim that there was no proper American copyright as the books that had been imported from Paris by the tourists certainly came to more than 1,500 copies. But he was prepared to give royalties to the author. The legal loophole also opened the way to other pirate editions, but the first publisher would scoop the reviews and get a big sale for at least a few weeks if the publicity was right. Shortly before Minton's edition appeared, with Maurice still considering what legal action was possible, he was approached by Walter Zacharius of Lancer Books. Zacharius was willing to pay a twelve per cent royalty if he had a contract to bring out a paperback edition, but the contract would have to be signed that day because time was short. He pointed out that Girodias could keep all the royalties as damages, because the authors had signed an illegal contract with Minton. Zacharius intended to bring out his own paperback edition just two weeks after the Putnam hardcover. He would get the benefit of the reviews and of the publicity that Minton had paid for. The Putnam edition would be published at $5.00; the *Lancer* paperback would be only 50 or perhaps 75 cents. Girodias was persuaded and he signed the contract, calculating that he could expect at least $200,000 from the deal. The bills of the restaurant were mounting and he would need it.

In the meantime the Winter Garden had been built, and Girodias turned it, for the time being, into an after-theatre restaurant at reasonable prices aimed at a younger clientele. He came across a black American chef called Leroy Haines, who already ran a little restaurant near Pigalle. Married to a tiny Frenchwoman, he had been chased out of his own restaurant by his diminutive wife – Maurice was amused by the difference in size between the black American giant and the tiny Frenchwoman, and speculated about the nature of their sex life – and Haines now proposed to Girodias that he should specialize in creole specialities such as Southern Fried Chicken and black-eyed peas. These dishes were first offered in the Winter Garden, but then Girodias encountered a statuesque black American blues singer called Mae Mercer. He moved Haines upstairs into a newly decorated American Blues Bar, where hamburgers, hot dogs and other typical American foods were added to the menu, all cooked by Haines. Mae Mercer did two shows nightly, sometimes together with Memphis Slim, a well-known jazz pianist, who had been in Paris for some time.

Mae became another of Girodias's mistresses, and perhaps the most memorable. Large, but well proportioned, she was taller than him, stronger willed and brooked no nonsense. She accepted Girodias as a lover for a while, but his many relationships with other women were too much for her. When she discovered that he was sleeping with one of the other stars of his complex of restaurants – at this point he had three – she threw him out of bed and chased him through the streets of the *cinquième*. In spite of her size and the heaviness of her breasts – they were both totally naked – she eventually caught up with him. It was dawn on a fine summer morning, and she was chasing him, not as has often been claimed with a butcher's knife from the restaurant kitchen, but with a high-heeled shoe. Eventually she managed to hit him so hard on the head with its stiletto heel that he carried the mark on his skull for the rest of his life.

Nevertheless Maurice's fascination with Mae was not just a casual fling. Her frankness and lack of embarrassment at those moments when French women want to be most private, when sitting on the lavatory for instance, intrigued him. She would keep up a constant stream of banter and conversation during her ablutions, took sex as a natural activity that is performed the way we eat a meal, and switched from being a private woman to the professional singer as circumstances required. She considered it perfectly natural to be faithful to the man she slept with, but what shocked her – as a strictly brought-up Baptist – was the content of Girodias's publications. She had never heard of most of the sexual practices that he put into her hands, her eyes growing big as she read, and he loved to see her shocked innocence as he deflowered her mind. It was a genuine love affair, although it did not last long.*

The restaurant had now expanded into different sections. The ground floor became a Russian restaurant, which Girodias called "Chez Vodka". It featured a balalaika band, led by a handsome young white Russian named Marc Laudchek, whose beautiful blonde wife, Olga, sang with the band, but she also ran the restaurant. She too became a Girodias mistress, apparently with the complaisance of Marc. Maurice met Marpessa Dawn, the star of *Black Orpheus*, a film which had recently taken Paris by storm. Set during the Brazilian carnival in Rio de Janeiro, it is a love story that emphasizes interracial harmony and equality, but also the contrasts between the lives of the poor in the shanty towns and the ultra-rich, differences which are temporarily forgotten in the colourful euphoria of carnival. The dusky beauty of Marpessa had made a mark on every Frenchman who had seen the film, and Girodias knew that she would draw in the customers. He engaged her as hostess and entertainer for a Brazilian nightclub, which he installed in the basement. She too became his mistress. At one point he was having affairs with all the three ladies who managed and entertained in different parts of his building, and the electricity between them was dramatic.

But the uses of the building did not end there. Part of the ever-enlarging basement – Marcos was still excavating – was now turned into a small theatre. Here he put on a number of plays, usually, but not always, with a strong erotic element. The first was an adaptation by his brother Eric Kahane of de Sade's *La Philosophie dans le boudoir*. The production was chaste enough in terms of action, because the novel is really a long dialogue leading to the seduction of an innocent young girl, who by the end of the book is not at all innocent in terms of her knowledge of what sexuality is all about. But the language, elegant eighteenth-century French, deals in much detail with bodily functions and emotions, and could be very titillating to an audience. It was well reviewed by some Parisian newspapers, but the priest next door lodged a complaint with the police, and before the end of the week, when it was playing to full houses, it was closed down. Other fairly harmless productions followed, including a Dadaist farce by Marc O, a name that was then fashionable, but Girodias was incapable of keeping so many balls in the air, and he soon accepted defeat as a theatrical impresario.

Whereas one restaurant, properly managed, might have paid its way, it was too much to expect to keep three going. Girodias, sleeping in some kind of rotation with three different beauties who worked on different floors, drinking much of the profits of his own bar – assuming that the barman had left him any profit – and running a publishing house, had to leave his sister Sylvie to do most of the management. Sylvie had no experience and obviously could not deal with the mounting deficit, the daily theft by employees and the decreasing receipts, as customers, having satisfied their curiosity, stopped coming. The prices were high, the food not that wonderful in a city where diners knew the difference, and the *accueil*, the all-important presence of a welcoming host or hostess, very erratic. Sylvie filled some tables by inviting groups of her friends to make it look less empty, but none of them paid, and Girodias, when he used the restaurant himself – and he frequently went elsewhere – was usually entertaining friends and authors, none of whom expected his hospitality to cost them a penny. The monkey-gland treatment, which he presumably still took, may have given him additional energy, but with practically no sleep and mounting debts, disaster could not be much longer averted.

This was the time when money was coming in from *Lolita*, *The Naked Lunch* and other books he had successfully subcontracted, but none of the authors' share of these rights was leaving Girodias's hands, at least not in the direction of the authors. He needed every penny that came in to pay his restaurant suppliers, his staff salaries and his printing bills. Authors living in Paris could no longer count on walking away with cash in their hands, and when they did get something it was a pittance. He never knew what he owed. William Burroughs turned up in Paris. He had gone back to Tangiers from London, where he was then living, in the knowledge that considerable amounts were due to him from the recently published Grove Press edition, and Girodias had received advances from me as well. Burroughs's frantic appeals for money to be sent to him in Morocco were ignored, and when he finally managed to get to Paris and went to see Girodias, he was greeted with the words: "I have a terrible confession to make." His publisher was facing bankruptcy, and there was no way he could meet his obligations to his authors.

Girodias's new secretary was now Marilyn Meeske, who had replaced Miriam Worms. Miriam, married to a sociologist who, like many of his contemporaries, was very involved in protests against the Algerian war, had enough to think about in her life without sharing all the problems of La Grande Séverine and Olympia Press, problems which were insoluble.

The Algerian War was a larger concern. It played little part in the lives and consciousness of expatriate writers in Paris, but it convulsed French intellectuals, and the majority of the population simply wished to see the conflict ended, even at the cost of losing a valued colony. The wave of Algerian nationalism was now too powerful to be halted, and books about the atrocities of the French Army in Algeria, especially those committed by the paratroopers and the Foreign Legion, the latter at that point dominated by German ex-SS men and others who had fought with the Nazis and had then fled to North Africa after 1945, had greatly influenced French public opinion. In Britain, I had myself published Henri Alleg's *The Question*, a book describing the methods of torture used by French soldiers during the Algerian War, at a time when it was banned in France.* I had also written in the *New Statesman* about the "Audin Affair", the torture and disappearance of an Algerian communist named Maurice Audin, following this by editing a large composite volume on colonial atrocities committed by both the British and the French armies, which at the time led to calls for my arrest for treason by right-wing newspapers and some members of the House of Lords.*

Miriam had had enough of Maurice's follies and absorption in his own affairs at such a time of national crisis, and she left him to work for a small political newspaper which was dedicated to the cause of Algerian independence. Walking out of her new office building for lunch one day with another member of the staff, she became the victim of a plastic bomb left there by the "ultras", the right-wing militant terrorists, who were subsidized by the French *colons*. Paris at this time was a dangerous place, emptied of most tourists, because bombs were planted wherever Algerian sympathizers lived and in the places they frequented. Her friend was killed. Miriam was lucky enough only to be wounded, but she lost one eye. Girodias felt guilty. Had she remained with him she would be whole; he had never meddled in Algerian politics, and it was his craziness as her boss that had forced her to leave! Miriam made a full recovery, except for the eye, which from that time onwards she covered with an eye-patch, drawing attention to her loss by making it a fashion feature: henceforth she always wore a piece of material over her eye that matched her skirt or her costume.

Marilyn Meeske was, like Iris Owens, a New Yorker, Jewish, sexy and full of vitality. She had a younger sister, equally attractive in a different way, Patty Welles, and they both exuded sexuality. Marilyn and Patty contributed to the Olympia list of pornographic literature, although not everything they wrote was published because of Girodias's present and forthcoming problems. Marilyn in her early days in Paris, frequented Café Tournon and the Old Navy and met there the survivors of *Merlin* and other American and anglophone groups. Girodias, when he met her, instantly liked her and commissioned work from her. When Miriam Worms left, Marilyn moved into her shoes and became both secretary and editor to Maurice.

She took the pen name Henry Crannach after Lucas Cranach, a favourite painter, and thought that with a man's name she could let herself go more than with a woman's; after all, Trocchi had done the same the other way round with some of his novels. *Flesh and Bone* was her first db and she followed it with a book that she intended to be a serious novel, *The Porridge Tasters*, which horrified Girodias with its lack of sexual content, so he declined it. Later she agreed with his judgement and added some erotic content. During the period when she was writing, but had not yet worked for Girodias, she managed to get a job through Marlon Brando, working as an extra on a film he was making in Paris. Somehow the word went around the set that she wrote pornography for Olympia and she became the most sought-after girl in the production. "How do you get your material?" she was asked, as well as: "Aren't a lot of those books true?" and "Do you practise what you write?" The obsessions of make-up men, production men and technicians, constantly hounding her for details of her personal life and its relationship to her writing, made her finally leave the set. As for Brando, he was less interested: he had scalded himself with boiling water while serving tea and insisted on being doctored and babied for several days.

She became good friends with Norman Rubington and Terry Southern, as well as with the various inhabitants of the Beat Hotel at 9 Rue Gît-le-Coeur, including Gregory Corso, whom she had first met at the Hôtel Alsace-Lorraine, where she and Vali, a girlfriend, were both staying. Corso had a way of intruding his presence on those who did not particularly like him, including Vali, but the most embarrassing incident happened when Marilyn was being visited by very conventional relatives from the States, on whom she wanted to make a good impression. She was already suspect in the family because she had once nearly been expelled from school for owning a book by E.B. White and James Thurber with the word "sex" in the title. On this occasion she was sitting with them having an aperitif in Les Deux Magots when to her dismay she saw Gregory Corso approaching, looking like a typical beatnik. She tried to avoid his eye, but he came over and sat at the table without invitation. Her unfriendliness released a torrent of abuse from Corso and a long denunciation of her character in front of the speechless relatives. This helped to clear the throng at the tables around them, and Corso then also left while Marilyn Meeske tried to make up some explanation. He made amends of a sort: she found a poem outside her door the next morning, entitled 'An Apology Flower':

> As a child I saw many things I did not want to be
> Am I the person I did not want to be?
> That talking-to-himself person?
> That selling-old-fruit-on-the-street-corner person?
> Am I he who on museum steps sleeps on his side?
> Do I wear the cloth of a man who has failed?
> Am I the looney man?*

In Paris Marilyn met the Kronhausens, a very strange couple, who seemed to have switched their sexes in their first names. "Ebe", the husband, was a German who had been tortured by the Gestapo and had at one point had his balls crushed by their boots. This made sex difficult if not impossible for him, but it in no way diminished his interest in the subject and the activity. "Ebe" was short for Eberhard. His wife, "Phil" (Phyllis) was an attractive American blonde, past her youth but still with a high sex drive. They had met in the States at university when they were both studying to become Doctors of Psychiatry; both were obsessed by sex to the extent that it was difficult to engage them in any other subject. They were to write many books in the next few years and one of the first, *Pornography and the Law*, became a best-seller.* They were then planning an exhibition of erotic art that was to successfully tour many countries. The Kronhausens were living in the Rue de l'Odéon, and, having met Marilyn, they told her that they wanted above all to meet Girodias, who was up to his neck in problems at the time and trying to avoid social engagements. But Marilyn insisted and told Maurice, "They'll amuse you. They're an extraordinary couple, naive as anything. That's their real strength: they're very naughty, very naive and very well organized. To them you will be like Moses coming down from Mount Sinai to speak to the chosen people. Don't be such a snob."

"Well, we'll see. Maybe later…"

It was a few days after that, when Girodias was having a drink with Marilyn at an outside table at the Café de Flore, that she suddenly called out: "There they are!" Girodias, seeing them approach, had already observed the strange appearance of a couple walking up the boulevard. On the one hand they looked like typical tourists, casually dressed, the man with a Rolleiflex around his neck, but their walk was jerky and out of synch with each other. He had a small head, was abnormally thin, and his face looked older than the rest of him. She, a small blonde with a determined air about her, seemed to be on some mission. They stopped suddenly, and it was obvious to Maurice that they had recognized him, as well as Marilyn. Girodias was convinced that they were about to pounce and devour him – it was indeed the Kronhausens – because they had been trying for some time to make an appointment. But Girodias ignored them; he had a number of men as well as Marilyn with him at the table, including Mason Hoffenberg, who at this point had still not signed the contract with Walter Minton. Girodias could see in their eyes that they suddenly suspected that he was a homosexual. They hesitated and walked on. Later that afternoon Maurice was in a favourite bar, Le Nuage. He was in the process of beginning to seduce a beautiful young woman he had just met there, and made sure there was no doubt about his intentions. The Kronhausens stopped and gasped at the sight, all their suspicions being suddenly destroyed. He was a heterosexual man after all!

3

Marcos was still excavating under the graveyard. He hoped to find treasures, having heard that many cemeteries contained corpses with jewels and gold buried with them, but if this was true, he was in the wrong graveyard. He found nothing of any value. But the premises became larger. There were now two cellars, one of them containing Marpessa Dawn's Brazilian nightclub, the other, which became his little theatre for a while, was to be a future restaurant, perhaps even a French one! The bones were taken out after the restaurant and nightclub were closed, and Marcos's truck worked until dawn removing the debris: 257 skulls and thousands of miscellaneous bones, together with rotten wood, stones and earth were removed. Marcos and his workmen swore in Spanish as they raked through the human garbage, finding no precious metals.

Girodias had not paid much attention to the disposal of the rubbish. At the end of a year of excavation he had a second underground space and what was not lined with polished stones was now panelled in white wood. But the neighbours were getting agitated, and Marcos finally admitted that it was getting too complicated to find remote disposal areas and empty stretches of river. He had been using the local rubbish dumps, and even putting bones and skulls into the restaurant's garbage bins on occasion. He eventually admitted to using those of the neighbours as well.

Girodias was lucky to be in an Arab quarter. Tongues were undoubtedly wagging, and he could feel the hostility of his neighbours when he walked through the streets, but the Arabs knew that the police were no friends of theirs. If they were to report the skulls and skeletons turning up in their rubbish, they might easily find that some crime was being pinned on them. They undoubtedly grumbled, but there was no incident.

No money had come in from the Lancer sales of *Candy* and Girodias decided that it was time to go to New York to find out what was happening there. He booked into the Chelsea Hotel, left his suitcase, and went directly to the address of Lancer Books. If he telephoned, they might put him off to another day. It was better to take them by surprise. When he gave his name, the receptionist looked at him with round eyes, and without even waiting for his next question, told him: "Mr Zacharius is not in."

"Mr Stein then."

"Mr Stein is not in."

At that moment an office door opened and a pretty young black woman came out with a no less pretty smile. "Maurice Girodias! What a pleasure to meet you. My name is Sarah, Sarah Uman. I'm the assistant to Irving and Walter. Come into my office."

While he sat on the sofa, she filled time with light conversation, asking after his trip and saying that she was sure they had many friends in common. She had heard so much about him. But then she went on: "You should have warned us. Walter will never forgive himself for missing you. He just left half an hour ago for his plane."

"Where to?"

"Well, he's gone to Mexico."

"And what about Irving Stein?"

"No, Irving isn't here either! You really should have telephoned—"

"Where's he?"

"In the Congo," she replied without flinching. "You didn't know? He's gone for a long trip. What would they do without me, those two? Always travelling! But they have confidence in me to look after things."

"I'm sure it's justified. But that's not the question. We made a contract in Paris. Walter was going to ring me as soon as he got back to New York. I've heard nothing. Now be serious, Miss Uman. Three telegrams with no reply. Many useless telephone calls and I never get through. So I came personally. Where are they? Why are they hiding? What are they afraid of?"

Sarah laughed. "Afraid? Why should they be afraid of you? That's funny."

"Because if they're up to something fishy, I have a signed contract, and they won't get out of it easily."

"I'm sorry," said Sarah, "but they're not here. It's about *Candy*, isn't it? What a wonderful book. I love it! I know you discussed it with Walter and he brought back a copy, which I devoured…"

Girodias's temper was mounting. Should he hit her or pull off her pants? This was a real little tease who knew just what she was doing.

"Since Putnam published it, it's the only book that's discussed," she rattled on. "It's going to be a real best-seller…"

"I know that. And it belongs to me."

"I thought that it belonged to the author, Maxwell Kenton."

"That's only a pen name. Stop playing games. I've come across the Atlantic for only one reason. To find out what's going on! And to settle my accounts with Walter. If you're not going to tell me anything, I shall remain here until he comes out of his hole—"

"I understand, Maurice," she interrupted. "I'm sorry you feel that way. But they're really not here. If you want to talk about legal problems, perhaps you should have a word with our lawyer, Hymie Schlockman."

"Why didn't you say so before? Can I call him from here?"

"Please. Use my phone. Here's the number. I'll leave you alone." She left the room, no doubt to listen in from another extension.

"Mr Schlockman?"

"Yah!" Maurice did not like the sound of the voice. He told him his name and why he was in New York.

"Well, what can I do for you?" Maurice started to explain why he was there, but was quickly interrupted. "Now listen to me. You signed a contract for a book for which you don't have the rights. A book without any copyright, which has just been published by another publisher. Isn't that true?" He exploded over the telephone, almost shouting. "That contract was an attempt to cheat my clients. If they had consulted me at the time, I would have told them to sue you. So why are you wasting my time? Go back to your own country, old man. You're out of your depth. You've got nothing to do here."

"Now listen—"

"You listen. If you want to know something interesting, it's that Lancer are publishing tomorrow. Just try to stop them. Have fun!" And he hung up.

4

One of Olympia Press's new authors was Gregory Corso, whom Girodias put into the second category of authors who combined a certain literary quality with erotic appeal. Olympia's green-backed series of Traveller's Companion paperbacks all had either some original quality or were literary in the sense that, however much Girodias asked the authors to keep up a certain level of sexual content, they viewed themselves as serious writers making art. The books in the second category were not expected to end up on American best-seller lists, but to have a reasonably good sale based on the popular appeal of the series.

Girodias did not have any *Lolita* or *Naked Lunch* ready for publication in 1961, but Corso's novel *The American Express*, which he ranked in the school of psychedelic, delirious and poetic writing, would do for the time being. It also had little in it to interest the Brigade Mondaine. It also occurred to him that the estimable institution from which the book took its title might threaten him with a lawsuit for stealing the name from them, in which case he could turn the publicity to good advantage. The novel itself had little to do with American Express, but, in the prologue, which was set in an American Express office, a young woman asks a young man to make her pregnant, an offer that he willingly accepts, but the sex act is not described. The author jumps instead to the birth, which *is* described and in the following manner:

> They wheeled her into the basement of the American Express, they held her down, they spread her legs, they plunged into her womb, they yanked the child from her, they punched it into life, they threw it out into the street, it lay there until dawn – Dawn, and something small and sad rose and walked into the world.*

This is how Gregory Corso presents to the reader the birth of Simon, the hero; his other characters have names that include Dad Deform, Mr D., Scratch Vatic, Angus Plow, Wolfherald, all of them belonging to the author's personal mythology. The publisher decided to give a big party for the book's publication in the cellars of La Grande Séverine and he invited the Paris Director of American Express, but received no reply. The cover of the book showed the façade of the American Express itself, in such a way that the sign over the entrance became the title of the book. Girodias was being as provocative as possible.

There were about thirty members of the press present, but nearly all of them worked for the *New York Herald Tribune*'s Paris edition. Girodias looked them over and realized that there was not a single critic or columnist of note among them. They were minor employees of the paper who had come to have a good time, and eat and drink at his expense. There were also about a hundred beatniks, some of them invited by Corso, but most of them friends of friends, who had heard about the party on the grapevine. Gregory Corso came in looking unusually elegant, wearing a shirt he had borrowed from a waiter and with a cigarette-holder he had borrowed from a call girl. A group followed him that included Allen Ginsberg and a number of hippy musicians with Tibetan instruments, which soon persuaded the orchestra Maurice had engaged for the evening to give up.

The high point of the party turned out to be Allen Ginsberg and a few of his friends doing a ritual striptease, accompanied by the hand-claps of his sycophants, while the maze of incense, hashish and marijuana made them almost invisible. The *Herald Tribune* staff began to disappear uneasily. Girodias observed a man standing apart, watching all this, who obviously was not part of the press or one of the hippy invaders. He was wearing a tie, a three-piece suit and had polished shoes. Maurice went up to him and asked if he was enjoying the occasion.

"Not particularly," the man replied.

"What a pity. Perhaps you're here for professional reasons?"

There was a pause. "Are you the owner of Olympia Press? Girodias?"

"Yes."

"Then I must tell you, that I have been asked by American Express to investigate the way in which their name is being used. My own name will hardly interest you and as I have no desire to find it in one of your books, I'm not going to give it."

"I hope your report will not be too nasty," said Girodias. "The author's reason for using the name is quite innocent. He picked it because American Express has been like a cradle for several generations of cosmopolitan young Americans—"

"Well that says it all," said the stranger. "Thank you for your hospitality. I must congratulate you on the decor. Your taste in that respect I can only admire. As for the rest..." His hand indicated the psychedelic crowd in front of him and he added, "I hope you can live with it. Goodnight." He was gone. And there were no further consequences.

Chester Himes was another American writer who came into Girodias's orbit. Like Gregory Corso he had spent some time in prison in the

States. Corso always said that his three years in prison had given him a better education than most of his contemporaries had enjoyed at Yale or Harvard, and it pushed him into the beatnik fold. But Himes refused to be part of any group. He had a strong power of observation and a spontaneous sense of humour, which gave a vivacity and a certain satirical hilarity to his writing. Girodias heard that Plon had accepted his novel *Mamie Mason*, the subject of which was a circle of successful American black socialites who were as snobbish as their white counterparts, for translation into French. The principal character, whose name was the title, was a high-flying figure of fashion with ebony skin and consenting thighs.

Girodias was intrigued by what he had heard about Chester Himes and when he learnt that he was in Paris with his white, blonde wife, he contacted him and asked if he would call at his offices and let him see the English manuscript. Having taken an evening to read it, he asked for a second meeting and offered $1,000, payable on the spot, as an advance against English-language rights. His only condition was to ask Chester to add half a dozen sex scenes, preferably within a fortnight.

"It's a deal," said Chester laughing. "But I would like to ask for another favour. I've heard all about your nightclub where Clay Douglas is singing the blues. I hear he's great. Could I come one evening with my women?"

"Whenever you like," said Maurice, and, a few nights later, Chester Himes was entertained with his wife and Ellen Wright, the widow of Richard Wright, who had recently died. Girodias had known Dick Wright reasonably well; he had come frequently to La Grande Séverine in its very early days, but Maurice had not previously met Ellen. It was a good evening, with much drink and enjoyed by all. Himes soon produced not six, but more than twenty sexy scenes of such erotic and comic quality that Girodias regretted not knowing him earlier: he might have guided his talent away from cops and robbers and towards pornography. *Mamie Mason* was followed by another novel which Girodias wanted to call *Zebra Stripes*, but Chester found a better title: *Pinktoes*.

Beckett had always wanted his three novels, *Molloy*, *Malone Dies* and *The Unnamable*, to be published as a trilogy, and Girodias had the copyright to the first of them, which he had subcontracted to Barney Rosset for the US and to me for Britain. We had each acquired the second two from Les Éditions de Minuit. My first Beckett publication was *Malone Dies*, which did not receive good reviews. It was published on the same day as Sadeq Hedayat's *The Blind Owl*, and they were reviewed together in a column of crime fiction in the London *Sunday*

Times. "Mescaline might help," said the reviewer, "but don't count on it." For economic reasons I imported *Molloy* for a while, either in the Olympia or the Grove edition, but then in 1959 decided to put the three into one volume, which was Beckett's wish. But Girodias made difficulties and I could not do so without his consent. I then suggested that I subcontract the second two novels to him to sell in Europe, and this was finally agreed. The trilogy then came out in three editions, with Girodias's in the familiar green-backed Traveller's Companion series. This was perhaps the most positive fruit of the Girodias-Rosset-Calder axis that had been planned at that lunch in the Quasimodo, the only time that all three had collaborated directly on a project. Girodias in his memoirs complains that he got the worst of it; he had brought Beckett to us, as well as many other authors, but he had made the least out of it because of the rival editions. He also says that both Barney and I were reluctant to be too closely associated with a man whose reputation was as a pornographer, whereas we saw ourselves as avant-garde literary publishers. To alleviate Girodias's paranoia, I put "Published in association with Olympia Press" on the title page of my own edition, something that Barney did not do.

In helping Barney Rosset to get the American rights to *Tropic of Cancer*, which he did partly to continue his association with Miller, and also because he hoped to distribute the novel in Europe, Girodias had several times received the assurance that he would not be the poorer for it. Girodias took this to mean that he might expect some commission or a lump sum from the deal when it was completed. But no money was forthcoming after the contract was signed between Miller, Hachette (owning the world English-language copyright) and Rosset. Girodias had spent much time over two years getting the deal cemented, but then he found himself out in the cold, and at a time when he badly needed money for the restaurant. Barney, on the way back from Hamburg, where he had finally signed with Henry Miller (in that town because Miller was having an affair there with Renata Gerhardt, Ledig-Rowohlt's secretary), stopped over in Paris with his new girlfriend, Christine, about to become his third wife. They went to La Grande Séverine where Maurice gave them an excellent dinner. As they were leaving, Christine whispered something into Barney's ear.

"Oh, yes, I was going to forget," said Barney. He drew from his pocket a flat object wrapped in tissue paper and offered it to Maurice. It was a round cigarette box, silver-plated, probably bought at an airport for about ten or fifteen dollars. Maurice looked at this present in stupefaction. Barney was not a timid or ambiguous person. This little piece of junk had been bought for a single purpose: to make it quite clear how little he thought of Girodias's help and goodwill in the negotiations he had just completed and to cut short any claim he might make for a sizeable cut from future profits on Henry Miller.

5

La Grande Séverine became something of an office as well as a restaurant. Maurice's customers, booksellers who imported his books into the States, the UK and Canada, came to visit him there and quite naturally expected a free dinner for themselves and their wives or girlfriends. They all made good money out of importing pornography and could quite easily have offered to pay, but Maurice was too timid to suggest it, and also he liked to play the successful publisher and businessman, never admitting how close he always was to bankruptcy. There were visits from Cliff Scheiner, the Soho bookseller who smuggled Olympia titles into the UK, Remington and Marty Gartleboob from Toronto and Bill Door from Los Angeles. The latter owned his own nightclub, sold pornography by mail-order, and was an excellent customer for Olympia. But when in Paris he wanted to practise what he read in pornography as well, and he counted on Maurice to guide him to interesting brothels and orgy houses, about which Girodias really knew nothing. He had to go around to the porters of hotels to get some addresses for Bill Door, who was surprised that the "King of Porn" did not practise what his books preached. He left Paris promising to send an enormous order with instructions as to how the books were to be smuggled into the States, disguised as other merchandise. Maurice was pleased to be rid of Door and even more pleased to receive a telegram a few days later saying, "Everything fine, letter follows." Then nothing happened and weeks went by. Finally Girodias contacted a friend in Los Angeles and asked him to get in touch with the Crescendo, Bill Door's nightclub. Two weeks later, his friend wrote to him. Bill Door had been found in a ditch beside a mountain road with his current girlfriend; each had their hands tied behind their backs and a bullet in the back of the neck. The killing had been efficient and economical.

The Gartleboobs from Toronto were a bizarre couple of brothers. One of them presented his card to Maurice with the words: "With a name like mine, it's better to see it in writing. Unfortunately the printer got it wrong. He's made it Gartlebob." His brother protested that he should have had the card reprinted, and during the ensuing argument,

Girodias understood that the two were nearly illiterate; it was not the printer, but one of the brothers who had made the mistake. They were incapable of reading the books they imported! Before they left, having given Girodias an order, they also gave him a present: it was a "French tickler", made in Hong Kong. "Put that on your dick," said the elder Gartleboob, "and you'll drive all your women wild. My wife doesn't care that I can't read as long as I use that on her."

Maurice always enjoyed the little quiet spell before the restaurant opened its doors. The first couple would enter, the pretty lady on the arm of her escort crying out, "Oh, we're the first!" George, the doorman, would take the man's keys and go to park his car, then Monsieur Rivaux, the maître d'hôtel would come forward, bowing and smiling, and Rolande, the coat-check girl, also all smiles, looking aristocratic and welcoming, would take the furs and remove them to safety. "We have the finest fur coats in Paris," she would whisper to him as the customers were ushered to their tables.

One evening the glass doors were opened and a familiar silhouette was seen, first outside, and then surging through the entrance, squealing thrilly.

"Daaarling!" screamed Rosemary, waving her silver swizzle-stick towards the barman. "Darling, my precious own love, I'm back at last. Didn't I tell you I'd be back? How many women do you have now? Send them all away, all you need is me."

Rosemary was superb, but also problematic and dangerous. Maurice knew that their previous encounter had cost him dear, and was almost certainly the reason he had lost all benefit from *Candy* in the US. He had not really expected to see her again. He let her throw her arms around him without too much enthusiasm and offered her a drink, pouring out her glass himself. It was impossible not to invite her to dinner and he was uneasy about what would follow. She rattled on through the meal, telling of her life and how much she had missed him.

While she was talking he noticed two small scars on her wrists. They told a tale of loneliness and despair very different from the confident sex-bomb she appeared to be. He might be the Prince Charming of her fantasies, but the wrists were a potent witness of her disappointments and humiliations. Maurice imagined how men she met in nightclubs treated her, and what she had left out from her bubbling flow of bright conversation.

"What about Walter?" he asked.

"Walter, that creep!" She spat out the words with such violence that Alain, the barman, recoiled as he was refilling her glass. She had never received the two per cent commission he had promised her for *Lolita*. Walter Minton had never confirmed it in writing. She had slept with him, unwillingly, just to get it, but Walter had used her, not just for sex, but to get his revenge at the same time. They had no sooner finished fucking than he had put on his clothes and sneered that he had better waiting for him at home. She had thrown a vase at him and they had slapped each other across the little hotel room where they had arranged to meet. He had promised to bring the money with him, a cheque for $200,000, which represented less than a two per cent royalty, but of course he had no intention of paying her anything at all. She had attempted to sue. *Time* magazine had made a story out of her role in Putnam's acquisition of *Lolita* and there had been witnesses to the promise. But it was all pointless. He was too rich and could afford the best lawyers. In court there would be too much prejudice against her: she would be reviled as a common prostitute. So she had given up.

Girodias reflected that were he a heel like Walter Minton, he would at this moment bundle her into a taxi, send her off, and point out that he owed her nothing. She had been, unknown to him at the time, responsible for all the money he had made from *Lolita*, but also for all the losses resulting from Minton's current hostility to him. She had already been in Paris for three days and had rented a little furnished studio nearby. He was under siege: what to do?

"Look, Rosemary, let's talk seriously." He tried not to look at her eyes, now brimming with tears. "I can't give you my liberty. I'm like everyone else, you know, neither better nor worse. We get on very well, but I have other ties. You have to understand that you can't build too much on the one night of love we had together…"

They were sitting now at a remote table at the very end of his restaurant in the cellar. She put her head in her hands and shook with great sobs, while the whole restaurant watched. "That bastard Girodias is torturing yet another woman," were the words he saw in some of their eyes. He felt helpless. This woman, so beautiful, young and in her way intelligent, seemed destined to follow the sad future of all women who became striptease girls or whose bodies, one way or the other, belonged to the lecherous public. How could he intervene in a life of such intensity and innate tragedy? He ordered another bottle of champagne.

"Listen, Rosemary, I'm your friend—"

"Who cares! You can keep your friendship. I want you to *fuck* me, you understand? *Fuck and fuck and fuck.*"

This anecdote ends the second volume of Girodias's memoirs. There is no evidence that he wrote any more, and what happened that night or the ones following is not recorded. But Rosemary was not long in Paris, and others occupied his bed while he tried to deal with the problems of the restaurant. I was present one lunchtime when he was entertaining two fast-talking public relations men, whom he was asking to do publicity for La Grande Séverine. We four – I had only arrived at the end of their lunch, and was having coffee – were the only ones in the big restaurant in the cellar, the only part of the complex still open at that point. They were giving him promises that sounded wholly unconvincing to my ears.

"We'll do what we did for the Tour d'Argent," one of them said. "We'll invite the journalists and get feature articles about this place into the papers. We'll need an expense account, and an advance for our work. And a percentage of a year's profits. But look how well it all worked for the Tour d'Argent and other restaurants that are fashionable now because of us."

As he and his colleague talked, I could see that the despondent Maurice was as unbelieving as I was, but he had to give himself some hope. Excusing myself, I left them to it. The restaurant folded a few weeks later.

Marilyn Meeske had two younger sisters, twins called Patty and Barbara. They were, like Marilyn, very good-looking and sexy girls from the seemingly endless bank of New York girls with Jewish backgrounds answering that description. Maurice had slept with them both. Barbara died young in 1966, but Patty went through five marriages, the last but one to Leon Friedman, who through her introduction ultimately became Girodias's much put-upon, patient and always loyal and supportive New York lawyer. Her final marriage was to a London barrister. She was one of the very few of Maurice's sexual liaisons willing to talk about their relationship. He was apparently at times quite brutal in a playful way – on one occasion, when following her up the stairs of a hotel, he aimed little kicks at her legs from behind, and then looked unconcerned when she glanced back in exasperation, as if someone else had done it – and she did not stay with him long. She found some of his other oddities, like his parlour trick of eating his wineglass at the table in restaurants, more than she could take. But she nevertheless always retained an affection for him; the childish side of Maurice's character undoubtedly brought out a maternal quality in many women, and not just his lovers.

Maurice encouraged the two sisters, Patty Welles (a name she adopted both as a pen name and, eventually, her legal one as well, and which she kept through all her marriages) and Barbara Lebost to write a book for him. Entitled *Mouthing Off*, it took the shape of a conversation between two sisters having lunch in a smart New York restaurant (I believe it was El Morocco), talking about sex. Their conversation consisted of reminiscences, fantasies about erotic situations and techniques they would like to try, comparisons of lovers and the like. Maurice found the resulting manuscript very arousing and intended to publish it as an Olympia db in Paris, but he was closed down before he could do so. He then intended to publish it in New York, after moving there, and the book was set in type, but it never came out. The proofs were lost, as was the original manuscript in the course of events. Patty went on to write other, successful commercial novels, one of which, *Baby Hip*, sold well and was filmed, something which gave her several years of financial security. After her last divorce she remained in London and continued writing.

1965 and 1966 were years of great difficulty for Girodias. He was fighting the Brigade Mondaine; his authors, having been established by him, now wanted to leave in order to benefit from the new liberal climate – which Girodias himself had done so much to bring about – and to be published in the US and the UK; and La Grande Séverine, making heavy losses, was like a millstone around his neck. And yet he would not give up or admit his failure.

Correspondence with authors and lawyers was taking up even more of Maurice's time. The *Evergreen Review* published two articles about him, one in the summer of 1966 by Austryn Wainhouse entitled 'On Translating Sade' and another by Vladimir Nabokov the following February. Wainhouse described his relationship with Girodias, called him "bitter and reckless", and gave on the whole a jaundiced but not inaccurate picture of the eccentric workings of Olympia Press. Like others who have described him before and since, the Wainhouse article interprets Girodias's extraordinary absorption in his own life and projects, and his vagueness in business matters, as sharp practice rather than as incompetence and laziness in dealing with routine matters. The Nabokov attack was more venomous: Girodias was called a vulgarian, a pornographer with no principles whatsoever and an exploiter of the talents of others. Girodias wrote a long letter to the editor of *Evergreen* in which he said:

There are several points of significance which are common to those two articles by Austryn Wainhouse and Vladimir Nabokov. Not only the bitterness, the self-pity, the grandiloquent egomania and the tone of offended virtue, but, essentially, the underlying theme. They both try to convince their readers that they have been badly abused and cheated by me. The truth is quite otherwise, and they certainly cannot state that they ever lost a penny because of me: in fact they don't, although they constantly do their damnedest best to suggest it without saying it in so many words. I have always treated Wainhouse in a friendly and loyal manner. As to Nabokov, I sincerely believe that he was most lucky to come across a publisher who did as much for his book as I did. Instead of being fair and sensible about it, he has been assiduously trying to have our contract invalidated, ever since *Lolita* became, much to his surprise (and mine) a money-making best-seller. He is in fact now, at the time of writing, trying harder than ever, and we have a lawsuit pending before the French courts. Must we look further for an ulterior motive?*

During the same year he wrote a letter to the *New York Review of Books* complaining about a review that Gore Vidal had written of *The Olympia Reader*, a large anthology that Girodias had put together and edited for himself and Grove Press, which I was also supposed to publish in the UK. I was finally unable to do, because of the difficulty of clearing copyright for some of the extracts. The anthology contained a long introduction by Girodias. Vidal in his article tore the whole anthology to pieces, called the selections "junk", and the editor "a peddler of dirty books" and "a merchant of smut". In his letter Girodias pointed out that the world was not as intellectually free as Vidal imagined, that censorship was still everywhere to be seen, and concluded:

> Does Mr Vidal seriously contend that he would have been able to publish *The City and the Pillar* twenty years ago if the way had not been cleared first of all by drooling pornographic pigs such as my father and myself? Social prejudice is as thick and heavy as molten lead, and it takes a bit of fibre to fight it.
>
> I have done some fighting: much more so than any of the distinguished publishers who today in America are reaping the financial and moral harvest of my little literary discoveries. And that I have not done my fighting for money, at least that Mr Vidal grudgingly admits (... and hastens to add that it is only due to my "incompetence": read stupidity).*

He calls on Vidal to join him in his crusade and to "fight for a really free society: free morally and intellectually, as well as economically and politically". He accuses him of only being interested in the freedom of homosexuals and the abolition of prejudice in their regard, and ends by calling for a common front by all against those who would restrict freedom as a live ideal.

In early 1966 Girodias sold *Candy* to Tandem Books in London, receiving an advance of £5,000. Knowing that the authors were also trying to find a British publisher he was delighted to have got in first. But the problems came over the cuts that Tandem demanded. Ralph Stokes, the editor, wanted to omit dangerous lines and episodes, fearing a prosecution which Girodias, the white knight of anti-censorship, could hardly countenance. Then he heard that Max Reinhardt claimed to have also bought *Candy* and that Panther Books were planning a paperback. Girodias's letters to his American lawyer, Leon Friedman, became longer and wordier as he saw rivals everywhere trying to rob him. A film deal was in the offing, but held up by a Paris court case with Hoffenberg and Southern who were trying to establish that *Candy* was theirs and not legally "written" by Olympia who had commissioned it. Maurice was certain that the authors were doing secret deals to get more money from interested parties, but he was carrying out his own secret negotiations at the same time. He said, "Everyone is lying to everyone else, but isn't that better if it is done sincerely? The big thing is to save everyone's face."* Matters between Maurice and Leon Friedman were further complicated by the former having contracted *Mouthing Off* from Patty Welles, his wife, and because the lawyer was working on a contingency basis over *Candy*.

Everything to do with Girodias at this juncture was complicated, and he did not let his right hand know what the other was doing. He extracted money from a sleazy London publisher called Jeanspress for UK rights of *Candy*, presumably because Stokes of Tandem could not get his directors to finance a book that might be prosecuted. He was trying to arrange a tax-free, under-the-table payment of $30,000 to himself from French film director Christian Marquand for his agreement to the film sale of *Candy* to United Artists, in addition to his "public" payment of only $5,000.

Girodias also involved Friedman in his war with Grove Press. Austryn Wainhouse had contracted his Marquis de Sade translations to Barney Rosset and Maurice claimed that as he had commissioned and paid for them, they were his. In his letters to his lawyer he gives many portraits of Barney's two sides, the crusading anti-censorship publisher, and the business man with no scruples about stealing what he wanted. He was certain that Barney would publish a lookalike series to his Traveller's

Companion (Grove's Victorian Library, although mainly devoted to flagellation and sado-masochism, could be so described, so he was not totally wrong). Other Olympia titles ended up on the Grove list. Barney bought the first four volumes of Frank Harris's *My Life and Loves* from Hachette, then paid a pittance for the fifth volume, a Trocchi forgery. Girodias was furious that Grove not only achieved a good hardback and paperback sale in the US, but sold British rights to WH Allen, who in turn received £25,000 as an advance from Corgi for paperback rights. Girodias felt he was being cheated all round.

One of the unkindest cuts came when he discovered that Barney Rosset had bought *Histoire d'O* from Pauvert and had had it retranslated. Girodias had never even had a contract with the real author, although he might have had one with Paulhan, who had brought the book to him. The name of the author was still unknown (although, as was noted in an earlier chapter, it has since been confirmed as Anne Desclos, a Gallimard editor and mistress of Jean Paulhan). That his old office partner and friend should do this to him was an unexpected and nasty shock. In a long letter to Friedman, Girodias outlined his relationship with Pauvert and the circumstances under which Pauvert had published the manuscript brought to him by Paulhan, *only* because he, Girodias, had persuaded him, with much difficulty, to do so. He said that he and Pauvert had considered themselves to be, and had acted as, partners, that he had paid him a lump sum for each printing, but they had never bothered to make a contract. He had had to "weather several bans and prosecutions" and his English version had suffered much more than Pauvert's French one. He found it unthinkable that Pauvert should have taken advantage of his trust and sold world rights to the book that might never have been published were it not for his being the first to read it and for his enthusiasm. But there was nothing he could do about it.

Barney Rosset says that Girodias and Pauvert were not friendly at this point and that Pauvert nursed a grievance. It is more likely that Pauvert had seen enough of Maurice's extravagances and follies to discount him totally; he was, in any case, almost as unaccustomed to signing contracts as Maurice: nearly all his books were in the public domain, and he was having his own financial difficulties at this time. A contract for *Histoire d'O* for the US must have seemed like manna from heaven and it is doubtful if any thought of his erstwhile partner ever seriously crossed his mind.

The *Candy* controversy continued. Minton sued Zacharius and others who had brought out pirate editions. Girodias tried to establish a deal whereby his rights as originator and commissioner of the novel was accepted; he would agree to pay royalties on the French edition while collecting one third of the $100,000 the authors had received or were about to receive from Minton. At the same time Leon Friedman negotiated to establish copyright in the name of Olympia with the Library of Congress, and in this he succeeded. As a result Girodias ultimately received a piece of the money paid for film rights, but legal and other professional fees reduced the $200,000 payment to about half that, and Maurice ended up with only about $25,000. A contract involving all parties and finally bringing peace, was signed in January 1967. As Friedman put it to me in private conversation: "Everyone was crazy, Maurice, the authors, Minton, and others who had a claim or thought they did." Maurice did make some money from British rights: Candy was part of the deal when the New English Library set up an Olympia Press in the UK, but the collaborative novel, costing so much time and money, was a considerable overall loss.

But Girodias never lost his bounce. It was a time with many deals on the horizon, including the establishment of other Olympia Presses in Germany and Italy, all under the aegis of a local publisher with whom he had done business in the past. But the problems in France were too great, especially where the restaurant was concerned.

The end came in December 1966. The restaurant had closed its doors a few weeks earlier, and with great sadness Maurice applied for bankruptcy. The assets, such as they were, were auctioned. But the Olympia offices remained for the time being, and Maurice, now planning to expand his publishing programme into other countries, was as certain as ever that future good fortune awaited him. He still had his flair and his reputation as the "King of Porn". He simply had to avoid such follies as La Grande Séverine.

Chapter Nine

The Expatriate Diaspora

1

The generation of young writers, and their contemporaries in the other arts, who went to Paris around 1950 had mostly gone by 1960, usually back to their own countries. Dick Seaver ended up with Grove Press as Barney Rosset's senior editor, and became mainly concerned with the European list. Samuel Beckett, Alain Robbe-Grillet, Marguerite Duras, Eugène Ionesco, Fernando Arrabal and Robert Pinget were now Grove authors, and all of them were shared with my British company for the English-language publishing market – until the *Tropic of Cancer* war made cooperation impossible, and then we had to commission our own different English versions of these authors. Barney Rosset's decision cost him the use of the excellent translations of Barbara Wright and Donald Watson, and in return I lost those of Richard Howard. But I still collaborated with other New York publishers, George Braziller for example, who shared with me the English translations of the novels of Nathalie Sarraute and Claude Simon. Pinget at one point wrote a letter to Grove complaining about the way he was described in a blurb; this was not uncommon for French writers, who usually received careful and respectful handling from their original publishers and expected their complaints to be taken seriously, but Rosset was not convinced by Pinget, a rather gentle writer of Swiss origins, whose work had not received the same favourable critical attention in the States as Robbe-Grillet's, and he used this as an excuse to drop him. Pinget, as a result, was not available in English in the States for some years, until he was taken up by Red Dust, a small press run by Joanna Gunderson, and I began to distribute my own editions of his earlier work in the US.

Grove Press now had their house journal, the *Evergreen Review*, to lure authors, and it was an ideal medium for good short writing, such as Leroi Jones's *Dutchman*, Albee's *The Zoo Story* and short prose by Beckett and Pinter. Between them they increasingly attracted the best of the nonconformist American writers, especially the Beats, and Barney Rosset and Grove Press were always much in the news. Barney himself was frequently interviewed and asked to speak about the *nouveau roman*, about the new dramatic writers from Europe and the States who were being performed in small off-Broadway playhouses and published by Grove, and about new American writing in general. Often his editors were better qualified than he to explain the importance of these authors and what their work was about, but Barney liked the limelight and made all the appearances himself. At the same time he was publishing some novels in imitation of Olympia's Ophelia series, soft pornography that appealed to his own sexual interests, including titles devoted mainly to the "English" vice of flagellation, usually giving only "Anonymous" as the author; these appeared under his Victorian Library imprint.

Austryn Wainhouse left Paris in 1956 and went to Austria for two years. He had separated from Muffie and was not in particularly good odour with his father, whose career as a diplomat was certainly not helped by having a son who translated the Marquis de Sade, widely regarded as the most evil writer that had ever lived, and who was connected with a bohemian group that published in their magazine modern authors like Genet, an open homosexual and former convict whose work was considered obscene, and Sartre, whom the State Department viewed as a communist fellow-traveller. From Austria, Wainhouse moved to the south of France, where he bought a patch of ground at Castagné in the hills behind Nice. Here he built a house with his own hands from local stone and timber in an open-plan Scandinavian style. It was light and airy with a fine view, but he had access to it only by a footpath. The local farmer was not friendly and did not want a house built next to his land; access other than by the public footpath was refused and all building materials had to be laboriously carried by hand along the track. I visited him there once and, over a delicious meal, wondered at the inconvenience of his life, because he still had the same problem with his neighbour. He stayed there until 1971, and then sold the house. Four years later he returned to the US and started a private little press in Vermont, but he was by now receiving royalties for his translations from Grove Press.

Trocchi left Paris after five years there, still experimenting with drugs and taking them regularly, but not yet fully addicted. He did some travelling after Paris, first in Northern Europe, and then, during the summer of 1955, in Italy, Yugoslavia and Greece, arriving back in Paris and going on to London at the end of the year. He had started *Cain's Book*, but had not yet given the novel its locale. His heroine, Moira, was in many ways a composite of Betty and Jane, and he was still writing frequently to the latter. She was now Mrs J. Griscom, but not happily married, and she had already broken off the relationship by the time Trocchi arrived in America. On his way through Paris he had bought the Indian turquoise ring she had once admired; to her surprise it arrived in the post one day: it was his way of trying to get back into her affections.

In London Trocchi was suddenly depressed at the lonely state in which he now found himself. *Merlin* was dead, the group that had admired, listened to, and followed him was scattered; in addition he had failed so far to make a reputation as a writer. Since leaving Scotland he had always taken his creative talent for granted and believed public recognition to be his due. He still had enormous confidence in his abilities – had he not proved over and over that he could do anything that he set out to do? – but he was only known among his peer group and the readers of Olympia dbs, who would not even recognize his real name. He told Christopher Logue that he had even considered suicide, but that was not in his nature, and it is doubtful that his remark was any more than an effort to garner some sympathy. He still had grandiose plans to succeed as a writer (he had confided to the William Morris Agency in New York all rights to sell his available work for the next three years), and for both financial and sexual reasons he set about falling in love and starting an affair with Jane Fonda, who was now in London; but the relationship was of short duration. He attended the wedding of John and Sue Marquand in Chelsea at the local Registry Office. This was followed by a reception at their Cadogan Square flat attended by Kingsley Amis, Mordecai Richler, Henry Green, Elias Canetti and many other notable literary figures. Iris Owens came over from Paris for the occasion. He started to work on a screenplay for *Young Adam*, which was under offer to a publisher in New York, because a small film company had shown some interest in it, and he produced a few stories and prose fragments in a not very organized fashion. He also managed to get another girl pregnant, this time a teacher from North Africa, which necessitated another abortion. Then he left for New York.

He arrived on 30th April 1956 and his passport described him as a writer. He only had one suitcase with him and this contained for the most part unfinished prose in various stages of progression. He contacted some of his old Paris friends, in particular George Plimpton and Peter Matthiessen, both of whom lent him a little money, while Plimpton occasionally let him stay briefly at his Upper East Side apartment, and at the nearby offices of the *Paris Review* for longer periods. But it was Jane who met him off the boat, and although she did not want to get involved with him again, she let him stay at her apartment in Greenwich Village at West 11th Street for some weeks.

Trocchi managed to get a job, ideal for a writer of his kind, as captain of a scow with the New York Trap Rock Corporation. It offered him free accommodation and a small salary for very little work. A scow captain was basically a caretaker who occasionally had to attach the scow by catching a rope from a tug, which would then pull it to a mooring to be filled with cargo. This usually consisted of building materials, which were then towed to the point of discharge. When applying for the job, to another Glaswegian known as "Scottie", he claimed to have had "experience with small craft", and the man who took him on expected that a fellow countryman would be reliable and trustworthy. Trocchi was later to get jobs on other scows for his friends, including Mel Sabre and Mason Hoffenberg, both of whom also had drug problems.

Trocchi began using drugs much more intensively in New York, sometimes experimenting with substances he had not previously tried. He met a chemist who was carrying out experiments with addicts, and, always game for a new experience, Trocchi allowed his body to be used as a guinea pig; but the man measured out a dose of the heroin-additive he had developed in milligrams instead of micrograms, and this knocked Trocchi out for some hours. The worried chemist, having removed all identification from Trocchi's body, then reported it and called an ambulance, which he followed in his car. As Trocchi began to come round in the ward, the man declared that he was a doctor treating this young addict on behalf of a well-known family: his patient had escaped and he wanted to bring him back without any press publicity that might embarrass his parents. His authoritative manner convinced the hospital, and Trocchi was allowed to leave with him by taxi.

But Trocchi was soon not just a drug-user, but a drug-peddler as well; it was difficult to be one without the other in his circumstances, because he had to earn money to pay for his own habit. Selling drugs was very dangerous as a new law had just been passed in New York State, making the supply of drugs to minors a capital offence. Trocchi was now risking the electric chair. But the overreaction of the press to the growth of drug-taking, and the passing of the law itself, coupled with the rise of a new "Beat" ethic that was often drug-related, did produce a strong hostility towards the establishment and the law from the growing counter-culture, fed in particular by the first Beat novels to appear from Kerouac and by the poems of Ginsberg. Trocchi, without knowing it, was living a life that well represented what the beats were advocating, and he belonged to a peer group that was both envied and despised. As he puts it in *Cain's Book*:

> We were regarded as the lowest form of animal life on the waterfront. It was a job for no-goods and all kinds of vagabonds.*

Trocchi was paid about $100 a week as captain of the scow, but there was little to do other than to caretake, keep the boat clean and let it be towed. The scows were basically small floating apartments and the captains, if so inclined, could take aboard – as well as food – women, drink, drugs, and whatever else they needed or could afford for the trips around Manhattan or up Long Island Sound. The dock labourers who loaded and unloaded did all the work and were often incredulous at the scenes they witnessed from the denizens on board the scows. Trocchi became even more isolated on his, free to inject himself unobserved, free to have his reveries and occasionally write, while he contemplated the lights of Manhattan. He kept his heroin in a watertight jar, dangling below the waterline.

The mail occasionally brought news from what was left of the old crowd in Paris. Terry Southern had moved to Geneva, but still had stories about the Bonaparte and the Old Navy, as well as the jazz clubs the Caméléon and the Tabou, where Austryn Wainhouse, Iris Owens, Sinbad Vail (the latter two now a couple) and other members of the group reminisced about him and toasted him. When he could get ashore Trocchi would go to the Greenwich Village bars that often contained people he had known in Paris, and make new acquaintances; these were a mixed lot, writers and artists, some real, but more of them phoney bohemians, drunks and junkies. Increasingly he identified himself with the latter. It was cold with heavy falls of snow during the winter of 1956–57, and he shivered in the cab of the scow, contemplating his situation and writing from immediate experience. *Cain's Book* was coming along slowly. The dock workers became curious when they heard his typewriter. No other scow captain had one.

According to Andrew Murray Scott's biography, Trocchi had at least two homosexual experiences in this period, mainly out of curiosity, and to experiment.* He also seduced Dorothy, the one-legged wife of his friend Mel Sabre. She came to live with him on the scow for a while, and then returned to her husband. Dorothy is the model for Jacqueline in the novel. When on shore leave he visited Jane, using her apartment to write during the day when she was working at Brentano's bookstore, and he frequently borrowed from her and from other rich young

Americans he knew in order to buy drugs, while occasionally attending their parties. He had a constant need to feed the habit, while restlessly he searched for an outlet for the literary talent that he was convinced was as great as ever; it drove him from moods of self-destruction to others when his confidence returned, convincing him that fame and fortune would somehow alight on his shoulders at any moment. This above all drove him to return to his typewriter. What emerged on the page were fragments of experience, moments of observation, glimpses of past association and memory, and the local colour of a junkie's life. Like *The Naked Lunch*, *Cain's Book* was being written as a series of episodes, not yet linked together.

There were enough people in New York who remembered or had known Alex Trocchi in Paris to ensure that his name came up from time to time and that he was invited to literary parties. He excelled at these, exerting all his old charm, and on one such occasion in the Village he met Lyn Hicks from Hicksville. Her full name was Marilyn Rose Hicks, and she was twenty-one and beautiful, with brownish blonde hair and soft blue eyes. She worked for *Printer Ink*, a weekly magazine for the advertising industry, was a Smith graduate, and had a comfortably conventional family background. She had developed some literary tastes in line with the interests of her age group, had taken the *Evergreen Review* and the *Paris Review*, and had seen Trocchi's name there among the contributors. Lyn was an unconventional girl from a family that worried a great deal about her, and who hoped she would meet a "regular" young man who would give her a normal married life.

Using all his charm, Trocchi picked up Lyn in the same way that he had picked up Jane Lougee, and they instantly started a relationship. Trocchi, proud of himself for having landed such a beauty, took her round to meet Jane, who was not impressed and described her as a rather obvious showgirl. Alex decided that he had to leave his job, which, although convenient in many ways, was badly paid and had no future. It seemed a good time to see more of America. First he asked Jane if she would travel with him; although he was sleeping with Lyn at the time, he knew that Jane had the money to make the trip more comfortable. When she refused he took Lyn. He acquired an old coupé and they drove off in the early summer of 1957, travelling through the south and ending up in Mexico, where Trocchi tried peyote and mescaline. They returned to the States via California and stopped for a while in the Mojave desert. In Mexico he had seen a lawyer and gone through a divorce court to annul his marriage to Betty; now he married Lyn.

Both were on drugs. It has been said that Alex would not sleep with Lyn until she had taken heroin, on the grounds that "they had to be on the same plane of consciousness" and Trocchi confirmed this to me; but this is doubtful. It would probably have put her off at the time, and Alex was never someone to delay a seduction for something that would happen in the end anyway. By the time they arrived in California she too was an addict. It was in the Mojave desert that he started to paint bits of driftwood, picking up whatever he found with an interesting shape, and inventing an art form that was really a kind of doodle, but became a habit that he kept up for the rest of his life. Painting pieces of wood in bright abstract colours was a soothing occupation, and the patterns he painted became smaller and smaller as the years went by, paralleling the concentration induced by heroin on ever tinier points of mental experience.

California was cheap and the climate pleasant. There were many drifting "hipsters" (in Norman Mailer's newly coined phrase), who were becoming the Beat Generation. They met each other casually, lent each other what little they had, food, money or drugs, and lived in communities. Venice West, on the beach on the southern side of Los Angeles, was becoming a centre for the more artistic beats; here Ginsberg wrote some of the poems in *Kaddish*, and others who moved in and out included Kerouac, Neal Cassady, Gregory Corso, Gary Snyder, Philip Whalen, Ken Kesey and Jim Morrison, many of whom were there at the same time as Trocchi and Lyn. Alex was now thirty-two, older than most of the other denizens of the artists' colony at Venice West, and he became a leader and a guru to the group. He was again what he had always loved being, the centre of a circle which listened to him, fawned on him, created art around him and joined him in drug-taking. Not everyone was on hard drugs, but the use of marijuana was universal in "Trocchi's pad", where each person was trying to create art in his own way, without value judgements or competition. It can be assumed that Alex managed to support himself mainly from the contributions of all those who surrounded him and used his pad. The scene is described in *Sheeper* by Irving Rosenthal, who had gone to Venice West on the recommendation of Ginsberg:

The play of truth and moral beauty in that apartment was like lights, and Trocchi's Scotch burr scratched my heart, and for months I judged everything I saw and did as inadequate and cowardly compared to what went on in Trocchi's pad... I used the honesty I gleaned, there among rats and amphetamine heads, as a model for my own life as an artist.*

During the time of his departure, Trocchi, then as later, whenever he found himself the centre of an admiring circle, did no literary work of any consequence. Back in the East he heard from Girodias who wanted more dbs from him, and from Terry Southern who had a serious novel published in New York, and he found that Jane was about to be married to Baird Bryant, who had been one of their *Merlin* colleagues. The wedding took place at City Hall and Alex was the best man. The Trocchis managed to take over a loft on West 23rd Street between Sixth and Seventh Avenues: it was a large space that could have been made comfortable with some money, but they had none, and it was too large a room to heat in winter. On 18th September Lyn went into hospital and Mark, later to be called Marcus, was born the next day. The need to earn money was now paramount, and Trocchi managed to get some reviewing work, but mainly he looked for contracts to write books. He managed to sell *Young Adam*, with four short stories to bulk up the volume, to Castle Books, and this appeared in a volume entitled *The Outsiders* in 1960. He wrote a long poem based on Greek mythology that he entitled *The Sacred Grove*, which he offered to a number of magazines and periodicals, but all turned it down; it was lost on his subsequent travels. The agreement with the William Morris Agency to handle all his work was ignored by Trocchi, who now negotiated everything himself. He had the idea of producing a volume of Sappho's poems, most of which would be his own forgeries – after all he had successfully forged the last volume of Frank Harris's memoirs – and he dreamt up a complicated cover story to explain how the poems had come into his hands. The book, partly a biography of Sappho, the ancient Greek poet from Lesbos, and partly an anthology of her poems, with an explanatory introduction by Trocchi who presented himself as the editor of this spurious work, was eventually published by Castle Books, also in 1960. But the publisher was worried about an obscenity prosecution and he did little to promote it or sell it widely. The intended hoax, which might have been successful and have attracted major attention in the literary press, or, if discovered, still have given Trocchi an interesting reputation, simply misfired. Nevertheless, the book, in a quiet way and usually in pirated editions, remained continuously available for some years. Castle Books also pirated some old novels he had written for Olympia and brought them out under new titles without telling Trocchi or making any payment for them. Not only did Trocchi receive no remuneration, but the pirated editions prevented him from bringing them to a serious publisher.

Trocchi was also in contact with Seaver, who wanted to help, and they did collaborate on some editorial projects, including a collection of new fiction entitled *Beyond the Beat*, which was designed to give a respectability to the Beat writing movement. It was later republished as *Writers in Revolt*, containing work from Ginsberg, Burroughs, Genet and Hermann Hesse, as well as pre-war writers like Artaud, and even Baudelaire. But the important project was of course *Cain's Book*, which Trocchi finally finished. It was now based largely on his heroin experiences in New York, and particularly his time on the scow. It is a powerful book that gets totally inside a junkie's life and into his head. Its descriptions of the ritual of injecting heroin are totally real, accompanied by Trocchi's justifications, and his attacks on a society that he depicts as judgemental and hypocritical:

And when someone who hasn't used junk speaks easily of junkies I am full of contempt. It isn't simple, any kind of judgement here, and the judgements of the uninitiated tend to be stupid, hysterical. Anger and innocence... those virgin sisters again. No, when one presses the bulb of the eye-dropper and watches the pale, blood-streaked liquid disappear through the nozzle and into the needle and the vein it is not, not only, a question of feeling good. It's not only a question of kicks. The ritual itself, the powder in the spoon, the little ball of cotton, the matches applied, the bubbling liquid drawn up through the cotton filter into the eye-dropper, the tie round the arm to make a vein stand out, the fix often slow because a man will stand there with the needle in the vein and allow the level in the eye-dropper to waver up and down, up and down, until there is more blood than heroin in the dropper – all this is not for nothing; it is born of a respect for the whole chemistry of alienation.*

Lyn now did the same service for Trocchi that Allen Ginsberg had performed for Burroughs: she collated the various episodes and put them in order. Although Trocchi could perfectly well have done this himself, his addiction encouraged him to work in bursts; writing new material was easier and more interesting than sitting down to go over existing work, changing and editing it, reordering the sequences – work that needs continuity, which is difficult if you have to constantly interrupt yourself to tie up and give yourself an injection. Dick Seaver then proceeded to publish *Cain's Book* in April 1960, and although there was a hardback edition, the Evergreen paperback came out simultaneously; I certainly had the impression at the time that it was the first new novel that Grove Press published as a paperback original.

Drug addiction was a talking point in 1960 because it was receiving much sensational press coverage, and selling drugs could now be a capital offence. Lyn was as addicted as Alex, but her constitution was not as strong as his, and she took the addiction less well; she sometimes had the delusion that her arms were covered with cockroaches, which Alex was unable to make her believe did not exist. She would pick at her arms until they were covered with scabs according to the accounts, but it must be remembered that cockroaches are only too numerous in New York, especially in the kind of accommodation where the Trocchis were liable to find themselves. It is unlikely that Alex, with all his other problems and his addiction, would have bothered too much about "bugs", and Lyn's obsession may have been at least partially true.

Drugs were an issue of great public concern. Nelson Algren's novel *The Man with the Golden Arm* had been a best-seller a decade earlier in 1949, and the film starring Frank Sinatra – his debut as a serious actor – had also been a success, bringing home to a large public the realities of drug addiction. The junky was being viewed at the time of *Cain's Book* as both a menace to society and, in some circles, a romantic outlaw. But it was increasingly recognized that both hard and soft drugs were very profitable for the organized crime syndicates; they were also, heroin particularly, a new and frightening cause of street crime because the addict's need would drive him to any action to feed his habit.

About this time, Maurice Girodias paid a visit to New York. He was interviewed by the press, lunched by publishers, photographed by the *New York Times* and invited to dinner by ex-authors now living in New York. He spent one evening with the Trocchis in their loft on 23rd Street. Trocchi had apparently forgotten the invitation because he was out to meet a drug-dealer when Maurice arrived. Lyn apologized, explained the situation and asked him to wait. Trocchi eventually returned, took off his jacket, rolled up his sleeve and prepared the syringe. Lyn and Alex were both sitting on the sofa, and he offered her the rubber tube that they used to tie up.

"Here you are, you go first," said Trocchi.

"Oh no, Alex dear, go ahead. I can wait," responded Lyn. While they took their fix, according to Girodias, Marcus, now a year old, trotted around naked and emptied a half-full glass of beer. He was already on small doses of heroin, and had of course been addicted while in the womb. Lyn, casting a loving look at her baby, told Maurice: "He's so funny, he loves beer. It probably tastes better than mother's milk."

Once high again, Trocchi became a genial, charming and entertaining host, complaining about the terrible city where he now found himself, while Girodias, impressed by the youth and beauty of Lyn, so apparently innocent of the world and natural in an unnatural environment, reflected that they were in the process of killing each other, but that the miserable and glorious death they had chosen seemed, under the circumstances, to be entirely respectable and justified.

The publication of *Cain's Book* was greeted on the whole with good reviews, but even those that were less good made people want to read it. Norman Mailer's comment appeared on the paperback: "It is true, it has art, it is brave. I would not be surprised if it is still talked about in twenty years." Although Trocchi was now receiving money from his various literary efforts, it was never enough. His habit had become more demanding, and he did not even attend the publication party that Grove Press gave for his book. Much of his time at this juncture was spent looking for drugs; the new, harsher penalties had driven up the prices and it was difficult to score. At the time, when he was afraid that he might be stopped and searched by the police, he carried a portable pulpit around with him in order to resemble a hot-gospelling street preacher; it was a deceit that did not always work. He was arrested several times and thrown into the police cells, known as "the tombs", which he had to share with other addicts.

Now that Trocchi had a police record he could expect regular surveillance and his living quarters to be frequently raided. Lyn became adept at hiding drugs in their apartment, once disguising a syringe inside a child's turd floating in the lavatory. They moved to Saint Mark's Place in the East Village where the sidewalk was usually lined with junkies staring into space; Mark, growing older, now had to play in the street among them. Once Alex was arrested in the Bronx where he had gone to obtain heroin from a Puerto Rican dealer; the man's pad was under surveillance, and the narcotics squad raided it just after Trocchi had entered. On that occasion Lyn contacted George Plimpton, who bailed him out, and with the help of a good lawyer got him off because he did not have any drugs on him when he was arrested; the police had arrived slightly too early.

Trocchi put Lyn back onto the streets and she was a successful prostitute, having little difficulty picking up men. Because of her prettiness and air of innocence, she did not always have to give her body; some of her "johns" just wanted to hear her story and look at her. Trocchi seemed to have no compunction about being a pimp, and even boasted of how he had "cooled out of a bust" by telling Lyn to "make it with the fuzz" in the back of a police car, which probably involved giving them a blow job. He was now borrowing from every possible source and constantly wheedling a little more out of Plimpton and others he had known in Paris or met in New York. He harassed John Marquand after his father's death because he assumed that John would have inherited a large sum of money. Marquand denied being any better off, but helped out of old loyalty, even at one point selling his furniture to pay Trocchi's rent; the money went, not to the landlord, but to the heroin dealer, and on a subsequent occasion, Marquand, to Trocchi's great annoyance, paid the landlord direct.

There had always been a devil in Trocchi that drove him to the most extreme edge of danger, and he had an arrogance that enabled him to persuade himself that he could somehow talk himself out of a predicament or find some way to escape catastrophe. By now everyone who knew him had realized this, but he still received help, however grudgingly. Barney Rosset was one person who resisted. When Trocchi importuned him, Barney ignored him and went away, although he claims that he did contribute to the last big whip-around for bail. Seaver too, although he paid Trocchi for various literary projects, did not reach into his pocket. It was mainly George Plimpton who found most of the money in the end. Trocchi could have returned to the UK at any time and existed comfortably as a registered drug addict under the sensible British Home Office policy of keeping drugs away from crime. There is no question but that his New York friends would have found the fare to get him off their hands. But Trocchi stayed on, knowing that he was in danger of ending up in the electric chair because he was dealing in drugs in every possible way to feed his own habit. Even after his most serious arrest, he refused to recognize his real danger and become circumspect.

The crunch came in April 1961, just a year after the publication of *Cain's Book*, which by itself had made him a target. He was charged with supplying drugs to a minor, a sixteen-year-old girl, and although Trocchi, then and later, claimed that he was not guilty and the victim of circumstantial evidence, that evidence was damning enough to possibly cost him his life. Plimpton realized that, however generous he might have been in the past, he now had either to raise a large enough sum to bail out and defend Trocchi, or else finally abandon him. The bail was set at $5,000, a large amount in those days and one that the judge could feel confident would not be met. But George Plimpton found it: he felt that he would have Trocchi's life on his conscience for ever were he to back out now. Others made contributions towards the bail, including, possibly, a small amount from Rosset on this occasion (although there is some doubt about this), but the bulk of it came from the gentle, much put-upon editor of the *Paris Review*. Trocchi, in temporary freedom, then made a stupid gesture of bravado, and appeared on a national television programme about drugs in which "for demonstration purposes" he gave himself a fix in front of the cameras. There could not have been a more effective way of making himself the most hated image in America, public enemy number one. It must be remembered that at no time while in America, or later in his last years in the UK, did he ever agree that drugs were bad for him, or for other people. His line was always that everyone should be free to make his or her own decisions about drugs and not be hindered by the law.

While on bail, Lyn and Mark went to Hicksville to see Lyn's parents. A conventional couple, they were in a state of permanent grief because of the evil destiny that had overcome their daughter. Plimpton, together with Sue and John Marquand, had at one point gone as a delegation to persuade them, unsuccessfully, that their son-in-law was not as bad as he seemed to be. The Hicks' only concern now was to break up the marriage and rescue their daughter and grandson. There is no record of what transpired during that final visit of the three Trocchis, but it can hardly have been a happy occasion. On the way back to New York, while changing trains and waiting on the platform, Alex and Lyn gave themselves a fix, apparently thinking that the other waiting passengers would not realize what they were doing. The train came in. They were of course being followed by FBI men – how could they not be, given the charges they faced? – who moved in to arrest them. But Trocchi, abandoning his wife and child, began to run, and he just managed to jump onto the train as it left for New York. The Feds were waiting for him at Grand Central Station, but he somehow evaded capture again and managed to get to the Phoenix bookshop on Cornelia Street, a hangout for bohemian writers, owned by Larry Wallrich. Here he was hidden for several days while his friends made plans to get him out of the country.

He was brought food and dope for three days, and Baird Bryant brought him his own passport. Enough money had been collected to enable him to travel to Toronto. Trocchi then went across Manhattan to Plimpton's apartment on East 72nd Street – a long walk. Plimpton was away, but he obtained entrance (there was always a number of people staying or hanging out there), and dressed himself in two of George's Brooks Brothers suits, one on top of the other. Then he walked, the following day, to the Port Authority Bus Terminal and bought a bus ticket to Niagara Falls. This was not the shortest route to Canada and therefore less likely to be watched with vigilance. His photograph would be at every border, and as a wanted fugitive the police everywhere would be looking for him. The bus ride was twelve hours, and Trocchi was awoken in the morning by a customs officer, who was shaking him. He was at the Canadian border, in view of the Horseshoe Falls. He was asked his name and gave it – W. Baird Bryant – after a moment's hesitation.

"What does the 'W' stand for?" he was asked.

Trocchi searched his brain and then remembered. It was Wensel. "If you were called Wensel," he joked, "you'd say W. Baird Bryant." The tension eased and he was let through to Canada and safety.

From there he travelled to Montreal, where he made contact with Leonard Cohen, then a relatively unknown poet, except in Canada. Cohen put him up for a few days. He had brought nothing with him, his manuscripts and possessions were in New York and his wife was under arrest. He had no option now but to return to Britain.

2

In 1962, Henry Miller was still living in Big Sur, but was visiting Europe more frequently than previously. Money was rolling in from the sales of the *Tropics*, but somehow he seemed to be no better off. The reason was that he had been prevailed upon by lawyers and accountants to avoid tax by turning himself into a corporation and his financial advisors were now giving themselves salaries, offices and secretaries out of his income. He was constantly having to ask his various publishers for more money to meet these expenses and was borrowing in advance of future royalties.

In addition he was as susceptible as ever to feminine charms, and he had fallen heavily for Renata Gerhardt, Ledig-Rowohlt's secretary. She was a tall brunette, lively and enthusiastic with literary tastes, and she succumbed to his attentions, which began to cost Henry growing amounts of money, because he agreed to back her in starting her own publishing house. She moved to Berlin because at the time there were considerable benefits to be had from living and working there; the government was anxious to keep West Berlin, which was surrounded by communist East Germany, alive and flourishing, and there were inducements of subsidy and tax benefits to be had if you established or moved your business there. But Renata always needed more money to pay for her new books, and most of Miller's German income was being diverted to her from Rowohlt in Hamburg; but their personal contact was increasingly through correspondence, most of hers asking for more money.

A month after his appearance at the International Writers' Conference,* which I had organized as part of the Edinburgh Festival in 1962, Miller moved from Northern California to Pacific Palisades, just outside Los Angeles, where he eventually acquired a house at 444 Ocampo Drive, which was equipped with greater comfort than he had previously known, and with a swimming pool. Here he settled down, still working on *Nexus*, which he really did not want to complete because he had a superstition that once he had finished it he would die. He found a new circle of friends, spent much time in the pool, bicycling and playing ping-pong, and devoting more time to painting in water colours than writing. He also met Hoki, a Japanese-American nightclub performer and once again fell in love. It is doubtful that she gave Miller much sexual satisfaction, but she agreed to marry him, and she used his money to live her own life. At one point, some years later in 1967 when Hoki was coming to London, Henry Miller wrote to me and asked if I would look after her. She was staying at the Dorchester on Park Lane and I asked her to lunch. It was obvious that she had no intention of being looked after by Henry Miller's publisher; lunch consisted of bored conversation – Marion Boyars, my partner, and I had great difficulty in drawing her out on anything – and from her badly disguised beard-burn it was obvious that she had not spent the night alone. She declined to be taken to anything that was on in London or to see me again. A few weeks later Henry came to England on his way to Paris, and I used the opportunity to give a lunchtime reception for him at the Savoy, which included a press conference. There were interviews, articles and photographs in the press, which gave a new impetus to the sales of the Miller titles we then had in print. I took Henry around London – there were several places he remembered from the past that he wanted to look at again – and he asked me if I would drive past the Dorchester; he wanted me to stop across the street from it, alongside Hyde Park. I turned off the engine and for several long minutes, without saying a word, Henry looked at the hotel. It was obvious that he was voyeuristically imagining exactly what Hoki might have been doing there. Then he shook his head as if emerging from a dream and asked me to drive on, but conversation lagged and his mind was elsewhere. After two days in London he went to Paris, where Joseph Strick was making a film of *Tropic of Cancer*; he had been invited to watch the filming.

Thereafter he stayed in Pacific Palisades, keeping up a voluminous correspondence with Lawrence Durrell, Girodias, Ledig-Rowohlt and old friends, and writing to authors whose books he liked, such as Erica Jong, who made a special trip to visit him there. A local publisher in Santa Barbara, Noel Young of Capra Press, managed to publish some of his later writings and some earlier ones that were not available, and he too became part of the Miller circle. I was to visit Henry for the last time in 1976, four years before he died. He had broken his hip and was no longer able to use his bicycle, which had always been a major pleasure, and was not even able to bathe in his own swimming pool; nevertheless, he was in good humour. He had just received a long letter from Durrell, and he said approving things about Girodias. He was also in love again. He did not tell me the object of his affections, but his secretary was very beautiful and it was not hard to guess. I had one little surprise: when I went to his bathroom I found that the bath mat on the floor was covered with breasts and nipples made from foam rubber. He must have enjoyed walking over them, sexually orientated to the last.

Henry Miller died aged eighty-eight on 7th June 1980; it was the middle of the American Booksellers' Conference in Chicago and his death became the talking point of the convention. Barney Rosset filled the Grove Press stand with a large, black-lined notice of his death, in homage to the author who had helped make him famous and had caused Grove so much legal cost. Henry Miller had played a crucial role in the opening up of modern literature to sexual frankness and in bringing about the demise – but probably only for a few years – of censorship.

Henry Miller died a stoic at the end of a long and productive life. He left the following words of advice to his children: "About my death, take it with a smile, don't panic. Just think of it as the end of an act, the curtain falling. I've led a great life, a full life. I welcome my death with open arms, so should you."*

Henry Miller and William Burroughs had first met at the Edinburgh Writers' Conference at one of the evening parties. Burroughs was anxious to express his admiration for the older man, but Miller, not talkative on that occasion, inhibited him. "So you're Burroughs," he said.

Bill looked for words, and finally came out with: "A long-time admirer." They smiled and that ended the conversation. The next day they met again and Miller repeated his remark as if they had not previously seen each other. But they did manage to communicate a little more before the end of the Conference, especially on the last night. Burroughs certainly continued the Miller tradition and was probably his most important successor, opening the door considerably further onto the landscape of obscene literature as a way to view the obscene world, and extending the limits of what can be imagined, described and published. There are many similarities between Miller and Burroughs: each eventually became accepted by the literary world and they were both elected to the American Academy and Institute of Arts and Letters, the symbol of respectability, which at the very least meant that if they were attacked, their fellow members had an obligation to defend them.

But Miller, although not in any way censorious, did not really like Burroughs's writing. As early as December 1960, having been asked to read the manuscript of *The Naked Lunch* by Girodias, he had written back:

> I've tried now for the third time to read it through, but I can't stick it. The truth is that it bores me. The Marquis de Sade bores me too, perhaps in a different way, or for different reasons...

> However, there is no question in my mind as to Burroughs's abilities. There is a ferocity in his writing which is equalled, in my opinion, only by Céline. No writer I know of made more daring use of the language. I wish I had read him on some other subject – read him on St Thomas Aquinas for example, or on eschatology. Or better still on 'The Grand Inquisitor'.

> I know that no one could reach to that frenzied kind of description, at once vile and horripilating, without being serious in his intent... the effect of the book on the average reader... would be the very opposite of what the censors feared... To read that book is to take the cure.*

Miller's letter might have been one of the factors that held up the first Paris edition for so long.

Burroughs was Grove's candidate for the second Prix Formentor, which was moved from Majorca to a castle near Salzburg, because Franco would not allow the publishers and their entourages to return for a second year. Mary McCarthy was on the jury and having known Burroughs from Edinburgh she backed him; but unaccountably, during the middle of her nominating speech, she broke down into tears. The prize, in the end, went to Nathalie Sarraute. Barney Rosset naturally wanted to show the maximum "respectable" support for Burroughs at Formentor, because he was being asked by a number of American booksellers, facing seizure and prosecution, to help them financially, but after his experiences with *Tropic of Cancer*, he was reluctant to do this. He did, however, defend one case in Boston, and employed Edward de Grazia, who was on retainer with him, to handle it. De Grazia had assured him that this was a once and for all case, and he should defend this if no other. At one point during the trial Ed found himself in the men's room with the prosecutor, learnt from him that the case had been brought reluctantly, but the Attorney-General had to take cognisance of the "old ladies" and pressure groups who kept up a constant barrage for this or that book to be banned. Several eminent witnesses appeared for the defence, including John Ciardi, a Dante translator, who found many comparisons between *The Naked Lunch* and *The Divine Comedy*, Norman Holland, Norman Mailer, Allen Ginsberg and a number of academics. But the judge, an Irish Catholic, had obviously made up his mind in advance, and he found the book obscene. De Grazia appealed and on 7th July 1966, the Massachusetts Supreme Court ruled, by a vote of two to one, that the book was not "utterly without redeeming social value" and was therefore not obscene. The dissenting justice said that he had found the book to be "literary sewage", but he was outvoted. This was the last case to be brought in the US against a book with the rank of a modern classic.

During the Sixties, in spite of his difficulties with Girodias, Burroughs was able to support himself adequately most of the time, but his major cross was now his son, Billy. The product of his marriage to Joan, killed with a revolver by Burroughs in their "William Tell Act", Billy had been brought up by his father's long suffering parents, who had also kept their own son alive on an allowance until he began to earn money from his writing. Burroughs had little contact with his son, who began to become delinquent as a teenager, and increasingly curious about his distant father; he wanted to be with him. There were a number of incidents, including one where he accidentally nearly killed a friend with a .22 rifle that his grandparents had given him; at this point Burroughs agreed to let Billy come to stay with him. It was 1963 and the boy was sixteen. He flew to Tangiers where Burroughs was living at the time, and he was entered into the American School, the headmaster of which was Omar Pound, Ezra's son. Burroughs decided that his long-nursed guilt feelings about his wife and his son could now be repaired.

But Billy was being brought into a highly unconventional household, where his father lived with two English homosexual lovers, Ian

Sommerville and Michael Portman. There was only a couch for him to sleep on. Ian lost no time in trying to seduce the boy, who was also subject to the advances of the many other queens in the area. He was introduced to kif-smoking on arrival, and had little else to do except hang about the house, with no friends, while his father worked on his typewriter or sat in his orgone box. The father, taking little notice of his son's age and innocence, simply made him another member of his bohemian household. He had given little thought before Billy's arrival to his needs and to what his responsibilities as a father really were.

Billy started school and left after three days. He was not interested in learning; he preferred to sit around with his father and his circle, and his only immediate ambition was to learn to play flamenco on his guitar. Soon Billy began to miss his grandparents, who had been loving to him, and Palm Beach, where he had spent the last few teenage years. While in Tangiers, Billy deliberately and frequently behaved in a way that annoyed his father, in order to get back at him for the years of neglect; it soon became clear that the present arrangement would never work out. After much discussion Billy was returned to Palm Beach, and he was busted on arrival for possession of *majoun*.

Partly because of Billy, who had deliberately flaunted the native taboos, in particular by going up on the roof to see the women who were unveiled while they gossiped and did the washing, Burroughs began to have trouble with his neighbours. Ian Sommerville in particular was very promiscuous with the local Arab boys, and the time of tolerance was coming to an end. In addition, Burroughs never gave any employment to the local Muslims, which would have softened the hostility. The Istiqlal, a Moroccan nationalist party, was increasingly objecting to the presence of so many foreigners corrupting the local Muslim population. In 1964 the influx of American hippies swelled considerably, and their behaviour, very different from that of the discreet established foreign residents, could not be ignored. The foreign population that had enjoyed extraordinary privileges because it was not too visible, and had usually practised its pleasures and vices behind closed doors, was now endangered by the loud, over-obvious and anything but discreet hippies. Burroughs, because of the tension, decided to move to New York and join Brion Gysin there. The latter was trying to market his 'Dream Machine' through a toy manufacturer.

Burroughs arrived in New York at the beginning of December, where he was held and searched for three hours at customs. They were looking for drugs, and they leafed carefully through the quantities of books, newspaper cuttings and manuscripts that he had brought with him. Gysin was waiting for him outside and the customs officers said to him: "Are you a friend of that man in there? He sure writes some filthy stuff."*

Playboy gave him an assignment to write about his home town, St Louis, and he paid a nostalgic visit there, visiting childhood haunts and their memories, taking pictures of remembered buildings and seeing a few old acquaintances. But the result, *Return to St Louis*, was rejected by *Playboy*, although finally published by the *Paris Review*. Burroughs moved into the Chelsea Hotel, a long-time haunt of New York bohemians and artists, where he came to know some of the writers, painters and eccentrics who lived there permanently, then went to Palm Beach for the funeral of his father, who had just died. Bill would have liked to thank his father for the years of support and for adopting his son, but it was too late now. Billy was in boarding school and unable to attend the funeral. Burroughs then found a loft at 210 Center Street in Soho, and I remember visiting him there. I had trouble finding it, and not knowing New York well, thought it a particularly seedy and dangerous area; the large warehouse buildings were just being made residential, there were few people on the streets and it seemed to me to be a muggers' paradise. But Bill told me it was relatively safe, in spite of appearances, and that he was still able to run fast, and he showed me a weapon that consisted of a long wire-coil hidden inside a walking stick that was intended to whip a potential mugger across the eyes. He was, as always, fascinated by weaponry, and he was building a collection of unusual instruments of defence and assault. But Soho was usually safe because of the proximity of Chinatown and Little Italy. Both communities kept a neighbourhood watch and street robbers, according to Bill, were likely to end up in the chop-suey or made to disappear by the Mafia, who wanted no petty crime on their own patch: they even had their own internal patrols to police the areas and escort young girls from the subway to their homes.

Another of Burroughs's old Paris supporters, Gaït Frogé, was now living in New York. She had followed Norman Rubington there, and realizing with dismay that he was not willing to continue their old intimacy in the new world, had hastily returned to France, but failing to recover the premises of her old bookshop, had once again flown back. This time she met and married Jerry Westman, a not very successful graphic artist with whom she moved to Texas. That did not work out well for the two of them. Back in New York Jerry died, and Gaït lived by doing freelance editorial work for publishers, and odd jobs and translations for the *New York Times* and *Le Figaro*. Norman Rubington urged her to start writing, but after a few attempts, including work on a film scenario, she gave up. She thought of opening a bookshop in New York, but it was too difficult to get the financial backing, and she realized that she would never receive the generous credit that publishers had allowed her in Paris where she was often the only outlet for serious literature in the English language.

She did some secretarial work as well, and spent two or three days a week as personal assistant to Niccola Lindenberg, a French painter and sculptor, who lived in the Chelsea Hotel and became her best female friend. Gaït Frogé had always been a sociable person, one of the necessary traits of a good bookseller, and she hated being alone; every evening she went out to see friends or engage in cultural activities, visiting art galleries, going to poetry readings and to dinner parties with other émigrés, entertaining in her own apartment when she could. On one of her evening sorties she was badly mugged, and although she continued to go into the streets, it was with much nervousness, which did not improve her health; she was also drinking and smoking heavily, and she began to suffer from severe attacks of asthma. When Burroughs was in New York, she went to see him wherever he was living – both he and Gysin were indebted to her for publishing *Minutes to Go* from her Paris bookshop – and to his readings, but he was now moving in a more American circle, where she did not always feel welcome. She had a number of lovers after her husband died, one of them a very handsome Cuban, but her friends became more limited and she was lonelier as she grew older; French vivacity was not enough in New York without looks or money. I was to meet her once again with Maurice Girodias in the early Eighties: it was an intimate evening with the three of us having a simple dinner in her small apartment and reminiscing about Paris. She eventually died alone of an asthma attack in November 1988.

Gaït Frogé was a typical Breton, combining an independent and outgoing spirit with a strong need for friendship and affection. She was unfailingly generous and open-hearted all her life, very feminine in a typically Gallic way, never allowing her depressions to show, and always genuinely interested in other people's enthusiasms and careers.

Through Brion Gysin, Burroughs met Peter Matson, who became his American agent. Matson was a young man who at the time was trying to find a manufacturer to take on Gysin's Dream Machine, a kind of flickering kaleidoscope intended to appeal to the psychedelic generation, but he was unable to attract any serious interest. Gysin increasingly came to dislike New York which he saw as a matriarchy that brought out and justified all his misogyny, but Burroughs was now becoming a social success, much invited to parties, where he met all the leading painters and photographers, poets and novelists, including Marisol, Ted Berrigan, Ron Padgett, Frank O'Hara, Diane Arbus, Richard Avedon, Larry Rivers, Andy Warhol and others who were then coming into fashion. Burroughs began to build his own new circle. His public readings were a success and much talked about. He was not above gimmicks: on one occasion he tore down a white sheet that had been hanging behind him during his reading to reveal a giant rubber tarantula stuck to the wall. On another he gave a reading under the auspices of the American Theatre for Poets in a 129-seat theatre on East 4th Street; the hippie audience of young people, wearing the newly fashionable miniskirts, jeans and leather, packed the little theatre to hear the Underground's new guru. Burroughs came through the red curtains wearing his conventional three-piece suit with a topcoat and felt hat, and carrying a briefcase. He slowly removed his exterior layers, placed coat and hat on a white chair, together with an umbrella, and then began to read. His Midwestern voice with its Harvard overtones, so like T.S. Eliot's, and his sartorial appearance, so different from that of the audience, together with the obscenity, humorous satire and extreme unconventionality of his reading material, created a surreal and hypnotizing effect on the audience, who laughed, gasped and applauded. He then played a cut-up tape where all the voices were his own, mixing elements from his work with official dispatches from the Vietnam War and the newspapers. When he was finished he disappeared behind the curtains and did not come back for applause.

Burroughs was always a dualistic person. Externally he was quiet, apparently unexcitable, reasonable (except where certain complexes and obsessions were concerned), modest and unremarkable looking. His manners were good and gentlemanly, and his speech, except occasionally when drunk, careful and polite. He dressed like a typical office-worker or the manager of a small bank in a small town, and he talked like one. No one could have looked more conventionally middle-American. But inside that head a whole bizarre world, akin to that of Hieronymous Bosch or Dante, was present: his fictional orgies and ritualistic cruelties, his vivid descriptions of what can be done by those who achieve total power over the bodies and minds of others, are unforgettable and rank him with the greatest of the libertine writers, especially de Sade. Only occasionally could one observe, in Burroughs's company, a slight smile playing around the corners of his mouth, and see a certain brightness in his eyes, giving some hint of the private world hidden behind the normally fixed, unsmiling mask and the bored, dead-looking eyes.

He and his closest friend Brion Gysin were of a kind: Brion a hunter, potentially a cat-like killer, Burroughs more akin to the scavengers, jackals and crows, who follow in the killer's wake. But it is Burroughs who will be longest remembered as one of the most extraordinary writers of his century, an artist who caught part of the essence of his time, especially in his satirical descriptions of prototypes. The day may come when Burroughs is again not allowed to be read, as happened for more than a century with de Sade. Although he may well have had his tongue in his cheek when he claimed that his intention, in his more extreme descriptions of sex and death in *The Naked Lunch*, were based on Swift's *A Modest Proposal*,* his work does have that effect on the reader, namely to make him aware of certain impulses in himself that he did not realize were there, or had been throttled down. It is possible to imaginatively change one's sexual orientations when reading Burroughs, so that homosexual erotic descriptions can arouse the heterosexual reader and vice-versa. Only a good writer can bring this off; Genet springs to mind as another. Burroughs has said that the execution scenes in *The Naked Lunch* were intended as an attack on capital punishment, just as *A Modest Proposal* was an attack on English indifference to the Irish famine. *The Naked Lunch* enables the reader, in an age when, in the democracies of the West at least, executions are no longer public spectacles, to realize the link between Eros and Thanatos, and the erotic pleasure that so many can find in the contemplation of others suffering and dying.

3

John Giorno was a young poet who managed, in the Sixties, to sleep around with a large number of gay writers and artists who were prominent on the scene at the time. He came from a well-to-do family in Roslyn, Long Island, and had graduated from Columbia in 1958. He spent four years on Wall Street before joining the New York counter-culture, and he first became known when his lover, Andy Warhol, made a six-hour film of him sleeping. This put him into the avant-garde social set, and at a party given for Burroughs by Panna Grady, a wealthy hostess of Hungarian descent, Giorno met Gysin and became his lover. They lived together for a while at the Chelsea Hotel, doing fourteen acid trips together. Gysin was himself widely read, a fascinating conversationalist and a man of wide, worldly and artistic experience; Giorno fell passionately in love and became an acolyte and pupil as well as bed-mate. In 1965 they went together to Tangiers, and it was during that time that an interesting happening occurred involving the Bowleses.

Brion and John were staying in a flat next to Jane Bowles, and one day Paul rushed in to report that Jane's parrot, Seth, had dropped dead off its perch. The parrot had been perfectly well and healthy, and had just eaten some food which had been prepared by Jane. The assumption was that the food had been poisoned. An alternative theory was black magic. Suspicion fell on Cherifa, Jane's lover and servant, who it was widely believed was capable of both; it was also a time in the Muslim year when black magic was most practised and feared. The veterinarian was called, and he diagnosed that the parrot had died of an embolism caused by terror: either poison or magic might have caused this, but an autopsy for poison would have involved going to the Pasteur Institute, and Jane refused this, apparently afraid of what might be discovered. She was having an affair at the time with Princess Martha Ruspoli de Chambrun, a wealthy French-American, separated from her husband, one of the Tangiers mountain set. Martha Ruspoli was herself a controversial character, rumoured to have murdered a previous male lover and to be engaged in occultism, but it was obvious that Cherifa had the stronger motive. It was a time of high tension in the Bowles circle, and although Cherifa remained as cook and companion to Jane, the atmosphere grew steadily worse. Both Brion and Paul distrusted Cherifa, and her hostility towards them both was evident. In a letter to a friend, Andreas Brown, who later was to buy New York's legendary literary bookshop, the Gotham Book Mart, Paul Bowles predicted that the women in his household, excluding Jane, would eventually undo Brion, just as the latter's former partner had ruined him in his restaurant days, and this time would land him in jail.

In Tangiers Brion Gysin worked on *The Process*, a novel that was largely about the Beat Hotel and its denizens. He was still disappointed at his failure to get his "Dream Machine" produced commercially as a psychedelic toy, and he was half-way through his contribution to *The Third Mind*, which he had been writing together with Burroughs for some time. Giorno liked Morocco, which he found cheap, with drugs readily available, and he fell naturally into the life of the American expatriates. He was still deeply in love with Gysin, but the latter was not made for monogamy, and in any case he preferred Arabs; he became increasingly bored by the younger man, whose fawning had become an irritant. Giorno, deeply disappointed by Gysin's increasing indifference, returned to New York that August.

His next lover was Robert Rauschenberg and then Jasper Johns. Giorno wanted excitement and a full sexual life, and to be part of the political scene as well as the artistic one, but Johns was interested only in his art. The Vietnam War was not his concern, nor the rock scene, and he did not care, unlike Giorno, what the students at Berkeley and elsewhere were demonstrating about.

In 1969, John Giorno started "Dial-a-Poem", an experiment that he talked the Museum of Modern Art in New York into accepting. Twelve poets each recorded a two-and-a-half-minute poem, which you heard when you dialled the advertised number, getting by chance whichever line – and poem – came up at random; there were twelve telephone lines. This was so successful that the museum was soon getting 20,000 calls a day. Giorno began to make the recordings more political, using to read them, Bobby Seale of the Black Panthers, Abbie Hoffman, leader of the Yippies, and Diane di Prima. The latter described how to make a Molotov cocktail. On the day that a bomb exploded in the IBM building, a poem was coincidentally read about making a bomb, and the *New York Times* made a scare story out of it. The museum trustees hastily ended the Dial-a-Poem programme, but the New York Telephone Company used Giorno's idea for their other products.

Panna Grady, whose maiden name was de Cholnoky, came from an aristocratic Hungarian family on her father's side and a wealthy American mother and developed into the offbeat hostess for the avant-garde scene during the Sixties. She had grown up in Greenwich, Connecticut, had come out as a New York debutante before going to Wellesley and Berkeley, and while at the latter had involved herself in the Beat Generation poetry scene at City Lights, where she met Allen Ginsberg. Panna de Cholnoky decided that she preferred the beats to the high society of her parents and married a poet called Grady – the marriage did not last long – and then set about making herself the queen of the New York Beat scene, giving frequent parties in her large apartment in the Dakota. When she met Burroughs she decided that she had found the right man. He was polite and kind, well-mannered at all times, able to talk to her naturally without putting her down, or taking her and her money for granted the way so many other artists she had entertained had done. He was never condescending. It was not sex that interested her, but companionship, and she felt that a writer of Burroughs's stature would be the ideal companion for someone like herself, willing to give all she had to art.

In the spring of 1965 Panna Grady gave a party in Burroughs's honour that was gatecrashed by everyone in the Village who had heard about it, so much so that she had to tell the doorman to admit no one further. It was unfortunate that the first person to be turned away was the black writer Leroi Jones, who *had* been invited, and he got into a fight with one of the doormen. The party soon became legendary, partly because many of the guests, invited or not, behaved badly, and there was no lack of insults traded between rival writers and painters present. Burroughs at this point did not like parties and he left as early as he decently could.

Panna decided that she really loved Burroughs. He might be homosexual, but he was a manly homosexual, had been married before, and she was certain that with her money she could enhance his career, give him a comfortable life and enjoy the reflected fame. She gave constant dinner parties for him and he seemed to respond favourably. Herbert Huncke, prominent on the counter-cultural scene, found that he had a useful source of income in selling gossip about Bill Burroughs to Panna, and he regularly received a few dollars every time he came up with some anecdote about him. It was through Panna that Burroughs first met John Giorno, who now joined his entourage and became a permanent member of it. During the period that Burroughs and Gysin were working together on *The Third Mind*, a mixed bag of a book that included theory, explanation of method, cut-ups, collages and fiction, Giorno was often the third party present, eating with them at the end of the day. The painter David Budd often made a fourth; through Budd, Burroughs became interested in the stream-of-consciousness last words of the New York gangster Dutch Schultz after he had been shot. These are quoted in a book about the period* which fascinated Burroughs, who had always been interested in the gangsters of the Twenties and Thirties, subject of much of his early reading. He used the "last words" in a cut-up tape in his public readings and eventually wrote a film scenario about Schultz's death, which has not yet been made into a film: *The Last Words of Dutch Schultz*.*

The Soft Machine and *The Ticket that Exploded* were both published by Grove Press and by me in Britain. The American sales were disappointing, because these books were principally composed by cut-up and fold-in with much less pornographic material than *The Naked Lunch*. They sold better in Britain than in the States because Burroughs's reputation there was by now more as an experimental writer than as a shocking one. And *Dead Fingers Talk*, which first introduced Burroughs in Britain, but had never appeared in the States, continued to sell almost as well as the other three books, both in my own hardcover editions and then in mass-market paperback.

Nova Express, which had been commissioned in advance by Dick Seaver for Barney Rosset, was the next to appear, selling rather better than *The Soft Machine* and *The Ticket*. Part of the motivation in commissioning the book was to get world rights and give Barney the power to exclude me from publishing it in Britain, in revenge for the British publication of *Tropic of Cancer*. Barney then took great delight in sub-contracting it to Jonathan Cape, one of my principal publishing rivals in London. Burroughs, once he had realized what he had done, apologized to me, but said there was nothing he could do about it; he promised, however, that this would not happen again: Grove would only be allowed to buy American rights in future. As it turned out, both Grove and myself, were to lose Burroughs's later work, but for a very different reason.

Allen Ginsberg was away from New York for much of the year that Burroughs was living in the loft on Center Street. He had been travelling in Europe and had had a particularly bad time in Prague, where a police provocateur attacked him in the street, calling him *"bouzerant"* ("fairy" or "queer"), and in the subsequent confusion, which enabled the police to obtain and read through his notebooks, he was told that he was unwelcome and must leave immediately. He was hustled to the airport and put on the next plane to London. Back in New York, he reported his disgust with all totalitarian regimes and their strict codes of morality, which included a determination to keep the Beat scene out of their countries. Hippies at the time were simply not allowed in, and the accepted, although still-criticized dress of western youth – miniskirts and jeans – were simply banned in Eastern Europe. This disapproval also applied to some extent to West Germany and Austria. On one occasion in the mid-Sixties I was driving through the Tyrol and my car broke down. I had three women with me, including my wife, all wearing miniskirts. The entire population of the little mountain village came to gape at this provocative sight, and the comments were not friendly. Marion Boyars's sister, a medical doctor at a hospital in Hamburg, was severely criticized by colleagues for wearing a shorter-than-knee-length skirt in her office. Casual dress in Germany continued to upset the traditional German mind for some years, and radical students in the Sixties announced that: "Jeans are not trousers. They are ideology."

Towards the end of his New York year Burroughs began to pine for Europe. The drug scene was getting heavier, with many more arrests, and there were too many agents provocateurs, who in particular wanted to catch the better-known names of the counter-culture. Herbert Huncke was approached by a narcotics agent and asked to help set up Burroughs and Ginsberg by planting drugs on them before a raid. As soon as Huncke reported this to him, Ginsberg went to see the Mayor, John Lindsay, who made a formal apology on behalf of the city. Although Burroughs was free of heroin at the time, he still indulged occasionally in pot, and the New York newspapers, in their hyped-up reporting of the drug scene, gave the public the impression that there was no basic difference between soft and hard drugs. The entire press, except for a few small-circulation opinion journals, was right-wing and unsympathetic to the mood of the young, while the older generation attacked the new freedoms that their children were enjoying, created by the greater affluence of the time. Anti-communism of a totally illogical and virulent complexion – communism certainly posed no danger to America – was still very prevalent in the general consciousness; McCarthyism was not dead although McCarthy was, and there was much support for such extreme measures as obliterating Russia or China with a sneak atomic attack.

Paul and Jane Bowles showed up in New York. Jane had had her stroke and was now badly brain-damaged. She could only see with difficulty, had a speech impediment and dragged her feet. Burroughs went to see them at the Chelsea Hotel and came to the private conclusion that Paul really wanted to get rid of Jane and was making it easy for the doctors to kill her with dangerous treatments. At this point Paul Bowles was not doing as well as previously with his novels; he accepted a commission to write a book about Bangkok, which would involve spending a year there. This meant leaving Jane in Tangiers with Cherifa at a time when her condition was deteriorating; she was swallowing her medicines without proper supervision, never remembering whether or not she had taken her pills, and drinking heavily at the same time. But in spite of her illness, from which it was obvious she would never recover, Jane's novels and collections of stories were having a successful revival with her London publisher, Peter Owen, just at the time when interest in Paul's writing was at a low ebb. There were various academic appointments open to him, and he was eventually to accept one, teaching "Advanced Narrative Writing" and "The Modern European Novel" in California.

In early September 1965, Bill Burroughs returned to London. He had old friends and lovers there, and he felt that away from New York, where he had found little time to write, other than his collaboration with Brion Gysin, he would be able to return to a regular routine of work. He had some trouble on arrival with British Immigration, because his was now a well-known name, associated with drugs and literary controversy, and his passport was stamped with permission to stay for only one month. But he went to see Lord Arnold Goodman, then the most fashionable lawyer in London, who was also the personal solicitor of the Prime Minister, Harold Wilson, and of the Labour Party, which had been returned to power the previous year. Goodman was soon also to become Chairman of the Arts Council, which was beginning, under the enthusiastic new Arts Minister, Jenny Lee, to expand its influence and activities with a massive increase in public subsidy. Goodman was able, without difficulty, to obtain an extension of Burroughs's right to stay in Britain from the home Secretary, Roy Jenkins.

4

Iris Owens returned to New York at the beginning of the Sixties. She had lived with Sinbad Vail, editor of *Points*, for the last of her years in Paris and they remained good friends thereafter. Five of her books had appeared with Olympia, and most of them were to be republished by Grove Press in the Eighties, still under the pen name, Harriet Daimler. These included *Darling*, *Innocence*, *The Organization* and *The Woman Thing*. Her first meeting in Paris with Walter Minton, at the Café de Flore on the occasion of the rumpus at the lesbian nightclub, did now bear some fruit, although it quickly turned sour. Minton gave her a contract to write a novel for Putnam; no doubt he saw it as a chance to spite Girodias. She started to write, but found herself stuck in the middle, and abandoning it, suggested another manuscript instead. But this did not interest Minton. There is some confusion over the unfinished manuscript, which at one point passed through the hands of Bill Targ, then a senior editor of Putnam, who was told to do Minton's dirty work for him. Targ considered Minton an ignorant upstart for whom he had no respect. The manuscript of the commissioned novel, *The Hope Diamond*, was never completed, but Iris went on to write another, *After Claude*, which was accepted by Farrar, Straus & Cudahy. Minton considered this grounds enough to sue. Bill Targ, a man of mild-mannered courtesy, working under a boss for whom he had no respect, suddenly had a provocative and threatening letter to Roger Straus, written in his own name, thrust under his nose, and was told to sign it, which he reluctantly did. He apologized to Straus later, privately.* The case went as high as the Supreme Court of the State of New York, where Iris Owens finally won. The judges, in handing down their decision, spoke of the Putnam contract as a form of "indentured serfdom" which had no place in a free society.

In New York she met Rosemary Ridgewell again and they became good friends. Rosemary had continued her lawsuit against Minton in spite of her doubts, and she was eventually awarded $100,000 from Putnam, less than half the original claim, but a useful amount. She also found a permanent relationship, so Maurice's premonitions about her future were happily ungrounded. Iris ran into Gaït Frogé and Marilyn Meeske as well, and the old friendships of the Saint-German-des-Prés cafés were renewed in Greenwich Village, while those other émigrés who had returned to London began to meet in Bernard Stone's Turret Bookshop in Kensington and the pubs and coffee bars of Soho. Many of them frequented my own offices in Sackville Street, above a tailor's shop.

Mason Hoffenberg also ended up in New York where, like Trocchi, he became a junkie, worked on a scow on the river, and he eventually died young. He never received much in royalties from Minton for *Candy*, although he ended up with some money. Girodias had always thought of Hoffenberg as a "loser" compared to the well organized and more astute Terry Southern, and in that he was proved right.

Patrick Bowles turned up in London with a beautiful girl called Gail that he had met in Paris at the offices of the American Express, and came to my office to claim royalties for his translation, in collaboration with Beckett, of *Molloy*. He also asked for freelance editorial and translation work. He soon became known as an available and obliging stud, having a fling among many others with Marion Lobbenberg, before she became Boyars. Christopher Logue had already been back in London for some time and he was pursuing his career as a poet, playwright and occasionally an actor. When *Private Eye*, the satirical magazine that mocked people, events and pretensions – always struggling through a plethora of lawsuits – started up, he began to derive a steady income from it with a regular column of "True Stories". Alexander Trocchi returned to Britain from Canada on a tramp steamer that took thirteen days to reach Aberdeen. There were no drugs to be had and it was thirteen days of hell because of his withdrawal symptoms, which became more painful with every passing day. He had brought some Demerol with him, which helped to knock him out, and he hardly stirred from his bunk for the whole trip. From Aberdeen he took a train to Glasgow, where he was met by an old school friend who let him stay with the family for a few days. Trocchi immediately went to Boots the Chemist, explained that he was an addict, and managed to get a little heroin. He then registered as an addict, which entitled him to get a free daily ration. Britain did not have a drug problem because the liberal attitude of the day kept the small number of addicts away from the crime scene.

In the meantime, Lyn was in jail in New York and he had to find a way to get her out and to bring her and Mark to Britain. Knowing nothing of Trocchi's past at this time, except what is related in the novel, I was negotiating with Grove to publish *Cain's Book* in Britain, and I eventually signed a contract with them. It appeared in the spring of 1963, not long after I had brought Trocchi to the Writers' Conference, which also made his name well known. He managed, in the meantime, to sell *Young Adam* to Heinemann, and I put a group of his stories into a new experimental series entitled *New Writers*; this was intended to publish short work by emerging talent and use up some of the oddments that every publisher gets sent by his literary authors: poems, short stories, essays and some prose fragments. Trocchi managed to get journalistic assignments and reviewing, and after his Edinburgh appearance was frequently in demand to appear on television panels and discussions on the radio, which in Britain, unlike America, were usually quite well paid.

Royalties due to him were now building up in New York, but he never received any of them. Frederick Fell of New American Library, which had been the last of the publishers of *Young Adam* in New York, sued and managed to get all of Trocchi's royalties from various books blocked; soon the IRS was also suing and instructing Grove Press to pay all royalties to them. He had, of course, jumped bail, but Plimpton, the biggest loser, did not add to the claims and counter-claims that were made by those who had paid advances for unwritten books, or had lent him money.

It is difficult to disentangle truth from lies in the various claims that Trocchi now made. He demanded back from an old friend, Cecil Strachan, a large, carefully selected personal library that he said he had entrusted to him on leaving Scotland. Strachan denied ever having seen such a library and even knowing that it existed. He did get money from several publishers, including myself, for signing contracts for books he was never to write, and one such, *The Long Book*, aptly titled, seems to have been offered to every fiction editor in London, several of whom gave him contracts and an advance. When in 1963 I moved offices from Sackville Street to Brewer Street, I had to leave in a hurry because the old building was due to be torn down as soon as I departed. It was impossible to hunt through the store rooms, full of old galleys, manuscripts and correspondence with authors – archive material that would in the normal course of things be valuable one day, as so much literary history was there. I took what we could find in the short time available, but had to leave the bulk of the archives. Then Trocchi, as soon as my staff and I had departed, went to work with half a dozen friends he had recruited, and rescued tons of folders with correspondence, galleys corrected by Beckett and other important writers, as well as books, manuscripts and assorted correspondence. Through Bertram Rota, the rare book manuscript dealer, and in some cases by means of direct correspondence with university libraries in Texas, Vancouver and elsewhere, he managed to net a tidy sum for the material that would otherwise have ended up with the rubble of the old Queen Anne building, as it came down to make way for the enlargement of a department store. I never found out how much Trocchi earned in this way, but £10,000 would be a conservative guess.

After two years Trocchi did manage to get Lyn and Mark over to Britain. She had been released from jail some months after Trocchi escaped, and went to stay with her parents, who were determined to prevent her from returning to Alex. She held a number of jobs, but it took a long time to get her passport back. In the meantime she worked mainly for a local radio station in Stamford, near her parents' home. During those two years Alex bombarded her with letters and tried to get Dick Seaver and Don Getz to use their good offices to obtain a passport for her, and to keep it out of the hands of her father. Don Getz was trying to make a film of *Young Adam*, and he had promised Alex a substantial advance against royalties, but the deal never came off. Trocchi did manage, during the time of separation, to send some money to Lyn, but it was never used as he had hoped to enable her to get herself out of the country; it is probable that she had never kicked the heroin habit during the time she remained in the States; certainly she was on heroin when she rejoined Alex.

They had their reunion at Prestwick airport outside Glasgow. Lyn had escaped from her parents, obtained her passport and flown with Mark, keeping her plans secret. They now settled down in London where Trocchi's career, although it would no longer be productive, was not yet ended. But he was never to fulfil the early promise of the Glasgow philosophy graduate, whose professors had been so certain that he would in a few years bring literary renown to the city of his birth and education.

Chapter Ten

The Sixties and after

1

May has always been a month associated with trouble in Paris, although other summer months have their share of revolutions and notable events. It was in May ten years earlier that the *coup d'état* occurred in Algiers that, but for the hasty return and decisive action of General de Gaulle, would have plunged mainland France into a military dictatorship. May 1968 saw another insurrection, but this time it was the students who rose. It started on 3rd May when Jean Roche, the rector of the Sorbonne, called in the police to break up a small demonstration in a courtyard of the university. Exams were close and he wanted to have no political activity to divert students' attention away from them. It was an act that contained a symbolic importance, because the university had always been considered a place of sanctuary, and to allow the police to enter and make violent arrests was unpardonable, a gross error of judgement on the rector's part. That night students paraded down the boulevards of the Left Bank, arms linked, shouting slogans. The University of Nanterre, east of Paris, followed suit. It had its own grievance: the university had been trying to expel an activist, Daniel Cohn-Bendit, a sociology student, who was German-Jewish, on grounds of nationality, because he was an agitator and a nuisance. The arrested students were hastily tried, and, to make examples of them, sent to prison for two years with no right of appeal. Their fellow students rose in fury, were locked out of the university and roamed the streets, overturning cars, breaking shop windows, insulting the police, and beginning to battle with them in every part of the Saint-Germain, Saint-Michel and Luxembourg districts. The riot police, the Compagnies Républicaines de Sécurité (CRS), were called in and were soon breaking heads with their long batons. The students crossed the river, marched massively down the Champs Elysées and extinguished the undying flame at the Tomb of the Unknown Soldier under the Arc de Triomphe, which had last been put out when Hitler drove over it. Suddenly Paris was at civil war.

For weeks the battle went on. Barricades were erected in the narrow streets of the Left Bank, as they were during the time of the Liberation, paving stones were torn up to be used as weapons and Molotov cocktails made a reappearance. The Sorbonne was broken into and used as barracks. Thousands of others, workers, political activists, many of them carrying the black flags of the anarchist movement or the red ones of revolution, joined the students. Behind the walls of the official buildings the students celebrated their unity. Wine and food were brought in, there was singing, dancing and a good deal of copulation. At the art school posters were hastily designed and printed. Manifestos and leaflets, which called for the resignation of the government and reform of the educational system, including the abolition of exams, were written, printed and circulated to the world outside.

The government of Pompidou decided to defuse the situation by withdrawing the police. There had already been many student casualties and others – bystanders, journalists and tourists – were also attacked by the police, chased up the stairs of buildings where they had taken refuge, beaten with clubs, dragged out onto the streets again and left for the ambulances to pick up later. Given the respite, the students organized a massive march, with reputedly a million marchers, from the Place de la République in the north-east of the city to the Place Denfert-Rochereau in Montparnasse in the south-west. A huge banner led the march proclaiming the "Solidarity of Teachers, Students and Workers", and "De Gaulle Assassin" was one of the slogans shouted by the marching throng. Three demands were made of the government: the reopening of the Sorbonne, the release of the students who had been arrested and sent to prison and the withdrawal of the CRS. Pompidou, realizing that only surrender could stop further violence, capitulated and agreed to the demands. The Sorbonne turned into a gigantic celebration.

Ten days after the start of the insurrection, the unions had called for a national general strike. By 23rd May, three weeks after the trouble began, three million striking workers were paralysing the country. All transport stopped, the delivery of mail was suspended and the telephones did not operate except where automatic systems still functioned. It was impossible to enter the country or to leave it. De Gaulle had been on a state visit to Romania, and during his absence the opposition parties had tabled a motion of censure on the government, which narrowly avoided a defeat. The students knew the affair was not over and began to prepare for the next round, cutting down trees to build more barricades and arming themselves.

De Gaulle returned and made an ineffectual speech that did nothing to create a sense of confidence, while the unions and the Communist Party made plans to bring down the government by collaborating with the students. There were massive marches organized by the trade unions. De Gaulle suddenly disappeared: he had gone to Germany to consult his generals, who were stationed there, in particular Massu, who a decade earlier had been about to invade Paris from Algiers. By now, the students were better organized and were led by Daniel Cohn-Bendit, a natural leader and orator. The Odéon, Barrault's theatre, was taken over by Jean-Jacques Lebel, a poet and the son of a famous art critic, who romantically saw himself continuing in the great revolutionary traditions of 1830, 1848 and 1871. From behind the barricades he had hurled paving stones at the CRS, and now, having invaded the Odéon, he turned the stage into a tribune where orator after orator held forth, anyone of note turning up there out of curiosity being invited to make a speech. The whole Latin Quarter was by now a no-go area, and the students set up their own militia to run it and to try to control the anarchy. Thousands of cars had been overturned, usually to create a foundation for the barricades, while others were set on fire. Shops had been looted and windows broken, but many shopkeepers had helped the students by feeding them or giving them shelter from the police charges, as had some of the residents living overhead.

The workers had taken advantage of the student rising to strike and make their own demands, and younger workers joined the students in their defence of the barricades, while the older ones took their place in the marches. But the relationships between students and workers were tenuous. "Poor workers begin every morning at eight," a student leader, called Castro, said on television, apparently unaware that many of them begin at six. Many workers disdained the students, who, however revolutionary they sounded, and however anxious to make an alliance with the proletariat they were at the present moment, remained, nevertheless, their future bosses.

The École des Beaux Arts became one of the principal centres of activity. In addition to putting out pamphlets, the art students, many of whom were extraordinarily striking and talented, produced hundreds of poster designs. In the future months and years many of them were to be exhibited and reproduced in art books. Literature justifying the uprising poured out on all sides from students in pamphlet form, and the Paris publishers turned out quickly written books from journalists and pundits about the events.

The bourgeoisie, including the parents of the rioting students, reacted in different ways. Some supported the rising in principle, while trying to find ways to keep their particular children, by one ruse or another, away from the violence and the danger. Others disowned them: one father, having heard from his own son how he had set fire to cars in the Latin Quarter, went out to burn his son's car in a rage. The government showed itself to be impotent and only just survived a vote of no confidence from the combined opposition. During this time, all the arts came to a stop: theatres closed and only a few churches had concerts, and they were impromptu and mainly free, in order to bring people into the churches and away from the danger zones. There were few tourists and the remaining expatriates were either caught up in events – a few went to the barricades – or joined the throngs that came to watch history in the making.

Uninvolved curious sightseers came in great numbers, and from whatever vantage point was available watched the students behind their barricades and the CRS confronting them; they witnessed the police charges, the throwing of paving stones, and the street battles. Inevitably, many onlookers were injured; journalists, who had to be close to the action to see what was happening, suffered most; in any case the riot police did not much like being photographed and their actions reported: journalists were a natural target.

Because food and all essential supplies soon ran out, there was a rush into Paris of suppliers hoping to take advantage of the shortages. Main roads were blocked by trucks and all the ordinary streets had cars moving inch by inch through them. The main trade unions announced that they could hold out for at least four months, but it was obvious that the main population could not. Banks closed or opened for limited hours only, allowing only minimal withdrawals. Three weeks after the trouble began nine million were on strike, but the cooperation between workers and students had worn thin. The Communist Party in particular was distancing itself from the students and making quite different demands, treating the students like interfering social workers. Their attitude was that the students were thinking with their stomachs; the Party was the brains who should be leading events. Nevertheless, as during the war, social life in Paris went on, with dinner parties – restaurants away from the Latin Quarter always full – and many small shops taking advantage of the strikes by underpricing unionized employees in the big ones. Amid the talk of civil war, adrenaline ran high: these were exciting days to be alive.

Cohn-Bendit was now a national celebrity, "Danny le Rouge"; he appeared frequently on television and was seen putting his point of view in opposition to those of the government and police spokesmen, as well as being interviewed by radio and press commentators and by international journalists. For the young the excitement continued to mount, but for the old, unable to get their pensions, their medicines or to move around the city to find food and other essentials, life was pure hell. Those who could, hoarded, including the shops themselves. When the emergency ended, many shops were found to have kept back supplies that at the time they had complained were sold out. Horror stories abounded, both about the activities of the police and of the wild excesses of the students.

May 1968 changed many things. One of them was the state censorship that under de Gaulle had kept radio and television as the voice of the party in power, allowing no balance of opinion and no dissent from the official state line. During the insurrection dissident voices were at last heard in panel discussions and interviews. Hotels were taken over by their staff, including the Right Bank luxury hotels, the Georges V and the Plaza d'Athénée, which had banners outside announcing that "The Personnel has taken over the Responsibility of Running the Hotel". Visitors, however, were treated with the usual courtesy and important ones were informed politely that the manager could not receive them personally as he was locked into his suite. Factories too were taken over by the employees, but most of them kept on running and paying out wages. Genêt, Paris correspondent of the *New Yorker*, described the scene at the Odéon theatre:

It is a degrading sight. The words "Ex-Odéon" have been painted on the walls and the metal fire curtain, the aisles and the entrance were filthy, with students asleep in the boxes or playing their transistors in the front row. Smoking had been forbidden and the toilets were locked, so there was no danger of fire or flood, but the loveable little eighteenth-century playhouse, in its last refurbishing dressed in red velvet, looked like a gypsy camp.*

The Sorbonne was more than a gypsy camp. It was a non-stop party, a giant orgy where the students celebrated with wine and free love: everyone copulated everywhere and as one student later told me: "It wasn't the army that ended the revolution but the hot piss." Gonorrhoea flourished. But after a month the enthusiasm began to tail off and the activities of the trade unions and the workers dominated the news instead. And there was the backlash from the middle classes, many of them parents of the revolutionaries. A massive pro-de Gaulle rally and march was held on 30th May. Shouting slogans, many of them calling for the expulsion of foreigners – with no doubt Danny Cohn-Bendit principally in mind – and in support of the police, they marched down the Champs Elysées to the Arc de Triomphe. The right-wing parties joined in enthusiastically, and there was an ugly air of popular fascism in many of the banners and the tracts handed out to bystanders.

By the middle of June the revolution had come to an end. Massu's paratroops, brought back from Germany, ringed the capital and the students knew that if they attacked, it would not be with clubs. The insurrection ground to a halt, students went home and the workers returned to normality. For a time it had seemed that a civil war was possible, but de Gaulle's firmness, and the threat of the army, punctured the balloon. It was the normal police, not the CRS, who reoccupied the Sorbonne and the École des Beaux-Arts. The cost of dilapidations was totted up: 150,000,000 francs. Some of the workers derived an advantage: there was a massive increase in wages, especially in the automobile industry. Otherwise France returned to normal, but with more repression on left-wing and revolutionary groups.

The events in Paris attracted enormous attention in other countries. In Germany student revolt continued with sit-ins and demonstrations, and the German counterpart of Daniel Cohn-Bendit, Rudy Dutschke, was shot in the head and paralysed, only dying in 1981. The "Days of May" had been a tourist attraction for the adventurous young of Europe who were willing to brave hardship and danger for the sake of the excitement. The rising inspired literature and drama; in Britain, Trevor Griffiths's *The Party*, showing British reactions, was controversially put on at the Old Vic by the National Theatre company. But it proved that the use of force was perfectly condoned by the bourgeoisie, which massively supported de Gaulle in the next referendum. That same year Mayor Daley put down demonstrations at the Democratic Convention in Chicago with similar force and baton charges: among those taking part in them were Allen Ginsberg, William Burroughs and Jean Genet. It was a year of history. The Russians invaded Czechoslovakia that autumn, Robert Kennedy was assassinated, Nixon elected President. It was also an important year for me in London.

2

To some extent this book is a record of the battle against censorship: it is that which drove so many to Paris. Writers went there because the climate was fresh and because the French have never, at least not where its considerable and influential intellectual community was concerned, subscribed to the mentality of the nineteenth century, an attitude that has more to do with maintaining a social order and the values on which empires are built than morality. This applies equally to the political and commercial empires of American commerce and industry, built with the full support of the government and its agencies. But the subtlety was mostly gone by the end of the century. Nonconformist thinking and "free" and pleasurable lifestyles have always been seen as a threat to the building of empires and the making of money.

Girodias was therefore in the right city, a centre to which creative artists of all kinds flocked, because Paris was a good place to live and work, and although Paris always had its problems, especially under de Gaulle, a publisher like Jean-Jacques Pauvert had no difficulty in doing what he wanted with a minimum of interference. Girodias found trouble because he looked for it: he was a willing martyr, more a revolutionary than a reformer by temperament. His career would have been brief anywhere else, as indeed it was when he left Paris.

Barney Rosset was not a particularly good tactician. He had courage, but more importantly he had money and he spent it all, either on his pleasures and obsessions, the smaller part, or on his crusades, the larger part. He had the support of a generation – hippies, intellectuals, academics and adventurous readers – but he was brought down in the end by bad planning, lack of self-control over himself and his inability to take advice from those who could have and wanted to help. My own position was not based on ideology and my problems were mainly caused by limited means and bad luck; I was caught up in the course of events in changing times, and had to use psychological tactics to publish books that obviously had to appear eventually in Britain – the world is too much of a global village for even an island to remain remote for long from a knowledge of what is being read, thought and discussed elsewhere. But lack of capital diminishes choice. I had to move before other publishers did when the risk was present, and while my bigger and richer rivals were still hesitant. They could afford to pay big advances for potentially commercial books if they could be reasonably sure that they would not be prosecuted. I paid small advances and took the risks, but not without giving much thought to ways of circumventing prosecution by the establishment.

I was lucky in that I knew how the establishment thought and reacted – after all, I had grown up in it. In his excellent history of the British censorship of the time, John Sutherland contrasts the careers, personalities and tactics of Girodias, Rosset and myself. He says of the former: "Girodias displayed an odd mixture of the desire to scandalize and to evangelize." Rosset he describes as a would-be tycoon, trying to make big business out of publishing sexually explicit literature. In my own case, he describes me as "a gifted organizer", citing my Edinburgh Conferences (I also organized others elsewhere that attracted less attention) and my establishment of the Defence of Literature and the Arts Society (DLAS), and characterizes my "colours" as "modernist, anti-censorship, international". He goes on to say:

> Calder contrived more successfully than Rosset or Girodias to escape prosecution. This was not because his choice of books was tame, nor because the British climate was more favourable to obscenity. His immunity was the result of strategy and what in court would be called "excellent character".*

It is always difficult in retrospect to remember what one's motivations were and why certain decisions were made. I certainly do not remember agonizing over decisions. It was always clear what I had to do. I knew what I liked and wanted to publish, but only a few titles were ever commercial. When it came to books with controversial material, it was a matter of opportunity and chance. I published Henry Miller because I had the opportunity to do so, and the Edinburgh Writers' Conference of 1962 convinced me that most thinking people were on my side. Even if prosecuted, I believed that the public would stump up the cost of defence. I proved this to be so when I finally was prosecuted over Hubert Selby Jr's *Last Exit to Brooklyn*.* The opportunity to publish it came naturally, because I had already succeeded in publishing books where other publishers were afraid to take the risk. I never really believed that I would make money on controversial titles, but of course hoped to do so. In the last century there is little evidence that "risk" publishing has ever done the publisher much good. Barney Rosset sank a fortune into Grove Press and ended with nothing other than his reputation and a place in the legal history books. Girodias never recovered from his bankruptcy, although to the end of his life, personally penniless, he still hoped to start new ventures.

A look at other independents only proves that those who are motivated by the spirit of adventure, and enthusiasm for the life-enhancing power and spirit of art, do badly; those only interested in money do well, but they are mostly soon forgotten. James Laughlin, founder and publisher of New Directions, was, like Barney Rosset, a young man who had inherited a fortune, but he never took risks with obscenity or libel. He was effectively willing to risk his income, but not his capital. His press was a distinguished one, but the caution associated with it took away much of its colour. Giangiacomo Feltrinelli, a publisher in Italy, was similar to Rosset: politically radical, interested in good literature, and a man of energy and excitement. He was assassinated while in hiding, wanted by the police for possible terrorist activity, in circumstances that made his obvious political killing look like an accident. His firm continued after his death only because it was supported by the Italian Communist Party.

Giulio Einaudi, whose father had been the first post-war socialist President of Italy, ran a distinguished publishing company, but went bankrupt; he was only saved by a consortium who effectively pushed him out of control. Einaudi, with a big international list, was really only interested in a few local writers; he bought what was prestigious but this involved him in too high an editorial overhead, and, like Feltrinelli, his real interest was in politics. His list reflected the talents and interests of the editors he engaged to find the best authors. In this he resembles Rosset, who also published much on the advice of others. They both wanted the best and to do well, but the personal touch was not always there. Ledig-Rowohlt, son of one of the century's greatest German publishers, never had the personal commitment of his father, but he loved literature, loved taking risks, while always remaining a businessman at heart. He sold out to a larger firm and was still around at publishers' gatherings in a social way for the rest of his life: indeed he died at the Congress of the International Publishers Association in New Delhi in 1992.

Siegfried Unseld took over the established firm of Suhrkamp after the war and made it into a publishing giant. He typified the attitudes of a country in which, after the Hitler period, everyone wanted to be seen as progressive, liberal and intellectual in the tradition of German culture, which had Goethe as its icon. He built a prestigious list of the most important European intellectual authors, commissioned many translations and found his new German writers from both the East and West sides of the country. His stars were Bertolt Brecht, Max Frisch and Samuel Beckett, and he cultivated the German avant-garde, giving it time to become fashionable. He also started a theatrical publishing company that controlled dramatic rights, but this eventually became independent. Unseld was an empire-builder who acquired other companies for different types of books. He entertained royally during the Frankfurt Book Fair and was pleasant but arrogant in personality, especially to those he respected. He must have had a Nazi past because he was the man at Doenitz's naval headquarters who opened the telegram announcing Hitler's suicide.

There were others, like Christian Bourgois in Paris, who took certain risks, but always with the money of the parent publisher who financed him. Bourgois had good, but not impeccable taste, and basically published the discoveries of others. Rob van Gennep in Holland lost interest in the avant-garde after the age of fifty, and thereafter made money with remainders. Carlos Barral, founder of the Prix Formentor, seemed to sink into conformity after the death of Franco. He died young and his place was taken by the house of Anagrama, also in Barcelona, run by Jorge Herralde. But around the world there were always new publishers emerging, and they usually conformed to the same types: enthusiasts with money who pursued causes and went under; avant-garde publishers lucky enough to have a few years of fashion and success who then turned commercial or else failed after twenty or so years, left with a mountain of unsold books and no liquidity; and others who continued, although more invisibly, because they adjusted to the times and became smaller, continuing through rigid economies, but inevitably having to sacrifice the excitement and applause of their high noon. Changing times and mortality was their nemesis. I put myself principally into the last category.

There is one significant publisher who has so far only received brief mention, an unflamboyant personality in a flamboyant world. He was Jérôme Lindon, publisher of Les Éditions de Minuit. To him must go the credit for discovering Beckett, whose pre-war novels were totally unknown, even by Lindon when he took on the Irish writer, and the large, varied group of French novelists who became known as the *nouveaux romanciers* and their works as the *nouveau roman*. There have been various other schools of post-war fiction. The beats were one. The Gruppe 47, founded by German intellectuals to recreate a German literature after the demise of Hitler and the Third Reich, was another. This last produced Günter Grass and Heinrich Böll among many others, and it was a new bridgehead for expressionism, but it is no longer thought of as a school. The *nouveau roman* has remained so, principally because its popular acclaim has always been limited and because its publisher, Lindon, was a man who eschewed excitement and let the press do his promotion for him. His success was hardly noticed outside the French book trade for many years, but he received major press coverage when he died in 2001. He was certainly the most highly respected publisher in his own country, both by the government, which gave him more help than he liked to admit, and by his colleagues. He prospered, lived quietly, never travelled, worked long hours and knew exactly what he was doing. He lost some authors to bigger publishers without too much complaint, and often saw them return to him. His daughter Irène learnt the business under him and took over after his death. Lindon took on other publishers' authors only when they suited his list. When attacked during the political days of the Algerian war – he had published some of the most important documents of that unhappy time – he defended himself ably, but he had books banned all the same. He was not easy company, had a reputation for stinginess, and his personality was best described as dour. But his high seriousness had never been in question. There was no rubbish on his list and he certainly had read every book that bore his imprint, and had personally edited a large number of them. Lindon was active on committees and was trusted by the Ministry of Culture as hardly any other publisher was, both for his honesty and his integrity, as well as for his nose for talent. He was the de Gaulle of French publishing, but none of the categories of "enthusiastic" or "adventurous" publishing as defined above quite fitted him. Beckett trusted him absolutely, but had to be more reserved with him than with other friends and colleagues; one could not imagine Lindon totally relaxed! He became Beckett's literary executor on the author's death, a role that later passed to Edward Beckett, Sam's nephew. Lindon always refused to speak or pontificate about Beckett, or about his other authors, and it became obvious that his extreme modesty was genuine and his aloofness natural. In terms of real publishing accomplishment (that is, other than just making money) Lindon was the most remarkable and successful publisher of his time.

3

Paris was still the Garden of Eros after the events of 1968, and it continued to attract immigrants involved in the arts. They included American, British and other anglophone writers and editors – all enthusiasts for literature, art and a life of freedom; in many ways intellectual life became more like the scene as it had been in the Twenties and Thirties.

But money was more important now, life was more expensive and there was also a growing seriousness. The anglophone presence was a little smaller, but many had established themselves permanently in Paris because life there remained pleasant and many English-speakers found that learning French was less necessary because the English language, in spite of the protests of French purists about the invasion of their language by "franglais", had become the language in fashion. When Samuel Beckett won the Nobel Prize in 1969, he was claimed by both the French and the Irish, helping to cement the growing friendship and reciprocal interests of the countries who shared the British Channel and the Irish Sea. The Vietnam War was at its height. The My Lai massacre, for which Lt William Calley stood trial, stirred up public opinion, but as the bulk of Americans in Europe were opposed to the war in any case, it did not create much tension for Americans in Europe. Many were there to avoid the draft, including Henry Miller's son, Tony. In Paris, Peter Brook was now well established; the French had adopted him and made him their own, so he could not really be considered a part of the Anglo-American community of expatriates. Jim Haynes, on the other hand, became its epicentre.

Jim Haynes was an Edinburgh bookseller who had helped me with both the Edinburgh Writers' Conference of 1962 and the Drama Conference* of the following year. He was also the founder of the Traverse Theatre, one of the best known experimental theatres in Europe. He had become involved in two new ventures: a newspaper, the *International Times (IT)*, and a new theatrical centre, the Arts Lab. The *International Times* quickly became the voice of the underground, catering to the new classless, but largely working-class in origin, young generation that had money and wanted to spend it on a good time. The newspaper openly advocated the legalization of soft drugs and was certainly not opposed to the use of hard ones. It featured sex, youth, pop music, the newly fashionable Zen Buddhism, and the arts – not the traditional arts, but new, young ones, mainly freaky experiments in performance art that were, for the most part, superficial but exciting. Among those involved were Barry Miles (who never used his first name), Jack Henry Moore, John Hopkins (a photographer with the *Observer*), Tom McGrath, a playwright, who became editor of *IT*, and a large number of young people who were trying to get into the media and the current London scene. Trouble came quickly from *The Times*, objecting to their name being used and threatening to sue; within a short time, the *International Times* had to change its name and simply became *IT*.

IT featured an "IT girl" on its masthead: this was a photograph of Theda Bara, but it should have been Clara Bow. The paper came out fortnightly and listed more or less everything going on in London and in other places where the paper had correspondents. It carried articles about people in the news, and events and topics of interest to the young. The first printing was 10,000 copies. When the first issue arrived Jim Haynes went to stand outside the Aldwych Theatre where Peter Brook's *US* was playing (I had published the book), because this was currently the most important production to be seen in London, attracting the kind of audience for which *IT* was largely intended. It sold well. On Saturday afternoons he stood on Chelsea's King's Road, the copies going like hotcakes. Circulation grew and soon it was selling at newsagents all over London. Tom McGrath, the first editor, was eventually replaced by others, but he gave it its shape and colour: anti-authoritarian, youth-orientated, outspoken about politics and current issues and opposed to the traditional and always supporting the new and experimental. It could often be silly, but was always eye-opening. It epitomized an age that elevated trivia and immediacy above seriousness and anything that looked to the future, but it did no harm and added to the gaiety of life. It quickly became commercially viable and lasted until its novelty wore off, and the advent of more professional journals such as *Time Out* that did the same job, but better.

The Arts Lab was closely linked to *IT*, and many of the same people were involved. It was opened in an abandoned warehouse on Drury Lane. Jim rented it in the summer of 1967 and raised money mainly from people in the theatre: cheques came from Peter Brook, Timothy Beaumont (a rich clergyman who helped to finance many projects and causes, and was a constant source of funds to the Liberal Party), Fenella Fielding, Fred Zinnemann, John Schlesinger and many other, lesser-known personalities; Kenneth Tynan and David Frost gave moral support and allowed their names to be used.

Certain publications were a central part of the "swinging London" scene, but they also precipitated the beginning of the backlash. Jim sent a copy of the first issue of the *International Times* to Lord Goodman, who definitely did not approve. He immediately detected its attitudes towards drugs, and support for the campaign for the legalization of cannabis. Goodman had a ward, Nigel Samuel, son of Howard Samuel, owner of a large chain of popular jewellery shops who had drowned shortly after buying into the radical weekly opinion journal, the *New Statesman*, leaving Nigel a large fortune; Nigel had a taste for the Sixties bohemian scene and put money into both *IT* and the Arts

Lab; Goodman was opposed to both and he refused any further Arts Council support to Jim Haynes's new enterprises, even with Jenny Lee urging him to help them. Michael Astor, younger brother of the editor of the *Observer*, had been one of Jim's supporters and a patron at the Jeannetta Cochrane, but, after looking at the Arts Lab, he decided that it was too crazy and declined to be involved; he was only one of many who ceased to support Jim from that time. I myself, in a passive way, did the same, but not from disapproval: I simply did not feel comfortable in an environment that had no observable artistic standards or ambitions, and I was in any case very taken up with producing operas and other events at Ledlanet, an arts centre in Scotland. The Arts Lab put on some interesting plays, and one of them, Jane Arden's *Vagina Rex and the Gas Oven*, I published, although I never saw it on stage.

But interesting plays were a minority. Increasingly after the first year people went to the Arts Lab principally to sit about, smoke grass and talk, not to get involved in any intellectual activity. Jim was little interested in what it was: hazard was the governing principle. London had too many layabouts with ambition but little talent, and they took advantage of Jim's inertia. Many stories circulated about the Arts Lab, which became increasingly a drug hang-out, and occasionally an orgy palace. Creditors would come to Jim to get their bills paid and find him in bed with a woman; he would roll off for a minute to find the cheque book and a pen and return to lovemaking. Privacy was neither possible nor important at the Arts Lab, and many flopped out at night on a mattress on the cinema floor. But in the early days it received much publicity, was featured in television programmes and articles about "swinging London", and visited by tourists as one of the sights.

A laboratory it certainly was, as well as being one of the places to be seen because it was filled with the famous and the beautiful, the scandalous and the infamous. Dick Gregory, James Baldwin, Christine Keeler, Yoko Ono, John Lennon, Michael X, Alexander Trocchi, Paul McCartney and Brian Epstein were just a few of the users, and the performers were as varied as the patrons. Anyone who wanted to perform just had to ask Jim. Marion Javits, the wife of Jacob, the New York senator, came, was enthusiastic and offered to help Jim set up an Arts Lab in New York. David Bowie borrowed space to rehearse, Christopher Logue and Trocchi did poetry readings. There were "happenings" and one of them, entitled *Tea with Miss Gentry*, consisted of chalking up an announcement of the production, for which about ten people had to congregate at a given time by the notice board; they were then led to Miss Gentry, a lonely lady who lived in a room on a nearby street, several floors up. The ten or so people then proceeded to have tea with her, while she talked about her old days as a hat designer for theatrical productions.

As with all such enterprises, the Arts Lab always needed money. Having been turned down by the Arts Council, Jim Haynes was entirely dependent on private generosity and most of the time it was forthcoming. But money was spent without budgets being made, or any concrete idea of how much was needed, and this prevented other funding institutions, which in the climate of the day were often willing to help, from doing so. Jim approached the Gulbenkian Foundation and a grant was being considered when the director with whom Jim was negotiating suddenly died; but it is very doubtful if he could, in the end, have helped. One generous young lady, living in Paris, had a reputation for helping unusual enterprises in the arts and Jim, on a visit there, met her at the Café de Flore. She gave him a cheque, and when he looked at it after her departure, he saw that it was for £5,000.

But fashion moved on, and the Arts Lab became tackier and attracted more undesirables and more police attention. Jim tried confrontation and went to see the police. He asked for their advice as to how to control the drug problem, telling them that he took nothing himself, but he knew no one under twenty-five who didn't. They were sympathetic, but said nothing. As the rent fell into arrears, and rates owed to the local council were unpaid, the "beautiful people" stopped going, and the Arts Lab faded and died. For all Jim Haynes's dislike of boards and committees, he discovered that nothing can function for long without them and without proper management. It closed at the end of 1969.

After the closing of the Arts Lab and *IT*, Jim moved first to Amsterdam, a city noted for its tolerance, where with friends he started a sex newspaper called *Suck*. The friends and collaborators who edited this new publication included Bill Levy, an American poet, Germaine Greer, an Australian, then coming into prominence as a feminist writer and polemicist, Heathcote Williams, a talented but over-the-top poet and playwright of an anarchist and freak-out disposition, his girlfriend Jean Shrimpton, then a top fashion model, Willem de Ridder, who ran a pop magazine in Amsterdam and allowed his offices and facilities to be used for the purpose, and Haynes himself, still accompanied much of the time by Jack Moore. The first issue appeared, some copies circulated around London, and de Ridder and Haynes were soon visited by plain-clothes officers from Scotland Yard, accompanied by apologetic Dutch policemen playing host to them. The British policemen asked questions, which were politely answered, and went impotently back to London:

THE GARDEN OF EROS

they could not stop a newspaper in another country, and the Dutch police, with their tradition of tolerance, were not willing to cooperate with them. *Suck* was of course instantly banned in Britain, and its first editor Bill Levy, who had gone to London from Baltimore in the Sixties to study and do research on Ezra Pound, and had worked on *IT*, was also banned from re-entering the UK. *Suck* had only a brief but eventful life and ten issues. The first was probably the best, containing erotic texts, mostly told in the first person, of sexual experiences, adventures and descriptions, much graphic and photographic illustration, which mainly depicted couples and group sex, but also contained a certain amount of wit as well as much deliberate provocation. I carried a copy of the first issue through Switzerland on a train to Austria and the reaction of other passengers overlooking the paper was dramatic. It was really only juvenile masturbatory material at bottom, and after the first couple of issues the editors found little new to put in their publication except more photographs of orgies, with Jim Haynes usually very prominent in them. To quote Jim, who tried to differentiate *Suck* from such American sex magazines as *Screw*, then appearing in New York: "No matter what it is, they [*Screw*] joke about it. On the other hand *Suck* was primarily a sexual liberation newspaper which represented the entire pendulum of sexuality."* But the opposite was true: by reducing sex only to mechanical performance, it made it impersonal and therefore ultimately boring.

Jim was also one of the founders of the Wet Dream Film Festival in Amsterdam, an erotic film week that first grew out of a plan to throw a monster *Suck* party, i.e. orgy. There were two festivals, a year apart. The films were shown in a cinema on the Leidesplein and on one occasion on a large hired boat that went out to sea for the screenings. The boat was equipped with a "love room" for orgies and another to listen to live chamber music, and for food and drink. There were late sex parties every night in Amsterdam and the festival lasted a week. About four hundred people attended and Jim somehow managed to raise some money in order to give cash prizes to the winning film-makers. Richard Neville, late of *Oz*, Germaine Greer and other old friends of Haynes made up the jury.

But Jim stayed only a short time in Amsterdam and soon settled in Paris. Jack Moore followed him everywhere and became a combination of housekeeper, manager and assistant to Jim, while earning some money by pursuing his own career as a technician working with films, video and television. Haynes very quickly fell on his feet. First he obtained a job teaching media studies at the experimental University of Vincennes at Saint-Denis, a radical centre that invited such fashionably left figures as Noam Chomsky to come to lecture; Jim appeared to have absolute freedom to talk – and in English – about anything he wanted, mainly to a class of attractive young girls. His students were mostly trying to improve their English as well as getting credit for a course that can never have been onerous. This went on for many years until Jim achieved tenure and was increasingly well paid for a single day's work a week. The University eventually moved to the Northern suburb of Saint-Denis and Jim went with it. One of France's leading feminists was teaching there at the time, Hélène Cixous, a brilliantly intellectual lady, then living with a boyfriend, also teaching at the University and a good friend of Jim's. When their *ménage* broke up, Cixous reportedly tore her department of the University in half: anyone who talked to her ex-lover became a bitter enemy. Although she lived very near Jim in Montparnasse, she would never speak to him again. I published her big study of Joyce in English translation, one of her novels, *Angst*, and one of her plays; but such was her growing militant feminism that, being a man, I eventually lost all contact: she simply would not speak to me, or allow me to publish more of her work.

Jim Haynes found a large studio apartment at the southern end of Montparnasse in 1973. This was "No. 1A" in a long row of artists' studios overlooking a private garden in a flowery tree-lined *impasse* sealed by a metal gate, at 83, Rue de la Tombe-Issoire, the street that had once been the main road south out of Paris. The long garden became part of Jim's entertaining facilities, because in good weather his guests could stretch down it for a hundred yards. The studio became in a short time one of the principal meeting places for Paris anglophones, and a casual call at any time would find a mixture of journalists, writers, film makers, students, models, actors and visitors to Paris, some of whom he had casually met or picked up in odd corners of the world from Mexico to Albania; some would have been sent to him by others, some of them would be staying with him, either in his spare room or sleeping on the sofa, or in sleeping bags or mattresses on the floor at night. The large cellar, stacked with video and recording equipment, and cassettes of all kinds, was the domain of Jack and his circle. The studio seemed to stretch to accommodate any number of people, not very hygienically. Jim became a constant traveller, increasing his enormous acquaintanceship, so that the volume of callers in Paris never diminished. A constant stream of waitresses he had picked up in restaurants or table-neighbours whose conversation he had invaded, or people he met at airports, train stations and at parties, would turn up in Paris. Sunday night became an open salon, where you paid a modest amount for all you could eat and drink – the food varied according to which volunteer was doing the cooking and the wine was *ordinaire* – but an astonishing mixture of people would come together there, from academics to actresses, and the famous and notorious were usually well represented.

A group quickly began to gather around Jim, as had happened in Edinburgh and London, including anglophone Paris residents who were successful enough in their careers to be able to live comfortably in the city that had so much to offer in terms of its quality of life. Mike Zwerin, a previous *Suck* editor, who wrote regularly for the *Village Voice* in New York on jazz, now began to write for the Paris edition of the *Herald Tribune* on diverse subjects. Garry Davis, the first man to have given up his American passport to become a world citizen in 1948, hoping to start a world movement that would bring wars to an end, moved around Europe and was frequently in Paris. He issued his own passports to those who wished to support or emulate him; they could only be used in those countries like Sweden and Norway that were tolerant enough to accept them, but the possessors always kept their own in reserve. For a while Jim Haynes was Davis's Paris agent, selling the passports to those who wanted them, mainly for a joke; they were of course very necessary to the genuinely stateless, but Jim had to desist after a visit from the French police, who warned him that he was endangering his right to stay and work in France. On a visit to New York, he met an actress at a party, and she and Jim became lovers, then close friends, then literary collaborators. Jeanne Pasle-Green subsequently came to Paris where she and Jim co-edited *Hello, I Love You!** which he published himself in 1974. It advocated free love, casual flings and allowing oneself the pleasures of the minute: love should never be clinging or an inconvenience. And love should always be at first sight! It was an extension of *Suck*.

La Coupole continued to be the main meeting place for Paris expatriates, as it also was for much of *le tout Paris*, the smart chattering classes, but Jim made it practically his office. He could nearly always be seen there from ten or eleven at night until two or three in the morning; all the waiters knew "Jimmy" and would give him messages that had been left or regale him with the latest gossip. I had spent many nights there during the Fifties and early Sixties, sometimes staying all night, but in the Seventies the restaurant began closing much earlier, usually staying open until five at latest. For Jim Haynes it was a place to meet new backers and to recruit new girlfriends.

Jim began to put out a newsletter, usually running to several pages. It was an account of his travels and contacts, of the people he met, what they did and particularly what they did with him. As with *Suck*, it was uninhibited and shameless, telling all, and not everyone was pleased at having their private life revealed to the growing number of recipients of the newsletter. Jim also started putting books together to express his relaxed personal philosophy. After *Hello, I Love You!* came *Workers of the World, Unite and Stop Working*, the point of which was that if you enjoyed what you did in life, you were not working but "fullering", a word he coined from the name of his guru of the moment, Buckminster Fuller. He had an imprint now for his second title, Handshake Editions.

But as the climate began to change and the Sixties faded into memory, Jim found that his do-all and tell-all attitude was creating considerable resentment. Jean Shrimpton was one of the top models of the Sixties, a cover girl for *Vogue* identified with the scanty boutique clothes that looked so well on her. She had been involved with both *Suck* and the Wet Dream Film Festival, was obviously interested in everything erotic, but, although sexiness was part of her image, the other part was girlishness and innocence. She distanced herself from Jim and his outspoken frankness, which he saw as a kind of betrayal, but her commercial image could have been at stake. Permissiveness may have been the keynote of the Sixties, but it was not always wise to flaunt it, and the Sixties were over now. Nixon had become President of the US in 1968: the business society he favoured quickly began to recommercialize lifestyles, attitudes and freedoms. In Britain the Conservatives returned to power in the summer of 1970, promising lower taxes which brought higher prices, and with them came a return to middle-class values. The closing of the Arts Lab and *IT* made the trend clear enough, and even Amsterdam began to crack down a little on the more extreme manifestations of sexual and behavioural freedom. Germaine Greer's defection from Jim's group was better publicized than Shrimpton's. She wrote a long letter entitled 'Why I Resign from Suck!' giving Jim permission to publish it, but either in full or not at all. There had been an agreement to publish nude pictures of all the *Suck* editors in a particular issue, but in the event only Greer's nude photo appeared. She objected strongly to being used in this way and also to the graphics that surrounded her photo and the whole context in which it was published. There were orgy shots including herself that had appeared without her knowledge or permission. One can detect from her letter that she felt that *Suck* had become less an organ of sexual liberation than just another exploitative commercial enterprise, and she attacked the "spuriousness of your [Jim's] pseudo-revolutionary aims".* *Suck* died as did the Wet Dream Film Festival after two years.

Jim Haynes found himself on the edge of the film world for a while. The notoriety of *Suck* and the Wet Dream Film Festival brought many people to his door, and several times he played small parts or was an extra in films, but he was also approached by would-be film-makers who had a little money and wanted his help to make something erotic; Jim's role was usually to round up good-looking people willing to make love on camera, especially if they were already known. One such would-be-Fellini, Max Fischer, an Amsterdam man who owned an advertising agency, actually made such a film with Jim's help, but it was an artistic disaster. Both Heathcote Williams and Jens Thorsen, who was later to court controversy for a film project (later abandoned) entitled *The Love Life of Jesus Christ*, had a major participation in putting it together (different sections were made by different people), but Fischer, who edited everything into a pornographic hotch-potch, having severed his connection with those who had done the filming, eventually put out *Wet Dreams* (stealing their title did not delight Jim Haynes and his associates), which was later reissued as *Dreams of a Young Girl*, but neither Jim nor the others were paid or received any part of the profits: none of them had a commercial mind or taste for contracts.

Suck at its peak achieved a circulation of 30,000 copies and opened some surprising doors to Haynes. In Budapest apparently, one copy circulated to around 2,000 people. The European editor of the *Times of India* invited Jim to dinner with two Indian cabinet ministers, both fans, and the magazine and its shenanigans was the only topic of the evening. Salvador Dalí, whose Paris orgies were famous, was also a fan, and Jim spent an afternoon with him being quizzed about it. He had briefly entered the commercial world, and *Suck* was making a good profit, but the group that invented it, mainly for fun, were quarrelling, and worried about their individual images. Sex for fun in private is one thing, in public something else.

Handshake Editions grew out of the same dislike of contracts that brought down more than one subject of this book. Jim Haynes met the black American Jazz poet Ted Joans soon after arriving in Paris and he agreed to bring out a small edition of his new poems. The deal was sealed with a handshake, hence the name. A number of other small texts appeared under this imprint, including Jim's own rather eccentric books, until Faber accepted his autobiography. Jim would sell his books, but especially *Hello, I Love You!*, around the cafés of Montparnasse; La Coupole was usually good for a few copies a night, although a pretty girl might get one free.

In Paris Jim Haynes became the centre for the famous and the infamous, a contact point who was nearly always available. John Lennon and Yoko Ono were good friends who came frequently to Paris. Yoko had made a film in London, which consisted only of people's bare bottoms (both Jim and I declined to be filmed, but I did add a few sentences to the medley of voices on the soundtrack). Kenneth Tynan, and his new wife, Kathleen, who had during my Edinburgh Drama Conference sneaked away from her husband to join Ken in Edinburgh, both used Jim to meet other people and as a kind of unpaid social secretary, but hardly anyone who knew him didn't. Jim just liked helping people. His next venture was the *Cassette Gazette*, a magazine on an audio cassette, but in spite of an impressive list of participants and editors, nothing much came of it. Over the Seventies and Eighties Jim was always on the fringe of a new idea to do with films, publications, recordings, or some venture for which vague large amounts of money had been promised from somewhere. He believed in everything that was about to happen because he wanted to believe, he was trusting until let down, and he retained his basic innocence where business was concerned: nothing with him succeeded for long except his amazing talent for meeting and getting on with people, but he had the security of his job at the University, which enabled him to save up for a venture, then lose those savings and start to save again. His personal needs were in any case modest. Simply by applying, using Studio A1 as his portmanteau name, he acquired credentials that enabled him to attend, as a journalist, every Cannes Film Festival, every Frankfurt Book Fair and to get into the Paris exhibition openings and other events that interested him. He returned regularly to Edinburgh at Festival time, and was usually interviewed by a newspaper or radio or television programme about his past in that city; with time he was able to exaggerate the role he had played in my two Edinburgh Festival Conferences and other ventures in the arts, although his activities at the Traverse tended to be forgotten as the one-time avant-garde theatre became part of the Edinburgh establishment; it moved twice in the next twenty years to end up in the late Nineties between Edinburgh's biggest concert hall and its civic repertory theatre, the Lyceum.

Haynes managed to travel everywhere in the world that he wanted to go, or as was said by many, where he was sent; how he managed it financially was one of the mysteries of Paris. He was too old to hitchhike, and although he had friends everywhere that he could stay with, travel does cost money. There were rumours of CIA contacts or involvement with other secret services, but never evidence of anything concrete. There was a certain circumspection about Jim after his first year in Paris, and he had a disingenuous explanation for everything. But by general agreement, he could do no harm to anyone. The two common factors in all his activities were people, usually clustered about him like a swarm of flies, and women: although he liked his lovers younger as the years passed, and his catchword as he turned his head in the street was frequently "I've just fallen in love", he liked and lusted for women of all ages and had little difficulty in attracting them. The non-involvement was of course part of the attraction. You could enjoy a night with him, but never a romance. Haynes was a light eater who never smoked and seldom drank – a glass of wine at most – and he changed little over the years. He was a Peter Pan or a Dorian Gray, sometimes growing beards or moustaches or removing them, his full head of hair longer or shorter, but always remaining a tall, lanky American with a gleam in his eye, a smile on his face, dressed like a Paris bohemian expatriate. Jimmy Stewart in his prime could have played him perfectly. A few never trusted him. Maurice Girodias, once he was back in Paris, became very guarded about Jim, convinced he was a CIA agent, but he always responded to Jim's friendly gestures.

In the early Nineties Jim Haynes put together a series of guidebooks, based on his globetrotting; which were published in Edinburgh by Canongate Press. These volumes, under the series name *People to People*, were books of contacts for travellers, listing names and addresses with telephone numbers of individuals, most of them single, in different Eastern European cities. Each entry describes the person, his or her tastes and appearance, and what the individual was willing to offer in accommodation and services, always with the possibility, not stated, of sexual availability. In the Eighties Haynes was commissioned by Robert McCrum, a counter-culture figure, who eventually became editorial director of Faber, to put together his scrapbook to make a kind of autobiography. It is a publication full of useful and fascinating souvenirs, mainly of the Sixties and Seventies linked by a sparse account of his life and career, with press-cuttings, photos, reproduced letters and even solicited testimonials, some of them, like Charles Marowitz's, not very flattering.

Marowitz points out that Jim's love of everyone, including "strangers and down-and-outs" is only a form of narcissism and, because it is uncritical and undiscriminating, irreconcilable with art. That is true. To Jim art is people, and he cannot separate the two. But he had never claimed to have any critical perception or standard of judgement, and it is unfair to attack him for not being what he has never claimed or wanted to be. The arts for Haynes were simply something else you could enjoy in life, because they are there, and artists are better company than people who dislike them or are frightened by them.

Thanks for Coming starts with the words: "This book is for", followed by twenty pages of closely set names from Susan Abbül to Mike Zwerin, and the list ends with: "and all those closet hippies everywhere."* His address book, several thick volumes, is voluminous, and has private notes about everyone in it, which includes birthdates and zodiac signs. Jim always knew with whom you shared your birthday. His ambition seemed to be not only to know as many people as possible, but to share and be part of the lives and experiences of everyone he met, so that he could always claim to have played a part in whatever activity made them celebrated.

Jim's ideas have not faded with time. Jack Moore, who was very able with television technology, helped him to set up a cable station from his basement to a number of apartments in and around his block. From the extensive stock of video cassettes, films and other materials stored in his studio, all copied from some source by Jack, programmes went out regularly until the impetus waned. Jim still had dreams of running a regular cable station from his home up to the end of the century. Alésia is an interesting area of Paris, thick with artists, well away from the tourist areas of Montparnasse. Henry Miller's Villa Seurat, scene of much of *Tropic of Cancer*, is two streets away. Giacometti's studio was about a hundred yards from Jim's, Lenin lived nearby, and it is only a few minutes' walk to Beckett's old apartment on the Boulevard St Jacques. Jim would often meet Sam on his walks around the area, especially on his way to the Parc Montsouris, a large green public garden with interesting statues.

A new English bookshop opened in Paris in 1982 called the Village Voice. It was owned by Odile Hellier, an attractive French woman who had lived and studied in both the Soviet Union and the US. But the relationship did not last long, and Odile continued on her own. Jim Haynes soon discovered her and frequently helped as a volunteer, remembering his old Edinburgh bookselling days. His knowledge of books was still good and he was a superb salesman, so the shop did particularly well on the days he was there: it gave him the opportunity to meet even more people, especially young women. But friction sometimes developed. Jim was not into profit and he often sold books too cheaply when Odile was away, especially the dwindling piles of Olympia titles she had acquired from various sources, for which there was always a steady demand, but little chance of obtaining replacements. For a while Odile Hellier also ran a coffee bar, selling sandwiches, espresso and light snacks: but she found that too many people were coming in for a cheap lunch – almost all Americans – who never bought a book. She stopped catering, gave more space to books and her sales increased. An ebullient Englishman, Michael Neal, later joined her and became an essential part of the operation.

By the late Eighties the Village Voice had become known as the best English-language bookshop for literature and serious subjects in France, perhaps in mainland Europe. When I pointed out to Maurice Girodias, whom I introduced to Odile and the shop one day, that it had taken the place of Gaït Frogé's English Bookshop two decades earlier, he demurred, thought about it a moment, and reluctantly agreed. Gaït's memory was still strong! Soon after he gave a talk there, recalling the history of Olympia and its authors. As with its predecessor, the Village Voice at 6 Rue Princesse, a small street running south from the Rue du Four, two blocks from the Boulevard Saint-Germain, soon became a meeting place and a hangout for writers and those who wanted to meet them. Odile had her difficulties in the early days; it takes time to get known and there is always competition in selling the more popular titles from the Right Bank bookshops, and from three or four on the Left Bank, but no other bookshop carried such a wide and discriminating stock, and she was willing to stock French authors in translation as Gaït had done. A good bookshop that is also a warm and friendly rendezvous is essential to the literary health of an expatriate community. After the Sixties that community changed a little, but it continued with new faces.

4

There were still a few survivors from the Thirties. Maria Jolas only died in 1987 at the age of 94. Having sold her house to de Gaulle after the war and having survived Eugene by many years, she continued to live alone on the Rue de Rennes, translating Nathalie Sarraute, a friend with whom she often quarrelled because they supported different sides in the Arab-Israeli dispute, and they temporarily stopped talking to each other every time the shooting started. Richard Ellmann had spent months talking to her when writing his biography of Joyce, and she regularly attended meetings every time the James Joyce Society met in Paris. Young Americans flocked to see and question her about the great expatriate days pre-1939, but she had never spent much time in Paris cafés, or outside the *transition* circle. Her role in literary history had been as hostess, but she remembered well the many evenings entertaining the master while he was writing *Finnegans Wake*, which had first appeared in instalments in *transition*. When talking of Joyce, a gleam would come into her eyes as she remembered anecdotes, occasionally criticizing Ellmann for mistakes in his book, or coming out with: "I forgot to tell that to Ellmann." She started, but never finished, her own autobiography (although many years later some of it was published in America, as was Eugene's); she was active and generous from her shrinking means in supporting left-wing causes in Paris,* was always available to translate some student manifesto into English, criticized her own government's international politics and, when she won the Scott Moncrieff Prize for one of her Nathalie Sarraute translations, at the French Embassy in London, she used the occasion to denounce the Vietnam War. Her daughter Betsy, although she retained her American nationality and taught composition in California as well as in Paris for part of the year, was really part of the French musical avant-garde, a composer whose works were regularly heard in France; had she gone permanently to live in the States, where serious contemporary music is known and appreciated by only a tiny coterie, she would have had no career, except perhaps as a teacher.

Another member of the old Joyce circle, although marginally so, was Édouard Roditi, the son of an American father, who lived and did business in France, and an English mother. Born in Paris in 1910, he was educated at English public schools (at Elstree Joseph Conrad once convinced him he should become a writer) and at Oxford. While still at university, he translated St John Perse's poem *Anabase* before discovering that T.S. Eliot had acquired the rights to do so, and he then corresponded with Eliot, who was working at Faber as poetry editor. The correspondence was a sophisticated one, and when they met, Eliot "practically fell off the chair when he saw he was dealing with a kid".* During the Thirties he joined Breton's surrealist group (he had been involved, while still a student, in Dada and surrealism as translator, partner in a new publishing company and with his own poetry), but being homosexual, was eventually expelled; Breton became a homophobe in the Thirties. He only visited the US for the first time at the age of nineteen, but as a young man was incredibly active as poet, translator, editor and publisher. He did work for and was published in many English periodicals, including *transition*, T.S. Eliot's *Criterion*, and Éditions du Sagittaire in Paris (which he had helped found and partly owned), and he also worked as a teacher. Roditi did post-graduate studies in Chicago and California, taught in Kansas, and became a man-of-all-literary-work, always of the highest quality. He occasionally spent time in Berlin, where he became a friend of Stephen Spender and Christopher Isherwood, even well into the Hitler era, which must have been dangerous as he was a Jew. Roditi passed the war years in the States, working mainly for French shortwave broadcasting from New York under the auspices of the Department of the Army, and he stayed with the government service as an interpreter. His great moments as such were at the San Francisco Conference that set up the United Nations, and at the Nuremberg Trials where in 1946 he had to interrogate the top Nazi war criminals.

Roditi was a friend and correspondent to a wide spectrum of leading writers and artists until his death in 1992. Paul Bowles had been a close friend since 1931 and Roditi became a frequent member of the Tangiers literary circle; he knew nearly all the more serious members of the Paris expatriate groups, as well as the leading figures in French and European literature. This may well have been the reason for the disgraceful way the American government treated him. McCarthy, and the Un-American Activities Committee before him, decided at some point that anyone with his cosmopolitan and literary background must be suspect. Although he had never taken part in political activities or expressed opinions on issues, and belonged to no party, he was, after Nuremberg, gradually demoted to ever lower-level postings until he was forced to resign. He took freelance work, but the FBI continued to persecute him and he was eventually, but only for a short time, expelled from France because of its influence. His name crops up constantly in the biographies of his contemporaries and the literary memoirs of later generations. Although he knew Beckett when they were both contributing to *transition* in the Thirties, they had no further contact until they met one day in the library at Tangiers in the early Seventies and over coffee reminisced about Paris in the Thirties. Roditi was an active homosexual with a large number of lovers, and he even as a young man had a one-night stand with Lorca, although he did not know who the older poet was at the time. His sexual inclinations may have damaged his career in some circles. He was an eclectic who never really became identified with any school, other than surrealism in its early days, and he attributed his lack of world reputation, except among intellectuals, to his outspoken rejection of writing and art that lacked clarity, or became bogged down in techniques and language that required generations of academics to explain. In his own poems and other writing his aim was clarity above all. Ezra Pound was an obvious target for Roditi, but he also had little time for the lesbian writers, Djuna Barnes, Gertrude Stein and Jane Bowles; he felt they were overrated because their lives were interesting and because they made good journalistic copy, or interesting subjects for biographers. Roditi believed that the "cult of personality" had done much to reduce the level of craftsmanship, and therefore the quality, of the arts in our time. David Applefield, the editor of *Frank*, interviewing him for another magazine, elicited a quotable aphorism: "Journalism has corrupted our sense of values, and literary criticism too is all too often degenerating now into a kind of gossip columnist's art, as if the world of letters were an adjunct of café society." Roditi died in Spain on a visit at the age of eighty-two, bitter that so much early promise and committed activity had received little recognition, but leaving a large manuscript of his memoirs that may yet prove a valuable addition to the archives of literary history. He was negotiating for its publication when he died. It is in four volumes under the title, *The Age of Improvidence*, which well describes the whole twentieth century.

Another Paris old-timer was Georges Pelorson, renamed Belmont, who, as has been related, was considerably helped by Girodias during his period of disgrace from 1945. He eventually obtained a job as an editor at Julliard and was responsible for many of their English-language acquisitions, as well as editing new French writers. But he had to keep a low profile: known collaborators continued to be pariahs in Paris, and in his case there were whispers that while working in the Vichy Department of Education he must have been responsible in some measure for the deportation of Jewish children. Beckett, his pre-war close friend, would no longer see him, and if they happened to meet accidentally in the street, Belmont would be treated politely but without any of the old warmth. After Beckett died in 1989 there was a spate of Beckett conferences around the world, and Belmont would appear at some of them as Beckett's oldest surviving friend, first at Monte Carlo in 1991, then at Dublin later that year. Slightly older than Beckett, he had remained in excellent health and was expected to contribute to the growing flood of literature about the man who has already had more written about him than anyone else born in the century. But his retirement was discreet and uneventful. He died in 2007.

5

Remembered in Paris and New York, but no longer able to go there, Alexander Trocchi was living in London from 1963, first in a bedsit in Heath Street in Hampstead, then at a series of other addresses, until he found a large flat at Observatory Gardens in Kensington. He was receiving money from National Assistance, payment from odd jobs, such as reading manuscripts for publishers, and advances and royalties derived from the publication of *Cain's Book*, money for the translations he undertook, some of which he completed, but also advances for novels that he offered to write that were never even started and that in many cases he never intended to write. He also derived an irregular, but not insignificant, income from interviews and appearances on the media. But it was never enough.

His father died while on a visit to the Isle of Man and Alex attended the funeral with Lyn; she fell ill and was admitted to the local hospital as an addict, but as a voluntary patient who wanted to be cured. The doctor warned Alex that it was near-impossible for his wife to kick the habit if he himself did not. Temporarily off heroin, she then returned to London with Alex.

There were negotiations for European editions of *Cain's Book*. Helmut Kossodo, a small literary publisher producing books in German in Geneva, a man with whom I had many amicable dealings, signed a contract; he was having financial problems and never produced the book. Rowohlt finally did. In other countries contracts were signed, but no one saw *Cain's Book* as a potential best-seller; the tendency, as happened in Italy, was for a larger publisher to buy it and pass it on to a smaller one. Trocchi himself was too involved in his schemes and new ideas to spend time actually sitting down to write another novel, although he had accepted advances from several publishers to do so and always promised to deliver a manuscript soon.

But Trocchi managed to keep his name in the swim. He was mentioned and quoted in news items and articles about trendy London, associated with a number of activities, frequently seen at the Arts Lab, the ICA, the Round House, a fashionable figure everywhere. Drug addicts were few at the time, and considered interesting rather than dangerous or pitiable. Had not some of the great figures in English literature been addicts, such as Coleridge and de Quincey? The liberal British laws were still successful in keeping the crime syndicates out of selling drugs. Not only could a registered addict get a daily dose, but it was free. Most of the addicts in London at the time were American hippies. They would congregate outside Boots the Chemist in Piccadilly Circus, which was open all night, prescriptions in hand, waiting for midnight, the beginning of a new day, when they could obtain a new supply. But the few resident addicts were better organized than that and usually knew their chemist personally, able when necessary to get their National Health subscriptions filled in advance. Although a guru to the hippies, Trocchi had little intellectually in common with them. He was still interested in literary theory, was trying to invent a new attitude towards the arts and promoting an art-orientated society that would have no time or interest in war, in which the arms-race would become a thing of the past, and the state would give everyone convivial jobs and a pleasant lifestyle. "Sigma", an international but loosely linked association of artists and writers was the vehicle. Visitors to London in those days included Robert Creeley and his wife Bobbie, often visiting their great friend, the American artist R.B. Kitaj, who, having studied in England under the GI Bill of Rights, was living in London and had become one of the leading painters of the day; there was also Gregory Corso, the poet Victor Bockris (whose poems I turned down for publication and who was later to write some successful biographies of counter-culture figures, including Andy Warhol), Bill Burroughs, Allen Ginsberg, and dozens of others whom Trocchi had known or now came to know; they increased his sense of his own importance as a man of destiny who would do great things: he was only in his early forties in the middle Sixties. Joseph Strick negotiated with Alex for a screenplay of *Ulysses*, but he eventually wrote it himself. Trocchi's name appeared in *Penthouse* and *Playboy*, but only in features. Victor Lownes, who had come to England to run the Playboy Club and the magazine for Hugh Hefner, told me that some American friend suggested he should call on Trocchi as an important figure on the "swinging London" scene. He rang him and was invited to lunch. Alex had made no preparation – in fact he had almost certainly forgotten all about it – when Lownes turned up, but he realized quickly that this was potentially an important new contact for him. He and two friends who were present – also junkies according to Victor – found what food they could in the house, mainly lettuce leaves, and put some on a plate for him, then discovered some bottled salad dressing and poured a little of it over the lettuce. Alex tried to behave as if everything was normal and to charm his guest, but all Lownes remembered about him was the lettuce. The visit had no follow-up.*

Many film-makers continued to make plans for a film of *Young Adam*, but it never materialized until 2003. Trocchi's use of drugs interested many psychiatrists including the fashionable R.D. Laing, whose theories of madness were being hotly debated. Laing, another Glaswegian, was also a poet, and his theories were used by some writers as literary material: David Mercer's television play *In Two Minds* was based on Laing's theory that schizophrenics are not really mad, or no more than the rest of us, but different and living in a world that is very real to them. Laing and Trocchi became good friends, each using the other as a sounding board for his ideas.

Another successful man who befriended Trocchi was Sir Roland Penrose, founder of the Institute of Contemporary Arts which grew from being an art gallery for experimental work in Mayfair, that also promoted many talks and lectures, to a new Arts Council-sponsored centre (again under the benevolent ministry of Jenny Lee) that contained a theatre, cinema and catering facilities as well as a large gallery capable of mounting large exhibitions, on the Mall, London's most prestigious public avenue, which runs from Trafalgar Square to Buckingham Palace. Its neighbours were the royal residences that border the famous processional street. Penrose was Picasso's first biographer and the translator for much of his writing, including his two plays. He had been a friend to many modern painters of the Paris schools, cubists, Fauves and surrealists in particular, and was a good painter himself. He found Trocchi very like the bohemian friends of his youth, befriended him as such, introduced him to others who could help him and almost certainly regularly lent (gave) him money. When Trocchi moved to Observatory Gardens in North Kensington, he was only a few doors away from Penrose.

At the time Trocchi was still producing his little painted sculptures, to which he gave the name "Futiques". Some of these were exhibited in galleries and I used one for the cover of *Cain's Book*. It was shaped rather like a curved penis. I used another one, a squat oval shape, for Creeley's novel *The Island*. It was a time when anything called "Art" was treated as art, and Trocchi also earned a little money, probably through Penrose's influence, lecturing on sculpture at Saint Martin's School of Art. Many of his classes were very disorganized and used mainly to spread the dogma of Sigma. He invited his friends, mainly poets, to come to read, and give the students a wider perspective on "Art". It was a time when you could get away with such things without protest. I would lecture myself occasionally at Art Colleges and I was amazed at the lack of formal training and discipline that I occasionally

CHAPTER 10

encountered; students were often not even taught to draw. Years later
when the Turner Prize became a talking point, there was a similar
eclectic view of art.

A year after the publication of *Cain's Book*, when the second printing
was selling well, some copies were seized, together with forty-eight
other novels and nearly a thousand different magazines, in a police
raid on Sheffield's seedier bookshops. I could and should have ignored
it. A few copies would have been destroyed and no one would have
been any the wiser, but given that the book had received a good press
and Trocchi was a famous character, I decided that it would be well
worthwhile to mount a defence. I had had no trouble over Miller or
Burroughs after steering through all the risks and cautions, and I had
reason to think, especially after my Edinburgh conferences, that the
age of censorship was over. A vigorous defence would give *Cain's Book*
renewed publicity and start the sales all over again. The police had of
course seized the book by accident. It was a hardcover published at
twenty-five shillings, a price higher than most novels and certainly the
dirty-book trade had not considered it until then a book of interest
to their customers, unlike *Lady Chatterley* and *Tropic of Cancer*.
Pornography addicts wanted raw sexual description, not a novel about
the daily life of a drug addict on a scow in New York.

The case was heard before three magistrates in Sheffield on 15th
April 1964. A magistrates' court does not need barristers and our
solicitor Bruce Douglas-Mann was qualified to plead. Defence witnesses
included the popular television broadcaster, writer and critic, Kenneth
Allsop, who had reviewed the book favourably, Walter Keir, a Scottish
critic, the Sheffield City Librarian and Kathleen Knott, an imposing
senior poetess. I gave evidence and so did Trocchi, the latter against
the will of our solicitor, but as Trocchi was present it was impossible
to stop him. I did have a little difficulty in the witness box explaining
a quotation from de Sade that precedes the opening of the novel. It
concerned the joys of doing evil, and could hardly be called an integral
part of the book, but it implied that some writers like to corrupt
other people. I gave my opinion that books could teach, they could
enlighten and instruct, and that all knowledge was not pleasant; but I
had never known anyone to be corrupted, saddened perhaps, but not
corrupted, by a book. The purpose of literature was to make readers
more aware. Trocchi followed me into the box and said exactly the
opposite. If he had thought that his book could not affect behaviour,
he said, he would not have bothered to write it. The magistrates had
probably already made up their minds, but Trocchi's evidence almost

283

certainly clinched the case against us. We were found guilty and those copies of the book that had been seized were ordered to be destroyed. This applied also to the twenty copies in the Sheffield Public Library, about which the Librarian had given evidence.

The trial took a single day. That same evening I was booked to give a talk on the novels of Max Frisch on the BBC, but they had someone to meet me off the train to tell me it had been cancelled. The judgement was in all the evening newspapers and I had become too hot for them. We had no option but to appeal and we lost again in a surprising verdict that brought a new concept into the law, that descriptions of drug-taking, which was not itself illegal per se, were themselves illegal. Fortunately the verdict, at both levels, unless a national case were brought against us, would only apply to Sheffield. And fortunately the prosecution ended there.

Some little time later, in June 1965, because of the presence of many poets in London, including many visiting Americans, a large poetry reading was planned and Trocchi became involved and made himself a central figure. Because the climate was right and so many well-known names would be present, the Albert Hall was rented. The poets from Britain, the US and Europe included Christopher Logue, Adrian Mitchell, George MacBeth, Michael Horovitz, Harry Fainlight, Dan Richter, Allen Ginsberg, Laurence Ferlinghetti, Peter Brown, Tom McGrath, Anselm Hollo, John Esam, Gregory Corso and of course Trocchi himself. Much advance publicity was given to the event by the newspapers and a press conference was held on the morning of the day on the steps of the Albert Memorial at which Trocchi did much of the talking, and as a result he was elected to compère it. It turned out to be a long evening with the house full. The tickets were five and ten shillings and over £2,000 was taken at the box office. Trocchi turned out to be a good chairman. He did not allow any poet to go on too long, not even Ginsberg, who delivered a long mantra and seemed determined to hold the floor for half an hour at least. He was finally silenced by cries from the crowd, including a Scottish voice shouting, "This is McGonagall!" and by Trocchi's restraining hand, which finally took the microphone away from him. The whole hall reeked of pot and the spotlights had difficulty in cutting through the haze of cigarette smoke and marijuana. Among the more unconventional moments some people undressed, and a group of about twenty of R.D. Laing's patients, bewildered and frightened, were visible to all on a raised platform at one side of the hall, walking around, flapping their arms, obviously distressed by the lights and the noise. For Laing it was a form of shock therapy. Perhaps it was to convince his patients that their own "real" world was better that the other one.

Trocchi took the opportunity to attack the Sheffield magistrates in a speech that acknowledged his own applause, and he basked in it as he had done in Edinburgh. It was certainly the highlight of his public career as far as London was concerned. He was now a major counter-culture figure, his face familiar from television and his ideas taken seriously by the pundits. Because of this he certainly helped to popularize drug-taking among the more impressionable younger people, who saw him as a role model. If drugs could make you famous, as he was, and apparently have little harmful effect as he always claimed, then why not indulge? Certainly the taking of hard drugs, negligible until then, increased, not because of *Cain's Book* and *The Naked Lunch*, which very few read, but because cult figures took them, especially in the world of rock music. This eventually led to a change in government policy and a crackdown on junkies. Some of the long-established addicts continued to get prescriptions, but doses were much reduced and some doctors who had prescribed over-generously were heavily criticized; one such was Lady Frankau, a fashionable psychiatrist, who had mainly the well-heeled and the famous among her clients. A few doctors were knocked off the register. One of Burroughs's dictums was that pushing was just as addictive as using, and there was much truth in it. The government policy in cracking down is understandable, but it was wrong because crime finally got its hold on the addicts. It was one thing to be tolerant to a few dozen, not to hundreds or thousands. Criminalization was perhaps inevitable.

The poetry festival at the Albert Hall was certainly one of the larger events of the Sixties' hippie era but it did not end happily. It was successful with the public and it received good press, but the manager of the hall was furious at the unrestrained scene and announced that such "filth" would never be allowed there again. He was referring as much to the people as the poetry. The big shock came over money. Everyone expected to be paid, but most of the £2,000 taken at the box office disappeared. Christopher Logue later cleared up the mystery for me. He had wandered into the box office in time to see John Esam, a New Zealand poet, who had put up much of the money to hire the hall, and Trocchi, both stuffing the box office takings into bags. They looked embarrassed when they saw him. "Help yourself to some," said Trocchi and he went on stuffing. Esam also took the BBC facility fee for recording the evening, and all that most of the poets received was a small fee from the BBC. Esam subsequently disappeared, and when the BBC tried to contact him they found that he was not reachable at any address. There was a major row among the participants with many accusations, threats of legal action and letters to the press, but it died down eventually. Trocchi lamely announced that the accounts had been disorganized, money had disappeared, and he was sorry. The row slowly faded into memory.

Trocchi was not to write anything else of significance. He made some good translations, most of them with the help of another translator, with himself shaping the final draft to get the style right. In the case of one Dutch book, *Ik Jan Cremer*, an autobiographical novel by a man very like himself, he was well able to catch the picaresque braggadocio of Jan Cremer's exuberance. The book sold well in English, but it had already had an enormous success in Holland. The Dutch press kept ringing me to ask if it was true that I intended to tour the author around Britain in a gold-plated Rolls-Royce. "Perhaps a silver one," I told them.

Trocchi opened a bookstall for antiquarian books in the Portobello Road, where there was a weekly market for old silver, bric-a-brac and books. He had an eye for a rare edition and the ability to be persuasive in interesting collectors. Trocchi's stall was later moved to other locations and finally into the Kensington Hyper-Market. He always had helpers to work with him, necessary as he was never able to stay away from a fix too long, and a market stall cannot be left unattended. He was involved in legal trials: on one occasion during Girodias's London collaboration with NEL, after many books had been seized in a police raid, he had to give evidence about his own past writings. He was also mixed up in a suspected jewel robbery at a hotel, and I went to court to give him a "character", saying that he was a distinguished writer who could not conceivably be involved in anything shady. The same happened when he was accused of selling heroin (from his ration), but he got out of that one too. He told me he had given, not sold it, to a friend. This was Michael Portman, Burroughs's old lover and sycophant. "Never again", he wrote to Bill afterwards.

But he soon found himself as much the victim as the instigator of con tricks. Various American publishers of the shadier variety came to see him to get hold of his libertine novels, which Girodias was also trying to negotiate. Some titles which were published by Brandon Books in the US had very good sales, but Trocchi was never paid in spite of meeting with Milton Luros, the publisher, who made big promises, and even sent contracts for Alex to sign, but never returned them when he did. Girodias sued some of the American pirates including Brandon, and sometimes succeeded in getting a decision in his favour, but he never received back even the cost of his actions.

Tragedy hit all the Trocchis in London. When Lyn became very ill, I sent Alex to see Tibor Csato, my own doctor, an unusual Hungarian intellectual, who looked after the medical needs of much of the Hungarian colony in London, including the Kordas, a name his secretary always confused with my own. Csato knew how to treat artists, especially the bohemian ones: he was sympathetic and never judgemental, a better psychiatrist in practice than any I had met, although not qualified as such. He had Lyn admitted to hospital, both for her malady, hepatitis, and her drug addition. She had gone off heroin several times, but had always resumed the habit, and she died not long afterwards, in November 1972. Her funeral was a simple one, a cremation with no ceremony, except that Alex made a short speech and read, because it was traditional, the twenty-third psalm, 'The Lord is my Shepherd', very beautifully. Trocchi had a mellifluous voice and an actor's sense of timing. Afterwards, outside in the sunlight, he seemed not depressed, but full of energy. "I must finish *The Long Book* now," he said, and not I think just for my benefit. "I must do it for Lyn."

Mark died six years later, of a cancer that started with a spinal infection, almost certainly drug-related. Alex carried on, painting his futiques, selling antiquarian books, earning bits of money here and there, but always unreliable, with his own health visibly deteriorating. He was still surrounded by acolytes, loved holding court and talking about the problems of the world and how he was still going to change it. He went into hospital to have a cancerous growth removed from his lung, and came out again, relieved it was no worse. I had managed earlier, after years of trying, to get hold of his collected poems, for which I had paid an advance and which I knew existed. Lyn had let me into his flat one day when he was out; I found a pile of verse in the drawers of his desk and removed them. They were in a terrible mess, only a few in a finished version from when he had done a public reading, but with creative editing I was able to put together a small volume. Once I had them, Alex was pleased and let me do what I liked. In one case I edited two versions of the same poem without realizing it, and it ended as two different poems. I published the volume in 1972 under the title *Man at Leisure*. There was never any sign of *The Long Book*, for which I and several other publishers had signed contracts and paid advances. I had looked for traces of that too during my poetry raid. Trocchi continued to promise everything to everyone, articles, books, translations, manifestos, and he was talking about writing an autobiography during his last year. But his energy was gone. He would meet friends in public houses in the late morning and spend the afternoons at a drinking club in a nearby cellar, anything to avoid having to face the blank page. His energy and his health deteriorated together, and in April 1984 he caught a cold which developed into pneumonia; taken into hospital, he died on the 15th. He had, for a man who had been constantly on heroin since the middle Fifties, and for about thirty years, long outlived his natural expectancy. He just missed his sixtieth birthday.

During his last years Trocchi was still attractive to women and was usually seen with a succession of young women, mostly in their twenties. The last came as an au pair, and her name was Sally Child. She had been recommended by Robert Creeley, whose wife Sally had met in New Zealand. She fell in love and ended by living with him for the last six years of his life. She was only twenty-three when they met, but it was a love match, and Sally became a foster mother to Alex's younger son, Nicholas. When Alex died he was cremated and Sally kept his ashes together with the jar containing those of Lyn, Marcus and two cats who had died. It had been Alex's intention to bury all the other ashes together and plant a rose bush over them, but he never got round to it. One day Alex's own ashes disappeared. No one ever found out who took them or why. A year after his death, an accidental fire destroyed most of his remaining manuscripts, books and papers. The final tragedy came when Nicholas, now eighteen, went up onto the roof one day in 1985 and walked off it, killing himself in the fall. He had been depressed, was not getting on well with his studies, and undoubtedly the tragedy of the House of Trocchi had preyed on his mind.

6

William Burroughs liked England for a number of reasons, not least that his international fame had started in the British Isles, and that he found many young men to his liking there. Ian Sommerville and Michael Portman were both important to him, and the latter, although spoilt in almost every way, was usefully rich, or at least had a generous spending allowance from his wealthy and aristocratic family, which was paid to him by his godfather and guardian Lord Goodman. Burroughs inevitably derived some of the benefit, although not in a deliberate way. There were attempts by Michael's sister and mother (whose Greek boyfriend suggested cutting off the young Portman's allowance) to separate Mikey Portman from Burroughs, but Lord Goodman defended the relationship, mainly because he realized that Burroughs was trying hard to wean Michael off heroin, and he was then too old to be a wild beatnik and lead him into trouble.

Burroughs's needs were always fairly simple and he liked routine in his life: when untroubled he was a workaholic, spending all day with his typewriter, after which he would relax with alcohol and sex, usually eating very little. He had his own circle in London and was happy to stay in and talk. In 1962, shortly after his Edinburgh appearance, he met Anthony Balch, a minor film-maker who for years had tried to think up a way to film *The Naked Lunch*. Balch was an immensely tall, suave and good-looking young man from an English public-school background, rather on the edge of the film world; he never became well known and his name is not listed in the current or later standard film reference books, but he was very persuasive and just the kind of Englishman who had always fascinated Bill. At Burroughs's request I gave him a contract, but no advance money was ever paid or even a script established. There were many film-makers – Kubrick was one of the more eminent – interested in filming the novel after Balch, but when it was finally made, by David Cronenberg, it had little to do with the book, using only a few episodes and characters from it in a biographical film that was mainly about Burroughs in Tangiers. Balch had made some horror films and had distributed European soft-core porn movies in the UK but he had no real reputation. He did however make one film with Burroughs which was partly shot in Marion Boyars's London flat near Paddington. Young actors in outer-space costumes with toy machine guns were firing ping-pong balls at each other and Marion decided to keep out of the way until it was finished. The film had other scenes in London locales, one of them in the board-room of the British Film Institute in Dean Street in Soho. Burroughs himself played in the film as chairman of the board of an interstellar corporation. In fact, as was evidenced by his successful readings, he was always an excellent actor.

After his first long New York stay, Burroughs was mainly in London between the beginning of 1966 and February 1974. His old boyfriend, Ian Sommerville, had taken up with a very camp working-class boy from the North, Alan Watson, and the situation was a repeat of Ginsberg and Orlovsky in Tangiers, with Burroughs unable to control his jealousy. He began to use the young male prostitutes who could be picked up in Piccadilly, just a minute away from the flat on Duke Street, St James's, that he had rented shortly after returning, and with two such "dilly boys" he had a long-term relationship. During this period he also became interested in Scientology and went through both the complete elementary course and then the advanced one which must have cost him a great deal of money; Scientologists are very greedy. Scientology is a form of psychotherapy in which the patient is asked questions with his hands holding two electrified metal tubes attached to an E-meter, which measures the sweat in the palms. Every time a painful memory occurs or an association that has an emotional trigger, the needle on the meter jumps: it is basically a lie detector. Burroughs found that many of his complexes and his unconscious memories could be released in this way. Although he hated the people who ran the organization in the name of their always invisible leader, L. Ron Hubbard, who had started as a rather bad science-fiction writer, he knew that they were only applying a potent technique to make money. Their purpose was to mentally and emotionally enslave their patients into becoming addicts to the treatment; but Burroughs made many discoveries that would be useful to his work. He was investigating the occult side of his own nature, even perhaps going back to memories of previous lives. I met him for lunch in Edinburgh one day at the building where he was undergoing the advanced course. To qualify for this you have to be a "clear", already rid of the inhibitions and shock reaction to the questioning that you have undergone on the basic course. I picked him up at the Centre, a large building in the university section of the city on South Bridge, and while waiting for him looked at the young men and women standing around the hall and the office; they all looked glassy-eyed and moved like automatons, talking in disembodied voices as if to the wall. I felt that they were invaders from another planet, Burroughs characters from one of his interplanetary novels, or models from *The Invasion of the Body Snatchers*.

Over lunch we talked about his course. He was fascinated by the techniques and what he had learnt about himself, and he was trying hard to retain control of his mind against their efforts to dominate it. As they were by nature suspicious they had a number of traps to test his sincerity and the E-meter, being a lie-detector, made it difficult for him to conceal his real contempt for them. I felt, as so often in Burroughs's company, that there were two sides to him, one being part of the story he was always fabricating about himself, in which he played a character (the mythomanic Burroughs), and the other the logical person that could discuss things normally. He would seem to fall into his own fictions and then emerge from them again. I asked him if sinister organizations or secret services like the CIA were in any way involved with Scientology. "You're fucking right they are," he said. "The CIA are in it up to their fucking necks." I was not sure that he believed it, or that he did not cooperate with his "auditors" more than he admitted.

Some time later I dropped in on him early one evening in Duke Street to discuss some editorial matter. He was alone and had already drunk a fair amount. Editorial problems did not arise very often between us. When editing *The Naked Lunch* I had detected that some characters with different names were probably the same, and had found several other discrepancies. I also felt that some of the linking could be better done: the book was really a series of episodes or routines that had been put together rather haphazardly, either by Ginsberg, Girodias or Burroughs himself. On the second of the two editorial sessions with Bill, some years earlier, after agreeing with every suggestion I had made so far, he suddenly became bored and told me to carry on by myself. He wanted to get on with his new book and would leave it to me to do what I thought best. Unlike Beckett, who pondered every word and never agreed to any change I might suggest, Burroughs was never interested in past work.

Whatever it was I went to see him about that evening in Duke Street did not take long. I asked if he would like to go out to dinner and he jumped at the chance of escaping for a while from his lonely flat. It was past sundown – drinking, not working, time for Bill. I took him, unadvisedly, to the Caledonian Club, a rather stuffy place for London Scots to meet and Scottish visitors to use. Although there were not many people in the dining room, there were some, and voices are usually lowered, not to be overheard. Bill, quite drunk by the time we sat down, was unable to lower his voice, was unaware of the atmosphere, and kept talking on topics such as the CIA, politics, conspiracies and especially Scientology. 'Fucking' used as an adjective was in every sentence and we received several nervous glances from other diners and the staff.

"Please, Bill," I pleaded, "could you just be careful what you say in here." But it was no good. Fortunately he was not hungry and I managed to get him to a nearby pub, where it didn't matter much what he said, and where he could smoke. The Caledonian Club allowed no smoking in the dining room, and four times, after warnings from the head waiter, I had had to take a freshly lit cigarette away from him.

During Burroughs's time in London Brion Gysin became ill in Paris and had to have a number of painful operations. Bill contributed to his medical expenses. His old buddy Neil Cassady was already dead, and in October 1969 Jack Kerouac also died, news that came at a time when Burroughs was already deeply depressed. Panna Grady moved to London, began to give dinner parties and again frequently asked Burroughs. She was now living with Charles Olson, a poet who was not known in England at the time and was not particularly happy in London. She once again entertained lavishly, widening her circle of intellectual acquaintances, and she behaved much as she had in New York. When Olson died in 1970 she married Philip O'Connor, an author who had done a little work for Girodias and who was frequently in my office with a pile of manuscripts. O'Connor was undoubtedly talented, a rather wild literary critic as well as a writer in most established forms, who had a modest success with his *Memoirs of a Public Baby*. O'Connor had interesting theories about most modern writers, especially Beckett, Burroughs and others who had come from conventional middle-class homes and were therefore unable, as he saw it, to shake off an inherent conservatism which, whatever the milieu they had adopted for their lifestyle, was part of the baggage they brought with them, and coloured their writing. Panna Grady gave him at least a conversational platform for his ideas. He contrasted the avant-garde conservatives with the avant-garde "bohemians" who came from a more plebeian background: Céline, O'Casey and James Hanley for instance, who brought their own background into their style, which was more original because it had to be invented rather than refined from the work of their predecessors. O'Connor was a heavy drinker and this became evident towards the end of Panna Grady's parties, to which many London bohemian poets and artists were invited. William Empson, an eminent elderly poet, who looked like the grandfather of all the hippies with his ponytail and flowing beard, the man who, together with Arthur Waley, had done most to promote the literature of China and Japan in Britain, was often used as a senior figure to restore order when a fight broke out or the police came, following a complaint from neighbours.

But Burroughs preferred to keep his social life to a minimum and he was happier with old friends than the party scene. He came to very few of the parties that I periodically gave to launch a new book or to meet a visiting author. With London as his base he travelled fairly frequently to give lectures and readings or to attend conferences where his work was featured. He was asked to teach a course in Switzerland at an experimental "University of the New World". All the students were hippies and the local Swiss people in the mountain village, where the "University" was trying to establish itself, did not like the invasion and were uncooperative and unfriendly. Burroughs taught his course, being one of the only instructors to turn up, but he did not enjoy it and in the end he was not paid; nor were the local tradesmen who had been persuaded to give credit. He made visits to Paris and Tangiers and on one occasion was invited to Hollywood where Terry Southern had interested a producer in making *The Naked Lunch*. His fare was paid, but by the time he arrived the producer, Chuck Barris, had lost interest. Burroughs returned empty-handed.

Burroughs's London flat sometimes became a dosshouse for too many people, visitors from abroad, past and present boyfriends, and his income had dwindled. He received some money by selling his archives to Robert Altman, a financier operating from Liechtenstein, who wanted to set up a library of literary material. Brion Gysin, who still had many international contacts, was the prime mover in this deal, but the money had to be divided up with Miles (Barry Miles), who did the cataloguing, with Brion himself, and with others who had worked on the project, and Burroughs did not get as much as he had expected. He was visibly deteriorating and, like Kerouac who had died of cirrhosis, drinking too much and showing signs of senility. Ginsberg turned up in London, was alarmed at what he saw, and persuaded Burroughs that it was time to return to the States. He was sure that he could get him a teaching job in New York that would earn him some money and keep him positively occupied, and he was as good as his word.

Burroughs then left Europe for good. In New York he met a young admirer, James Grauerholz. A Midwesterner from Kansas, he was anxious to get into the artistic side of hippie New York, and he had written to everyone he could think of that he admired or could help him. He met Ginsberg who passed him on to Burroughs at a time when the latter needed a secretary and manager. He was accepted. There was a short sexual relationship at the beginning, but Grauerholz did not like older men that way and was successful in turning it into a friendship and becoming a professional manager for all Burroughs's literary and financial affairs. The latter now sank deeper into his preoccupations and his writing, getting gradually senile, but this did not affect his output. Grauerholz was able to exercise the kind of control over Burroughs that the Scientologists had failed to do. *Grau* in German means grey and he had become, as he had planned, an *eminence grise* to Burroughs, living on his money and supporting his lifestyle out of royalties and advances from publishers. These became much more substantial with time because Grauerholz brought in an agent, Andrew

Wylie, a sharp operator with a nose for big money, who specialized in taking authors away from their habitual publishers on the promise of higher advances from another one. By putting together a prospectus for seven books which Burroughs would undertake to write, Wylie held auctions, inviting bids for the package from all of Burroughs's publishers as well as others who were now interested in acquiring him as an established author. He wanted to get large advances in immediate money for future work. I had to back out: there was no way I could find a small fortune in competition with bigger publishers who could raise whatever they needed for projected books that might never be written; in any case Burroughs was hardly likely to write better books in the future. He was an accidental writer, more interested in the process than the result, unlike my other "star", Samuel Beckett, who was interested in both style and content, and the nearest he could get to putting the greatest amount of meaning into the smallest number of words in a perfect, unimproveable poetic utterance. Dick Seaver was in the same position. He had some time previously persuaded Burroughs to leave Barney Rosset at Grove Press and to move to Viking Press, where he now had his own imprint, Richard Seaver Books, and from there he took Burroughs and his imprint to Holt, Rinehart & Winston. With much anger he too had to back out of the auction. He had done much work in editing Burroughs, especially on what was probably his most important and readable book after *The Naked Lunch*, *Cities of the Red Night*, the first Burroughs novel to have a thoroughly professional editing job done on it at one time. He had thought that Burroughs, recognizing his need of a good editor, would have stayed with him, receiving his royalties regularly and good advances on his new books as finished; but he reckoned without Wylie.

Burroughs had lived for some time in a "bunker" on the Bowery, a street full of hoboes and drop-outs, lined with alcoholics all trying to panhandle any passers-by. Even motorists were reluctant to drive down it. Here in a warren of whitewashed rooms, mostly opening onto a central area, lived a commune of writers and others who ate at a large refectory table, and passed their time together. I presumed that many of them were on drugs and that the commune was homosexual, but on my two or three visits to see Burroughs I was politely ignored by the other residents. It reminded me partly of an old-people's home and partly of a hospital, but Burroughs was always largely indifferent to his environment. The West Village was now the New York centre for the punk scene, in which Burroughs was a cult figure, although very few of the young people whose lives revolved around brightly hued and eccentrically cut hairstyles and music of total mindlessness could have read much of him. But the homeless and the punks were what he saw every time he ventured outside the metal padlocked gates of the bunker. It is difficult to imagine William Burroughs, the conservatively dressed, long-faced, unsmiling writer, becoming a guru to the punks, who were themselves a revolt against the beats, but the titles of his books became the names of boutiques, restaurants and bookshops, and the reformed junky was now a role model for those who were starting on the road to addiction. Burroughs was now always called William by his New York circle, not Bill; this was Brion Gysin's idea, although some who had known him earlier, including myself, stuck to the old name. His celebrity attracted money: there were a number of wealthy admirers who saw a chance of making a little more from his work. There was a proposition to use his film script *The Last Words of Dutch Schulz*, but that fell through. Then Jacques Stern, a financier who had to live in a wheelchair because of polio, came forward with a project to film *Junky*. Terry Southern was brought in as screen-writer and Dennis Hopper as actor and director. Stern paid large advances to everyone involved, and for a year Burroughs and everyone around him had money in the bank and grew accustomed to enjoying Stern's hospitality. It seemed the film might really be made, but the eccentric Stern who was heavily into drugs and alcohol, suddenly lost his money and the parties and incoming cash ended, as did the whole project.

At the end of 1978 the first of a number of Burroughs festivals took place, organized by Victor Bockris, and it was called "The Nova Convention". Keith Richards of the Rolling Stones ran into Brion Gysin in Paris and said he would like to be involved, so his name was headlined on the poster. This helped to sell out the three nights of the 'convention', but in the event Richards did not appear: he had been busted for heroin in Toronto and advised not to connect himself with anything associated with drugs. But others who took part included John Cage, Merce Cunningham, Allen Ginsberg, Ed Sanders, Robert Anton Wilson, Timothy Leary and Philip Glass, as well as Burroughs himself and Gysin. Frank Zappa turned out to be an acceptable alternative to Richards.

Inevitably, surrounded by drug-takers, Burroughs began to indulge again and soon he was once more hooked on heroin. This was during a period when Grauerholz was taken up with problems of his own and his supervision of Burroughs's life and habits slipped, but Burroughs found a methadone clinic in New York that was able to wean him off. Methadone was however necessary for him from then on and he never dared be far away from it. He bought a property in Florida, but never developed it because there was no nearby clinic.

In October 1980 he went to Lawrence, Kansas to do a reading and decided that he liked the town. It was near James Grauerholz's hometown of Coffeyville and it did not take long for James and Burroughs jointly to come to a decision to move out of the bunker with all its temptations and follies and retire to Kansas where life was cheaper and Burroughs's income could be better regulated. James took an apartment and eventually lodged Bill – or William as he now was – in a little wooden frame house where he settled down on his own and continued writing, occasionally receiving visitors and going out frequently in the evening to have dinner with Grauerholz or others in the new circle that he entered there, mainly centred on the university. James confiscated his collection of weapons which Bill would handle in Grauerholz's apartment, brought him a daily ration of vodka, cat-food for his growing family of cats (Burroughs loved cats and hated dogs) and doughnuts for himself. Books continued to appear. Seaver had now moved on to Holt, Rinehart & Winston, where he had published *The Place of Dead Roads*. Books continued to appear from Burroughs, but from *The Western Lands* onwards, both Seaver and I were out of the picture. I spent days in Lawrence on different occasions, seeing Bill and calling on the university bookseller, and on the last of several visits I went through Bill's lectures, articles, and fragments, making up what I intended to be a second volume of his *Collected Essays*. Grauerholz took over all this and later issued his own collection under the title *Interzone*. Not long after that visit came the seven-book auction, and our correspondence quickly became hostile. As Burroughs's "literary" British publisher I stood in the way of Wylie transforming him into a commercial author. I had a contract for the first collection of essays, which I realized were a part of the seven-book series on offer. By not sending back proofs and by rejecting my proposed title *A Biological Mistake*, which until then he had liked, Grauerholz and Wylie, through Burroughs, were hoping to break the contract. I did the only thing possible: correct everything myself, copy-edit the typescript and proceed to publish. At the next Frankfurt Book Fair an American lawyer came to see me at my booth and tried to persuade me to relinquish my rights, but could give no good reason why I should. I pointed out to him that I had been lobbying for some time – I knew some of the international panel of advisors – to get Burroughs onto the Nobel Prize in Literature short list, but in view of events had ceased to do so. Greed and disloyalty were not an incentive.

From that time my long relationship with Burroughs gradually deteriorated. Girodias was long out of the picture; so was Rosset, although Grove still had the major works for America. Grauerholz not only kept Burroughs away from the big cities and the people he might meet there, but broke off his old contacts. He was certainly no help in Bill's relationship to his son Billy, who died in March 1981. The only friend who remained outside the US was Brion Gysin. In 1984 I was asked to put together a tour of some of my authors by Laurence Staig, the Literature Director of *Eastern Arts*, who organized literary events in Cambridge and the counties of East Anglia. Burroughs first agreed to come, but then cancelled. When asked, Brion Gysin replaced him, rather to my surprise. He turned out to be a fascinating talker, explaining Burroughs's cut-up and fold-in method with clarity and his own part in giving Burroughs the initial idea. On that tour we had Robbe-Grillet, Alan Burns, Trevor Hoyle (both English writers I published) and others. Although Brion was obviously in failing health he was excellent company, always cheerful and full of interesting anecdotes about his career as a painter and writer, his collaboration with Burroughs, and the Paris art and literary scene in particular.

He did not have long to live. He died in Paris on 13th July 1986. He had developed lung cancer, to add to his other ailments, a month before; but he was already dying of emphysema and was suffering after a colostomy. A heart attack finally carried him off.

I learnt about his death from Maurice Girodias when having lunch with him in Paris the day before the funeral. Maurice was living in a small apartment on the Rue Alésia that had a view of the crematorium. Sunk in his own troubles, he had developed a macabre humour about others. "I shall watch the crematorium chimney tomorrow," he said. There will be a puff of smoke. It is big for a fat man, small for a thin one. Brion will give off a big cloud. I thought of staying for the funeral, but I was booked on the first plane to London the next morning on a non-transferrable ticket. Only Maurice witnessed the puff, or perhaps not. According to Ted Morgan, he looked away.*

7

To a great extent the 1968 student rising coincided with the beginning of the decline of the avant-garde in Paris. The *nouveau roman* was already being replaced by a new generation whose work was clever but tended to be incomprehensible to most readers. Jean Ricardou, Claude

Ollier and a few others produced a *nouveau nouveau roman* which depended more on semantics and our subconscious understanding of words and language than on a reconstruction of the way the mind works, and at such public and recorded meetings as the Colloque de Cerisy-la-Salle the old avant-garde led by Robbe-Grillet argued with the new generation about the possibilities of the novel used as secular theology. A wave of critical books examined this new literature which seemed to have the purpose of impressing the public with the cleverness of its authors more than enlightening anyone about anything else. It was not a literature that could be described as helpful for those who wanted to understand their lives and the reasons for their actions. There was a renewed interest in psychoanalysis and much of it came from feminist writers like Hélène Cixous. But the relationship between language and meaning still dominated literary discussion; phenomenology was back with new twists, and *structuralism* became the dominant literary fashion, supported by the universities, so that the use of language, choice of words, ways of understanding them, and the significance we read into them, dominated the literary press. *Tel Quel*, a magazine published by Les Éditions de Minuit's principal intellectual rival, Les Éditions du Seuil, was edited by Philippe Sollers, who became the new intellectual guru together with his wife Julia Kristeva, Cixous's rival among the literary feminists. Sollers had started his career by writing a classic form of *nouveau roman*, and *The Park* had some success in France, but none in translation when published on my own list; he quickly switched to a literature that had more to do with philosophy and the mental sciences than descriptions of human behaviour. Because it was more academically based than the *nouveau roman*, which could be read for its entertainment value as well as its aesthetic and intellectual appeal, structuralism began to interest those teaching at American universities and at Oxford and Cambridge, because it was seen as a branch of philosophy rather than literature. It was hotly debated at Cambridge where Christopher Ricks used the intellectual academic battle to force Frank Kermode's resignation as Professor of English. But it was of little interest to the Paris exiles, who no longer had a Trocchi to breach the gap between literary anglophones and French intellectuals.

In Britain the generation of C.P. Snow and Graham Greene was replaced by a new Gothic school among which Iris Murdoch, now becoming very popular in French translation, and John Fowles were predominant. Muriel Spark steadily built her reputation, sometimes also entering the Gothic mode. The trend was increasingly away from intellectual rationalism and towards the psychological, the mystical and the horrific. The freedoms and eclecticism of the Sixties, which had been fought for so hard, were taken for granted and became gradually eroded as the Seventies turned into the Eighties. Consumerism was back with a vengeance and everyone wanted to make money. Writers would no longer attend conferences with only their expenses paid; they wanted a fat fee as well. American universities began to offer $1,000 or more for a lecture by a well-known name and literary archives from the Fifties went up in value as universities competed to build their collections, which would eventually bring literary researchers, historians and biographers into their libraries. Mammon was invading the literary as well as the art scene. Small publishers began to lose their authors as they became better known, editorial standards dropped, greed and profit became the only reason for doing anything and a new generation that was not collegial, and became unwilling to share with others, rejected flower-power for the fleshpots.

The situation was better in Paris, although the same forces were at work. French publishers tend to know each other, meet at the same restaurants and be friendly when they meet. The relationship between publishers and authors is much closer in France, where, even if the heads of big companies do not read the books they publish, they have senior editors who do and they know enough not to be embarrassed at a dinner party by showing their ignorance. The relative absence of literary agents in France, who do the author ego-massaging in New York and London, is also a factor in the friendlier and non-combative nature of publisher-author relationships. The boom in big advances for potential best-sellers never happened in France where local authors were concerned, happy to get smaller pre-payments and a regular income from royalties, rather than one lump sum which would probably never be covered by sales. The agent of course was only interested in the size of the advance. During the Seventies publishing patterns in France reflected the trends elsewhere, but only on a moderate scale. There was a bad period for bookshops when the government, in the late Seventies, abolished the obligatory publisher's fixed price on French books, but after a year the consequences were so severe, particularly for independent bookshops, that price maintenance was restored. The position of the author – a few fortunate ones earning large amounts of money at the expense of others as a result of a best-seller-orientated book trade – did not change drastically in France after 1970 as it did elsewhere. Jack Lang, a Minister of Culture who understood the complex problems of publishing and bookselling where his counterparts in other countries never did, must take the credit for this. The "loi

Lang" saved literary publishing in France as it began to decline in the English-speaking countries.

The Paris theatre continued to attract large audiences and Jean-Louis Barrault dominated it, eventually emerging from the years out of official favour that followed his dismissal from the Odéon by De Gaulle. After occupying a series of warehouse spaces where he produced his own form of total theatre in circular or semi-circular arena-like auditoria, he settled into the old Quai d'Orsay train station under a tent, which insulated both the acting space and a combination lounge-room and restaurant from the promenade area, inside the covered station. From here the government moved him to the Palais des Glaces at the Rond-Point of the Champs-Elysées to make room for a museum that Valéry Giscard d'Estaing intended to call after himself; this latter was still not finished when Mitterrand ousted him from the presidency of the Republic in 1981, so it became the Musée d'Orsay instead. Barrault's new theatre was renamed the Théâtre du Rond-Point, but in spite of making the interior look as close as possible to its predecessor it never achieved the same atmosphere in the centre of Right Bank Paris as it had on the Left Bank.

Arthur Adamov continued to have some success with his plays. He made a French adaptation of Gogol's novel *Dead Souls*, which played successfully at the Odéon and wrote a good play about the Paris Commune, *Springtime 71*: this was a Brechtian recreation of the popular revolt that came at the end of the Franco-Prussian War when the returning defeated French Army bloodily put down the insurgents who had taken over the city. The play was performed in many European countries, in larger theatres in Germany and at London's small left-wing Unity Theatre in a translation by Arnold Hinchcliffe. But Adamov remained always short of money, and he was usually drunk. He wandered around Paris bars, always in dirty old sandals and no socks, his face a stubble and his bad breath and body odour detectable two yards away. His long-suffering wife, nicknamed "Le Bison", who had frequently left him in the past and had always returned, now left him for good. He appealed to Martin Esslin, then Head of Drama at BBC Radio, a faithful supporter since the early Sixties, who would have sent him money – Adamov had long ago worn-out any chance of getting deeper into debt with Gallimard or myself – except that Esslin never received the letters. An eccentric postman had stolen and hoarded several hundred mail-sacks in his flat, and for no particular reason (he never opened them). The BBC was in his delivery area and it was months before he was caught; during that period Adamov took his own life.

Another of the three leading "absurdist playwrights" (Martin Esslin coined the phrase) was Eugène Ionesco. He was anticipating his own death, although he still had many years to go, and his work, now commissioned largely by the bigger German theatres, seldom left the theme of his own mortality: he lived in constant fear, both of death and of being forgotten. A heavy dreamer, he used his dreams for the subject matter of much of his drama, as his great predecessor Pirandello had done; his plays were increasingly nightmare-like structures where the living and the dead mingled socially on the stage, conversing together and watching the horrors of life converging on them. Although they remained funny in their situations and dialogues, his later plays were all tragedies. His success continued because he was an established author – but on a lower level – and his early plays were critically preferred to the later ones. He was no longer earning the big royalties of the late Fifties and early Sixties, which became obvious as he moved from the fashionable (but not for an artist) Rue de Rivoli to the Boulevard Montparnasse.

I met Ionesco early one morning at Orly Airport. We were flying to London on the same plane, but he was travelling first class and I was in tourist, so we did not travel together. He was standing at the airport bar putting down one scotch after another. I suggested that it was a little early – it was about seven o'clock – to be drinking so much.

"I'm afraid," he said. "I'm terrified of flying. I drink to kill the fear. I only dare take short flights now. And I have to drink all the way to have the courage to fly at all."

We took a taxi into London together and later met for lunch. He could barely walk after it and was sleepy, so I put him into a seat in the back row of a striptease club next to my Soho office, where I went back to collect him a little later; he was gone, but I soon found him in a nearby pub. I knew he was having dinner with Tony Mayer, a cultural attaché at the French Embassy, and took him to Mayer's home. I was invited to stay and it was a strange meal, Ionesco sleeping for most of it in the spare room. He was terrified that his talent was passing away – he had never been able to understand his theatrical success, much as he enjoyed it – and his joint fears, of dying and of sinking back into anonymity, occupied all his thoughts. But it was from just this fear that his work in all its poignancy emerged. His early plays were above all based on the contrast of language, the Romanian of his infancy and the French that he learnt after he moved to Paris. The same objects have different names, catchphrases different connotations and associations in different languages, and in any case the cultural differences between nationalities mean that life has to be learnt again from a different point of view when you move from one country to another. When he started learning English in Bristol he was able to observe factors in English behaviour which were very different from those he knew from his past elsewhere, and this emerges strongly in his play *La Cantatrice chauve* (*The Bald Prima Donna*, or *The Bald Soprano* in the different American translation) where he investigates the nature of everyday English conversation, so different from European. My relationship with Ionesco varied widely from the years when I first knew him, living in a Paris suburb, still unaccustomed to his early success, to the later years when he became a fashionable literary figure, earning good royalties for a while from Germany in particular, and then settling down in Montparnasse to a more modest existence. He was always jealous of Beckett, especially of his indifference to celebrity, and furious when Beckett won the Nobel Prize in 1969 instead of himself. His fear of death was equalled by his fear of sinking back into anonymity with changing fashion. He had an easy death. Lying down after feeling unwell at lunchtime, he died in his sleep.

Ionesco's biggest problem was with drink. He had to do this as secretly as possible, as his wife was always hiding alcohol from him. On occasion when I went to lunch at their Paris apartment, he would empty my glass every time his wife left the room, calling for her to refill it when she returned.

My relationship with Samuel Beckett was of course very different, but from the Seventies onwards we seldom stayed up late. When in London, usually to supervise a production of a play at the Royal Court or Riverside Studios, he was often put up at the Hyde Park Hotel, overlooking the park where he had spent time in London before the war, and he would go to look for familiar old landmarks, such as the "cockpit" which plays a part in the novel *Murphy*. I would often pick him up there and go to a local fish restaurant. In Paris we just met for dinner and then separated. On occasion we met in other places, a couple of times in Berlin. On one such occasion in that city, as I have related in *Pursuit*, he again met Burroughs, but Beckett was very preoccupied with the play he was rehearsing and was not willing to give more than a few minutes to seeing Bill and a group of Americans, including Allen Ginsberg and Susan Sontag, who were with him. Burroughs was hurt because he wanted Beckett to treat him as a serious writer on his own level, but Sam read very few of his contemporaries and had never read any Burroughs. Of the three he seemed most interested in Susan Sontag, who was meeting him for the first time.

Beckett was always happy on these working visits because the Germans treated him with a courtesy and an understanding that he rarely found elsewhere, giving him as much rehearsal time as he needed, and never trying to impose actors on him as had usually happened in Britain and frequently in France. His brilliant production of *Waiting for Godot*, created for the Schiller Theater in 1975, had established him in German minds as the best possible director of his own work and thereafter he could do no wrong.* He was able to bring a lightness and a balletic quality to *Godot* that even Walter Asmus, his assistant on the Berlin production, who later published voluminous diaries and commentaries about that occasion and Beckett's working methods, was never able to accurately reproduce. Beckett's German had been good since the Thirties, but his working visits to German theatres and television studios enabled him to improve his mastery of it and he became totally fluent, and in the professional theatre developed a full technical vocabulary.

If Beckett's reputation, and his audience and readers, continued growing during the Seventies, the same cannot be said of the other writers in the Minuit stable. Robbe-Grillet remained the star of the *nouveau roman* group, but his interests had moved more towards the possibilities of films, not only because there was more money involved, but because the medium gave him more effective ways of portraying the workings of the mind and memory; he was not to do much more in the novel: *Topologie d'une cité fantôme* (*Topology of a Phantom City*), published in 1976, was really his last *nouveau roman*, until *La Reprise* in 2002. *Djinn* (1981) is really a clever academic exercise, which was written for American students of French; it is an entertaining thriller, where every chapter becomes more complex in its grammatical structure and style. The title is the French pronunciation of *Jean*. He continued to write film scripts and direct his own films, but the strong erotic and often sadistic content, usually meant that these ended up in sex cinemas rather than in art houses. His autobiographical volumes *Le Miroir qui revient* (*Ghosts in the Mirror*), published in 1984, and its sequel *Angélique, ou l'enchantement* (*Angélique, or the Enchantment*), published in 1988, read much of the time like novels and he has no objection to their being classified as such. "Call them novels if you like," he has said to me on more than one occasion. They were part of the vogue of the Seventies and Eighties where writers moving into their senior years began to look back to their childhoods or youth. Beckett's *Company* was part of it. Nathalie Sarraute brought out *Childhood*, in which the old lady in her Eighties which she had become, carries out a dialogue with her own childhood self of around six or seven years old, trying to understand why her mother had taken her away from her father in Russia to live in France. Her theory of "tropisms" is given a new dimension in the memory and the questions of the older women as they open up the mind of the child, trying to understand the adult world and the painful separation of her parents. Marguerite Duras published L'Amant (The Lover), an account – whether it is true or partly so, or entirely fictitious continues to be debated by her critics – of an early affair with a Chinese lover from a rich family. This became the top best-seller in France in 1983 and it also won the Prix Goncourt. I had been publishing Duras at no great profit for decades, not only her novels but also her plays and film scripts, but she abruptly left me as her British publisher, and Barney Rosset as her American one, the minute she could command large advances from big commercial houses. When I telephoned her to remonstrate and point out how much had been done for her over the years and at what cost, she was neither pleasant nor polite.

"I want the biggest, richest publisher I can get," she told me. "I owe you nothing. Adieu!" And she hung up.

Marguerite Duras had never been much personally liked. She was as demanding in the theatre as she had been to her various publishers in different countries, switching her allegiance between translators, and always believing any derogatory remark made by one against the other. In France she left Gallimard to go to Minuit, then went back, and then back again. Minuit were very lucky to have her at the time of L'Amant, but she returned to Gallimard the minute Lindon voiced the slightest criticism of one of her later novels, L'Amant de la Chine du nord (The North Chinese Lover), in which she plagiarized her own earlier success. Nathalie Sarraute often talked about Duras in tones of icy irony. "How wonderful it must be to be like her," she would say. "How lucky to be able to love yourself so much! How wonderful it must feel! I wish I could love myself that way." The thought probably gave her the title for the novel she wrote when over ninety: You Don't Love Yourself.

Minuit in the Seventies and Eighties developed a school of younger writers, who had little to do with the nouveau roman, which had begun to be derided as old hat, although I personally saw nothing in these successors that was as intellectually stimulating. There was a return to the well-written social novel, and Gothic tendencies came back as well, but perhaps even more with such other European writers as Umberto Eco, a Queneau-like philosopher who wrote novels with his tongue in his cheek, full of literary jokes and pastiche, mocking current literary fashions, best-sellerdom and the tendency of the writers to connect everything to everything else. There were many new formulas from authors like Michel Tournier who attracted large followings, but somehow the excitement of the earlier years in French literature had abated. There was no central figure around which argument could develop and the big names were disappearing. Jean-Paul Sartre had died in April 1980, still enunciating new ideas, still interested in politics, but no longer sticking to any fixed position. A year older than Beckett, he died much younger: they had an equal number of similarities and dissimilarities, both bohemian by temperament, generous to others, living largely in their minds, and familiar figures in the streets and cafés of Paris; but Beckett was more austere intellectually and never believed that anything he did, said, or wrote could ever change the course of events: people come to their own destinies, largely through chance, and he believed, with regret, that human nature is unchangeable – that of the individual and that of the masses. Beckett was basically an aristocrat in his thinking; he could sometimes help individuals but not populations, certainly not humanity as a whole.

During the Seventies and Eighties English-language literature continued to be translated into French, German and Italian, but there was much less done the other way. Publishers wanted best-sellers, and most European fiction was too clever or muted for American or British taste. I had a French novel, set in New York, that offered no particular difficulty to the reader with strong, raunchy homosexual content, and a strong plot, which was rejected by all the obvious New York publishers because it was "too well written". This was Yves Navarre's *Sweet Tooth*. Genre fiction took over, especially the spy novel, and of course crime and detective fiction kept its readership, although suffering a constant loss to TV. The excitement of the genuinely new was only occasionally present in the writing of the Seventies and Eighties, with cleverness admired more than depth. Saul Bellow became the great American writer, and even more so after he won the Nobel Prize in 1976. Literature was only newsworthy again when the fatwa was issued against Salman Rushdie after publication of *The Satanic Verses*.

Rushdie was one of a wave of Indian and Pakistani writers who emerged at about the same time in Seventies Britain, mostly dealing with the problems of the sizeable, but not very noticeable, community of immigrants from the Indian sub-continent that had considerably changed the quality of British life. Suddenly, from the Sixties onwards, it had become possible to shop for food and some other products after five-thirty in the afternoon and on weekends. This had previously been inconceivable because the British shopkeeper wanted to be at home, probably in front of his television set, by six; the convenience of his customers did not concern him much. The new immigrants were mostly small businessmen who wanted above all to survive and succeed, and they often needed to send money to their families and relatives back home; they became the new achievers, sometimes the butt of racialist attacks and certainly not much liked, because they did not mix much with the indigenous population. The Pakistanis in particular worked hard, saved money, and some became rich. Intellectuals emerged from among them because in the Labour years free education was available at all levels if you could pass exams. Some of them became writers who then described the communities that had produced them, including their segregated lives, their problems and the racial prejudice to which they were subjected, not only from sections of the public, but also from unsympathetic authority, including the police and officialdom. One such writer was Hanif Kureishi, whose plays were first performed at the Royal Court Theatre, where he became "Writer in Residence" and went on to write successful films about the Pakistanis in Britain. Salman Rushdie had been brought up in India, but educated in Britain, and his novels gave a sense of recent Indian history very different from the India pictured by British historians, where events were seen from the outlook of the Raj. Rushdie wrote novels set in both countries, and they detailed the problems of adapting to British life; the difficulties endured by Hindu and Pakistani immigrants were an important part of his subject matter. He brought a Gothic, imaginative and supernatural flavour into his novels, which were also often satirical, funny, biting in the way they attacked the outdated local customs, and the taboos of those who had brought their culture and way of life with them into an industrial society that had become radically altered in the Sixties. There could have been trouble in the Muslim community arising from Rushdie's earlier novels long before *The Satanic Verses*, but the scandal aroused by that extraordinary work gave a perfect pretext to a sizeable minority that was becoming affluent, but still had no respect or clout. Now it began to flex its muscles. Suddenly the British government, and authority generally, had to take this ignored minority seriously. Its vote could sway elections in marginal constituencies, and if it took to the streets the situation could become ugly. In a sense, Rushdie and his enemies in the Muslim world were working together to give a culture, that wanted to be part of, but at the same time different from, the British one, its *raison d'être*. The Muslims began to have their demands taken seriously, particularly the most important: education. They wanted their own schools to bring up their young in the Islamic tradition; and on the media, especially the BBC, time had to be found so that Muslim fundamentalists could air their views and beliefs alongside Christian or Jewish viewpoints, in everyday and religious affairs.

Although the old haunts of Saint-Germain-des-Prés and Montparnasse were still places where you met your friends, they were no longer areas where any but a few of the more affluent intellectuals could afford to live. The suburbs of Paris began to acquire their own little groups of writers and artists. This on its own encouraged many who intended to stay on in Paris to improve their French and become part of the local community. The new publications that now appeared were first launched in the centre: *Paris Métro* was successfully relaunched in 1976 and *Passion* soon after. The first was an imitation of New York's *Village Voice*, the second of *Interview*. *Frank* started in 1984, each issue appearing only when its editor, David Applefield, could afford it. It followed the formula of little magazines of the past: new fiction and poetry, critical articles on literature, interviews, extracts from works in progress. The editor, like so many before him, earned what he could by teaching, not only courses in Paris at those centres that had been set up by the American Cultural Centre and American universities that had Paris branches, but often giving or taking part in seminars outside France. He travelled when he could to find writers, even publishing an issue of mainly Congolese writers.* From the Rue Monge near the Sorbonne he moved to the suburban town of Vincennes, from which he began to issue little guides for anglophones about the things going on in Paris, which were paid for by advertisers, and he followed this with a more ambitious publishing venture, the "Inside Out" series of city guides that not only gave the usual information of where to eat, stay and shop, but catered to visitors who wanted to know more than the casual tourist and enjoy the city on a limited budget. *Paris Inside Out*,* for instance, told its readers about Jim Haynes's Sunday-evening open houses and other offbeat activities that would appeal to the adventurous, the young, the lonely and those with bohemian tastes. Affordable housing increasingly drew intellectuals to the outer perimeter of Paris where the café life was less colourful but no worse than in central Paris, only more French. Nevertheless English and other languages could regularly be heard, from the late Eighties, at suburban café tables, and the conversations were not very different from those at the Café Tournon and the Café de Flore.

Joseph Strick became a regular Paris resident from the time of making *Tropic of Cancer*, and eventually could be found, with his French wife, in an apartment block just opposite the Café Tournon itself. Here I sometimes met him. But the café had changed. In the Sixties and Seventies it was possible to stay until two in the morning and many tables had chess sets. I had played with Beckett there several times; there was one occasion when I watched a young couple playing, and at the end of their game was invited by the husband to play his wife: he then disappeared. I had the distinct impression that I was expected to do more than play chess with her, but did not follow the matter up. The Café Tournon, no longer a writer's hangout, began to close early and then the chess sets disappeared. After 1975 one only rarely saw customers reading proofs or writing in an exercise book, and the excellent second-hand bookshop next to it closed its doors; there were obviously fewer customers who would pay for a first edition or a Sartre novel or an edition of Rimbaud's poems printed on good hand-made paper and illustrated by a good artist. New boutiques began to replace the antiquarian bookshops, cheap cafés and little theatres around Saint-Germain and the Luxembourg. They sold convincing copies of the latest *haute couture* fashions and many of them had the names of top designers. The French yuppies were taking over the left bank.

8

Barney Rosset remained a cult figure throughout the Seventies, but he was having his difficulties and his fortune had shrunk. The departure of Dick Seaver meant a certain decline in Grove's high literary image, especially in European fiction and drama; the firm no longer acquired as much of the cream of the new novelists and playwrights, and many of their best-known names left them for other publishers. Dick Seaver first joined Viking Press, and when it was taken over by Penguin Books from England, he became Penguin's American editor, leaving his wife Jeannette to run his own small imprint, Richard Seaver Books, which consisted of some authors who had followed him from Grove and others who might have gone there had he remained. Later he moved on to Holt, Rinehart & Winston, which was later taken over by outside interests and separated into different companies. Seaver then became the publisher of Henry Holt only. But he was pushed out when the financial results were disappointing and next moved to Little, Brown who put him in charge of a new imprint, based in New York, Arcade Publishing, which he later bought out in a management takeover in 1992.

The formula that lured Seaver away to Viking was an interesting one that the larger publishing houses had devised to keep down their costs and to get the best editorial minds to work for them cheaply. The formula was simple: the editor-publisher was given a budget to produce a certain number of books a year, perhaps about twenty; the budget had to cover his costs of production (paper, printing, binding etc.), his entire overhead, including his employees, advertising, rent for the office space allocated to him, and of course, his own salary. If he paid himself too much or spent too much on his own expenses, he would have less with which to publish books, and hence lower sales and profits, which would probably lead to his contract being terminated. The prestige of having his own imprint encouraged several ambitious editors to be as economical as possible in order to show a reasonable profit and keep the arrangement going. Tony Godwin, who in the Sixties had been the senior editor in charge of fiction at Penguin Books in London, was lured to New York under such an arrangement, but he died within three years. Seaver, however, made it work, and when *Viking* and Penguin merged he was wearing several hats. This did lead to his neglecting his own imprint as he became more of an establishment publisher, divorced ever more from literary publishing by the need to find best-sellers. He was lucky, after Holt, to get a similar position at Little, Brown, and this led to his owning Arcade. But it also doomed him to being once again a small independent publisher, a situation which involves many sacrifices and the need to face alone the inevitable problems of a cut-throat world. Seaver's link with the serious literature of mid-century Europe and America was inevitably broken, although he did continue to publish some literary authors such as Octavio Paz.

Fred Jordan stayed on at Grove longer, but left twice to take up other senior positions, once with the American office of Methuen and once with Prentice-Hall. He returned to Grove Press after failing to produce satisfactory results for his other employers. Originally a German who had spent some time in England, he was familiar with European publishers, and through them with some authors; this helped him to acquire a number of prestigious but not necessarily saleable writers for the American market. His judgements appear to have been based more on authors' established reputations in their own countries than on any personal assessment. But he knew how to get Barney Rosset's protection when in trouble and how to ingratiate himself with a man whose temperament and lack of concentration made him depend on the work of others. Barney only knew how to be a boss: he could not do the everyday work of a publishing company. Jordan was always taken back at Grove, but when Barney finally lost the firm he had founded and financed for more than three decades, Jordan's loyalty went to the new management, where for a while he was the only employee who knew the list well enough to establish some continuity. Barney Rosset had done a great deal for him, but when the writs were flying and the battle of words were becoming ugly, he made it clear that he had no time for Barney and certainly did not want to see him return. "Barney had it coming to him," he said to me at the time that I was trying to make a rapprochement, and he did not speak well of his former mentor. After Barney Rosset left Grove in 1986, the expensive new management put in by Ann Getty and George Weidenfeld, the new owners (about whom more will be said later), soon ran into massive loss, and Fred Jordan, realizing that his own future there was insecure, applied for and was given the job at Pantheon Books, which had just been vacated by André Schiffrin, fired for losing too much money with a prestigious list, expensively acquired, about whom I will have more to say in a few pages. Fred Jordan had put himself into a possibly difficult future position with his move: he had never shown any special promotional abilities, and he was now in charge of an imprint with a record of losing money because of its inability to sell its books sufficiently well to make a profit.

Selling an intellectual author in the US or Britain depends – and I am speaking from personal experience – on a combination of factors, the most important of which are careful planning and hard work. A publisher has to find ways to get the names of his authors known and respected, and the best ways to do this is to obtain reviews and news coverage. It is not enough just to send a new book out to the review media. The publisher has to lobby literary editors, think up ways of obtaining publicity, both for the author personally if he is available and willing, and for the book itself, which means getting the author interviewed wherever possible. The book should be judicially advertised if there is money to do so, less for the benefit of the public than to catch the eyes of other authors and reviewers, often looking for their own names in advertisements. It helps to get the buzz going. Small publishers can afford to do little of this, but they can lobby, and most importantly they could, until the Nineties, spend time talking to booksellers, who used to like meeting and knowing publishers, about the nature and value of their list, rather than leaving it to publishers' sales reps, who with a few exceptions sell only what is easy. They take little time to learn about the merits of a literary author because they are interested primarily in commission. Reps, especially those who work only on commission, are unwilling to spend time on books that will sell in small quantities and perhaps not at all. This applied less to those who worked for larger houses on a fixed salary, but only very marginally less. I have always felt that a publisher can do as much good away from his desk as behind it, especially if he is spending time with booksellers. If he is enthused or at least taught by whoever selected the book originally for publication, he would pass some of that knowledge on to his customers. It is principally by word of mouth that small publishers eventually get their more difficult, but ultimately rewarding, writers established. André Schiffrin, a man of taste and knowledge, had a wonderful opportunity, but he never understood what needed to be done to create interest in an author by arousing intellectual curiosity and by hard lobbying where it did most good: among academics, among other writers, literary critics and pundits, and in the book trade, which, although dominated by big commercial chains, used to be always led in taste by a few dedicated bookmen who loved books, to make discoveries, and to be on the cutting edge of new work. They were the booksellers who wanted to read themselves but it was only the odd bookseller who was given sufficient credit on the cultural scene: Sylvia Beach in Paris and Frances Steloff of the Gotham Book Mart in New York were good examples, but most towns had such a bookseller, which is why there were remote readers for Joyce and Proust, Kafka and Beckett, Svevo and Olson, authors to whom one usually had to be brought by an enthusiast.

All this was to change under globalization which, spreading to the book trade, had the effect after the early Eighties in the US, and a decade later in Britain, of allowing commercially run chains to kill the independents by ruthless undercutting, made possible often by the willingness of publishers to offer massive discounts for large purchases of a popular title. Rumours abounded in the US as to the sources of the money that made this possible. Many saw it as a way to launder money into real estate or other properties that were above investigation. In Britain the empire of good literary and general bookshops, particularly those created by Tim Waterstone and which bore his name, was, because of too rapid expansion, and a series of financial takeover deals, eventually to fall into the hands of administrators with no interest in books other than making money from those that were the easiest to sell to an ever less-demanding public. Variety and choice were drastically reduced, the more specialized or intellectual titles ceased to be stocked, and bookshop staff became younger and cheaper to employ because neither knowledge of books nor interest in them was necessary. In fact either of these qualities, and enthusiasm even more so, was seen by head office as a negative quality because such staff would want to broaden the stock. 1997 saw the demise of The Net Book Agreement, and I was the only publisher willing to go to court to defend this crucial protection for good booksellers, which restricted the abilities of bookselling chains – now in fact more like supermarkets dealing in books but treating them as vegetables – to discount best-sellers in order to dominate the market and make more profit. In contrast the "loi Lang" in France protected culture against greed. But all this is a later story, included in this volume by hindsight.

Although Beckett is one of the most taught modern writers, and enjoyed while still alive the reputation of having had more books written about him in his lifetime than any other person in history, he is still the least understood, although that is gradually changing. He is taught more for the depth of his learning than for any other reason, an erudition that was unimportant to him and remains unimportant to all except the most industrious of his readers. Beckett is enjoyable to read once one has thrown the misconceptions, that some academics in particular have engendered, out of the window. He had a perfectly clear vision of what life is about, and saw it as an unfortunate accident, a tragedy, both because mankind has very little natural kindness, and man mistreats his fellow humans out of some innate cruel instinct; only a few civilizations have occasionally been able to control that cruelty for short periods in their history. Even if an individual is one of the lucky few, born into a period of peace and prosperity, and with creative abilities and appreciations, death soon ends it all: the cup is quickly snatched away. Given all that, Beckett's vision of the world is irrefutable, except by dogmatic fundamentalists and those who believe that life is only an ante-room to a better existence in some after-life; all we can do is to make the best of things. Beckett enjoyed what he could in life according to his frugal and aesthetic tastes, and being a writer he set out to open our eyes and entertain us at the same time. He is wonderfully funny when he satirizes religions and the placebos that are on offer from our different prophets and gurus. He can tell a story as well as anyone else, but his stories are not fairy tales; they are about real life, and can put off tender stomachs. But to anyone who can face the facts of human existence and not worry about some received dogma being thrown into question, Beckett is more rewarding than any other modern author; addictive is perhaps a better word. Here is where the bookseller of taste could come into his own: he must know enough about an author to be able to recommend him with a few words of background, and know enough about his customers not to recommend a "strong" author to a person whose mind is ringed around with caveats and can only get through life with the comfort of a religion that allows no questions, or a political outlook that is totally conventional or conservative. Many see Beckett as being profoundly political and they are not wrong, because he was a novelist who never left you in any doubt about where he stood, but he was not a proselytizer, because he believed that evil will ultimately always come out on top. Beckett became a man of political action during the Nazi invasion of France, but mainly out of loyalty to friends and because it never occurred to him to do anything else. He would shrug his shoulders when terrible world events were happening because, unlike Sartre, he believed that nothing he could do intellectually would make any difference. Academics are fascinated by him because they perceive him as a major literary figure, but unfortunately they usually overlook his entertainment value.

Beckett's black humour and his portrayal of basic truths, and the simple humanity that underlies his creative drive, can make him hugely enjoyable to the open-minded. It is to the enthusiasm of adventurous readers, often stimulated by booksellers who read, that has spread the word and is responsible for his fame. It is easy to imagine a situation in which this expatriate Irish writer never emerged from obscurity, like so many other major talents that were swallowed up in the horrors and indifferences of the twentieth century. It is our good fortune that he has been lucky enough to become widely known.

In criticizing some publishers who did not succeed in doing their job properly, that is to say by building a public for the discoveries they made and published, I have to recognize a basic difference between attitudes in Europe and the US (as well as in Britain), and it has to do with ego and self-perception, as well as with the atmosphere of offices and work patterns. An editor's job is done principally at home or in an empty office: he needs to be alone, which is not easy with visitors coming and going in a controlled and comfortable temperature and the knowledge that every square foot occupied costs real money. That was not how Trocchi worked in his heyday, nor Girodias when he was doing his real publishing, nor Kurt Wolff before he went to America, nor even Dick Seaver before he became part of the Madison Avenue scene. Bob Gottlieb, shortly after he moved from Simon & Schuster, where he was the "egghead" editor of such authors as Michel Butor (from the Minuit stable), to Knopf, told me that he did not believe in "printing paper", that is in producing good, literary titles without the personal will – or even the chance, when part of a big conglomerate like Random House – to be involved in the whole process; this would include planning the promotion and selling of each book oneself, instead of leaving it to someone in another department who would not even be interested in reading it. America still had some good small publishers on the European model, which is not usually departmentalized in the same way. Michael Braziller (son of George) of Persea Books, Noel Young of Capra Press, John Martin of Black Sparrow and John O'Brien of Dalkey Archive, some still alive, spring to mind. Barney Rosset, who has been woven like a filigree thread through the narrative of this volume, had exactly the right outlook: what he lacked was discipline and concentration. His taste was instinctively good and so was his attitude, and no one ever doubted his courage; his money enabled him to do what he wanted, but he lacked a sense of proportion and would allow no one to give him advice. He could not do real work, that is to read and select, edit what is chosen, deal with printers, write advertising copy and blurbs, and get away from his desk to sell his books to sympathetic booksellers on the same wavelength. That is why he eventually lost the company he built up, but he did resist becoming part of a bigger company, which is usually creative death, for many years. Schiffrin, on the other hand, always tried to work within the establishment. Unlike Gottlieb, he "printed paper". He never managed to get salesmen to seek out the literary outlets and his books became merchandised by the same machinery as all the coffee-table books and best-selling light fiction that Random House, his parent company, published. He either was not able to, or did not realize, the necessity of creating a different sales environment for titles that must build their reputation through the literary bookshops and in the universities. This suggests a laziness and a complacency that an independent publisher can never afford. But a laziness also lies behind Schiffrin's tendency to buy authors who had already been published by others, where most of the groundwork to establish the authors' reputations among the more discerning readers had already been done. There is a French expression that applies to him: a "*pique-assiette*", someone who eats off other people's plates.

Barney Rosset had published Marguerite Duras for many years, as I had done in Britain. Schiffrin had offered a large advance to obtain rights to *The Lover*, her breakthrough novel, thereby taking away from us both (because Collins, in London, followed suit for British rights in collusion with Pantheon) an author with a prestigious reputation that we had both worked hard to earn for her, at the precise moment when she became commercial. Few of Schiffrin's authors were his own discoveries. He only had to wait to make his offer until a smaller publisher would have difficulty in paying the large advance demanded. In the case of Duras, Barney Rosset could probably have found the money to equal the offer had he moved quickly, but he was numbed by what he saw as Duras's treachery. The shy and vulnerable side of Rosset always made him turn away and accept a situation where he felt let down, unappreciated or unloved. In my own case there was no way I could have met the Collins offer. Authors' loyalties were being much tested at this time and the role of the literary agent, who had increasingly supplanted the editor as the author's confidant and adviser, had much to do with this. The growth of the big publishing companies, brought about by mergers, takeovers and acquisition by conglomerates, and lack of continuity, as editors changed jobs, had alienated the author from the publisher, except in an ever-smaller number of cases. And as the big publishers were getting even bigger, the smaller ones were having increasing difficulty in maintaining even a small part of the market. Agents were often making decisions on behalf of their authors.

I was to have the same experience later with André Schiffrin over Claude Simon, an author who had long been published in the US by George Braziller. Braziller, however, followed commercial practice, even with his literary authors, who by definition would sell slowly and take years to develop a following, by remaindering when sales dropped too low. He never looked at a good and developing author as a long-term asset to be nurtured and continuously pushed, and as a result writers such as Simon were soon out of print, with publishing rights reverting to the copyright owner. In the case of Simon, another member of the Minuit stable of *nouveau romanciers*, rights came back to Jerôme Lindon, and I was able to acquire American rights at the same time as British ones. I had come late to Claude Simon, having always admired his work, but being unable to publish everything that suited my list, I let him go, in the Fifties, to Jonathan Cape in London. Cape, having more stamina than Braziller, kept his early novels in print until well into the Seventies, then dropped him. They had been encouraged until then by his high reputation among British academics who read French, and who saw him as a successor to Proust.

Claude Simon is an interesting figure, rather invisible as a personality in literary Paris, living mainly in a small village, Salse, in the Pyrénées, where he wrote his long simulations of the mind remembering and thinking, in sentences that often went on for pages. At the centre of his writing is a preoccupation with war, in particular the Spanish Civil

War that he had witnessed as a sympathizer with the Republic, and the Second World War in which he had fought as a cavalry officer. The events of 1940, and the fall of France as it had affected both French soldiers and civilians, are the subject matter of his best novels, but the events are seen – or remembered – by long stream-of-consciousness sequences, interrupted by free association, rather as if a camera were roaming over a battlefield, and remembered past episodes in the lives of those fighting, running away, or dying; these were constantly dissolving into flashbacks and then reappearing as present reality. Although Simon continued to enjoy high prestige and small but regular sales in France, his reputation had gone into decline in English-speaking countries after the Sixties, when I acquired rights to some of his principal novels. Then I continued to translate and publish the new ones. By a lucky accident, Simon had long had a supporter in the secretary of the Nobel Literature Prize committee, who lobbied hard for him in 1983. It went, after much argument to William Golding, and for the first time some of the squabbles that lie behind the Nobel Prize awards were reported in the press. Having not won, it was assumed that Simon's day had passed, especially as the secretary of the prize was retiring, but to the general surprise he won in 1985, although with much less publicity than when he had nearly won two years earlier. The novel that turned the scale in 1985 was *The Georgics*, a massive and complex work that contrasted two poles of human existence, living in fragile security in times of peace, and trying to survive in times of war and revolution. In France Simon was then lionized, treated as a national hero, with exhibitions about his career, including his war experiences, the basis of so much of his fiction, touring France and abroad. But elsewhere there were complaints about the difficulty of reading him, and when I published *The Georgics* in London and New York the results were disappointing, mainly because very few competent reviewers could be found, by even the major newspapers, to review the book. One reason, as I pointed out to Jérôme Lindon, who had to agree, was that the long introductory section, a description of the statue of one of the protagonists, a Napoleonic general, was extremely difficult to follow, and bore little relevance to the very exciting events of most of the novel. Nevertheless although sales were modest, they were better than most other intellectual titles that I was publishing in the States at that time (I had started a New York office in 1979) and I worked to keep the book and other Simon titles on bookshop shelves as a contemporary classic.

Then Schiffrin moved in, made an offer for the next Simon novel that I had naturally expected to publish in English as a matter of course, and repeated his manoeuvre with *The Lover*, acquiring both American and British right to *L'Acacia*. I noted with some grim humour that the total sales must have been in the very low hundreds, because I saw it in no bookshop in the States at a time when I was travelling around many of them, and that British rights were never sold. Shortly after, Schiffrin was dismissed, with much sympathetic publicity from the press.

Interestingly, André Schiffrin had been a later successor to Kurt Wolff, who, having been one of the great publishers of the century in Germany until Hitler forced him to leave, then became editor of this small but significant list in 1942. Later it became one of the prestige literary branches of Random House. Wolff, in earlier years, had been in an excellent position to carry out raids on the lists of smaller publishers, but he never did.

Losing authors was one of Rosset's later problems, and the main reason was his shyness and lack of follow-through where his authors were concerned. It was essential for a publisher like Grove to keep in touch with authors socially as well as professionally, to attend first nights of their plays, invite them to their parties and show an interest in what they were currently writing. Barney simply did not do this and as a result lost Tom Stoppard, Edward Albee, and others, including many who have been named earlier. For a time Seaver and Jordan cosseted authors when still at Grove, but there was no one to do so when they left. Rosset's sales and cash flow diminished, and he found that he was steadily losing money. Barney always remembered that his father had been a tycoon with a good head for figures and financial deals, and in imitation he played the stock market, gambled in property and tried to make up his publishing losses on Wall Street. During the Sixties he had bought a large building on Houston Street as an investment, but he then filled most of it with Grove Press employees, taking on more staff to fill the space. Any business that is not closely supervised by someone who knows what each member of the staff is doing is headed for trouble. There was no supervision at Grove and no incentive to work hard. People arrived and left when they wanted, and in the summer, when Barney tended to be away at East Hampton, 'summer hours' were liberally interpreted, nearly everyone leaving early after doing what I would consider very little work. Idleness leads to mischief. At one point the company was picketed by feminists, and Rosset had a strike of his female employees, their grounds being that much of his erotic publishing was demeaning to women. Barney claimed that he was a scapegoat for others and even that the CIA or FBI, neither of which liked him, were behind it. But for many of them a strike may simply have been a protest to relieve the boredom. A publishing company that could easily have been run by a dozen people was at one point employing two hundred. Eventually sanity returned, and at new premises in his fortress-like building on Houston Street, very near the old one, Grove Press and Barney himself, occupied different floors.

At one point with the banks pressing him hard, Barney decided on a confrontation. He told them that there was no way they could get their money back by pressuring. If the company were to go bankrupt, authors had the right to recover their copyright and go to another publisher; the only assets were the unsold books, most of which, with rights reverted, would become worthless except as waste paper. He reached an accommodation where most of the debt was wiped out. But the crunch came in 1985 when the company was once again in very deep trouble. Suddenly help was at hand in the portly shape of Lord Weidenfeld. George Weidenfeld had become a Baron (a member of the House of Lords), as a result of publishing one of the most unsaleable books of the century, the much sanitized memoirs of Harold Wilson, Prime Minister in the middle Sixties. Wilson had previously made him a knight and was often present at Weidenfeld's frequent and much publicized parties. George loved entertaining and bringing together well-known people from different areas of public life and the arts, and he himself never missed an opportunity to meet those who could be of help to himself, or to increase his acquaintanceship among the famous and socially prominent. He once pulled me aside at the Frankfurt Book Fair and accused me: "John, I hear you've been saying something beastly about me!"

"And what would that be, George?"

"I hear you've called me a snob."

"I don't remember saying that, George, but it's possible. I don't see your complaint. You *are* a snob. You know it as well as I do."

In fact George Weidenfeld's saving grace was his sense of humour. He could usually laugh at himself as well as at others and he was a shrewd observer of other people's weaknesses and foibles, which he exploited with delicacy. It explained his survival with a publishing list that was on the whole intelligently selected, but slow selling. I had brought him his biggest best-seller in *Lolita*, but few of his other titles sold well enough to cover his always heavy overhead and the cost of his entertaining. In the middle Eighties it was well known that he was in financial trouble. Always in the past he had managed, through his powers of persuasion and flattery, to raise more money when he needed it, but this time he was having difficulty. He did a typical thing, for him, and went to a health farm in California where he was certain to meet some very rich and, with luck, some very gullible, people. It was there that he met Ann Getty, wife of Gordon Getty, heir to the oil fortune, and a reclusive composer. He talked her into starting an American publishing company with him, but what he needed was not to start up a new one – that would have been difficult, and the Getty financial advisers would then have had to look closely into his own past track record in Britain – but to acquire an existing one. George must have known of Barney's trouble and he approached him to buy Grove, although it was not put that way. What he wanted to do, so he told Barney, was to help by putting more money into the company to keep their wonderful literary list going. Barney would continue to run it.

Barney took the bait, and control of Grove Press passed to the Wheatland Corporation, set up for the purpose of buying Grove with Getty money and Weidenfeld's experience. Grove might have terrible balance sheets, but at least it had prestige and glamour. At the last minute Barney had doubts and nearly backed out, but his situation was desperate. He had only owned minority shares in his company; most of the investors he had attracted over the years had mentally long written off their stake in Grove, but now they had money for their shares. Barney himself only received $400,000, all of which eventually went to pay taxes or lawyers.

New money was then invested in Grove by Ann Getty, the list was expanded, and Weidenfeld was able to obtain funds for his London company by starting Weidenfeld, USA which now shared its facilities and staff with Grove. New, high-powered executives went to work for Weidenfeld's American company to which Rosset and his staff were in effect subsidiary. I heard George's side of the deal over lunch in London where the question of my own firm joining the package was mooted, although this came to nothing. Weidenfeld told me of his bad moment when the whole Grove package nearly fell through because Barney, looking at the contract one last time, had become nervous. George had worked out the Getty family's revenue to the second and saw no end to the funds that would pour into his new empire. His American editors were buying books for publication, but mainly from packagers, and the titles were hardly exciting, a coffee table book on garden entertaining was one, and there was another on decorating Christmas trees. Large sums were paid out for books expected to become best-sellers, including an exposé of the *Pizza Connection* (on the Mafia) and Arthur Miller's autobiography. But Barney did not fit easily into a corporate structure: he was an individualist who had always been boss and was not accustomed to contradiction, other control or even cooperation. After a year he was suddenly fired.

It was the year of Beckett's eightieth birthday. Tom Bishop, Professor of French and Italian at New York University, a long-time devotee of Beckett and his work, and a brilliant organizer, put on, with the cooperation of the French Ministry of Culture, the French radio and such Paris supporters of Beckett's work as Jean-Louis Barrault, a big celebration at the Centre Pompidou in Paris. Barney Rosset came to it, bringing with him his current wife, Lissa, but also Anne Getty's son Peter, with a college friend from Yale. They all flew in on Concorde, Barney and Lissa at Grove's expense, a heavy cost. It was almost as if Barney was stretching his waning powers as "President" to the limit. The Getty boy had become a kind of protégé and Barney had promised to train him to be a publisher; he had even intervened at Yale to stop him being expelled. But Barney's obsessions could not be controlled, and even Peter Getty saw some of the bad side of his temper: Barney had conceived the idea that Lissa was attracted to Peter Getty because he was rich and young, and he threw a tantrum in Paris, which I witnessed.

This was of course during the time that Barney was still at Grove. The Paris celebrations were immediately followed by another Beckett-Fest in New York, also organized by Tom Bishop, and it was at this time that Rosset was told his contract was cancelled and offered a lump sum in compensation. He needed both press coverage and public support, and I took the opportunity, during an evening given over to readings of Beckett's poetry at New York University, which I was chairing, to make a gesture. Just before the last item, which I was to read myself, I made a short speech, announcing that Barney Rosset had just been fired from the company he had founded and had built into an American institution; I extolled his value to literature and American publishing. I asked for a protest and an appeal to reinstate him. The public response in the hall was warm, but Tom Bishop was a little uncomfortable; Ann Getty was a trustee of many institutions that received Getty charitable money, and one of them was New York University.

Barney then sued, but it got him nowhere. He bitterly complained that all that mattered in law was having big money and the expensive lawyers it could buy. But it was not the end of the road for him. He started a new publishing company, Rosset and Co., then changed the name to Blue Moon: most of the titles resembled his old Victorian Library imprint, the most profitable side of Grove's catalogue. But he also published one last Beckett. When ousted, he had asked Sam if there was any other text that he could bring out in New York under his new imprint to keep his old connection. The author thought hard: his first novel, *Dream of Fair to Middling Women*, had never been published; it had been offered to publishers in 1932, but rejected. He had gone on to complete a second book of stories, *More Pricks than Kicks*, and he had incorporated some of *Dream* into it. After the war he had refused to countenance publication of his juvenile novel, heavily Joycean in its style, and now, after reflection, he stuck to his decision not to release it. To help Barney, he decided to write a new text instead, and produced *Stirrings Still*, a short, very beautiful piece of prose, about a man, a writer, alone in a room, unable to leave it, who remembers nostalgically the world outside. It was his own situation very nearly. This was sent to Barney and I was told that I had the British rights. We both heard that he was continuing with a second section, and in this the man in the room finds himself outside, in the fields and the woods, although obviously only in his imagination. And then came a coda, a short last section, ending with a very Joycean cadence; it finished the work with a resigned acceptance of approaching death, quoting from one of his own late poems. If Barney had done nothing else in his life, to be the cause of this perfect, short, last prose work of Beckett's coming into existence, justified it. It was written for and dedicated to him. It is worth quoting the last lines:

> Such and much more such the hubbub in his mind so-called till nothing left from deep within but only ever fainter oh to end. No matter how no matter where. Time and grief and self so-called. Oh all to end.*

Stirrings Still, a work of only a few pages, was a little jewel, but Barney's problem was how to publish it. I came up with an idea and suggested that we should jointly issue a de luxe edition, limited to two hundred copies, and get an artist to illustrate it. Barney immediately stipulated that the artist had to be his first wife, Joan Mitchell. With some reluctance Joan provisionally agreed, and I spent a Sunday with her at her house outside Paris, reading the work together and discussing it. She said she thought she could do it. I then had to go to Australia to visit my bookseller customers. On my return I learnt that she had backed down. She had heard something adverse about me and used that as an excuse, but I think she was so much in awe of Beckett that she was unwilling to risk the challenge. I went to see Sam to discuss what other artist might be suitable. He was waiting for me in his apartment, and had, ready for me on his desk, a number of volumes illustrated by Louis le Brocquy, an Irish painter of his own generation, whose recent work had included several semi-abstract impressions of the heads of artists he knew or liked, mainly Irish painters and writers; he had already done Beckett's head several times. Whatever was acceptable to Beckett was of course fine by me, and I agreed. Barney, very upset by Joan's withdrawal, had never heard of le Brocquy, but after checking with his ex-wife, agreed with some reluctance. I went to France to see an art printer recommended by le Brocquy, who had worked with Matisse and Man Ray. *Stirrings Still* eventually appeared as an expensive well-designed limited, signed edition with le Brocquy's black-and-white graphics and a colour impression of the author's head. Beckett collectors thronged to buy it, and at £2,000 a copy both Barney and I made some profit. It was very necessary because I had my own financial problems at the time.

So did George Weidenfeld. I ran into him one Saturday afternoon at the Metropolitan Opera – a performance of *Götterdämmerung*. Unusually for him, he was on his own, and we had a brief chat about the performance. I thought him strangely muted and lacking his normal ebullience. The next day's newspapers told me why. Weidenfeld, USA had made a staggering loss, and although Grove Press's balance sheet gave no cause for joy, it was very much better than Weidenfeld's. In the next few weeks it was obvious that Weidenfeld himself had lost his credibility in the eyes of the Getty financial advisors, and probably in those of Ann Getty herself.

George Weidenfeld needs a little explanation. I first met him in 1949 in London, a time when post-war London was beginning to recover from ten years of austerity, when the Labour government was taxing the rich to the hilt, many things were in short supply, and there were opportunities for persuasive rogues to make some quick money. Those on the lower class level were known as "wide boys". On the top there were many whose guiles were stronger than their scruples, Robert Maxwell being a good example. George Weidenfeld was nearer to another English definition: he was a "character", that is to say a man of ambition, who advanced through contacts, taking risks, but always within the law, clever at getting backing from those with money to invest, a Falstaffian character who preyed on the vanity and social hopes of those trying to move in better social or intellectual circles, while charming and being useful to those already in them. He was living in a rather grand flat in Eaton Square, an address and a book-lined ambiance calculated to impress. He knew I had a rich uncle and wanted to meet him, and he could not help seeing that I had a very beautiful wife who had been a Hollywood starlet;

she led many to believe that I was much better off than in fact I was. He invited me to tea, at which, with a grandiloquent wave of his arm he casually announced: "I'm thinking of making a kind of Victorian-Edwardian marriage." In other words he intended to marry money. The lucky bride turned out to be the daughter of the managing director of Marks & Spencer, perhaps the most successful of Britain's chain stores, a girl whose last name was Sieff. Marks & Spencer were then financing him to produce Contact Books, a series of classics designed to sell only in their stores, and the forthcoming marriage undoubtedly put him into circles where he was able to advance his career, both commercially and politically, because he absented himself frequently to play a role in Israeli politics and had been for a time Chaim Weizmann's secretary. By ingratiating himself with members of the English literary establishment he eventually recruited Nigel Nicolson, the son of Sir Harold and of Vita Sackville-West to be his partner, and Weidenfeld & Nicolson was born. His Sieff marriage was short, but other rich ladies filled the gaps in subsequent years and restored his fortunes when they flagged.

During the period when he was receiving Getty money, George Weidenfeld travelled internationally with Ann, introducing her to the international jet set, including heads of state, royalty and important people in many walks of life. For George what mattered was to be visible and in the right circles, and he loved to play the host. The two of them were featured in many magazine articles and there was much speculation about their real relationship. Weidenfeld was elderly and fat but known to have been an ardent lover. He organized a conference on translation at Leeds Castle in Kent, one of England's most impressive settings, where international conferences normally take place, and announced a translation prize. Getty money was being quickly spent on dubious prestige. Because Gordon Getty was a composer and anxious to promote his music, George also organized a conference in Israel on the future of the symphony orchestra. A friend of mine, also a composer, who worked with the BBC, was invited on that occasion, and he went with his wife, an opera singer. Gordon Getty took her aside, and in the most humble way possible, asked if she would consider singing his songs. She looked them over and to get out of it said, "I'm afraid they won't suit my voice."

"Oh, that's no problem, my dear," he told her, "I can arrange them any way you like." Although he was generous to many musical institutions, Gordon Getty had considerable difficulty in being performed.

Tens of millions of dollars were lost in three years in the American publishing companies. George, knowing the bottomless depth of the

Getty purse, had simply assumed that as long as he kept Ann Getty amused, with pictures and profiles of her continuing to appear in the more glamorous magazines and newspapers, that more money would always be forthcoming. But it does not work that way in America. Ann Getty had been made to look stupid: losing large amounts of money is not acceptable in financial circles, however much prestige might be involved. Weidenfeld stopped crossing the Atlantic by Concorde, and keeping a suite at Madison Avenue's Carlyle Hotel. He disappeared from the American scene, while the two publishing companies were merged as Grove-Weidenfeld, and put under a professional commercial management. Eventually new editors were engaged, who acquired new authors and began to reprint the back list which had been largely ignored by the non-literary executives of the Weidenfeld years. Back in London, Weidenfeld kept an extremely low profile for a surprisingly long time. Then he sold out to Anthony Cheetham, then flush with money from having sold Octopus, a British group that he had earlier acquired. As with Barney Rosset, Weidenfeld remained the titular head (chairman) of the company. The Wheatland Corporation tried to sell Grove, but there were no serious buyers. A syndicate that Barney tried to put together in order to make an offer could not come up with any substantial amount of money. Grove by the end of 1992 was continuing to trade at a higher level under professional management, sustained by its back list. I had always wondered about the name of Wheatland, almost a translation of Weidenfeld's name: it apparently refers to Ann Getty's home town. Eventually Grove was merged with another publishing company, Atlantic, and Morgan Entrekin became the publisher of Grove-Atlantic. Apparently the Gettys still had a financial stake in it.

9

In early 1968 Maurice Girodias moved to New York and took an apartment at the Chelsea Hotel. He contacted Victoria Moorheim and asked her to work as an editor for the new Olympia Press that he wanted to set up in the US. With considerable misgivings and some reluctance, she agreed. He was already in touch with printers, including one he had met on a transatlantic flight, who had agreed to give him credit. He found an office on Gramercy Place and set about reprinting some of his old Olympia titles, starting with a few by Marcus van Heller (John Stephenson), but he used this pen name for other writers as well. Girodias was also looking for new titles and Vicky Moorheim was soon at work editing them. She set up a bank account for the new company, but knowing Maurice of old from Paris, insisted that she be in full charge of it, and that no cheques should go out without her knowledge; she also obtained his agreement that social security and New York taxes be accounted and paid as due. Girodias obtained a $10,000 loan from a printer in Arizona, but he used it to get himself an apartment as well as an office, ordering furniture from Macy's on credit. While getting the apartment ready to move in, he slept on the office floor on a mattress.

A serious novel, entitled *The House of Stairs* was accepted. It was eight hundred pages and Vicky Moorheim was told to chop it down to about two hundred and fifty. Clarence Major, a black writer, submitted a manuscript that was contracted and published. But trouble soon came over plagiarism, a spoof novel with which Maurice deliberately looked for trouble. Irving Wallace had brought out a novel about a pornographic trial, and Maurice Girodias was mentioned by name in it; the plot revolved around an imaginary novel entitled *The Seven Minutes*. Maurice had the idea to commission a real book, a db, and to call it *The Real Seven Minutes*. It was commissioned, written and published, with a dust jacket identical to the Irving Wallace book, giving J.J. Jadway as the author's name. It was not long before Irving Wallace's lawyer was in action, suing for damages and asking the court for a restraining order. Maurice used all his ingenuity to get around the problem, even contacting the author directly and threatening to reveal unsavoury information about him, but it did no good. An injunction was obtained and *The Real Seven Minutes* had to be withdrawn. It had been selling well at the time.

Other Olympia titles appeared, but there was always trouble. The account books were not properly kept, and in spite of his promise that this time he would not indulge in irregularities with the finances, it was impossible to restrain him. Maurice had borrowed a lump sum from someone he had met, and as usual the debt went to the back of his mind. He had obviously received some threat of physical harm, because $10,000 which he had obtained elsewhere, and which was earmarked to pay the production costs of books being printed, was diverted to pay Maurice's private debt. Money in escrow to pay social security and taxes was constantly raided by Maurice for his pocket money. When Vicky refused to allow him to use the cheque book as he wanted, he screamed at her 'this is not France,' but she was adamant. Relations became steadily worse and in the end Vicky left.

Leon Friedman had become his New York lawyer, and he was now involved in a variety of cases for Maurice. On no occasion would Girodias take Friedman's advice. Leon even took some shares in the company, mainly because Maurice could not pay his fees. One day Girodias told Friedman that he wanted to buy back his shares, giving no reason, and although the price offered was small, the lawyer was happy to get something rather than nothing. It then transpired that Maurice had found a broker who wanted to make the company public, and he was hoping to make a considerable profit by putting his shares on the market. But the scheme fell through and the offer to the public was never made.

Maurice's behaviour at this time in no way borders on the normal. At one point he persuaded a girlfriend to accompany him after midnight into Central Park and to sit there with him on a bench. He had never been mugged, but most people he knew in New York had been; he felt that he owed it to himself to undergo this experience. It was a fine June night, and they sat there talking and waiting. Then three youths were seen approaching in trainers, two of them black, one white. Maurice began to get nervous. Why had he been so foolish?

"What do you want?" he asked as they came closer, trying to keep his voice steady.

"We'd like some money," said the white youth, threateningly.

"Here's a dollar," proffered Girodias.

"Oh, thank you, sir. Thank you very much," said the youth. He took the dollar and the three of them walked on.

But the real trouble came over a book on Scientology that he had commissioned. It was entitled *Inside Scientology*, and purposed to expose the alleged methods and deceits of the organization, the way it extracted money from its victims and its links with the underworld. He announced it well in advance to get orders, and the Church of Scientology could not be unaware of the coming publication. Maurice had just lost his secretary at this time, a serious girl who, unreasonably from his point of view, expected to get her salary every week. It was just not part of his nature to do anything on a regular basis, or to consider the needs of others. In Paris his secretaries had become accustomed to waiting until he was in an amenable mood, and the social advantages of working for him – many free lunches and drinks, and the chance of meeting interesting people – made up for the inconveniences. A new girl presented herself, who in the words of Ed Ferraro, also working for Maurice at this time, was a little too eager to get the job. Following her hiring, correspondence disappeared, messages were not passed on, and Maurice was not told of impending problems until it was too late to deal with them.

At this point Girodias was also involved with Lyle Stuart in some joint publications. One of the books in question was written by a dominatrix from New Jersey, Monique van Cleef, and entitled *House of Pain*. An injunction with regard to it arrived at the office, but this also disappeared. Eventually realizing that his books were about to be confiscated, Girodias went to a warehouse in New Jersey where many of them were stored, taking his new secretary with him. There he walked into a trap: the police were waiting for him. They found marijuana and other drugs in his pockets which, so he claimed, had been planted on him, probably by his secretary. Girodias was arrested and taken to a holding pen. There is some confusion over this story, one version of which is that the secretary had suggested going down to the docks to look at the stars over New Jersey, a clear invitation to sex, and that they were engaged in making love when the police closed in on them. During the time he was in jail the secretary disappeared, and with her went everything in the office related to *Inside Scientology*. Girodias was released on bail, but the police now had many reasons to monitor his activities, and they were determined to have him deported.

One of those reasons was that he had attracted the attention of the State Department with another deliberately provocative title. Girodias had commissioned a scurrilous novel about the love life of Henry Kissinger, a man who needed to be satirized, but not in this way. Both Kissinger and the State Department took due notice, and a decision was probably taken at the time to have him arrested and deported as soon as possible. Maurice had not lost his penchant for making powerful enemies. Like his other publications, the Kissinger book attracted little attention from reviewers. He was now bringing out a wide range of titles, and some serious fiction was also coming from Olympia Press, but he knew nothing of the ways of American publishing, and the serious newspapers simply ignored him. There was competition everywhere, and he was far from the position he had occupied in Paris in the early Fifties when he was virtually the only English-language publisher, having a ready market in GIs and tourists for his wares, and the police little interested in books written in English. Even those American publishers he had despised as ignorant idiots maintained publicity and sales departments and ran their offices in a normal manner. Anne Patty, who joined him as a very young girl because she wanted a job in publishing, was astonished at his naivety in all matters pertaining to the office. He did not seem to know what questions to ask someone applying for a job, or even to describe what the job was. He did not know his way around the office or what needed to be done first. He had been fortunate in Paris to have a series of bright ladies to organize routine matters for him, but in New York everything was new and without precedent. Only Vicky Moorheim could run his first New York office, making it as near as possible to what he knew from Paris, but when he reverted to his old bad habits, she refused to stay. Maurice did not know where to buy anything or what it should cost. He relied on his luck and what fortune would bring his way. He totally misunderstood American business ethics, and was a natural sucker for any con man who came his way.

When bankruptcy loomed he was occupying offices in Park Avenue South. He sold all the office furniture, and his private things as well, to three different companies, that is to say the same objects several times over, and he also told his employees, all of whom were owed money, to come and take what they wanted before the furniture vans arrived. He also owed money to authors for books he had commissioned. One of them, Humphrey Evans, had written three books for him and never received a penny. At one point, a little earlier, surrounded by creditors, furious authors and unpaid employees, Maurice had taken a quick trip to India. While he was away Evans took over the office, cleared everything out that he could carry, removed whatever he could find in the basement, including three nude photographs he came across of three previous employees. There were of course many unpublished books, some of them in production when the office closed. One was *Mouthing Off*, the book by Patty Welles and her sister, mentioned earlier, set in the *El Morocco* restaurant. I remember reading it myself in proof, so it was not far from production, but neither Patty's husband, Leon Friedman, nor the author herself, could ever find the manuscript or any trace of it. Whatever there was in the office, was probably thrown out by the landlord when he reoccupied it.

During the last days of Olympia, Maurice had met a charming young medical student, just finishing her studies, and they fell in love. Lilla Lyon came from one of the oldest Massachusetts families – they were related to the Cabots and her ancestry went back to the *Mayflower*. Lilla's father was an ambassador to a South American country. When the police obtained a deportation order against Maurice Girodias she promptly married him; although it was certainly a marriage of convenience at the time – for his convenience – it was also a love match. When everything collapsed in New York, the marriage enabled him to avoid deportation, and he moved to Boston where Lilla began her internship, and Maurice continued writing *J'Arrive*, the first volume of his memoirs, which he subsequently translated into English.

Maurice's romance with Lilla started in February 1973. They had met at a party given by Leon Friedman for Maurice, and although at the time the latter seemed more interested in Leon's wife and other women present, Lilla thought he seemed "very nice". The *coup de foudre* between them came after subsequent meetings, usually little dinners of four friends where she at first came with someone else. They talked of going to France together, even of getting married there, but after the deportation order it was obvious that if Maurice left the country he would not be readmitted. Avoiding deportation was a very close thing, because it seemed that Kissinger himself was behind the move, probably with information being fed to the State Department by the Scientologists. Even the marriage only gave him a month's initial reprieve, but Lilla's contacts helped and eventually Maurice obtained a green card.

During Lilla Lyon's internship at Boston City Hospital, Maurice lay very low. He was there for two years from July 1977, and on two occasions I visited him. I did not meet Lilla on either occasion as she had to stay in the hospital on duty, but I remember a long lunch one Saturday in Boston Harbour when we got through three bottles of wine. I saw part of his English manuscript on that occasion. *J'Arrive* had already been published in Paris by Stock and I had read it in hospital while recuperating from a knee operation. I remember starting the first pages and laughing out loud as the surgeon walked into my room. "It's not often I find my patients laughing on the night before an operation," he said. Maurice was in fact a very funny writer and might have been an excellent comic novelist or a satirist had he known the limits of tact, but he always went too far in everything he did: he had to shock.

The English translation was given the title *The Frog Prince* – not his own idea – by Crown, who eventually published it. At that lunch in Boston we argued over his decision to turn down the perfectly adequate offer that Farrar, Straus had made for his book, in order to try to get a better one elsewhere. He was taking a bus the next morning (he could not afford a plane or train) to see Crown. I pointed out that Farrar, Straus was a far better imprint for a book of this kind and that the right publisher was more important than trying to get the top-possible dollar advance, but it was not a subject on which he could be persuaded.

After two years in Boston, Maurice, not made for a stable relationship, went back to New York, now separated from Lilla, but he was still in touch. Her internship finished, she went to work at a hospital in Baltimore. Maurice now found it possible to make occasional visits to Paris and return. He still dreamt of making a fortune in publishing, but the dream was getting dim. I remember one evening when I accompanied him to the home of a very rich French entrepreneur, where we ate off gold plates; he had recruited my presence to help him persuade his host to put a big investment into publishing, but nothing came of it. Maurice had adapted badly to the States and was becoming sour about everything American: the food, the wine, the culture, the ambience. He was missing the intellectual excitement of Paris and his old haunts. In 1981, having difficulties with his eyes, he realized that he could only have an operation under the French national health system if he re-established his residence there. He returned for good in 1981.

10

Back in Paris, Maurice Girodias had his operation for cataracts. As a long-time French resident, born in Paris, even though his passport was British, he was entitled to a free operation and it was successful. Later in 1986 he was to have another, this time for intestinal cancer, and some yards of his entrails were removed. But that too was successful, and, although he remained fearful of a return of the disease, he looked and felt well; it was not cancer that eventually killed him. He began to receive a French old age pension, only the price of a meal by the standards of his early days, but everything was welcome now. And he was helped out, both financially and in general support, by his brother and sisters.

He lived at various addresses, sometimes being given a room by an old friend or someone interested in his past career, occasionally by a girlfriend and sometimes he occupied his sister Sylvie's apartment in the same block as Les Deux Magots and, at his lowest ebb, allowed himself to be taken back by Laurette for a while, which cannot have been pleasant after years of estrangement. Eventually he found a small but pleasant apartment on the Rue d'Alésia in a modern block. It was high up with a view of the working-class districts of south-eastern Paris, contained very little furniture, and the walls had piles of manuscripts, his memoirs and many photocopies, which gradually grew as he worked on them.

Once settled, the memoirs went faster. He was finishing the second volume, *Les Jardins d'Éros*. His plan was to write three volumes in all, and give the series the overall title *Une Journée sur la terre*. The first volume was now unavailable in both languages. Crown, as I had predicted, had remaindered *The Frog Prince* after a few months, and there was never an American paperback or a British edition: several London publishers were interested, but Maurice, his ideas of grandeur in no way reduced, was still holding out for the kind of advance that only certain best-sellers could command. He still buried himself in causes and occasionally wrote articles for the press on subjects that interested him, or to give his own view of some past literary scandal or event. Two long-term projects still preoccupied him: one was an art book about Karnak, which in the Sixties and Seventies he had tried to negotiate as an international coedition, but without success; the other was a book about human beauty, largely illustrated, and with a text partly by himself, partly by others, that also never materialized. He put out several prospectuses both for a large art book, and for a series of books; he also saw it as a magazine.

Maurice became interested in the political rights of minorities. With him I met a Monsieur Person, one of the leaders of the cause for Breton independence, a man of charm and culture whom I had difficulty imagining with a machine gun behind the barricades, but he was ready for such an eventuality. The past persecutions of Jews, Protestants and heretics loomed large in Maurice's conversations: he spoke much like an idealistic young man with a long life ahead of him. Seeing him four or five times a year, sometimes for lunch, sometimes for dinner, I found his enthusiasm undimmed, his charm ever present, and his ideas for future projects as unrealistic as ever. At least I was not involved in any of his schemes, although occasionally I did him little favours, making enquiries or passing on messages. When I did not call him on one visit he wrote me an angry note, accusing me of having become too important to bother with him. I regularly received copies of his correspondence with interested publishers about his memoirs or other projects, letters to lawyers and presentations for book-packages that he wanted to put together.

His spleen was now aimed mainly at those he felt had robbed him of the authors and the titles that had started with Olympia, in particular Barney Rosset, who often tried to see him when in Paris, but was refused, and Dick Seaver whom he regarded as the main culprit in stealing the cream of the Olympia list. I too was guilty of taking advantage of him, as he saw it, but he did not hold the same rancour against me: I had never gone back on an agreement or diminished his role in finding interesting novels. The culmination of his hatred for Grove was an open letter to Samuel Beckett that he sent to the press, and to many individuals he had known or were likely to have an interest. It is an extraordinary document that is still obtainable, because the Paris magazine *Frank* reprinted it in 1991.* In the letter, after explaining to Beckett that he was currently engaged in writing "the Olympia story", and making a few references to Deirdre Bair's biography, he launches into his attack. He portrays himself as one of the few "individualistic publishers", possessing "a certain gift of intuition and sense of adventure [without which] no new authors would ever be set into print" and he cites Sylvia Beach and his late father among others in that category. He gives credit to Alex Trocchi, Austryn Wainhouse and Patrick Bowles for bringing *Watt* to him, but not to Seaver. He goes on to say, "Seaver's function within the *Merlin* structure was definitely menial," but that did not stop him from later claiming that he "ran the whole show at *Merlin* – a small magazine that never printed more than four issues all told and that he had founded Olympia." His bitterness is principally aimed at Seaver, whom he blames for self-aggrandizement to get into American publishing, and for stealing his authors.

The letter is very self-serving and often highly inaccurate, but there is more than a grain of truth in some of it. He confesses to having lost money on all his prestige authors except Nabokov, but he was willing to do this as long as his dbs made money. He gives credit to Barney Rosset and me for our battles against censorship, and thanks Beckett for his own position in that regard, but he is totally wrong when he says that it was through him that Barney and I discovered Beckett. He also forgets that two of Beckett's major novels, *Malone Dies* and *The Unnamable*, written in French and first published by Minuit, came to be published by Olympia in France in English, as an exchange for letting us publish *Molloy* in our own countries. We all three put the three novels together as a trilogy in our separate editions in 1959. In fact we both paid royalties for *Molloy*, none of which went on to Beckett, and received nothing back for the other two. For this we must blame ourselves: publishers seldom asked for royalties, assuming that they would arrive as a matter of course.

In his open letter, Girodias never once mentions La Grande Séverine and blames the pressure of the police and the courts for putting him into financial jeopardy. He had no way of surviving, he says, except to move to America and to cooperate with Barney Rosset. Although he undoubtedly talked to Barney, there was never any prospect of their working together in the same country. Such close cooperation was never really discussed; in any case, two such difficult individualists could never have worked together for even two days. Maurice cites his persuasion of Henry Miller to let Barney Rosset publish *Tropic of*

Cancer, as evidence of the deal he claims they were working out, but that came much earlier, long before he had to leave France. Talking of Rosset, he says:

> Our projected association, however, never materialized. It is during that period that all my great authors vanished one by one, in a manner of a classical Agatha Christie novel, only to pop up again on Grove's list. Being now bankrupt, with royalties still owed to some of the said authors, I was in no position to prevent the haemorrhage; Grove having given the example, dozens of mafia-type entrepreneurs set up publishing businesses whose only activity was to pilfer my list... Meanwhile Dick Seaver, who had strictly no experience in publishing, had been made senior editor of Grove, presumably because he knew personally most of the authors, translators and editors who had been connected with my firm in Paris; and this qualified him as "the Olympia specialist".

The open letter is very much an apology and a justification for his life, written, so he says, to put the record straight "for the doubtful benefit of the twenty-first-century school-children", and to explain his "creative passion". What it does is confuse the record even more. It is certain that a great deal of literature, that which he commissioned from the needy exiles in Paris, and accepted from writers who brought their manuscripts to him, would probably never have existed or found its way into print without him. But *Lolita* would sooner or later have found a publisher and have appeared, probably not under Nabokov's name. Girodias helped to put Beckett on the map, and Seaver, *pace* Maurice, certainly played a role here, but once *Waiting for Godot* became a worldwide success, the emergence of his other work was inevitable. The letter to Beckett received some mention in the French press, but little sympathy. Beckett himself made no response. When I saw him at the time he made no reference to it. In any case by September 1986 when the letter was written, Beckett, having more than once fallen down and lost consciousness on the street, and suffering from emphysema, had moved into a retirement home in Montparnasse and was not interested in such matters. Beckett's last years, confined to a small room with little privacy and few books around him, going out seldom and not liking the food, but never complaining or allowing friends to help him in any way, were a sad way for a great writer to end. But he would never allow anyone to really look after him (Suzanne, his much older wife, was herself bedridden and sinking), and at least he could see friends, have regular meals, read and reflect. One last work was to appear, a poem, written in French and then translated, *What is the Word*: it describes, painfully and accurately, the plight of a mind aware of its decline, trying to find a word, *the word*, to describe its own condition. Beckett died at the end of 1989, just before Christmas, six months after his wife. He had been born at Easter on a Good Friday, a time when death is celebrated, and had died at a festival of birth, giving double poignancy to Vladimir's most quoted line, "We are born astride of a grave, down in the hole, lingeringly, the grave-digger puts on the forceps."

Les Jardins d'Éros was finished and published in French. I had offered to read the manuscript, make suggestions, put right errors, but Maurice never gave me the opportunity. We had lunch, our last meeting, together with John Minihan, whose photographs of Beckett, Francis Bacon, Burroughs and many others are rightly famous, and Minihan took some excellent photographs of Maurice. He was in good form, the book was receiving reviews and publicity, and he had radio and television interviews ahead of him. When I subsequently read the book I was vastly entertained, but appalled by the many errors of fact and chronology, and the way he had twisted the truth to emphasize his own version of things. Maurice once again emerged as an excellent writer, but unreliable chronicler of his time. What is perhaps best about this large book is the way he was able to mock himself, make comic episodes out of his failures and disasters, and amusingly caricature both his friends and enemies. There was never to be a sequel: the third volume, nearly finished as he told his publisher and his friends, did not exist. *Les Jardins d'Éros* ends when he is still the eccentric owner of La Grande Séverine.

The character of Maurice Girodias is easier to describe than to analyse, and the contradictions that arise from differing accounts of his behaviour, including his own memoirs, make it difficult to portray him quite as sympathetically as he deserves. Maurice was, right up to the time of his death, exceptionally good-looking, well built, with a full head of hair, a fresh, handsome face that never became lined, that beamed openness, success and intelligence at whoever he was talking to, even with a hangover. He had an infectious sense of humour, laughed readily, and only looked serious when he could not persuade the person with whom he was dealing that the idea he was trying to sell or the amount of money that he was asking for was reasonable. If he was selling he multiplied the real value many times, if he was buying he saw no reason why he should pay anything at all. In other words he had no commercial sense and money was calculated in terms of his immediate needs. He never seriously looked ahead or planned, but fortunately he had others to do this during his most successful period, the middle Forties in Paris. Debts were ignored as long as possible and if he had a reasonable amount of money in his pocket he was happy. The childish side of Maurice was always dominant, but this was not obvious to others. Most people were charmed by his good looks, friendly manner and apparent self-confidence. His biggest faults were his deviousness and inability to see the point of view of others, especially if they were in opposition to him. He was certainly more at home in French than in English, which he spoke fluently with a light French accent. He could also write well in both and in a light, easy style. Maurice was always fun to be with providing there was not an argument. And outside of business he was generous with a cavalier, almost aristocratic, attitude to money, because it had no reality for him other than to meet the most pressing need. So much abuse has been voiced and written about Girodias that it is difficult to give a totally different view, but those who worked for him almost without exception genuinely liked him, and some loved him as well. He would refer to himself as a child, and in a sense he never grew up. His past ability to survive the war in German-held Paris probably lay at the root of his stubborn conviction that every problem would solve itself or blow over.

The decline of censorship, although it brought him money from sub-contracted editions, would eventually have made Olympia Press as marginal as any literary press that needs to find constant injections of new money to keep going. The more up-market Olympia became, the lower were its sales. But had it not been for the follies of which La Grande Séverine was the most monumental, he could have survived by taking reasonable care. Reasonable, however, is one adjective that no one could apply to him.

Girodias's interest in political issues was genuine, and his espousal of minority causes an outlet for a liberal inclination and a compulsion to be active. He supported the French socialist party, but only the more moderate, intellectual wing of it. But he never joined any party, and his dislike of doctrine would never have let him stay in one for long. He did write long, thoughtful letters to the press on issues that interested him, and they were good letters except where he himself was involved; then he could distort the facts out of self-pity and self-aggrandizement.

Everyone who met Maurice during his last months in 1990 remarked on how well he looked, how much he seemed to have recovered from his depression and his bitterness. I was a regular obituary writer for the *Independent*, and they phoned to tell me that Girodias had died, and they wanted a final paragraph for the obituary notice I had already written a year or so earlier. He had collapsed in the middle of an interview on a Jewish radio station, talking about his book. He had a heart attack in the middle of a sentence and breathed his last within a few minutes, a good way to go, without suffering, at a time when his fortunes were a little better. "He went on his cloud," said his brother Eric.

Because of Christmas, when travel to France was impossible, I had been unable to get to Beckett's funeral, attended by only a few in the Montparnasse cemetery on the previous 26th December. But I went to Paris six months later for Maurice's, arriving the previous evening and staying with Jim Haynes. It was a beautiful June day, and Jim and I found a large crowd outside the crematorium of Père-Lachaise, the majority being women, but not a single publisher was visible except Jean Castelli, who had worked as an accountant for both Maurice and Pauvert. There was no ceremony. We sat in the hall of the crematorium in silence while the body was reduced to ashes, listening, one after the other, to Mozart wind concerti, starting with the clarinet. As the first oboe concerto was nearing its end, an agitated Eric Kahane suggested we move outside. "If anyone would like to say something…" he ventured when we were on the steps; but the moment had passed, his virtues were not extolled, nothing had been prepared. I went with a little group to a bistro outside the cemetery gates; with us was a lady, who like so many others at the funeral looked slightly familiar, as if I had known her twenty or so years earlier – the cashier of La Grande Séverine. We drank to his memory and I returned to London. The ashes were deposited in a drawer at the crematorium by Eric. He had a plaque inscribed on it: "Maurice Girodias: Une Journée sur la terre". Eric himself was to follow Maurice before the end of the century.

A week or so later I was in New York. Many of Maurice's friends and acquaintances felt a need to get together to talk about him and we met at El Quixote, the Spanish restaurant under the Chelsea Hotel, where Maurice had often stayed. I circulated my obituary, the longest that had appeared. Present were Lilla Lyon, Iris Owens, Norman Rubington, Leon Friedman, Jerry Williams, Michael Golden, Ann Patty and some others. It was an alcoholic occasion, but not maudlin. Some antagonisms emerged and I did not stay to the end. We did however discuss Maurice's book: should it be translated? Should another book be commissioned? This volume, a chronicle of his time and of the activities of many others, is the result, because Ann Patty was also the editor of Poseidon. I borrowed Girodias's title, in the singular, but it is of course a very different book from his and about a much larger circle of people. It relies heavily on Maurice's memories, but more on my own and those of others who have been interviewed or have written their own books. Maurice Girodias was a centre around whom a whole offbeat literary world revolved, but he was not the only centre of that world. There was a story to tell that started in Paris. There is an overlap with my own later memoirs, *Pursuit*, published in 2001.

Postscript

This postscript is added nearly twenty years later because of what happened after that New York memorial dinner. The book was written, delivered to Poseidon just before that imprint was closed down after Simon & Schuster were purchased by Paramount Pictures. This led to demands for a totally different book, but even that fell into other hands when a new purchaser bought Paramount and editorial staff were again changed. I removed the manuscript, now in different versions, and offered it to another publisher who managed to lose much of the top copy. Finally, at Christmas 2002, I put together, as nearly as possible, the book I had originally been asked to write. More of the people in it have died – I nearly did myself in July 2002 – but as the story of Maurice Girodias and those associated with him, compiled largely at first hand, and otherwise from sources that have in many cases since disappeared, including Girodias's own memoirs, now out of print and difficult to obtain, it is still relevant, perhaps more than ever, because publishing in the globalized world of today is no longer an adventurous activity. If ever it becomes such again in the future this volume may prove useful to a new generation. But I hope that those who want to know something of the atmosphere and the history of the post-second-world-war literary scene that was centred in Paris and then spread elsewhere, and of the colourful characters that inhabited it, will find this chronicle entertaining and even inspiring.

Notes

p. 7, Maurice Sachs, *Le Sabbat: souvenirs d'une jeunesse orageuse* (Paris: Éditions Corréa, 1946). The English translation by Richard Howard was published by Jonathan Cape in 1965.

p. 9–10, *The taking of the Halle... police prefecture*: Maurice Girodias, *Une Journée sur la terre II: Les Jardins d'Éros* (Paris: Éditions de la Différence, 1990), p. 12. All English translations of passages from Girodias's *Jardins d'Éros* are my own.

p. 16, André Léjard, *Le Meuble* (Paris: Éditions du Chêne, 1941).

p. 18, Roger Vailland, *La Loi* (Paris: Éditions Gallimard, 1957).

p. 19, *I adore Laurette... prostituted me*: Maurice Girodias, *Une Journée sur la terre II: Les Jardins d'Éros* (Paris: Éditions de la Différence, 1990), p. 67.

p. 21, *Fuck your... not the society*: Henry Miller, *The Cosmological Eye* (1939; New York: New Directions Publishing, 1969), p.162.

p. 25, *His book*: Vice Admiral Muselier, *De Gaulle contre le Gaullisme* (Paris: Éditions du Chêne, 1946).

p. 26, Yves Farge, *Le Pain de la corruption* (Paris: Éditions du Chêne, 1947).

p. 34, *At that time... possible to follow*: Maurice Girodias, *Une Journée sur la terre II: Les Jardins d'Éros* (Paris: Éditions de la Différence, 1990), p. 151.

p. 35, *Only you can do it*: See Maurice Girodias, *Une Journée sur la terre II: Les Jardins d'Éros* (Paris: Éditions de la Différence, 1990).

p. 37, Vernon Sullivan (pseud.), *J'irai cracher sur vos tombes* (Paris: Les Éditions du Scorpion, 1947).

p. 37, *L'Écume des Jours* (Paris: Éditions Gallimard, 1947) and *Les Bâtisseurs d'empire* (Paris: Cahiers du Collège de 'Pataphysique, 1959).

p. 42, *I went to France... engagé as an outsider*: Andrew Murray Scott, *Alexander Trocchi: The Making of the Monster* (Edinburgh: Polygon, 1991).

p. 54, *Faut-il brûler Sade*: The essay appeared first in *Les Temps Modernes* no. 74 (1951), pp. 1002–33 and no. 75 (1952), pp. 1197–230. The English translation was published as *The Marquis de Sade: An Essay with Selections from his Writings* (New York: Grove Press, 1953).

p. 55, *a great lean rascal... not to be trusted*: Austryn Wainhouse, 'On Translating Sade', *Evergreen Review* vol. 10, no. 42 (New York: Evergreen Review, Inc., 1966).

p. 56, *a collection of stories*: Pierre Bourgeade, *L'Aurore boréale* (Paris: Éditions Gallimard, 1973).

p. 56, Sylvia Bourdon, *L'Amour est une fête* (Éditions Belfond, 1976). Barbara Wright's English translation, *Love is a Feast*, was published by John Calder in 1977.

p. 57, *with the... much-depleted man*: This quotation and the account of the meeting between Girodias and Wainhouse is taken from Austryn Wainhouse, 'On Translating Sade', *Evergreen Review* vol. 10, no. 42 (New York: Evergreen Review, Inc., 1966).

p. 61, *from the latter's*: For Girodias's account of the meeting, see Maurice Girodias, *Une Journée sur la terre II: Les Jardins d'Éros* (Paris: Éditions de la Différence, 1990).

p. 64, *or American publisher*: Deirdre Bair, *Samuel Beckett: A Biography* (London: Jonathan Cape, 1978).

p. 72, P.J. Kavanagh, *The Perfect Stranger* (London: Chatto & Windus, 1966).

p. 72, Richard Wright, *Native Son* (New York; London: Harper & Brothers, 1940).

p. 73, *He was tall... projecting forehead*: Robert Creeley, *The Island* (New York: Scribner's, 1963; London: John Calder, 1963).

p. 74–75, *a series of dialogues... abstract painters*: Published in *Proust and Three Dialogues with Georges Duthuit* (London: John Calder, 1965).

p. 81, Alexander Trocchi, *Cain's Book* (New York: Grove Press, 1960; London: John Calder, 1963).

p. 81, *Merlin, unpublished... and Christopher Logue*: Times Literary Supplement, 27th May 1955.

p. 81, *in its pages... both sides of the Atlantic*: Quoted in Andrew Murray Scott, *Alexander Trocchi: The Making of the Monster* (Edinburgh: Polygon, 1991).

p. 82, *a lot of style... made him impossible*: Peter Matthiessen, *Paris Review*, no. 79 (Spring 1981).

p. 86, *The day I arrived... appropriate climate*: Eugene Walter, *Paris Review*, no. 79 (Spring 1981).

p. 90, *people who feel... become a critic*: William Styron, 'Letter to an Editor', *Paris Review*, no. 1 (Spring 1953).

p. 92–93, *Through the long winter... mostly boring*: John Marquand Jr, *Paris Review*, no. 79 (Spring 1981).

p. 95, *The Revolution... plain reader be damned*: Eugene Jolas, 'The Revolution of the Word', *transition*, no. 16/17 (June 1929). It is reproduced in Dougald McMillan, *transition 1927–38:*

The History of a Literary Era (London: Calder & Boyars, 1975), p. 49.

p. 109, Brion Gysin, *The Process* (New York: Doubleday, 1969; London: Jonathan Cape, 1970).

p. 121, *It was not religion... Hitler and to Stalin*: Maurice Girodias, *Une Journée sur la terre II: Les Jardins d'Éros* (Paris: Éditions de la Différence, 1990), p. 239.

p. 131, Stanley Kauffmann, *The Philanderer* (London: Secker & Warburg, 1954).

p. 131–32, *If something does not pay... are wrong*: Arthur Schlesinger Jr, 'The New Mood in Politics', *Esquire*, January 1960 (published later in *The Politics of Hope* (Boston: Riverside Press, 1962).

p. 132, *We live in a heavy... dreariest in our history*: Eric F. Goldman, 'Goodbye to the Fifties and Good Riddance', *Harper's Magazine*, vol. 220, no. 1316 (January 1960), p. 27.

p. 141, *raped by Negroes... during the war*: Correspondence courtesy of Leon Friedman, New York.

p. 142, *I know that... safe from trouble*: Letter to Leon Friedman, 10th March 1964.

p. 153, *At the end of the afternoon... too often before*: Maurice Girodias, *Une Journée sur la terre II: Les Jardins d'Éros* (Paris: Éditions de la Différence, 1990), pp. 399–400.

p. 156–57, *For the analytical intelligence... my own insight*: Maurice Girodias, *Une Journée sur la terre II: Les Jardins d'Éros* (Paris: Éditions de la Différence, 1990), pp. 367–68.

p. 172, *when we quarrelled*: See my book *Pursuit* for a detailed account of these quarrels (London: Calder Publications, 2001).

p. 183, Michelle Green, *The Dream at the End of the World: Paul Bowles and the Literary Renegades in Tangier* (New York: HarperCollins, 1991; London: Bloomsbury, 1992).

p. 184, *everything around her... taken seriously*: Paul Bowles, *Without Stopping* (New York: G.P. Putnam's Sons, 1972).

p. 188, *a paranoid conceit... rich already*: Quoted in Ted Morgan, *Literary Outlaw: The Life and Times of William S. Burroughs* (New York: Henry Holt & Co., 1988).

p. 192, *Tanger [sic] is finished... list of hundreds*: Quoted in Ted Morgan, *Literary Outlaw: The Life and Times of William S. Burroughs* (New York: Henry Holt & Co., 1988).

p. 200, *did not last long*: Elicited from interviews with Marilyn Meeske Segal and Mae Mercer in Los Angeles, March 1993.

p. 202, *banned in France*: Henri Alleg, *La Question* (Paris: Les Éditions de Minuit, 1958), published in English as *The Question* (London: John Calder, 1958).

p. 202, *the House of Lords: Gangrene* (London: John Calder, 1959).

p. 204, *As a child... looney man*: Sent to the author in a private letter from Marilyn Meeske Segal.

p. 204, *became a best-seller*: Phyllis and Eberhard Kronhausen, *Pornography and the Law: The Psychology of Erotic Realism and Pornography* (New York: Ballantine Books, 1959).

p. 208, *They wheeled her... walked into the world*: Gregory Corso, *The American Express* (Paris: Olympia Press, 1961).

p. 216–17, *There are several points... ulterior motive*: Wainhouse's article, 'On Translating Sade', appeared in *Evergreen Review* vol. 10, no. 42 (August 1966). Nabokov's article, 'Lolita and Mr Girodias', appeared in *Evergreen Review* (February 1967). The latter was in fact a response to an earlier article, entitled 'Lolita, Nabokov and I', Girodias's own account of Lolita's publication, which appeared in *Evergreen Review* (September 1965). Girodias's letter in response to Nabokov's attack appeared in *Evergreen Review* (June 1967).

p. 217, *Does Mr Vidal... read stupidity*: Gore Vidal's review of *The Olympia Reader*, entitled 'On Pornography', appeared in the *New York Review of Books* vol. 6, no. 5 (31st March 1966). Girodias's reply was published vol. 6, no. 8 (12th May 1966).

p. 218, *Everyone is lying... everyone's face*: Letter to Leon Friedman, 10th February 1966.

p. 225, *We were regarded... vagabonds*: Alexander Trocchi, *Cain's Book* (1959; London: John Calder, 1963).

p. 225, *and to experiment*: See Andrew Murray Scott, *Alexander Trocchi: The Making of the Monster* (Edinburgh: Polygon, 1991).

p. 227, *The play of truth... life as an artist*: Irving Rosenthal, *Sheeper* (New York: Grove Press, 1967), quoted by Scott in *Alexander Trocchi: The Making of the Monster* (Edinburgh: Polygon, 1991).

p. 229, *And when someone... chemistry of alienation*: Alexander Trocchi, *Cain's Book* (1959; London: John Calder, 1963), p. 33.

p. 235, *Writers' Conference*: The International Writers' Conference, which was organized by the author, ran from 20th to 24th August 1962. A full account can be found in my autobiography, *Pursuit* (p. 193 ff.).

p. 236, *About my death... so should you*: Henry Miller, *Reflections* (Santa Barbara: Capra Press, 1981).

p. 237, *I've tried now... take the cure*: Quoted in Edward de Grazia, *Girls Lean Back Everywhere: Law of Obscenity and the Assault on Genius* (London: Constable & Co, 1992).

p. 240, *some filthy stuff*: Ted Morgan, *Literary Outlaw: The Life and Times of William S. Burroughs* (New York: Henry Holt & Co., 1988).

p. 243, *Swift's A Modest Proposal*: In Swift's satirical treatise of 1729 it is suggested that the Irish potato famine could be ameliorated by eating babies as meat. This shocking "proposal" was of course intended by the author to attract public attention to the extent of the Irish tragedy, but many readers took him seriously.

p. 246, *book about the period*: James David Horan, *The Desperate Years: From Stock Market Crash to World War II, a Pictorial History of the Thirties* (New York: Crown, 1962).

p. 246, William S. Burroughs, *The Last Words of Dutch Schultz: A Fiction in the Form of a Film Script* (New York: Seaver Books, 1970; London: John Calder, 1986).

p. 249, *later, privately*: In William Targ's autobiographical volume *Indecent Pleasures: The Life and Colorful Times of William Targ* (New York: Macmillan, 1975), there is a description of a publisher (pp. 302–304) that is obviously Walter Minton.

p. 257, *It is a degrading sight... gypsy camp*: Janet Flanner, *Paris Journal: 1965–1970* (Harvest/HBJ, 1988).

p. 260, *Girodias displayed... excellent character*: John Sutherland, *Offensive Literature: Decensorship in Britain 1960–1982* (London: Junction Books, 1982).

p. 260, *prosecuted over Hubert Selby Jr's Last Exit to Brooklyn*: See *Pursuit*, pp. 314–24.

p. 264, *Drama Conference*: The Drama Conference was held from 2nd to 7th September 1963 as part of the Edinburgh International Festival. For a full account, see *Pursuit*, p. 245 ff.

p. 268, *No matter what... pendulum of sexuality*: Jim Haynes, *Thanks for Coming!* (London: Faber and Faber, 1984), p. 223.

p. 270, *co-edited Hello, I Love You!*: Jim Haynes and Jeanne Pasle-Green, *Hello, I Love You! Voices from within the Sexual Revolution* (San Francisco: Jean Lafitte Editions, 1974).

p. 271–72, *Germaine Greer's defection... aims*: Germaine Greer's letter of resignation is reproduced in Jim Haynes, *Thanks for Coming!* (London: Faber and Faber, 1984), pp. 231–32.

p. 275, *This book is for... hippies everywhere*: Jim Haynes, *Thanks for Coming!* (London: Faber and Faber, 1984), pp. 7–26.

p. 277, *left-wing causes in Paris*: Born a Kentucky heiress, Maria McDonald went to Paris early in the century to study singing, met Eugene Jolas from Alsace in New York after the war, and backed him to start *transition*. Her family had owned slaves in the nineteenth century. She told me once that when travelling as a small girl in Italy, her mother had indignantly left the Villa d'Este, perhaps Italy's most celebrated resort hotel, because they had a "nigger" staying there, in this case the Aga Khan.

p. 277, *practically... dealing with a kid*: This quotation, as well as other material in this chapter, is taken from an interview with Édouard Roditi by David Applefield in *Gargoyle* No. 32/33.

p. 281, *no follow-up*: Related to the author by Victor Lownes in 1992.

p. 297, *he looked away*: Ted Morgan, *Literary Outlaw: The Life and Times of William S. Burroughs* (New York: Henry Holt & Co., 1988).

p. 303, *do no wrong*: For a detailed account of Beckett's own productions, see Dougald McMillan and Martha Fehsenfeld, *Beckett in the Theatre* (London: John Calder, 1988).

p. 307, *mainly Congolese writers*: Frank: An International Journal of Contemporary Writing and Art, no. 14 (1992).

p. 307, David Applefield, *Paris Inside Out* (Paris: American University of Paris, 1990).

p. 321, *such and much more... Oh all to end*: Samuel Beckett, *Stirrings Still* (John Calder: London, 1999), p. 22.

p. 332, *reprinted it in 1991*: Frank: An International Journal of Contemporary Writing and Art, no. 13 (1991).

Index